Pushkin's Tatiana

PUBLICATIONS OF THE WISCONSIN CENTER
FOR PUSHKIN STUDIES

General Editors

David M. Bethea
Alexander A. Dolinin

Olga Peters Hasty

Pushkin's Tatiana

The University of Wisconsin Press

University of Wisconsin Press
2537 Daniels Street
Madison, Wisconsin 53718

3 Henrietta Street
London WC2E 8LU, England

5 4 3 2 1

Printed in the United States of America

Library of Congress Cataloging-in-Publication Data
Hasty, Olga Peters.
    Pushkin's Tatiana / Olga Peters Hasty.
    288 pp.   cm.—(Publication of the Center for Pushkin Studies)
    Includes bibliographical references and index.
    ISBN 0–299–16400–4 (cloth: alk. paper)
    ISBN 0–299–16404–7 (pbk.: alk. paper)
    1. Pushkin, Alexander Sergeevich, 1799–1837. Evgenii Onegin. 2. Pushkin,
Alexander Sergeevich, 1799–1837—Characters—Tatiana. I. Title. II. Series.
PG3343.E83 H37   1999
891.71'3—dc21   99–6271

In loving memory of my grandparents

Где нет любви к искусству, там нет и критики.

[Where there is no love for art, there is no criticism.]

Alexander Pushkin

Contents

Foreword

In the early stages of her fascination with this project, Olga Hasty remarked that Tatiana is the Russians' Mona Lisa. Tatiana's image beckons us, but—or so it occurred to me at the time—it is difficult to say why; it is all but impossible to single out an ambiguous gaze or mysterious smile, since everything in Tatiana resists the concrete lineament. That this should be so is curious, for Pushkin had a vivid pictorial imagination. The *Onegin* manuscripts are full of self-portraits, renderings of antique sculpture, male and female heads, sketches of backs, torsos, legs, feet, stumps of trees, rowboats, the occasional demon, dog, rump of a cat, horse. Pushkin sketched Onegin himself (alongside his author) on the Neva embankment, and sent the drawing to his brother Lev in November 1824; a year earlier, on an *Onegin* manuscript page, we find in the lower left corner a handsome male head with raven locks—most likely, Lensky. One draft of Tatiana's letter (June 1824), heavily corrected and crossed out in Pushkin's compact script, is illustrated in the margins with what looks like classical statuary—two draped, grieving female figures, each with head cupped in hand, hair undone, no view of the face.[1] The closer we look at these figures, the more they appear to turn away.

Olga Hasty puts this reticent, partially concealed heroine at the center of her reading of Pushkin's great novel. Bypassing the garrulous narrator, she addresses the novel's events—and reactions to events—from Tatiana's vantage point. Given Tatiana's stature and charisma in the text, one would think the task easy. For several reasons, however, it proves most arduous and is all the more instructive for being against the grain.

First, Tatiana's role in Pushkin's tale both fits, and in crucial ways fails to fit, the classic "nonconsummated love plot" of the eighteenth-century French and English novel. What is that plot? In recent years, it has come under much reasoned—and also some unreasonable—suspicion by feminist critics. Experienced man comes in contact with innocent girl. Girl loses her head over man, who is moved, touched, gratified, but being true

to himself (and being in charge of the story), he cannot commit or reciprocate and must therefore withdraw. Girl cannot abide: she either pursues
the man, or dies, or both in sequence. The subtext here is male autonomy
against tenacious female need; and since these are gender essentials, the
resultant tragedy is above good or bad (although the girl, assuredly, usually remains in our minds as the greater good). In a nonerotic variant of
this plot, one that has enjoyed enormous popularity in Eastern Europe
throughout the twentieth century, man is put in prison for a "cause";
there he clarifies and simplifies his life, undergoes spiritual rebirth, im-
proves his writing skills, whereas the girl on the outside—harassed,
lonely, impoverished—becomes that distanced muse and conduit which
sustains and transmits (literally) the man's spiritual biography to the
world, with scarcely a thought to any story of her own. Withdrawal or
incarceration of the man (whose self-absorption is thereby justified and
complete) versus engagement, defilement by the world, and self-sacrifice
for the woman: both parties to the plot are ennobled, although their roles
are rarely reversed.

And Tatiana? As Hasty's account will demonstrate, she follows this
pattern only up to a point. She falls in love, risks all to reveal her feelings,
wins (instead of love) the man's kindly, condescending dismissal, suffers
quite terribly. But she neither pursues the man, nor dies. Nor does she reject the world. She demands nothing in return for her loss and refuses the
reward of that originary passion when it is finally offered by the originary
lover. Unconventionally for heroines in the "nonconsummated love" genres—where lack of consummation is so often compensated for by noisy
expanses of chat, soul-searching, remorse, or confession—Tatiana's gift
for silence and her sense of timing are exquisite. She knows how to take
her leave. Just as Pushkin exits from his novel with his hero compromised
and still on his knees (it's his problem now), so Tatiana, after delivering a
minimalist speech on the lessons she has learned over the past several
years, rises and returns to herself.

In its grace and discipline, the model is highly appealing. But the experience, again, is difficult to analyze, because so much of it (from Tatiana's external appearance to her inner emotion during moments of pain
and decision) is not shared with the reader. When, later in the century,
Russian artists expand on the "Tatiana prototype"—identifiable as such
by the misfired letters, the series of tête-à-tête exchanges on a bench in a
garden, and by giveaway unresolvable affinities between strong woman
and hesitant man—the heroine is provided with a palpably novelistic development. Turgenev's Natal'ia Lasunskaia in *Rudin*, Goncharov's Olga
Ilyinskaia in *Oblomov*, Tchaikovsky's image of Tatiana in his operatic
variant of *Eugene Onegin* are each allowed to express shame and frus-

tration, contemplate options, wonder out loud what it means to be in love. Paradoxically, self-expression of this sort both fills out and flattens the image. Pushkin's Tatiana, heroine of a "novel in verse," is more mysterious, still on the brink between compact lyrical image and a fully prose-worthy personality. Although she reads novels, augurs, and dreams, her reactions to these events are glossed only reluctantly in the text. And when she picks up and changes her fate altogether (travels to Moscow, marries a general, becomes a princess, begins to host an aristocratic salon) we are given no access to her inner life at all.

This restrained mode of behavior and its restrained presentation by Pushkin are bewitchingly attractive. Why is this so, and what are the dynamics of Tatiana's image as it matures within the text? The chapters that follow in this book provide a fascinating set of specific answers to these questions, but let me offer two general speculations. There are many good reasons for falling in love with Tatiana, but marital fidelity and regal bearing are not in themselves sufficient. Nor can her complex appeal be explained as Tchaikovsky so masterfully explains it in the opening scene of his opera, where an ensemble for the four female principals comes to represent all the ages of woman (aged nurse, nostalgic mother, awakened fiancée, as yet waiting maiden); this quartet culminates in musical variations on the wise maxim—part Pushkin, part Chateaubriand—that good habits not only take the place of happiness but, in the course of a life, can constitute their own high virtue and bliss. This is indeed part of Tatiana's wisdom. But as Hasty will argue, there is more of the proactive and creatively risk-laden in Pushkin's heroine than such a passive reconciliation with fate might imply.

Tatiana bewitches us, first, by her absolute lack of female vanity. In a novel where the menfolk spend a great deal of time in front of mirrors (Onegin, that Venus in fastidious drag, preens for hours before going out), she avoids any display of her self. Indeed, she would prefer not to be watched at all. This is not to suggest that she is unattractive—for although we have no way of knowing Tatiana's degree of beauty, intimations from the lovestruck narrator and her eventual social triumph as Princess N suggest some basic very good looks—but only to say that her impulse is to look *out* on the world, not to invite the world to look in. Her trademark, that which eventually will haunt the smitten and chastised Onegin, is a window seat looking out on an open field. In this, of course, she contrasts sharply with the hero, who values the world largely as an audience made up of people just like him, gazing back.

Female vanity perniciously obscures horizons. Tatiana's freedom from it permits her to see clearly, learn rapidly, and mature irreversibly, even under conditions of great insecurity and humiliation. But Tatiana captivates us for another reason. Whenever she has a chance to make a scene, she does not. Suspecting the worst after sending her impulsive letter, she would like to run from Onegin when she meets him in the lane but instead hears him out in silence. She dreams a terrible prophetic dream, but no one can help her understand herself through it. She almost faints at her name day party—for there are so many people, from Monsieur Triquet to the radiant Onegin himself, looking in—but regains her balance. Her excursions to Onegin's deserted library appear to promise relief, but for all the knowledge she gains on these visits, her despair is only deepened. The final declaration of love and leave-taking in book 8 is nothing short of spectacular. It is as if all the unnecessary detail has been burnt away and only those factors conducive to moral growth remain in place.

As Hasty reads the scene, Tatiana's response to Onegin is a most efficient rendering of all she has learned throughout the novel. Years earlier, at the moment of her greatest vulnerability, Onegin had advised her to "learn to control herself"—and now we see that she has. Although she sheds her tears in private, she is not ashamed to cry. She knows there is no going back (especially not to that which she loves and has lost). She accepts that her present is absolutely real. And she insists on seeing in Onegin, now as then, a man of integrity, honor, and pride. In the final scene, as in others of high intensity that we are privy to only briefly, Tatiana intuitively acts in such a way as not to bring out the weaker sides of those she loves. Compare—and Hasty will do so in scrupulous detail— the behavior of Tatiana with that of the heroines in her favorite novels. Everywhere, women in her position are designed to close down; Tatiana, one of Russian literature's best readers, acts in such a way that even her failures "open out."

Thus we can fairly say that this prenovelistic heroine of Pushkin's novel-in-verse inhabits a genuinely dialogic zone. For dialogue is not just having a face, making eye or lip contact with the beloved, walking happily hand in hand, being sketched by an author while conversing along the embankment. As Tsvetaeva rightly sensed, Pushkin's masterpiece is symmetrical but deceptively so: the moments of active confrontation and exchange between lovers are displaced along the diagonal, timed to go off when no one is watching, unbearably lonely. Most Russian scholars who have traced the evolution of Onegin's character throughout the writing of the novel concur that Pushkin, in his subsequent drafts, steadily reinforced his hero's disillusionment, superfluity, and indifference to the world of others.[2] Of the relatively few scholars who have devoted close attention to Tatiana, the best (such as John Garrard) acknowledge that, as compared with female heroines in literary works that Pushkin ambivalently admired, Tatiana is marvelously rounded and mature: "Unlike

Onegin," Garrard writes, "Tatiana learns from her experiences."[3] Olga Hasty does not take that insight on faith. What does it mean to learn? How do we prolong an experience, so that not all of us fails in it? In Tatiana's model of the world, all the hard work happens alone, before or after the crucial events into which we fall, sitting by the window looking out on an open field.

CARYL EMERSON

Acknowledgments

My manuscript has benefited greatly from the kind attention it received from various readers. In particular I am thankful to Caryl Emerson for her generosity of spirit and the unflagging interest she showed in this project. I am also deeply grateful to David Bethea, Ellen Chances, Christopher Hasty, Robert L. Jackson, and Stephanie Sandler, who read the entire manuscript with great insight and provided a wealth of suggestions that significantly improved this study. To Michael Wachtel go special thanks for his encouragement and the eagle eye he cast over the proofs. I also thank Susan Tarcov for copy editing, David Freedel for computer assistance, Nicole Monnier and Adam Mehring for proofreading, and Marguerite Johnson for helpful comments. I owe particular thanks to my editor, Juliet Skuldt, for her generosity, care, and patience in working with my manuscript. Princeton University provided a generous grant to offset publication costs, while the McIlwain Preceptorship gave me leave time and research support to pursue this project. For these I am most grateful.

Thanks go also to all my friends and relations who sustained me in the course of this project—most especially to Christopher and Kate for patience, nurture, and shoulder rubs.

Pushkin's Tatiana

Introduction

Nothing so difficult as a beginning
In poesy, unless perhaps the end.
Byron, *Don Juan*

There are as many Tatiana Larinas as there are readers of *Eugene Onegin*. Pushkin must surely have intended this to be so, for he provided surprisingly scant concrete detail about his heroine and, even as he created seemingly endless associative possibilities in his text, left great gaps in her story. In so doing, he invited, indeed demanded, that his reader participate actively in the process of creating the heroine of his novel-in-verse. Tatiana's characterization is infused with a rich polyvalence that grants her a stimulating, inexhaustible complexity both within her text and beyond it, and we can say that her uniqueness lies not in any particular feature, but rather in the meaning that she makes possible.

Pushkin's keen awareness of his reader is documented in his public exchanges with critics as *Eugene Onegin* appeared chapter by chapter over a nine year period. Within the text itself it is overtly demonstrated by the author/narrator's frequent apostrophes. It is implicit, moreover, in the prominent role he assigns reading in Tatiana's development. That Tatiana is an ideal heroine is reflected in the fact that she is also an ideal reader, and it would seem that the co-creativity to which Pushkin urges his reader can be learned from the very heroine to whom it is to be applied. The exhilarating experience of being drawn into a creative alliance with the greatest poet of the Golden Age has doubtless contributed to the extraordinary success Pushkin's heroine has enjoyed among readers whose enthusiastic response has fostered a "Tatiana cult." One of the most discussed and most elusive female characters in the Russian tradition, Tatiana is deemed the progenetrix of an impressive list of subsequent heroines, ranging from Goncharov's Olga (*Oblomov*) and Turgenev's Natalia (*Rudin*) to Bulgakov's Margarita (*The Master and Margarita*) and Pasternak's Lara (*Doctor Zhivago*). A commanding literary type, Tatiana is also held up as a putative model for flesh-and-blood women.

That Tatiana should play a prominent role in Russian culture and society is not surprising given Pushkin's significance in the history of Russian letters and the importance Tatiana herself assumed both in the text of *Eugene Onegin*, and in Pushkin's own creative biography. Pushkin's friend, the poet Kiukhel'beker, noted in his diary that "in his eighth chapter the poet himself resembles Tatiana."[1] This observation is very much to the point, for *Eugene Onegin* is a profoundly autobiographical work, and it is the *way* in which it is autobiographical that makes its heroine so important: Tatiana lives the dynamics of Pushkin's art. Pushkin does not become Tatiana, but his own becoming takes place alongside hers. Thus, Monika Greenleaf trenchantly summarizes, "[t]he story of Eugene Onegin turns out to be the story not of his career, marriage, or death, but of Tatiana's—and the poet-narrator's—*Bildung*."[2]

In *Onegin* Pushkin takes care to make the dates of both the related fictional events (winter 1819–spring 1825) and the time of narration (1823–30) readily determinable. Because the time of the narration overlaps the time of writing, the text, J. Thomas Shaw notes, documents an important period in Pushkin's creative biography: "The time spans of *Onegin* mark a time of crises—or at any rate, great changes—not only in Pushkin's way of looking at the world but also his mode of writing."[3] The autobiographical quality of Pushkin's novel-in-verse thus extends well beyond a commonplace interjection of recognizable personal details into the text to reflect the development of its creator in the very process of the work's unfolding over time. Indeed, the fact that Pushkin did not subject earlier parts to any substantial revisions once he had completed the text prompts us to regard what Pushkin called his "free novel" as a unique sort of "lyrical diary." It was here that the stuff of biography such as the triangular relationship of Aleksandr Raevskii, Elizaveta Vorontsova, and the exiled Pushkin of the Odessa period could become not simply the material of poetry, but a means for exploring what poetry is.[4] Unique in many ways, this "diary" engages novelistic characters and narrative events in the service of expressly poetical concerns. In it Pushkin documents his own growth and charts for himself a space of possibility.

The formation and topography of this space are best studied by moving through Pushkin's text side by side with his heroine, for even as he engaged his reader in creating her, Pushkin was putting his own artistic credenda to the test. Indeed, although he chose to name his work after its hero, it is through Tatiana that Pushkin projects his own thinking about literature and life in the course of those seven years, four months, and seventeen days, during which, according to his own calculations, he worked on *Onegin* (*PSS* 6:532).[5] It emerges that the characterization and story Pushkin crafts for his heroine are intentionally indeterminate not because it mattered little to him how she should be read, but because it was around such indeterminacy that his own ideas about the poetic enterprise evolved.

Yet Tatiana's potential-generating openness is not without its risks, for it leaves her particularly susceptible to partisan appropriation by her readers. The generous gaps Pushkin left in his novel-in-verse were easily made to hold the material of readers' own agendas. Once filled, the open spaces of Pushkin's text proved difficult to reclaim. Marks of various critical incursions became fixed in the landscape and persisted in subsequent readings of *Onegin*. Thus Tatiana came to be regarded not in the particular context Pushkin lovingly created for her, nor even in the larger context of that poet's thinking about his art, but in the light of the critical causes to which she was rallied. The co-creativity to which Pushkin urged his reader led to the usurpation of his heroine, and the muse who ever accompanied the poet was led away to stand instead at the critic's side.[6]

Even as Pushkin documents his own development in the course of writing *Eugene Onegin*, his ongoing exchange with early critics of the work reflects his conscious efforts to direct the course of a fledgling Russian critical tradition.[7] "*Onegin* was not simply another book," Clayton summarizes, "it was a continuing literary phenomenon surrounded by passionate partisanship and controversy."[8] It was not long before this tradition took a course that was decidedly different from the one Pushkin implicitly advances in his novel-in-verse, where he insists that the same principles govern the successful conduct of both literature and life. As critics insistently shifted the weight of inquiry away from literary concerns toward social ones, Pushkin's broad definition of life, which embraces human creativity and the poetic imagination, was reduced to a civic-minded purposefulness, which—even as it insisted on "realism"—narrowed the scope of what was "real." Over time *Eugene Onegin* came to be discussed—with little heed for Pushkin's intent—primarily in terms dictated by the realist novel. Designations like "realistic," "true to life," "depiction of reality" became constants in *Onegin* criticism and extended naturally to evaluations of Tatiana as well. Yet like the recognizable details of his own biography, so too the sociohistorical conditions depicted in *Eugene Onegin* are part of a project considerably more far-reaching than a merely representational one. A full hundred years after Pushkin's death, Marina Tsvetaeva still had cause to disdainfully parry criticism that centered on verisimilitude:

Быт? («Быт русского дворянства в первой половине XIX века»). Нужно же, чтобы люди были как-нибудь одеты.

[*Mores?* ("The mores of the Russian gentry in the first half of the nineteenth century.") People do, after all, need to be dressed in *something*.][9]

Because Tatiana was a crucial ally in Pushkin's enterprise, she had, in a sense, the most to lose when critics dwelt on social issues to the exclusion of anything else the poet sought to convey. In the rush toward a sociologically infused realism, Tatiana was studied for what she might be made to reflect of Russian society and national identity and neither for what she herself was nor for what she represented of her creator's artistic method. The complexity of her characterization over time was consistently reduced to a generalized image largely based on the last scene of *Onegin* with little regard for the dynamics of the whole. Tatiana's particularity and immediacy were absorbed into abstracted generalizations that did little justice to the openness to change that distinguishes her from the other characters in the work. The overriding tendency to consider Tatiana as a "type"—whether of an actual woman or an abstract ideal—drew attention away from the process of her becoming to fix her in a static image. The touted brand of "artistic reality" into which she was drawn had little in common with the reality of the poetic imagination that Pushkin championed, while the teleological, progressive view of literary development that was advanced ran counter to the principle of cultural synchronicity Tatiana embodied in his novel-in-verse. Clayton's summary of Pushkin's fate describes also Tatiana's, for she too "quickly [became] the object of national veneration, an icon to be fought over, to be praised or blasphemed, but rarely to be understood."[10]

Belinskii's influential ninth article on Pushkin (1845) and Dostoevsky's famous Pushkin speech of 1880—both of which exerted a lasting influence on subsequent discussions of Tatiana—are cases in point.[11] The unequivocal tone of these noteworthies' assessments of Pushkin's heroine overrode the carefully crafted openness and subtlety of her characterization, as each derived a creature of his own design from Pushkin's text. Belinskii, for whom *Eugene Onegin* was "an encyclopedia of Russian life," considered Tatiana in the context of the woman's role in Russian society. This perspective led him to enlarge on her rejection of Eugene as a morally suspect acquiescence to the dictates of prudish social norms. Belinskii construed Tatiana's development as a progression from the created worlds of the sentimental novels that predominated in her early years to a mature acceptance of an actual world in which imaginative constructs were left behind. This movement from the imaginative to the responsibly realistic that Belinskii attributed to Tatiana was in fact the course that he, together with other social-minded critics, advocated for Russian letters. As the poetic imagination was increasingly marginalized by radical critics of the 1860s and 1870s, Pushkin was branded a man of the past and his heroine was denied any relevance to Russian society. Tatiana suffered similar devaluation whenever the imagination was opposed to life rather than conjoined with it. Thus, for example, in the Soviet period, "Tatiana faded out of Russian literature, and Russian life [and was] superseded by . . . her sister Olga, now grown buxom, ruddy-cheeked, noisily cheerful."[12]

In his celebrated 1880 Pushkin speech, Dostoevsky countered radical critics but moved no closer to Pushkin's text. Recasting Tatiana in the image of one of his own self-sacrificing heroines, he imparted to her an aura of sanctity and proclaimed her "the apotheosis of Russian womanhood."[13] The issue of national character (*narodnost'*) that Belinskii found central to *Eugene Onegin* is raised again by Dostoevsky in connection with Tatiana and remains firmly ingrained in subsequent readings of the heroine. Thus, for example, when critical interest in Tatiana was revived in the 1950s, so too was the familiar preoccupation with the "realism" of her characterization and with her "Russianness"—couched now in terms of the heroine's ties with the common people. Even when V. Sipovskii broke with established tradition to insist that Tatiana's roots were European rather than Russian, he continued to speak of her not as a unique creation within Pushkin's text, but as a literary and social type.[14]

Whatever else she may have meant to critics, on the strength of her marital fidelity Tatiana came to be generally regarded as an exemplar of moral strength. She thus found herself securely fastened in the "strong woman–weak man" opposition that was prevalent in the Russian realist tradition. Ivanov-Razumnik's introductory article to *Eugene Onegin* in the 1907 Brokgaus-Efron edition of Pushkin's works presented what seemed to be the most widely accepted view of Tatiana: a strong woman who was prevented from self-realization only by the absence of an adequate male counterpart.[15] Implicit in Ivanov-Razumnik's assessment, which showed even the strong woman to be helpless in the absence of a worthy mate, is a view that limited the way Tatiana was read even when later critics moved beyond sociology and reinstated her in Pushkin's text. The autonomy as well as the erotic and creative energy that Pushkin invested in Tatiana remained without notice simply because these were not qualities conventionally granted women. Thus, whether she was praised or censured for it and whether it was seen as acquiescence to social demands or the fulfillment of moral obligation, Tatiana's rejection of Eugene was unquestioningly considered a typically feminine gesture of self-denial rather than a self-assertive statement of moral and (as I will argue) creative ideals at which she had arrived herself. So long as Tatiana's autonomy, sexuality, and creativity remained unrecognized, the profound correspondence of her role in *Onegin* with Pushkin's own aesthetic-philosophical thought could scarcely be appreciated. Thus even when the Symbolists and the Formalists turned to focus on questions of poetics, Tatiana did not figure significantly in their reevaluations of Pushkin's novel-in-verse. Indeed, it was only relatively recent Western scholarship that prepared the way for recognizing these crucial aspects of Tatiana.[16]

The loosening of the sway of sociology admitted new ways to regard *Eugene Onegin* and fostered a regeneration of the severed ties between Tatiana and her maker. Yet the recognition of the heroine as a poetical entity did not eradicate deeply ingrained notions of the woman's role in society. When linked to Tatiana, the idea of the poetical remained a curtailed one that prevented her image from springing entirely free of the norms to which it had been fitted. Thus, for example, in *The Sociology of Pushkin's Art* (1929) D. D. Blagoi ascribed to Tatiana an essential poetic quality that aligned her with Pushkin, and yet reverted nonetheless to familiar terrain to describe her last scene as a return to Russian roots that pointed the way to the possible salvation of an entire class of Russian nobility.[17] Ludolf Müller, among the first to consider *Eugene Onegin* thematically, discussed Tatiana in the context of other works by Pushkin, notably "The Snowstorm" ("Metel'") and "Dubrovskii," and yet arrived at a conclusion redolent of Belinskii's when he faulted Tatiana for disregarding the dictates of love and fate to enter into matrimony.[18] Leon Stilman's pathbreaking study did much to elaborate the question of genre in Pushkin's work. His assessment of Tatiana, however, echoed Sipovskii's in its claim that Tatiana's rejection of Eugene was dictated by her sentimental epistolary novels.[19] Yet even when readings of Tatiana did not keep pace with new critical perspectives, the welcome diversity of approaches that was increasingly brought to bear on *Eugene Onegin* expanded—even if only indirectly— ways in which its heroine could be discussed.[20]

For all the attention Tatiana has received, her role as Pushkin's aesthetic spokeswoman has been given surprisingly short shrift. The purpose of the present study is to recuperate the creative potentialities with which Pushkin invests his heroine. The approach is pluralistic, aimed above all at an appreciation of Tatiana's unique position within *Eugene Onegin* and thus also in Pushkin's artistic biography. The focus is on Tatiana as the controlling subjectivity of *Eugene Onegin* as we examine what David Bethea aptly calls this heroine's "psychology of 'reading the world.'"[21]

Pushkin imbeds his heroine in a rich medium of dissimilar literary and social contexts, all of which contribute in significant ways to her development. He aligns her with a dual tradition of Russian folklore and the European novels of sentiment that exert a formative influence on her, endowing her with the erotic energy of her preromantic literary predecessor, Bürger's Lenore (via Zhukovskii's translation). He gives her the ability to grasp the import of the romantic works she peruses in Eugene's library. And he finally acknowledges her as a hypostasis of the author/narrator's own fleetly metamorphosizing muse. Tatiana is exceptional not in her departure from existing literary norms and practices—these the author skillfully invokes to generate expectations in his readers—but rather in the "inclusivity" by which she is defined. Those very features that shape the Russian literary tradition and animate Pushkin's novel-in-verse animate its heroine as well. The "syncretic cultural matrix" William Mills Todd III sees in *Onegin* is vital also to Tatiana's constitution.[22] Amidst the generic, stylistic, structural, and thematic complexities of Pushkin's masterpiece Tatiana is the center that holds. In her, merely apparent choice recedes before an assimilative model that champions the creative coexistence of seemingly irreconcilable influences and points of vantage. The more she absorbs, as Pushkin demonstrates, the richer the context at her disposal for evaluating the surrounding world and her place in it. And it is precisely this constant recontextualization that has the power to rejuvenate a world that threatens to grow pale with repetition or anemic from attempts to avoid iteration.

Tatiana's significance derives from the fact that she embodies not only a moral ideal, but also a creative one with which the moral melds. At the same time, she is neither symbol nor allegorical figure, but a convincing representation of an actual woman. Even as Pushkin creates a heroine in whom to embody his thinking about his art, he accords her a significant measure of autonomy. Indeed, Tatiana's seemingly autonomous development projects a crucial tenet of the defense of poetry Pushkin advances in *Eugene Onegin*—the profound relevance of the poetic principle to the conduct of life.

Tatiana is not recognized as the author/narrator's muse until the final chapter of *Eugene Onegin*. But her exceptional qualities are registered from the very outset, and she is subtly but unmistakably distinguished both from literary heroines who preceded her and from the other characters in the work. In connection with the various antinomies that obtain in Pushkin's novel-in-verse—and among these are rural-urban, Russian-European, repeated-unprecedented, traditional-fashionable—Tatiana exemplifies the quintessentially poetical requirement that either/or be replaced with both/and. Unlike the other characters in the text, all of whom—with the exception of the author/narrator—are readily described within the bounds of preexisting categories (the idealist Lensky, the jaded late-romantic hero Onegin, the commonplace heroine Olga), Tatiana eludes determination.

Tatiana is distinguished by her innate sense of the inadequacy of her immediate surroundings, be they the rural Russian estate where *Eugene Onegin* begins or the glittering Europeanized capital where it ends. This leads her to nurture the creative imagination by means of which she can expand possibility at just those points where there appears to be none—

an activity in which Pushkin was himself highly practiced. The steady growth of Tatiana's inner world is directly dependent first on her receptivity to stimuli that have little resonance for the other characters and second on her exceptional capacity to synthesize what she absorbs. The resources at Tatiana's disposal are manifestly meager ones, but in the rich medium of her intense need for something beyond what is immediately available or apparent, they blossom with meaning.

As we study Tatiana, we come to recognize that the axioms Pushkin has her embody hold equally for the process of creating an individual heroine, an individual text, and for the process of literature itself. In creating Tatiana, Pushkin shapes a viable artistic biography for himself and charts, moreover, the development of Russian literature within the context of the Western European tradition. To understand Tatiana better means also to get a deeper look into how Pushkin construed literary process—individual and cultural—and how he translated his ideas about it into his own works. For Tatiana exemplifies the inspiring muse, the inspired poet, and the tradition in which they obtain. In order to appreciate the significance of her multifaceted role, it is necessary to read *Eugene Onegin* from *her* perspective, giving close attention to the way she interacts with the surrounding world.

Accordingly, this book is devoted to a Tatianacentric reading of Pushkin's novel-in-verse that closely follows Tatiana's development and focuses on her role opposite the other characters and vis-à-vis Pushkin himself. It considers Tatiana as an autonomously developing individual and as a heroine Pushkin created in response to specific literary circumstances and expectations. As we move through the text with Pushkin's heroine, we are afforded the opportunity to study closely how Pushkin defined the creative processes of literature and of life. Caryl Emerson offers the insightful suggestion that Tatiana "be appreciated not as tragic heroine or renunciatory object but as a special sort of dynamic poetic principle,"[23] and it is the purpose of this study to foster just such appreciation.

The opening chapter delineates the framework of oppositions that coalesces around Tatiana. Here we consider the issues Pushkin confronts as he sets out to create a heroine who is both new and lasting, who departs from the norm but is not determined by a quest for novelty. Both in her constitution and in her story, Tatiana negotiates the repeated and the unprecedented, the traditional and the newly invented. It falls to her, uniquely, to project a world in which experiences are not stretched out in a line, but form instead an interrelated organic complex.

Chapter 2 focuses on the specific literary genealogy Pushkin shapes for his heroine. Tatiana's reading calls up an important body of material against which she is to be evaluated. Significantly, Pushkin does not simply provide this genealogy for his heroine, but chooses instead to have Tatiana actively engage her literary predecessors. Richardson's Clarissa, Rousseau's Julie, and de Staël's Delphine become an integral part of Tatiana's own world. The works in which these heroines appear foster Tatiana's correlative emotional and imaginative growth and intensify the question of how she is to deal with her newly developing erotic sensibilities. Her story, as we recognize here, is driven not by a conventional novelistic plot—the quest for a husband—but by the more urgent question of how desire might be productively engaged. This question remains at the forefront of Tatiana's narrative to lead her beyond the expectation of her milieu and her readers—an expectation reinforced in Russian folklore and in the European novels she reads—that her erotic energies will be absorbed into matrimony.

Tatiana emerges an ideal reader, which means, according to the definition implicit in Pushkin's text, that she successfully interrelates what she reads with what she experiences. Outmoded literary forms are reinvigorated by the new context into which Tatiana's reading draws them. Works of bygone eras are thus endowed with a perpetual validity that argues against their retirement with the advent of subsequent generations of writings.

The novels she reads and reenacts in her imagination intensify Tatiana's feelings, which she can no longer confine to her private inner world. In Eugene, who now appears in the drowsy rural setting of her formative years, Tatiana sees an object from the actual world onto whom her powerful feelings can be projected. Finding no other outlet for her emotions, she composes a letter to Eugene. Chapter 3 is devoted to a close study of the text of this letter and the privileged context Pushkin crafts for its presentation. In it Tatiana engages vocabulary assimilated from her novels to both express and contain her overpowering emotions. In the process, the Eugene to whom she writes emerges not as a flesh-and-blood man whose attentions she seeks to secure, but as a muse who can replenish and enlarge rather then merely satisfy her powerful feelings. The composition of the letter emerges as a genuinely creative act demonstrating essential features of inspired writing as Pushkin defines it.

Although books provide Tatiana with the means to compose her emotions in both senses of that word, they do nothing to promote her understanding of Eugene. The hero who plays opposite Tatiana at this juncture in the text eludes the alternatives she frames in her letter, not intentionally, but simply because there is no point of intersection between his and Tatiana's radically dissimilar worlds. This intersection has yet to be effected. Chapter 4 gives careful consideration to the text of the monologue with which Eugene responds to Tatiana's letter. Eugene's speech reemphasizes the distance between hero and heroine, and this distance is foregrounded especially by Tatiana's success and Eugene's failure in what Pushkin projects as the correlative acts of reading, writing, and loving.

When her letter fails to elicit a satisfying response, Tatiana seeks other means to expand the options open to her. The folk rituals of divination in which she now engages translate her from a limited actual world of literal signification into a symbolic, supernatural space that is opened by the figurative potential inherent in even the humblest of signs. Individual destiny is shaped by the capacity to read beyond the meaning commonly attached to any given sign, and to expand thereby the limited possibilities afforded by the concrete world. The decoding processes that are emphasized in the course of the fortune-telling carry unmistakable implications for the reading of literary texts and, indeed, the text of life itself. The fifth chapter examines the rituals of divination that culminate in the risk-laden augury by dream. Indicated here are Tatiana's intense erotic sensibilities and, more important, the precarious translation between order and chaos, between the conscious and the unconscious, and between the literal and the figurative in which the poet must ever engage. The terrifying proximity of creativity and destructivity is revealed.

Chapter 5 concludes with a discussion of the ill-starred name day festivities that follow Tatiana's dream and a consideration of her subsequent discovery of the books in Eugene's library. The name day celebration underscores once again the failure of Tatiana's and Eugene's dissimilar worlds to intersect, and demonstrates the danger inherent in such failure. Loath to admit into his own life the unforeseeable that Tatiana courts, Eugene is preoccupied above all with maintaining his illusory control over events. His actions betray not only his irritation with Lensky but also his uneasiness in the face of Tatiana's unconventional behavior. The attentions he pays Olga and the duel with Lensky that follows mark Eugene's concerted effort to reassert the validity of that very code that has proved insufficient to explain Tatiana. Contrasted with the element of risk that is vital to the creative enterprise are the disastrous consequences of Eugene's refusal to admit the unexpected into his life.

Bewildered by Eugene's behavior, Tatiana seeks in vain to make sense of the conflicting signals she receives from him. It is only with her subsequent visits to his deserted library that, demonstrating once again her consummate reading skills, she learns how little Eugene resembles that hero/muse she has fashioned in his image. It is just as she loses her muse that Tatiana is taken, against her will, to the Moscow bride market where she must find a flesh-and-blood mate.

Tatiana's sojourn in Moscow marks a transitional stage between her maidenly life in the Russian provinces and her married state in St. Petersburg society. Chapter 6 discusses the transformation of Pushkin's heroine from callow rural miss to commanding princess in the capital and focuses on the dramatic shift in perspective that is occasioned by the author/narrator's own recognition of Tatiana as his muse. The renowned speech with which Tatiana departs from the pages of Pushkin's novel-in-verse crowns her development and provides the criteria necessary for revitalizing the jaded hero. The Eugene who now appears at her feet to proffer the love that he was incapable of experiencing earlier leads Tatiana to recollect a time of open possibility that preceded the loss of her muse and her entry into marriage. With this recollection, the image of her erstwhile muse returns to stand alongside the flesh-and-blood man before her, and it is between them that Tatiana must now make her choice.

Like her letter to Eugene, Tatiana's speech can be described as a controlled surrender. Neither the revenge nor simply the completion of a structural symmetry they are conventionally made out to be, Tatiana's words asseverate her adherence to a poetic imperative that informs her choice of the muse over the man. In refusing Eugene, Tatiana forgoes consummation of her love in favor of protracted desire; she avows her allegiance to an "other," by which she means not simply her husband but a broader imaginative realm that subsumes the contingencies of the actual world. At the same time, in freely admitting her love for Eugene even as she rejects his advances, Tatiana prepares her own modulation from flesh-and-blood woman into muse. Though the love story of *Onegin* may well be deemed a failed one, the promise of mutual inspiration that hero and heroine hold out for one another marks a success of a different order.

The epilogue to this study opens with speculation on why Tatiana has been consistently relegated to the role of loyal spouse to the detriment of the more far-reaching implications of her essentially poetic temperament. It then considers the significance she was accorded in the poetic self-presentations of two major Russian women poets. A discussion of Pavlova's *poema Quadrille* and Tsvetaeva's essay "My Pushkin"—texts that are grounded in readings of Tatiana—reveals the resonance Pushkin's heroine had in their thinking about poetry and their own place in the Russian tradition. As Pavlova and Tsvetaeva enlist Tatiana to champion female creativity, to legitimize their own entry into poetry, and to secure themselves a place in the tradition, they directly engage that creative impetus with which Pushkin invested her. The readings of Tatiana advanced by Pavlova and Tsvetaeva lend support to the recuperation of Tatiana's creative potential that this study promotes. Highly idiosyncratic, these readings are fully consistent with Pushkin's view that literary process is dependent on constant recontextualization and on the interrelation of literature and life.

1
Bildung

Change grows too changeable, without being new . . .

Byron, *Don Juan*

Poetry is by its very nature a reconciler of antinomies. In it intense emotions join with strict rational form, and yet remain vibrant; the most subjective of individual experiences open into universality and yet remain unique; the fleeting is endowed with permanence and yet loses none of its evanescence. Thus Pushkin may well speak of the "devil of a difference" between a conventional novel and *Eugene Onegin*,[1] for whatever else we may say of its hybrid genre, the very designation of the work as a "novel-in-verse" presupposes an expressly poetical enterprise. Although the novel can be absorbed into verse, poetry does not lend itself to absorption into the novel, and it is only in the poetic form that the seamless melding of these distinct genres is possible.[2] In the poetic project of *Eugene Onegin* Pushkin weds novelistic development of plot and personality potential with a verse form of his own invention to create a profoundly self-reflexive text. The principal exponent of this exceptional venture is Tatiana Larina who, by virtue of her ability to conjoin productively what other characters hold apart, stands side by side with her creator. J. Douglas Clayton's persuasive argument that "first and foremost *Onegin* must be seen as a lyrical poem"[3] is borne out by the role Pushkin assigns his novelistic heroine.

As he began his work on *Eugene Onegin* on 9 May 1823, Pushkin could not know where this project would take him, but with Tatiana's appearance in the work, the basic premises that were to guide the unfolding of his novel-in-verse fell into place. It is the purpose of this chapter to limn the fundamental issues that crystallize around Tatiana. We will consider how she is introduced, the attitude the author/narrator assumes vis-à-vis the reader when she is presented, her formative influences, the setting of her early years, and the features that distinguish her from the other characters. These elements of Tatiana's coming into being—all of which are novelistic in essence—will be examined for evidence of the far-reaching poetical concerns that propel the voyage of discovery Pushkin undertakes in *Onegin*.

From the very outset we find Tatiana imbedded in a fertile cluster of contexts: the immediate one created for her specifically within the text of *Eugene Onegin*, the broader one of the literary tradition against which Pushkin sets her, and the virtually inexhaustible implicit contexts that Pushkin's readers bring to the text. These various contexts are correlative, for addressed in each from the particular perspective it affords is the problem of engaging custom and novelty in the creative acts of reading, writing, and living. The crucial questions of reconciling tradition with innovation and conjoining the impulses of art with those of life are confronted simultaneously at the levels of the literary tradition, the individual text, and how the text is read. Pushkin's creative sphere, the fictional world Tatiana inhabits, and the actual world in which the text is received meld, and in discussing Tatiana it is important to remain aware of the configurations of the inter- and intratextual contexts in which she takes shape.

Tatiana is the last of the principal characters of *Eugene Onegin* to be introduced. By the time she makes her appearance in stanza 24 of chapter 2, the stage is richly prepared for her entrance. The settings—fashionable St. Petersburg and traditional rural Russia—that Tatiana will successfully bridge at the work's end have been described. The other major characters with whom she is to be compared have been presented, and the unique features with which Pushkin endows his heroine can be readily appreciated. As Tatiana appears on the scene, an entire constellation of oppositions falls into place, and these oppositions serve to delineate both the heroine herself and the larger issues Pushkin has her confront on his behalf. At their core is the tension between the repeated and the unprecedented, the traditional and the novel, the familiar and the unfamiliar, and this tension gives rise to the overriding question that is at the heart of *Eugene Onegin* and indeed of all art: how something can be made new and yet lasting, lasting yet new.

Tatiana's leading role in this exploration can be appreciated if we juxtapose this latecomer to the text with the other characters of *Eugene Onegin*. The comparison of Tatiana with her sister Olga underscores the problem the author himself confronts as he seeks both to create a new heroine and to avert the threat of her eventual absorption into the commonplace. Tatiana's mother, Praskov'ia Larina, exemplifies the dissipation of potentially creative erotic energy to the ease of habit—a fate that Tatiana, as we will see, successfully eludes. Counterposed to Lensky, who is predetermined by the German idealism to which he uncritically subscribes, is a Tatiana who does not fall in with any system and who re-

mains open to change. Opposite Onegin's pursuit of one thing after another is Tatiana's unique capacity for the synchronous engagement of disparate stimuli.

The characters who surround Tatiana in *Eugene Onegin* highlight
her defining features even as she offsets the insufficiencies demonstrated
in their constitutions. Although various, these insufficiencies can be
traced to an underlying single-mindedness that inhibits the otherwise dissimilar characters from going beyond the ready-made options available
to them. It is only Tatiana who successfully eludes determination. Her
privileged status within the text can be recognized from the moment of
her appearance in it.

Tatiana is first introduced in the context of an immediately preceding account of her sister Olga—a modest, obedient, cheerful, blond, blue-
eyed literary cliché of a heroine who has, as the author/narrator points
out, appeared in countless literary texts and now crops up in the "real life"
of *Eugene Onegin*. The reader is referred to "any novel" for a portrait of
the heroine the author/narrator now disclaims, and beyond whom he proposes to move his Tatiana.

> Всё в Ольге . . . но любой роман
> Возьмите и найдете верно
> Её портрет: он очень мил,
> Я прежде сам его любил,
> Но надоел он мне безмерно.
>
> [Oh, Olga's every trait . . . But glance
> In any novel—you'll discover
> Her portrait there; it's charming, true;
> I liked it once no less than you,
> But round it boredom seems to hover.]4
>   (2:23, ll. 8–12)

As he sets out to create a new heroine, Pushkin recognizes that he
must not simply consider how she will depart from the prevailing literary
norm, but must also confront the problem of how to forestall the threat
that she, in turn, will be superseded by another model, as is the heroine
to whom she is now opposed. Intimated here is that to adhere too closely
to tradition is to surrender further development to repetition and thus to
remain mired in cliché. At the same time, however, to depend exclusively
on novelty is but to postpone its inevitable recession into the commonplace. Pushkin must find the means to write into the literary tradition a
heroine who is new and yet not determined by the quest for mere novelty.

As part of this project, the author/narrator of *Eugene Onegin* provides no "portrait" of the heroine. Unlike her attractive but unremarkable sister who remains always the same ("vsegda" [always] is repeated three times in the first two lines of her description in 2:23), Tatiana is in flux and cannot be fixed in a static image. Defined by her openness to change—a quality which no other character in the work possesses, excepting the author/narrator himself—she comes to us not ready-made, but in the process of becoming. While the conventional "novelistic" heroine Olga has no unique features and fits perfectly into the role her humdrum, conventionally romanticized milieu predetermines for her, her "unnovelistic" sister is a misfit destined to chart a new course both within the setting of her text and within the Russian literary tradition. The juxtaposition of the two sisters emphasizes not only Tatiana's uniqueness, but also the interdependency, indeed the involution, of literature and life that remains at the forefront of *Eugene Onegin*, where Pushkin repeatedly demonstrates the rejuvenation of literary convention by life—life that has itself been saturated with literature.

Unlike Olga, who is presented as a set of features to which a name is then applied, Tatiana enters the text in name alone.[5] It is telling that her initial appearance is a disembodied one and significant too that Pushkin uses his heroine's name not only to call her into being but also to signal his departure from established literary practice:

Ее сестра звалась Татьяна . . .
Впервые именем таким
Страницы нежные романа
Мы своевольно осветим.

[Her sister bore the name Tatiana.
And we now press our willful claim
To be the first who thus shall honour
A tender novel with that name.]
(2:24, ll. 1–4)

In the footnote he appends to the first line of this stanza, Pushkin draws attention to "Tatiana" as both an acoustic fact and a sociological marker.[6] The stanza itself goes on to comment on the mellifluousness of this name and the associations it prompts—associations that situate it squarely in traditional Russian rural society. The larger project of Pushkin's work is thus encapsulated onomastically, for in "Tatiana" poetic qualities—the acoustic and associative properties of her name—are wedded to the novelistic—the name as a sociological indicator. Pushkin's new heroine is pointedly distanced from the fashionable urban world where novelty holds sway. At the same time, her old-fashioned Russian name is described as new in the literary context into which it is now introduced, a context that is in turn revitalized by this introduction. Thus, already in name Pushkin's heroine emerges from the locus of creativity: the intersection of the traditional and the unprecedented. In the naming of the heroine her destiny may already be glimpsed, for as we will see, it falls consistently to Tatiana to interrelate the repeated and the new, and to engage the creative potentialities inherent in the tension between them.

Tatiana's revealing onomastic introduction is followed by five stanzas (25–29) that present the reader with an account of a heroine who is defined predominantly in terms of what she is not.[7] Neither rosy nor vivacious like her sister, Tatiana is as out of place in her milieu as her name is on the pages of a novel. She shies away from family and playmates, and, eschewing childish pastimes, spends much of her time gazing out of a window. She herself cannot be gazed upon with concrete result, for the author/narrator provides his readers with no physical description of the heroine, focusing instead on how she relates to her surroundings and how she differs from everyone around her. Noted only is the fact that Tatiana does not resemble her sister in beauty or complexion:

> Ни красотой сестры своей,
> Ни свежестью её румяной
> Не привлекла б она очей.

> [she lacked her sister's beauty, lacked
> the rosy bloom that glowed so newly
> to catch the eye and to attract.][8]
> (2:25, ll. 2–4)

By creating a heroine whose physical appearance remains to be constituted in the mind's eye of each of her readers, Pushkin actively enlists his audience in her co-creation, a co-creation that can potentially support the project of ensuring that her vitality endure. Yet even as this strategy promotes Tatiana's lasting newness, it also foregrounds the conventions and expectations that govern reading and that threaten to close down those possibilities Pushkin carves out for his heroine in the space of the text. Thus, for example, on the strength of the familiar double heroine device that operates in the absence of a concrete description of Tatiana, readers are consistently led to envision Tatiana as a dark-haired, brown-eyed counterpart to her blond, blue-eyed sister.[9] This, of course, may well be how the heroine looked to her creator, and there is nothing intrinsically wrong in imagining a dark Tatiana. The danger here lies in how quickly and completely the possibilities resident in being *unlike* Olga are withdrawn if the unconscious dynamics of opposition lead readers to regard Tatiana as merely her sister's antithesis. This situation alerts us to the sterility of construing existence—whether literary or actual—exclusively in terms of contraries, for such a view reinforces precisely that either/or approach to life and text that the poet ever strives to subvert. In and of themselves, antitheses threaten to be not only meaningless but downright harmful, inasmuch as they create a false sense of choice just where available options have in fact been drastically reduced, and the fertile region where extremes can productively coexist has been obliterated. Although there is much to be gained from opposing Tatiana to Olga, to see her as merely antithetical to her sister is to curtail her development and to overlook the complexity that gives rise to her genuine, far-reaching uniqueness. It is clear that not only the successful creation but also the reception of a new yet also enduring heroine depends on considerably more than her mere opposition to an outdated model. Tatiana cannot simply be an "unOlga." If Tatiana is to be spared being read back into the narrow scope from which he frees her, Pushkin must lead his reader beyond the literary convention of the double heroine device, even as he exploits its potential.[10]

In sum, the reader's past literary experience is a rich resource for enlarging a literary work, and the various literary traditions Pushkin evokes as he develops his heroine enhance the creative opportunities at his disposal. And yet the business is also a risky one, for those very allusions to past conventions that can highlight the new perspective the author now offers threaten also to activate predispositions in the reader that could interfere with the fresh apprehension of the work and the appreciation of its uniqueness. Pushkin mitigates this threat by drawing the different contexts, the various meanings they generate and the different perspectives they afford into dynamic, ever-shifting interrelationships. The stability of any one construct is thus constantly undermined, and ever new ways of relating to the text are demanded. Pushkin, as William Mills Todd III notes, "has made sure that any monistic reading will sooner or later run aground on the ontological complexity of his novel."[11] This ensures that not only Pushkin's heroine herself, but also the ways she is read will remain in flux.

Having drawn attention to Tatiana's uniqueness as a literary heroine and to the role that he and his readers play in creating her, the author/narrator proceeds to supply material he is now purportedly recording rather than inventing. In this "biographical data" we recognize the essential features of Pushkin's literary project translated now to the terrain of a fictional world that ostensibly represents life itself.

Tatiana grows up on a secluded rural Russian estate far removed from the fashionable urban society that has already been described in connection with Eugene's upbringing. She neglects the prescribed activities—needlework, dolls, and games—in which other girls engage in preparation for the roles they are to assume in their adult lives, in favor of daydreaming and solitary nature walks that yield no concrete results. Her clear preference for the imaginative over the pragmatic can be regarded as both cause and consequence of her alienation. This alienation is rich with promise, for it provides her with a critical point of vantage on her surroundings, marks her lack of interest in the predictable future her place in society holds for her, and reflects her longing for something beyond the immediately available. Tatiana cannot—as does Eugene, for example—effect an actual departure from her limited and limiting world, but this circumstance serves her well, for it precipitates what Pushkin himself knew to be ultimately a preferable metaphoric departure into an imaginative realm that coexists with the conventional world and yet springs free from its narrow compass. From the very start, Tatiana is absorbed not in the day-to-day, but in the shaping and exploration of another reality that coexists with it. This is possible largely because her upbringing is one of benign neglect. Although her knowledge of French implies some formal schooling, no tutor or governess is in evidence to inhibit her natural, individual growth.[12] In place of these is a Russian nanny brimming with folktales, and a stack of outmoded Western European novels of whose potential danger to young girls Tatiana's parents remain unaware.

The folklore and the novels offer Tatiana two distinct yet complementary ways of construing existence—both welcome enrichments to the pedestrian day-to-day life of her immediate surroundings. The folktales she loves so well provide a dramatically expanded reading of the world around her, while the novels that she avidly reads open new imaginative and emotional expanses within herself. The stories her nurse tells suggest a vast supernatural dimension beyond the natural phenomena and contingencies of the mundane Tatiana observes daily. Here the individual surrenders self and destiny to those invisible, incontestable forces that govern the cosmos. Yet inasmuch as the supernatural beyond attaches itself to signs of the here-and-now, the ability to recognize transcendent meaning in the commonplace and the capacity to read and to manipulate such signs secure for the individual a modicum of participation in shaping the course life might take. The folk idiom—as we will elaborate in chapter 4—nurtures the imagination with a wondrous display of the polyvalence of signs and the breadth of meaning they are capable of sustaining. At the same time, the heedful structure of the oral text carves out a distinctly human space within the vast reaches of the natural world. The scrupulously maintained, ever-repeated patterns of the folk idiom supply the entire community with the means to coax order into an inscrutable universe that is tamed by repetition.

The English and French epistolary novels Tatiana reads shift the focus of attention from the universe that surrounds her to the one within. Here the project is to impart creative order not to the outside world, but to the protagonist's own emotional realm—a realm that, even at its most turbulent moments, can be formally contained by the written text. It is now the individual's sensibilities and the particular form in which she couches them that shape destiny as she selects the verbal signs that are to contain and convey her emotions. Distinctly at odds with the age-old repetition that characterizes folktales, the epistolary novels create a sense of immediacy and unrepeatability that derives from the intensely personal expression of private emotions at the very moment of their coming into being.

The mix of these two strains is crucial and animating. Commentators keen on foregrounding Tatiana's "Russianness" insist, predictably, on the importance of the Russian nanny and folk culture to Tatiana's development.[13] Those critics who argue that Tatiana is European in character naturally choose to focus on the significance the novels assume in her life.[14] Yet Tatiana is rich in character, imagination, and creative potentiality precisely because she successfully absorbs the divergent worldviews couched in the Russian folk *and* the European literary traditions and is thus determined by neither. What Russian folklore and Western European novels contribute to her development carries implications that are considerably broader than those of the opposition of East and West, for the distinct perspectives offered by these genres extend beyond questions of narrowly defined national identity. Together with the folktales and the novels, Tatiana absorbs, besides the opposition Russian/European, also those of oral/literary, natural/civilized, communal/individual, traditional/novel, and repeated/unprecedented. The synthesis of these antinomies expands that private inner world she nurtures in the course of *Eugene Onegin* and enhances the potentiality she brings to the text. It is worth noting here that the Russian folklore and European novels that figure prominently in Tatiana's early years play a definitive role both in Pushkin's own development and in the evolution of Russian letters. This intimation that the process of Tatiana's development might be regarded as analogous not only to Pushkin's individual creative growth, but also more broadly, to the emergence of the Russian literary tradition, is subsequently reinforced in the text of *Eugene Onegin*.

The epistolary novels of Richardson and Rousseau are given a special place in Tatiana's Bildung. Indeed, they come to overshadow the actual world and to dominate in her imaginative space:

> Ей рано нравились романы;
> Они ей заменяли всё;
> Она влюблялася в обманы
> И Ричардсона и Руссо.

[But novels, which she early favored,
Replaced for her all other treats;
With rapturous delights she savored
Rousseau's and Richardson's deceits.][15]
(2:29, ll. 1–4)

The "deceitfulness" of the novels (Pushkin rhymes "romany" [novels] with "obmany" [deceits]) is implicitly opposed to what is presumably the verity of the actual world they replace. For Tatiana, however, the novels she reads are not deceptions, but newly discovered realities that complement her actual experience and foster her individual growth.

Significantly, Pushkin postpones the mention of books, which in earlier drafts of *Eugene Onegin* appeared already in the account of her earliest childhood, preferring to introduce them instead at this later stage in his heroine's development.[16] Tatiana's absorption in Richardson and Rousseau thus marks what proves to be an interdependent blossoming of her imagination and her sexuality. Pushkin's heroine throws herself into avid novel reading not at the behest of fashion or custom, but out of an immediate, personally experienced need. The fact that the once wildly popular writers she now discovers are no longer in vogue means nothing, for to her these books bring fresh revelations about her newly developing self.

That reading should take center stage at this juncture in Tatiana's story is scarcely surprising in light of the fact that Pushkin has placed her in a setting that is markedly lacking in eros. There is no one in Tatiana's milieu who can help her come to terms with and direct the new sensations that she now experiences. Her mother is completely desexualized and evinces no residual traces of those emotions her "Grandison" once inspired in her. The account Tatiana's nurse later gives of her own arranged marriage, indeed her ignorance of the very notion of "love" (although conditioned, of course, by peasant norms), reinforces the pronounced asexuality of Tatiana's environment.

Nor can Tatiana turn to her younger sister. Olga, although contemplating marriage, shows as yet no signs of either the desire or the imagination that animates Tatiana. Indeed, Olga appears to lack not only a vocabulary of love, but the very capacity for powerful, sustained feeling. This mere replica of a conventional novelistic heroine who no longer excites readers, is herself incapable of individualized experience of intense emotions and is content with a conventional reenactment of love and courtship. Her beloved Lensky's experience and expression of feelings are predetermined by the German idealism to which he unthinkingly subscribes. His lyrical outpourings, though ostensibly inspired by and directed toward Olga, are in fact dictated not by overpowering feelings for a flesh-and-blood woman, but by a generalized ideal that he does not devise, but simply adopts as his own. The object of his abstract idolatry, cognizant perhaps at some level that the poems are not really addressed to *her*, remains unresponsive to them.

Onegin's later disdainful comparison of Lensky's beloved to a Van Dyck Madonna (3:5, l. 9) is not simply a detail included to exercise scholars determined to identify the painting, nor yet another bit of "the motley refuse of the Flemish school" ("flamandskoi shkoly pestryi sor"). It is a signal of Onegin's instinctive disapproval of Lensky's attachment to an abstract ideal in place of an actual woman. Superimposed on the opposition of repetition and novelty, we recognize here another opposition that is, as we will see, central to Tatiana's story—that of the abstract ideal and the flesh-and-blood individual. We can observe here that Onegin's juxtaposition of Tatiana and her sister in this conversation once again triggers the double heroine device to reinforce the suggestion that, unlike her bucolic sister, the melancholic Tatiana is possessed of sexual vitality. At the same time, the juxtaposition of the two male friends indicates that if Lensky falls short on the erotic front because he sacrifices an actual woman to an abstract, ready-made ideal (an ideal that, like Olga-the-novelistic-heroine, has had its zest sapped by all too frequent evocation), Onegin's erotic energies have been dissipated by their all too frequent physical exercise. Although a misfit in his rural setting, Eugene is, like its denizens, fervorless.

Tatiana's burgeoning emotions and inchoate desires alienate her still further from the markedly desexualized world around her and lead her deeper into an imaginative space that develops in accordance with actual needs. Thus she turns to Richardson and Rousseau—authors whose works excite those very passions against which they ostensibly warn—to learn the vocabulary of love and to derive welcome support for the desires she is beginning to experience. To say that the novels she now reads "replaced everything else for her" ("Oni ei zamenili vse" [2:29, l. 2]) is to say that at this stage in her development, Tatiana is focused on her correlative emotional and imaginative unfolding.

Far from being a sign of escapism, Tatiana's reading marks an earnest attempt to come to terms with what transpires within her. The imaginative literature that initially overwhelms her day-to-day life will be discussed in further detail in chapter 2. Here we need note only that Tatiana's developing erotic sensibilities are from the very start aligned with the imaginative realm. The creative imagination supersedes physiology, and a book serves as an acceptable substitute for a flesh-and-blood bedfellow. The potential danger inherent in this metonymic replacement is lost on her father, who, having read no novels himself, sees no harm in letting his daughter "sleep with a book":

Но в книгах не видал вреда;
Он, не читая никогда,
Их почитал пустой игрушкой,
И не заботился о том,
Какой у дочки тайный том
Дремал до утра под подушкой.

[But still, in books he saw no harm,
And, though immune to reading's charm,
Deemed it a minor peccadillo;
Nor did he care what secret tome
His daughter read or kept at home
Asleep till morn beneath her pillow.]
(2:29, ll. 7–12)

Tatiana's singularity within the text of *Eugene Onegin* is thus intensified by urges that are universal in both life and literature, but which are pointedly excised from the surroundings that Pushkin crafts for her. The isolation in which she must deal with her nascent sexuality and the absence in her milieu of ready-made models that anticipate and thus threaten to encroach on direct emotional experience lead Tatiana to seek out models in the realm of imaginative writing. Analogously, Tatiana's reading assumes this prominent role in her development because it is not fashion driven. In the absence of preconceptions and expectations, and of those models of social behavior that in the city turn largely on erotically charged competition and public display, Tatiana must find her own way. Under these circumstances she emerges as an ideal reader who brings her own experiences to the novels and actively integrates what she reads into her own life. Her sexuality and her imagination are drawn into powerful interaction, each deriving energy from the other, with the result that Tatiana's capacity for love is expanded far beyond the desires that fuel it.

The author/narrator's account of Tatiana modulates at precisely this point—that is, just as she is described sleeping with a novel under her pillow (2:29, l. 12)—into a brief biography of her mother, whose story augments the literary context in which Tatiana's development can be read with the context generated by what is ostensibly life itself. The account of the espousal and married life of Tatiana's mother shows the erosion of feelings by trivial day-to-day concerns. After her marriage, "Polina"—now Praskov'ia Larina—casts aside her romantic notions as easily as the fashionable conceits she cultivated in her days of youth. Her girlish fantasies give way to the actuality of a placid, markedly unexceptional life's course. With the complacent reenactment of custom, her life's energies are absorbed into habit. In the passage that describes Praskov'ia's married life, the words *privykla* (grew accustomed) and *privychka* (habit) appear three times in the space of four lines (2:31–32). Mere repetition keeps her in a holding pattern that precludes further development, and she is content to conduct her uneventful life with her husband according to tried and true customs:

> Они хранили в жизни мирной
> Привычки милой старины.
>
> [Amid this peaceful life they cherished,
> They held all ancient custom dear.]
> (2:35, ll. 1–2)

This "real life" alternative to Tatiana's fantasies demonstrates the threat that her environment poses to the emotional and imaginative energy that now animates her. In light of Praskov'ia Larina's progression from starry-eyed romanticism to mundane pragmatism, Tatiana's emerging erotic sensibilities and novel-precipitated withdrawal from the actual world can be construed as a passing stage rather than as a sign of a unique destiny. The mother's past emerges as a possible portent of the daughter's future and alerts us to the fact that Tatiana's feelings and vivid fantasies alike run the risk of being swallowed up by the quotidian. Although ultimately this pedestrian maternal biography serves as a backdrop against which Tatiana's exceptional one emerges with greater radiance, here Praskov'ia's "real life" story collides with the distinctly literary expectations set into motion by the description of Tatiana provided thus far. The question that arises from this collision is whether Tatiana's development will adhere to the conventions of literature or to the norms of life. The former course threatens to produce yet another Olga, the latter yet another Praskov'ia, neither of whom is a livable, growing model. It is clear that Pushkin intends for Tatiana to supersede these inadequate options offered by the distinct conventions of literature and of life in order to create a heroine who resembles neither her mother nor her sister. It is, as we will see, the dynamic interrelation between life and literature that ultimately ensures her success in this regard.

Tatiana is well prepared for charting this alternative course, for the author/narrator, as we have seen, has already distinguished her from her sister. He provides her also with a powerful safeguard against a fate like her mother's. Whatever the similarity of Tatiana's fancies to those Praskov'ia harbored in the days of her youth, a compelling difference prevails between mother and daughter. The romantic notions of Praskov'ia Larina's early years, as we learn, are not fueled by specific literary texts as are Tatiana's. They are instead determined by vocabulary extracted from fashionable novels that was common currency at the time.

Praskov'ia did not actually read the novels in question, but simply resorted to their idiom—and did so, moreover, with little heed for precision.[17] Thus *her* "Grandison" resembles not Sir Charles, that irresistible paragon of virtue Richardson describes at considerable length, but his irredeemable father, Sir Thomas:

> Сей Грандисон был славный франт,
> Игрок и гвардии сержант.
>
> [*This* Grandison was fashion's pet,
> A gambler and a guards cadet.]
> (2:30, ll. 13–14)

In Pushkin's unfinished *Roman v pis'makh* (*A Novel in Letters*), the heroine Liza writes from rural seclusion to a Petersburg friend: "Nadobno zhit' v derevne chtob imet' vozmozhnost' prochitat' khvalenuiu Klarissu" (It is necessary to live in the country to have a chance to read the celebrated Clarissa) [*PSS* 8:47]. Because, unlike her mother, Tatiana grows up on a rural estate, she has the time to experience at first hand those expansive novels that her mother only heard of and talked about. Tatiana's actual and literary experiences are unmediated. They do not follow the dictates of fleeting fashion, but are guided instead by nature and feeling— the very two forces that Liza of *A Novel in Letters* designates as "eternal."[18] The directness of Tatiana's apprehension and the emotional and imaginative intensity that distinguish her from her mother suggest that her burgeoning feelings will not be so easily erased from her life.

Here it is necessary to ask what sort of a fate this might portend, for we cannot overlook the fact that the plots of those very novels that intensify Tatiana's feelings issue a stern warning against allowing life to be ruled by powerful emotions. In the writings of both Richardson and Rousseau, erotic love is shown time and time again to have disastrous consequences for both sexes, but for the woman in particular. Thus Clarissa Harlowe dies, a victim of Lovelace's unbridled passions. Harriet Byron, heroine of Richardson's *Sir Charles Grandison*, having herself fallen prey to the excessive ardor of Sir Hargrave Pollexfen, advocates *comfort* over *joy*,[19] and suggests that a woman wait to marry until her "romantic age" is safely "over."[20] In Rousseau's *La nouvelle Héloïse* (*The New Eloise*), the expressly unerotic marital relations of Julie and Wolmar are presented as a preferable alternative to the heroine's passionate love affair with Saint-Preux. These works will receive further attention in the subsequent chapter, which is devoted to Tatiana's reading. For now it is important to note only that the novels that absorb Tatiana abound with compelling arguments against powerful feelings in favor of a stable, emotionally uneventful existence. Thus, although Tatiana's readings supply her with a vocabulary of love and nurture an imaginative space in which it can flourish, these books ultimately advocate a dispassionate surrender to matrimony, maternity, and household duties—a life's course, in short, very like her mother's. "Some of us are to be set up for warnings, some for examples," Harriet Byron notes in one of her letters.[21] The heroines of Tatiana's novels fulfill the former function, while her mother serves in the latter capacity. For all their obvious dissimilarities, Tatiana's actual world and the invented ones of her novels conspire in their insistence that intense emotions are potentially destructive and therefore to be excluded from life. Thus, to cite but one of many possible examples, when Tatiana's nurse later diagnoses her ward's love as a malady (3:19), she reinforces the very notion Richardson projects in *Sir Charles Grandison* with Clementina's story that powerful feelings are inevitably debilitating rather than self-affirming.[22]

Although they coincide in message with Tatiana's day-to-day life, the novels she reads nonetheless focus on those very emotions that now occupy center stage in her personal development. They offer a broader range of plots and possibilities than the surrounding world, and, perhaps most important, demonstrate compellingly the forceful energies resident in eros. Thus it is hardly surprising that at this point in her development Tatiana should find the "warnings" of her novels more compelling than the "examples" supplied by her own milieu.

Because she is not prepared to surrender the emotional energy that animates her life, Tatiana faces the question of how her feelings might be preserved from extinction, and yet also be prevented from destroying her. The problem before her is that she must neither sacrifice her emotions to habit as her mother did, nor yet allow herself to be undone by powerful feelings as did the heroines of her novels. It is precisely this concern, as will be argued here, rather than the conventional novelistic plot of securing a husband, that becomes the moving force in Tatiana's story. Its undercurrent is a distinctly poetical one, for the twofold project of enabling and yet also containing overpowering feeling is the provenance of poetry. The seeds of the "dynamic poetic principle" Caryl Emerson discerns in Tatiana are already sown.[23]

It is specifically in the context of her pedagogically unsound but imaginatively promising reading that Tatiana regards Eugene. We have noted already the effects of the double heroine device that Pushkin deploys to connect Tatiana to that literary tradition in which her sister has become a cliché, and yet also to disassociate her from it. We have seen, too, how Tatiana is compared to and yet also distinguished from her mother. We must turn now to examine the contrasts that emerge when we

juxtapose Tatiana with the hero she has not yet met, but whose development the reader has already witnessed. It can come as no surprise that it
is precisely this juxtaposition that propels the text.

Heroine and hero could scarcely differ more in background and
habit. The sleepy, custom-driven rural setting in which Tatiana's formative years are passed and her uninhibited natural development in ram-
bling woods and meadows contrast sharply with the frenetic bustle of Eugene's St. Petersburg milieu, where his development is governed—indeed
predetermined—by the artificial dictates of fashionable society. Tatiana
prefers solitude and the tranquillity of nature. Eugene, concerned primarily with the effect he produces on those around him, spends his time
at crowded social events. Tatiana absorbs the stimuli of her surroundings
and remains open to change. Eugene is all highly polished surface. The
stimuli to which he is exposed glance off without effecting any substan-
tive alteration in him. While Tatiana, a consummate reader, lives in the
world of her books, Eugene attends the theater where, from a distance,
he watches people act. His busy day ends at dawn, and he heads for bed
just as Tatiana rises to greet the new day. Eugene holds little respect for
the institution of matrimony and focuses instead on the quick, transient
gratification of frivolous erotic sensibilities. In Tatiana's milieu, sexuality
is neglected in favor of married life and the stolid, earnest business of per-
petuating the species. Opposed to the quest after novelty of Eugene's
world is the dedication to preserving the status quo of Tatiana's.

Considered against Eugene's upbringing in the European capital, the
account of Tatiana's early years in the Russian provinces emphasizes the
vast differences between their worlds. It is tempting to consider these
differences in terms of the conventional opposition of Russian tradition
to European civilization that haunts discourse on Russian culture. Although this opposition is a significant one, it is more productive to consider the sharp contrasts between the distinct worlds in which Pushkin situates his hero and heroine as deriving not from the tension between East
and West, but from the antithetical temporalities that govern their respective milieus. Pushkin's descriptions of life in Petersburg and in rural
Russia were praised by readers for being true to life. Yet for all their abun-
dance of "realistic" detail, the settings Pushkin crafts for Tatiana and Eugene are carefully contrived abstractions that project the consequences of
the divergent temporal constructs that inform their radically dissimilar
worlds. Tatiana emerges from a milieu that subscribes to a cyclic tempo-
rality and is governed by custom—repetition that remains impervious to
change. Counterposed to this cyclicity is the sequential linearity of Eugene's world, where fashion—the endless, sterile replacement of one thing
with another—holds sway and where what Pushkin has elsewhere called

a "blind prejudice for novelty" reigns. In the distinct temporalities that define the settings Pushkin creates for his hero and heroine, we find yet another manifestation of that fundamental challenge all artists must confront—the creative interrelation of custom and novelty.

The juxtaposition of St. Petersburg society and Russian provincial life graphically demonstrates the negative consequences of each of these distinct temporal constructs taken in isolation. With this demonstration the demand is issued to explore how they might be productively negotiated. If we recognize that it is precisely this temporal question that Pushkin himself confronts as he sets out to create a heroine who neither repeats nor merely succeeds her predecessors, we can appreciate the extent to which his own aesthetic searchings are tied up with Tatiana's story.

The inadequacies of the discrete temporalities of the settings juxtaposed in *Eugene Onegin* are very much in evidence. Although the author/narrator reserves a kindlier tone for descriptions of Tatiana's rural setting than of Eugene's urban one, it is immediately apparent that the divergent temporal constructs they exemplify—pure cyclicity and pure sequential linearity—have an unsettling tendency to coincide in the results they produce. As we compare Tatiana's milieu with Eugene's, we see that both in constant repetition and in constant flight from it, significance is all too easily lost. What were once meaning-laden rituals have paled with reenactment by innumerable generations into those empty gestures of habit that the text documents in Tatiana's rural world, while the relentless forward drive toward novelty in Eugene's urban setting has allowed no time for meaning to adhere to gesture. Thus too, ceaseless change, as Eugene's boredom attests, can become every bit as dull and devoid of significance as ceaseless repetition. Considered in terms of sexuality, the opposition of repetition and novelty collapses as it becomes clear that desire runs the risk being stilled by a sequence of ever-changing partners no less than by the recurrence of always one and the same of honest matrimony. A surfeit of passionate engagements proves as deadening to intense feelings as their complete absence. Eugene's series of conquests leaves him exhausted and unresponsive, while in Tatiana's provincial world, erotic sensibilities are stifled by the early habitual onset of matrimony.

Inasmuch as the *consequences* of the unalloyed temporalities that prevail in the settings Pushkin has devised for his hero and heroine are virtually indistinguishable, it is clear that the problem is not one of simple choice. Demanded here is the shaping of new possibilities, and it is precisely to the quest for such possibilities that *Eugene Onegin* is dedicated. Indeed, the very opposition of the temporal constructs designated as cyclicity and sequential linearity underscores the fact that their separation into alternatives diffuses their dialectical and productive potentialities. It emerges in the course of *Eugene Onegin*—and this is crucial to the work—that only their integration can satisfy the creative imperative of ensuring permanence through change and newness through constancy. Without recourse to the return and regeneration that tradition supplies, there is nothing to protect the isolated present from the doom of passage in which its presence will have been illusory—degraded to fashion. Without the rejuvenation of tradition by returns effected from new temporal terrain, there is nothing to protect its reenactments from the doom of stasis and ossification. The various pure antinomies represented in the text of *Eugene Onegin* demand productive integration. Although here we have focused on the opposition of cyclicity and sequential linearity, it is important to recognize that this holds true for all of the diametrically opposed constructs presented in Pushkin's novel-in-verse. As its hybrid generic form avows, *Eugene Onegin* is an eloquent argument for the creative momentum and expansion of possibility that can be derived from integrating what is apparently irreconcilable.

Like any truly creative being, Pushkin is committed to order but opposed to schematization. Into the structure of *Eugene Onegin* he consistently introduces shifts that disrupt the stability of the symmetries on which it is built. He thereby creates a dynamic balance that is both exquisite and precarious. Even as Pushkin establishes the antinomies dictated by the distinct temporalities that govern Tatiana's rural milieu and Eugene's urban one, he does not do the obvious. He does not let hero and heroine stand as representatives of these distinct temporal settings in order to bring them together in an ending made doubly happy by the wedding of opposed temporal constructs. Rather than resort to such a static, dully symmetrical solution, Pushkin chooses to tilt the aesthetic balance in his heroine's favor.

Thus we observe that Eugene fits easily into his milieu while the awkward Tatiana shies away from others and remains estranged even from members of her own family. Although on the surface this appears to be yet another in the series of dissimilarities that obtain between hero and heroine, it is in fact the detail that disrupts the symmetry of the oppositions that we have sketched thus far. The point is that Eugene's worldview coincides with that of the setting in which he spends his formative years. This view is firmly entrenched, and he neither questions it nor sees beyond it. By the time Tatiana is introduced, Eugene has already moved from Petersburg to his country estate, but it is clear that mere relocation has no significant effect on his development, for to rural Russia Onegin brings the baggage of his urban world. The novelty of country life quickly wears off for him, and Eugene, who can regard his surroundings only in the terms dictated by his own fashionable milieu—that is, as hopelessly outdated—cannot but fail to recognize the alternative to his own way of seeing that this different world offers. Such shortsightedness precludes the possibility of a productive integration of new outlooks that could further his growth. In his new setting Eugene is accorded the status of misfit. Although his estrangement suggests a link with Tatiana, it is at bottom merely a sign of the inability to acknowledge otherness on the part of both rural old-timers and urban newcomer. The series of amorous adventures, the masks and personae he dons and sheds one after the other, his inability to assimilate the perspective of Tatiana's world, and later his travels all bespeak the extent to which he is defined by sequence.

Opposed to the system of "one damn thing after another" to which Eugene unwittingly subscribes, is not Tatiana herself, but rather the milieu in which she spends her early years. Pushkin makes it clear from the very start that Tatiana is not to be considered a representative of her setting as Eugene is of his. She neither fits into the world around her nor wants to. Indeed, Tatiana's intuitive sense of the inadequacy of the options her immediate setting offers her sets her apart wherever she finds herself and prompts her to take every opportunity to seek beyond what is readily accessible. Drawing on whatever is available—nature, daydreams, folklore, her window, her books, and subsequently on her love for Eugene—Tatiana infuses her surroundings with more than they themselves offer. The energy of both her openness and her stability derives from her capacity to interrelate the various stimuli she so readily absorbs. The productive coexistence of Russian folklore and Western European novels in Tatiana's girlhood is indicative of her successful assimilation of the dissimilar worldviews that give rise to these distinct manifestations of human creativity. For Tatiana there are no immutable boundaries. The worlds of Russian folklore, her own daydreams, and Western European novels interact with one another and with her day-to-day life, opening new realms of possibility within the restricted and restrictive space of her setting. Tatiana emerges as an extraordinary literary invention. Even as she is accorded a convincing, albeit sketchy, biography, she acts as the agent for proving the insufficiency not of simply one side or another in those oppositions that are so abundantly supplied in *Eugene Onegin*, but of one-sidedness itself.

Having focused thus far on Tatiana's uniqueness in her own setting and against the backdrop of the remaining characters, we must note also how distinctly unexceptional individual features of her characterization are in a larger literary context. Thus, for example, even though Tatiana is the only one in *Eugene Onegin* for whom reading is from the very start a life-sustaining activity, if viewed from a broader perspective, this trait loses its singularity. Richardson and Rousseau were as wildly popular in

Russia as they were in Europe, and the readiness of readers to be ruled by fictions of the literary imagination of the eighteenth and early nineteenth centuries has been amply documented.[24] The perusal of novels was not only a commonplace in everyday life, but a familiar topos as well. Pushkin himself, as Sipovskii reminds us, includes novel reading in all his works that describe contemporary life.[25] From this perspective, there is nothing exceptional in the fact that Tatiana reads, in what she reads, or even in the fact that for her the fictive world takes on a reality greater than that of her actual surroundings. Nor is the unsociability that sets Tatiana apart from the rest of her family without precedent. Chizhevsky suggests possible hagiographic antecedents, while Nabokov and Lotman explain the trait alternatively as a commonplace of romanticism.[26] To recognize that the pleasure Tatiana takes in horror stories coincides with that of the preromantics, we have only to recall by way of example Gottfried Bürger's insistence that his *Lenore*—prototype of Zhukovskii's Svetlana with whom Tatiana is compared—should be read in a dimly lit room decorated by a human skull.[27]

Yet Tatiana herself is innocent of this larger literary context that threatens to absorb her defining features. Her singularity derives largely from the fact that her behavior—even when it coincides with preexisting models—is never convention-driven, but always individual, motivated from within. The extent to which this precept is applicable to Pushkin's own literary endeavor is easily recognized. Represented in Tatiana's story is a natural, unselfconscious development. In the course of her growth, the various influences to which the heroine and her creator have been exposed are neither emphasized nor avoided but seamlessly assimilated. Tatiana's uniqueness is dependent not on novelty, but on her capacity to integrate the material supplied by life and literature into the private world of her imagination—a capacity analogous to Pushkin's own ability to integrate the material supplied by life and literature into the world of his novel-in-verse. Thus too in the influences that shape Tatiana's early development, we recognize a sequence of literary schools operating in rich synchrony. The sentimental epistolary novel and the folklore that inspired the preromantics interact to enrich Tatiana's imaginative sphere, to be joined shortly also by the writings of the romantics she discovers in Eugene's library. Thus Tatiana has not one literary orientation, but an entire cluster of reference points that work in concert to enhance her complexity.

From myriad apparent irreconcilables Tatiana learns to derive and engage in her own life the same creative energy that vivifies her creator and that he applies to make his heroine ever new. In this regard it is she who emerges as the principal character of *Eugene Onegin*. The source of Tatiana's creative vitality is in her capacity—one that she shares with

Pushkin himself—to embrace and hold in interactive simultaneity seemingly incompatible constructs. This enables Tatiana's mediation between recurrence and sequence, between the repeated and the new, and permits her also to hold the actual and the imaginative in harmony. Assigned to Eugene is the role of demonstrating the causes and consequences of failure in such mediation, and he emerges as a reluctant student who, at the work's end, is unwillingly apprenticed to Tatiana. Couched in the story of Tatiana and Eugene's unrealized love is the story of a successful harnessing of antinomies to socially, morally, and aesthetically satisfying ends. The quest on which Pushkin launches his heroine is closely tied up with his own artistic and personal searchings as he charts Tatiana's progress toward that essential poetic translation of life-negating either/or into the liberating creative affirmation of both/and, and then holds out—on the strength of his heroine's example—the promise of similar progress for the hero who trails after her.

Thus *Eugene Onegin*, I suggest, is not simply or even primarily a love story—itself a hackneyed symmetry—but a quest for expanded potentiality that is furthered by the dynamic reconciliation of the various oppositions established in the text. The circumvention of the dangers inherent in both repetition and innovation is of considerable personal and aesthetic significance to Pushkin as he contemplates his heroine's growth, his own development, and the course of Russian letters. Without tradition, the context necessary for fully appreciating innovation is lost. And yet dependency on tradition—conscious or habitually blind—brings with it the threat that change will be inhibited and the new stifled by the preexisting. Here emerges Tatiana's ability to steer between the faceless universality represented by her bland sister, and that excessive, ultimately vacuous Byronic individualism embodied in Eugene. True creativity and growth, as Pushkin has Tatiana enact before his reader, lies not in the overthrow of the universal by the singular, nor yet in the replacement of the extant with the unprecedented, but rather in the consummate negotiation between them. As the text of *Eugene Onegin* unfolds, Tatiana exemplifies how an ever new heroine is to be shaped, and how literary tradition can maintain momentum without losing its bearings or severing itself from the life-giving sources of past eras. The axioms of human creativity that Tatiana embodies are applicable at all levels of literary endeavor, ranging from the coming-into-being of an individual text to the great process of literature itself. They hold too, as Tatiana's story ultimately reveals, for the successful conduct of life.

2
Love and Reading

Wax to receive and marble to retain . . .
                    Byron, *Beppo*

As Tatiana matures, the alienation that signaled her uniqueness as a child modulates into that loneliness and sense of isolation which accompany awakening sexuality. She focuses now on needs that, in the absence of support from her markedly de-eroticized setting, must derive sustenance from the world of the imagination. Within the scant actual biography Pushkin provides for his heroine, this stage in her development is accorded considerable prominence. Having been prepared by what might be called a prologue that suggests the complex significance she is to assume within the text, Tatiana's own story begins here. For it is at this juncture that we move from contemplating the static image she presents to the surrounding world to enter the dynamic space of her private sphere. By no means, however, does this suggest a separation of her individual story from the ideas about creativity and literary development that Pushkin has her convey in the course of the work. Quite the contrary, beneath what might be construed as a literary commonplace—the description of a lovestruck heroine—are auctorial reflections on three areas delineated already in Tatiana's "prologue": individual creativity, the development of a literary tradition, and the role of the reader.

The powerful attraction to Eugene that Tatiana experiences upon meeting him bespeaks an emerging need to interrelate her private world with the one around her. No longer content with an exclusively imaginary realm, and yet unwilling to abandon it for the mundane realia of her surroundings, Tatiana sees in Eugene an object of desire from the actual world that can be drawn into the sphere of her imagination. That this sphere is enriched by Eugene's appearance is signaled by the intensity and the responsivity with which Tatiana returns to reading her novels after she meets him. Eugene provides that drop of blood vital to the continued existence of the shades who populate her private inner world, and a swarm of novelistic heroes flocks around him in a vivid affirmation of the potentiality he holds for Tatiana.

34

On the strength of the emotions she attaches to Eugene, Tatiana moves from being a spectator of the events described in the novels she reads to become an active participant in them. She identifies closely with Richardson's Clarissa, Rousseau's Julie, and de Staël's Delphine. Even as these heroines expand the scope of her vision and promote her development, the outmoded texts in which they appear are revitalized by Tatiana's reading. "What fashion abandons," William Mills Todd III notes, "the imagination can recover for its own purposes."[1] Enlivened by the Eugene in her mind's eye, the works to which Tatiana returns intensify her emotions, and awaken in her an overpowering need to express her feelings.

Conditions that give rise to inspiration fall into place, and Tatiana emerges as a creative being guided by the muse she comes to recognize in Onegin. Eugene's role as muse will be elaborated in chapter 3, which focuses on Tatiana's letter to him. This chapter is devoted to two immediately preceding, closely interrelated stages in her story: Tatiana's reading and the entry of Eugene into her world. By way of introduction we describe the significance reading assumes both for Tatiana as a developing individual in the text and for the author who guides this development in full awareness of literary tradition. We then discuss the effect of Eugene's appearance on Tatiana and, in particular, on the way she relates to her books. Finally, we turn to consider the stories of the specific heroines with whom Tatiana identifies in order to examine the notions about female sexuality that they project. Implicit in our discussion is what his heroine's reading reflects of Pushkin's own attitude to the individual reader and to the tradition she helps to shape.

Pushkin knew of Rousseau's wish that Julie d'Etange (*The New Eloise*) be regarded as an actual woman and not as a literary character of his invention.[2] Indeed, he showed a similar interest in having Tatiana develop in seeming independence of auctorial design. And yet in creating her, Pushkin eschewed the literary tactics generally deployed to such purpose. Unlike his French literary predecessor, who gives his readers immediate access to Julie's innermost thoughts and emotional and psychological states through her letters, Pushkin preserves for his heroine an extraordinary measure of privacy. Tatiana remains pointedly undemonstrative in the text. Her story is thickly mediated by a narrator who, admitting his own partiality, invites the reader to join him in admiring her. The unreliability of this narrator and the absence of markers that distinguish whether he is relating "facts" or conveying his own fantasies about Tatiana combine with her own reticence in a text that indicates but does not reveal its heroine. What are traditionally regarded as crucial moments in the story of a literary figure are not divulged, but must instead be pieced together from the scant information supplied by an author/narrator who repeatedly enfolds his readers in the pronominal embrace of his "we." (Tatiana has only two moments of conscious self-revelation in the text—the letter she writes Eugene, which I will consider in chapter 3, and her speech to him, which I will discuss in chapter 6.) The reader is left with a distinct, stimulating impression that, together with the author/narrator, he must work at getting to know Tatiana. Because she is a heroine who is in the process of becoming rather than one who comes to the text ready-made, the illusion that she is an autonomous being is significantly enhanced. It is as if Tatiana brings to the text her own potentialities, the realization of which the author/narrator can observe and marvel at, but not necessarily direct.

Crucial to the enterprise of deriving the heroine are the various contexts that are evoked in the text—contexts in which the sparse details relating to Tatiana can blossom with meaning. The novels Tatiana reads in chapter 3 of *Onegin* constitute one particularly important potential-expanding domain in which to consider her. Clarissa, Julie, and Delphine join the models supplied by Tatiana's milieu and the urban socialites with whom the author/narrator compares Tatiana to expand significantly the context in which we are to make sense of Pushkin's heroine.

The literary-historical significance of the sentimental epistolary novels Tatiana reads has received serious scholarly attention.[3] The particular heroines with whom she identifies, however, indeed the very fact that she identifies with them, are usually treated dismissively, while the imagination nurtured by the novels—when it is considered at all—is mentioned as if it were a childhood disease that had to be gotten over. Scholars differ in their assessments of the role Tatiana's heroines assume in her life, but the basic premise is that she falls under the sway of her novels and that this is not entirely to her credit. Thus, for example, Stanley Mitchell praises the Tatiana with whom *Eugene Onegin* culminates for her strength "to throw off literary fashion and become a real person."[4] Michael Katz, who by contrast regards Tatiana's behavior at the conclusion of the work as a "reenactment" of what she has read, writes that "[t]here can be little doubt that she vaguely recalls the fates of her favorite heroines."[5] A closer look at what and at how Tatiana reads suggests, however, that her reading plays a more important role in her development and in the overall design of *Eugene Onegin* than is generally allowed.

Pushkin's incorporation of the novels of a past literary school into his text advances two ideas that are central to *Eugene Onegin*: that literary development and creativity, like life itself, are more productively construed in terms of an interactive synchronicity of phenomena than of a mere succession of events, and that the dynamics of this synchronicity derive specifically from repeated intersections of what is already familiar with what is still new. Even as Tatiana enacts this notion on Pushkin's behalf, she is granted her own agenda, for she herself reads and reacts to the novels in question.[6] It is of considerable consequence that Pushkin does not simply provide a genealogy for his heroine but chooses instead to have Tatiana directly engage her own literary predecessors. Unaware of the temporal issues that preoccupy her author, Tatiana discovers in her reading a resonance of the powerful feelings she experiences, but for which she finds no encouragement in her surrounding world. Her novels fuel her emotional and imaginative development, but leave in place, indeed intensify, the overriding question of how the creative energy resident in eros might be productively engaged. For all that Tatiana learns from the heroines she studies, it remains for her to resolve this crucial issue for which they offer no viable solution.

Because Tatiana's reading is central to her own development and to the literary issues Pushkin explores through *Eugene Onegin*, the project of examining the works she reads is a rewarding one. Pushkin's selection of those heroines who are to tutor his own draws attention to the specific literary models with whom he aligns Tatiana and beyond whom he has her develop. Even as Tatiana's favorite heroines serve to expand her world, they throw into high relief those very features that promote both her development as a creative individual and her evolution as a literary heroine. Familiarity with Tatiana's reading material enables us to perceive more clearly the collision of codes and values that Pushkin orchestrates when he brings together a hero and heroine who, in Mitchell's well-chosen words, "stand at either extreme of their author's trajectory."[7] And only against the unvarying role assigned to women in these works can we come to appreciate what Pushkin accomplishes with his own heroine. Before we proceed to examine what Tatiana stands to learn from Clarissa, Julie, and Delphine, it is necessary first to consider the import of her meeting with Eugene and the effects it has on her rapidly expanding inner world, for it is in this context that the importance of her reading can best be understood.

The epigraph for chapter 3—the one in which Tatiana falls in love with Eugene—is taken from Malfilâtre's *Narcisse, ou l'île de Vénus*, "Elle était fille, elle était amoureuse." The applicability of this quotation to Tatiana is immediately apparent. If understood to be in a causal relationship, its two statements indicate that Tatiana's amorousness is both natural and inevitable at this stage in her development. Yet however natural, this emotional state, as we have already seen, is excised from Tatiana's surroundings and warned against with considerable eloquence by the authors whose works she reads. Lurking beyond the idea expressed in the epigraph, moreover, is what the subsequent lines from *Narcisse* convey: the culpability of a woman who allows herself to be guided by the dictates of love, and the power of a man to either forgive or condemn her for so doing. "Je lui pardonne; Amour la fit coupable. / Puisse le sort lui pardonner aussi!"[8] Given the context in which it appears, we can discern in Pushkin's epigraph a subtle indication of the incongruity between natural development and the social and cultural norms within which a woman operates, a situation that preoccupies the author of *The New Eloise* and that Tatiana both reads about and witnesses at first hand.

We have already noted that the absence of eros from her surroundings and the desexualization of her mother and nurse urge Tatiana to develop an imaginative inner space into which she absorbs the novels that at least acknowledge the female sexuality they warn against. As her emotions grow in intensity, however, Tatiana cannot remain content with her books, or with that inner world they have nurtured. The correlative development of her emotional and imaginative capacities has now reached a stage that demands cross-fertilization of the imaginative with the actual. Thus Tatiana needs an extraneous object toward whom her feelings might be directed. Whether or not this object is accessible, appropriate, or likely to reciprocate matters little just now. Of paramount importance is that her diffuse, inchoate desires be brought into focus and projected into the outside world. As the resources of Tatiana's imaginative sphere are depleted by the swelling intensity of her emotions, there arises the correlative need that they be replenished with something from "real life." Had he arrived much earlier or much later, he could scarcely have come to play such a crucial role in Tatiana's life, but it is precisely at this moment of unprecedented need that Eugene Onegin enters Tatiana's life to become the unwitting mediator between the actual and the imaginary worlds she inhabits. Anticipating further developments, we can observe that this particular role is one traditionally assigned a muse.

It is not given to the reader to witness Tatiana's first meeting with the hero destined to play such a significant part in her life. Indeed, Pushkin goes out of his way to trivialize the event textually. The visit to the Larins' home that Onegin undertakes at Lensky's behest is absorbed immediately into custom and denied singularity. Recorded is only the ritual of hospitality that the appearance of the two guests sets into motion:

> Явились; им расточены
> Порой тяжелые услуги
> Гостеприимной старины.
> Обряд известный угощенья.
>
> [And on arrival duly meet
> That sometimes heavy, but good-hearted,

Old-fashioned Russian welcome treat.
The social ritual never changes.]
(3:3, ll. 2–5)

No mention is made of any of the partakers of the feast, and even the enumeration of traditional Russian delectables served to the guests peters out very quickly, leaving the stanza a full six lines shy of completion. The event it patently fails to record is of considerable interest to the reader and would seem to be of import to Tatiana's story as well. Yet instead of a description of the conventionally privileged first meeting of hero and heroine, the curious reader is served up only a trail of ellipses. Nabokov argues that Pushkin canceled the end of this stanza "because of two flaws he could not correct without rewriting it," flaws which Nabokov himself is, naturally, quick to spot.[9] Yet Pushkin was not known to shy away from subjecting his manuscripts to frequent, rigorous reworkings, and it is difficult to believe that at this seemingly crucial point in his heroine's story he would choose to exhibit auctorial sloth or even to merely thumb his nose at readers and novelistic conventions. It would seem rather that Pushkin is urging his reader to recognize that what is important to his heroine must be sought not in this particular moment but elsewhere. The point is that Tatiana's is not love at first sight, but, more accurately, love well before first sight. Her meeting with Eugene is not to be regarded as a "cause"—the starting point of a love story that drives the heroine's plot. Pushkin chooses, in other words, to privilege not the isolated, fleeting moment of Tatiana's first encounter with the hero, but rather the entire process of her becoming into which that meeting is absorbed.

At the same time, Pushkin's pointed gesture of omission indicates the privileging of Tatiana's imagination over actual experience, for already at this relatively early stage in the text, Eugene is relegated to a role that is ancillary to the cultivation of Tatiana's imaginative sphere. From the very start, it is an abstract, incorporeal Eugene that is of greater import to Tatiana's story than the man himself. Small wonder that he should continue to serve in this capacity at the work's end. The emphasis thus naturally falls not on the encounter, but on what frames it: Tatiana's heightened receptivity and her reaction to Eugene.[10] Accordingly, the subsequent stanzas describing Tatiana's newfound "love" focus on the extent of her readiness for it, both in terms of the inevitability of the maturation process ("Pora prishla, ona vliubilas'" [The time came and she fell in love] [3:7, l. 6]), and in connection with the heightened imagination that is correlative with heightened desire:

Давно сердечное томленье
Теснило ей младую грудь;

Душа ждала . . . кого-нибудь,
VIII
И дождалась . . . Открылись очи;
Она сказала: это он!

[Long had a throbbing agitation
In vain sought in her bosom room;
Heart thirsting for . . . it knew not whom
VIII
Now found him . . . And in wonder gazing,
She could but whisper—It is he!][11]
(3:7, ll. 12–14—3:8, ll. 1–2)

The intensity of Tatiana's anticipation is demonstrated by the interstanzaic enjambment that appears at this juncture. Stanza 7 spills over into stanza 8, in a graphic demonstration of the potential vested in anticipation and desire to override conventional boundaries. The "he" Tatiana recognizes as an object toward whom her emotions can be directed is not merely a flesh-and-blood male who might be expected to fulfill the desires she already harbors. More important, he is a catalyst who intensifies feelings that are already in place before his appearance.[12]

Its effects are similarly more important than the meeting itself. Onegin's response is registered in his conversation (alluded to in the preceding chapter) with Lensky as they speed home after the evening spent at the Larins'. Eugene professes to be bored—neither more nor less than usual. He ascribes his yawns to "privychka" (habit). Seeking relief from his "boredom" by taunting his gullible friend, Eugene underscores that he has remained unaffected by the visit. Before the enamored Lensky, he parades his own imperviousness to arousal and flaunts his indifference to those very charms that excite his friend. He speaks first not of Olga as he surely knows Lensky would wish him to, nor yet of Tatiana, as could well be expected, but rather of Praskov'ia Larina, a woman far removed from the sway of eros. (Only Tatiana's nurse could have been a less likely recipient of Onegin's attentions.) Eugene then goes on first to allege his inability to distinguish between what we know to be the two very different sisters, and then to argue for the superiority of Tatiana over Lensky's chosen one. In so doing, Eugene says nothing about Tatiana, but speaks only of Olga's insipidness—this specifically in terms that belittle the woman Vladimir loves even as they debunk the aesthetic system to which he subscribes:

«В чертах у Ольги жизни нет.
Точь в точь в Вандиковой Мадоне:
Кругла, красна лицом она,

Как эта глупая луна
На этом глупом небосклоне».

["Your Olga's look is cold and dead,
As in some dull, Van Dyck madonna;
So round and fair of face is she,
She's like the stupid moon you see,
Up in that stupid sky you honor."][13]

(3:5, ll. 8–12)

The comparison of Olga's features with those of a Van Dyck Madonna bespeaks, as we have already suggested, Eugene's disapproval of his friend's deification of a flesh-and-blood woman and of his replacement of eros with abstract idealism. The moon to which he likens Olga derives from the set of stock images that define Lensky's borrowed aesthetics.[14] As Monika Greenleaf notes insightfully, "In what amounts to a dress rehearsal for their later duel, Eugene with one stroke destroys both tenor and vehicle, leaving only the carcass of Lensky's poetic language."[15] Applied to the vacuous Olga, the image is, as Eugene senses, as commonplace and sterile as Lensky's relationship with her. Yet we can note parenthetically that in the subsequent text of *Onegin* the jaded lunar orb that Eugene slights is revitalized by its alignment with Tatiana's creativity.

While Onegin speaks of Olga in this conversation, Lensky describes Tatiana, and does so in terms that suggest what is perhaps an unconscious yet clear acknowledgment of that very quality he does not recognize in her sister. Comparing Tatiana to her rhyme pair Svetlana, Lensky implicitly acknowledges her erotic energies. And yet in so doing he also removes them immediately from life to situate them in a literary setting that warns of the grave consequences of female eros. As is the case of any true rhyme, the significance of the juxtaposition of Tatiana and Svetlana extends well beyond their acoustic kinship. *Svetlana* (1808–12, pub. 1813) is one of Vasilii Zhukovskii's three reworkings of Gottfried Bürger's *Lenore* (1773).[16] In Bürger's ballad, the heroine's erotic urges lead her to damnable behavior and a grisly death. Driven by powerful desire, the unhappy Lenore follows her beloved not to a bed of consummation, but to a coffin where she perishes in the embrace of his putrefying remains. In *Svetlana*—Zhukovskii's version that infuses German preromanticism with Russian ethos—both the erotic and the grisly are prettified.[17] By removing Bürger's explicit connection of sexual desire with death from his own heroine's waking hours, Zhukovskii mitigates the horrific outcome of the German prototype. Svetlana remains unconscious of her sexuality. Her erotic desires and the terrors attendant on them surface only in a dream from which she awakens to the safe return of her intended and the promise of many unclouded years of matrimony. By the ballad's end, all traces of fear and sexuality have been erased.

Where Bürger sounds a terrifying warning against female eros, Zhukovskii creates an example of its felicitous domestication. Lensky's comparison of Tatiana to Zhukovskii's heroine reminds the reader of the strong possibility that Tatiana too might eventually surrender those powerful feelings that are now at the center of her existence to conventional matrimony. Certainly the resemblance Tatiana bears to Svetlana suggests the likelihood of such an outcome. The intense longing that alienates Tatiana from her surroundings and the many hours she spends gazing into the distance from her window link her with Zhukovskii's heroine, who is similarly riveted to her window by intense anticipation. The similarity between Svetlana and Tatiana is further reinforced by Pushkin's choice of two lines from Zhukovskii's work for the epigraph of chapter 5 where Tatiana's dream is recorded: "O ne znai sikh strashnykh snov / Ty moia Svetlana!" (Oh, never know these frightful dreams, / My dear Svetlana!).

Yet the possibility also remains that rather than surrender her erotic energies to matrimony like Svetlana, Tatiana might suffer the fate of that heroine's prototype and, like Lenore, be undone by them. Once again we find Tatiana's development suspended between the same inadequate alternatives that have been suggested on the one hand by her milieu and on the other hand by the novels that she reads. The complex and dynamic field of literary interactions in which *Svetlana* is engaged, however, reminds us that repetition does not necessarily presuppose replication.[18] Tatiana is aligned with a heroine who has been repeated many times, but always with a difference. Whatever her similarities to that literary prototype, she too, as it emerges, has a significant alteration to bring to the story.

Among the Larins' less literary-minded friends and neighbors, eros is not countenanced at all, and a conventional matrimonial plot precludes any other possibilities. Certain already that Olga and Vladimir will marry,[19] they proclaim Eugene to be Tatiana's betrothed, embellishing this ill-founded premise with highly specific, concrete detail intended, apparently, to authenticate it:

> Иные даже утверждали,
> Что свадьба слажена совсем,
> Но остановлена затем,
> Что модных колец не достали.

> [Some even knowingly conceded
> That wedding plans had long been set,
> And then postponed till they could get
> The stylish rings the couple needed.]
> (3:6, ll. 9–12)

The triviality of this fabricated impediment to the marriage stands in laughable contrast to the gravity of the problems that keep lovers asunder in the novels Tatiana reads. The "realistic" details supplied by gossips are as false and divorced from the actual situation as Tatiana's imaginative constructs are true and grounded in actuality.

It is worth reiterating here that Tatiana's absorption in the novels that prepared her for "falling in love" with Eugene is triggered by a personally experienced need to find support for a burgeoning sexuality that naturally comes to the fore even in that absence from her surroundings of all that "hints continuation of the species."[20] Tatiana's emotional development cannot therefore be ascribed solely to the effects of the novels she reads any more than it can to Eugene's entry into her life. Rather, this development is a consequence of that highly productive and necessary interpenetration of life and literature, of the actual and the imaginative that Pushkin champions throughout his novel-in-verse. The individuality he carefully crafts for Tatiana is based on the concurrent, indeed interdependent, development of her sexuality, which is foregrounded by the expressly unerotic setting in which he situates her, and of her imaginative capacities that take her well beyond that setting.

It is significant that in Tatiana's response to Eugene, eros and the creative imagination are virtually indistinguishable. For her to remain connected to the creative potential resident in eros, and thus to emerge as a viable heroine who projects, moreover, Pushkin's own aesthetic searchings, Tatiana's newly developing sexuality must be neither stifled, nor allowed to run amok. She herself is prepared to surrender neither her intense emotions nor the imaginative sphere that they fuel. Thus even though she is irritated by the neighbors' gossip about her impending marriage, Tatiana experiences pleasure in thinking about an unspecified, erotically charged condition in which Eugene is neither named nor assigned a specific role, but in which his presence is strongly felt:

> Татьяна слушала с досадой
> Такие сплетни; но тайком
> С неизъяснимою отрадой
> Невольно думала о том.

> [Tatyana listened with vexation
> To all this gossip; but it's true
> That with a secret exultation,
> Despite herself she wondered too.]
> (3:7, ll. 1–4)

The prepositional phrase that in the original designates what Tatiana wonders about is vague, for the Russian *o tom* can mean either "about the one [who]" or "about that [which]." Rather than refer specifically to Eugene, this imprecise reference indicates the broader imaginative, erotic field into which he has been absorbed. Rhymed with this "o tom" is the similarly vague "ob odnom" Tatiana evokes in her letter, which will be considered in the subsequent chapter. Looking ahead, we find a direct parallel to these equivocal designations in the "drugomu" (to another someone or something) that appears in Tatiana's famous speech to Eugene, which we will examine in chapter 6.

Tatiana's primary personal quest is not finding a husband as those around her expect, and her story differs from those of the other women in *Eugene Onegin* precisely because she seeks not the "cure" of marriage, but a means for the protraction of her "illness." Her response to Eugene suggests that she is interested in him less as a potential husband than as a much-needed object for those emotions that feed her imagination and are in turn fed by it. The question of matrimony is incidental to this more pressing need. In Eugene the imaginary and the actual intersect to create a realm of possibility for Tatiana—a realm of possibility (and not of actualization) where desire is sustained rather than diffused or satisfied. Up to now Tatiana has nurtured a private imaginative space closely aligned with her unfolding erotic sensibilities, yet removed from the surrounding world. Eugene's appearance fosters what has become a necessary interaction between the inner world she chiefly inhabits and the one around her. It does not urge the replacement of sexuality by matrimony any more than it does the displacement of the imagined by the actual.[21] Indeed, as a consequence of Tatiana's meeting with Eugene, the imagination stimulated by her reading and her awakened sexuality come together. The imagery in the stanzas describing her love (7–8) is infused with the heat of desire and serves to emphasize the convergence of nature and imagination in the emotions Tatiana now experiences. Thus we find references to the vivifying fires of spring, to the imagination burning with sensuality and longing, and to Tatiana's hot, solitary slumber.

> Так в землю падшее зерно
> Весны огнем оживлено.
> Давно ее воображенье,
> Сгорая негой и тоской,
> Алкало пищи роковой.

> [Thus, dropped into the earth, a seed
> is quickened by the fire of spring.
> Long since had her imagination,
> consumed with mollitude and yearning,
> craved for the fatal food.][22]

$$(3:7, \text{ll. } 7-11)$$

Tatiana's recognition of a love object intensifies her desire. Now it is not the "deceptions" of Richardson and Rousseau that fuel her imagination and dominate her life, but the image of Eugene. While it may initially appear that at this stage in her development Pushkin's heroine is incapable of distinguishing between literature and life, it is precisely at this point in her story that Tatiana, no longer content with a book for a bedfellow, becomes conscious of the fact that her sleep is both "hot" ("zharkii") and "solitary" ("odinokii") (3:8, l. 4). And it is now too that she experiences a dissatisfaction that extends both to her actual world, which she finds irritating beyond measure, and to that of the imagination, which has apparently lost its power to satisfy her needs. More jealous than ever of the solitude she has always treasured, Tatiana absorbs Eugene into her reveries, where he serves not as a potential husband but as a catalyst for the further development and intensification of precisely those correlative urges—the erotic and the creative—that fostered her receptivity to his appearance.

If reading promotes love, so too does love promote reading. Tatiana's imaginative intercourse with fiction continues to be interrelated with actually experienced physiological and emotional needs.

Теперь с каким она вниманьем
Читает сладостный роман.

[With what attention she *now*
Reads a delicious novel.][23]
(3:9, ll. 1–2, my emphasis)

However many readers her novels have had, and however outmoded they are in fashionable urban society, Tatiana's experience of them—even as she now rereads them—is just as immediate and unprecedented as her experience of the stages in her personal development to which her books speak. It is of no concern to her that her emotions and her readings have borne endless repetition. The freshness of her apprehension revitalizes both feelings and texts. Tatiana does not simply rehearse the plots of her novels to herself. Her incorporation of literary material into her imaginative sphere and her translation of feelings she personally experiences into the books she reads are indicative of a highly productive interdependency of reader and text. Tatiana reads creatively.

As she interrelates her own world with the worlds of the novels she reads, the divide between life and literature proves as permeable as the boundaries between the various texts. Her love for the newly discovered Eugene animates the heroes of her novels, and the Eugene of her mind's eye emerges as an exuberant, if unlikely, amalgam of some of the greatest heartthrobs of eighteenth-century Western European literature.

Счастливой силою мечтанья
Одушевленные созданья,
Любовник Юлии Вольмар,
Малек-Адель и де Линар,
И Вертер, мученик мятежный,
И бесподобный Грандисон,
Который нам наводит сон,
Все для мечтательницы нежной
В единый образ облеклись,
В одном Онегине слились.

[Those figures fancy has created
Her happy dreams have animated:
The lover of Julíe Wolmár,
Malék-Adhél and de Linár,
And Werther, that rebellious martyr,
And Grandison, the noble lord
(With whom today we're rather bored)—
All these our dreamy maiden's ardour
Has pictured with a single grace,
And seen in all . . . Onegin's face.]
(3:9, ll. 5–14)

That her composite of Saint-Preux, Malek-Adhel, Gustav de Linar, and
Werther could scarcely resemble the man she has just met goes without
saying. Given the brevity of her acquaintance with Onegin and the limited scope of her experience in the actual world, it is scarcely surprising
that Tatiana should draw on literary experience in her attempt to make
sense of the man she has just met. Recognizing him as a misfit in her rural
milieu, as an other who brings new promise, Tatiana situates Eugene in
the fictional world on whose sustenance she herself has thus far relied. We
are reminded here of an observation made by one of Tatiana's favorite
heroines: "I think that in general it is easy for a man of cold temperament
to attract the love of a passionate soul; he captures and holds your interest by leading you to suppose a secret beyond what he says."[24] Tatiana is
such a "passionate soul," and whatever else he may be, for her Eugene remains a compelling enigma—one, as it emerges, that neither her actual
experiences nor the old-fashioned novels at her disposal enable her to
solve. The newly arrived hero must remain a mystery to Tatiana until his
library yields up a disappointing solution. In the meantime, she fills Eugene with content far beyond what he can himself encompass.

The heroes Tatiana rallies to fill the void of Eugene's identity come
from works that, though of unequal quality, enjoyed tremendous popularity among both Russian and European readers. Hailing from England,

France, and Germany, they easily crossed national and cultural boundaries to capture the hearts of innumerable readers. Noteworthy here is the perfect ease with which Tatiana settles on the vacuous Eugene an intense simultaneity of disparate characters and characteristics. The surfeit of content with which she endows him attests to the generosity of her imaginative spirit and highlights the promise of expanded possibility his image holds out to her. However unlike the actual man, the Eugene yielded up by Tatiana's compendium of renowned heroes gauges accurately the intensity of those emotions out of which this image springs.[25] The flesh-and-blood man serves to house an ideal that Tatiana shapes from the very different sources at her disposal. Her composition of an unprecedented hero out of preexisting material is distinctly analogous to the way Pushkin himself creates *Eugene Onegin*, indeed Tatiana herself. Here Todd's observation that Tatiana's "creative use of conventions comes closest to the author's" is very much to the point.[26]

At the same time, Tatiana's amalgamation of the dissimilar heroes of her novels into the heady image of Eugene alerts us to the common ground shared by these literary figures. The heroes are without exception extremely attractive, and their allure is generated by the intensity of the emotions they themselves experience and thus evoke also in their readers. These are heroes whose activity (Grandison, Malek-Adhel) and inactivity alike (Saint-Preux, Werther) are subsumed by their concerted struggles with passionate love that is either unreciprocated (de Linar), or barred from realization by duty, society, religion, or morality (Saint-Preux, Malek-Adhel, Sir Charles Grandison, Werther). The abstract forces that act as powerful barriers to legal, sanctified, or socially sanctioned fulfillment intensify their love and shift the focus of attention from consummation to the experience of heightened, protracted desire. Although powerful feeling is both as problematical and potentially destructive for heroes as it is for heroines, the difference—one that the novels housing Tatiana's heroines highlight—lies in the far greater range of activity open to men into which superabundant sexual energies might be channeled. Thus, for example, although they do not necessarily succeed, Saint-Preux and Werther can at least try their hand at civil service, Malek-Adhel can devote himself to military duties, while Sir Charles Grandison can keep busy doing all manner of good at home and abroad. Whatever the dissimilarities between Onegin and the heroes with whom Tatiana would have him correspond, he, like they, can range beyond the immediate sway of those intense emotions that—according to Tatiana's novels, though not her immediate setting—must remain always at the center of a woman's life. Indeed, one notion that prevails across the boundaries of the various literary schools invoked in *Onegin* is that men naturally have many interests in life, but that women remain confined to what de Staël describes as "a destiny whose only events are feelings."[27] In this, even writers as dissimilar as Richardson and Byron fall into perfect agreement.[28]

In the society represented in *Onegin*, Eugene is granted more alternatives and greater mobility than are allowed Tatiana. As will be discussed in the next chapter, for example, Eugene's response to Tatiana's letter centers on his own decision to eschew marriage—an option that is not viable for Tatiana. Yet, as we will see, although a broader range of possibilities is open to Eugene than to Tatiana, it is she who successfully attains from within her restricted compass a productive alternative to the limited choices suggested by her surroundings and her readings.

If Tatiana's amalgamation of heroes in the image of Eugene is a tacit recognition of the variety of possibilities that are open to him, her own alignment with novelistic heroines reflects a need for an expanded range of possibilities. The humdrum plot of actual life as construed by friends and family, who can envision only uneventful marriage in a reassuring perpetuation of the status quo, is augmented by an imaginative range of possibilities in stories that, although perhaps not liberating in and of themselves, introduce a welcome variety into an otherwise all too predictable future. Even as her Eugene emerges as a complex composite of all the heroes Tatiana can muster to his definition, she herself is not content with the guise of any one heroine, and chooses to align herself with three: Richardson's Clarissa, Rousseau's Julie, and de Staël's Delphine.

> Воображаясь героиной
> Своих возлюбленных творцов,
> Клариссой, Юлией, Дельфиной,
> Татьяна в тишине лесов
> Одна с опасной книгой бродит.
>
> [Her fancy-fed imagination
> Casts her in turn as heroine
> Of every favorite creation,
> Julie, Clarissa, or Delphine.
> Dangerous book in hand, she wanders.][29]
> (3:10, ll. 1–5)

Of the three heroines with whom Tatiana identifies, only one (Julie) plays opposite a hero with whom Tatiana has aligned Eugene (Saint-Preux), and this argues eloquently for her lack of interest in assuming a predetermined role vis-à-vis her new hero. Tatiana is no mere composite or understudy of these heroines. Her reading is an urgent exploration not only of the new worlds the novels open to her, but also of the self and the possibilities open to it. Accordingly, these works remain important sources of self-knowledge rather than mere purveyors of plots she might reenact. Unlike the random and congested list of popular heroes she rallies around Eugene, the three specific heroines who now animate her imaginative sphere are of considerable literary import and interconnectedness. If we are to evaluate Tatiana's development as an individual within the world of *Eugene Onegin*, and to understand the intersection of tradition and invention that lies at the center of her characterization, we must turn now to look more attentively at the heroines whom she selects as her mentors. Here it is important to consider the literary tradition into which Pushkin enters his heroine and to examine in some detail what her heroines' stories offer Tatiana.

There are unfortunately no known surviving drafts of stanzas 7–24 of chapter 3, and we have at our disposal no concrete evidence of how Pushkin worked toward arriving at this particular list of heroines for Tatiana.[30] Yet even a brief consideration of the novels in which they appear yields up coherent reasons for why these particular works should be singled out from among Tatiana's books, and suggests plausible explanations for Pushkin's choice.

Like all the novels included in Tatiana's library, the three in which her preferred heroines appear enjoyed a wide and enthusiastic readership. Pushkin was himself thoroughly familiar with these works and held them in high esteem.[31] *Clarissa* (1747–48), Richardson's moralistic epistolary novel of action, met with great acclaim on its native soil, on the Continent, and in Russia. *La nouvelle Héloïse* (pub. 1761)—*pace* Voltaire, who regarded its success as one of the infamies of his century—became a seminal work for the preromantic period, and was so wildly popular that lending libraries charged patrons an hourly fee for its perusal. The publication of *Delphine* in December of 1802 was a major literary event not only in France, but in England, Switzerland, and Germany as well. Unlike others of the works in Tatiana's library, these three, besides enjoying great popularity, played a highly influential role in the development of the novel and of novelistic heroines. The works that house Clarissa, Julie, and Delphine are, moreover, interrelated within a coherent literary tradition that Pushkin augments with his own heroine. Rousseau lavished extravagant praise on *Clarissa* (which he read, like Pushkin after him, in Prévost's translation),[32] and singled it out as the work that most powerfully affected his *New Eloise*.[33] Germaine de Staël, in her preface to *Delphine*, included both *Clarissa* and *La nouvelle Héloïse* in her brief list of "novels we will never cease to admire,"[34] and referred repeatedly to these works as particularly important to her own writing. Thus we see that Pushkin has Tatiana subscribe not to an arbitrarily chosen group of popular literary figures, but to a series of seminal heroines whose interdependency exemplifies the processes of literary continuity and change.[35] Tatiana is not simply one of myriad enthusiastic readers of Richardson, Rousseau, and de Staël, but a heroine whose evolution draws on the worlds of these writers even as it goes well beyond them. Like Rousseau and de Staël before him, Pushkin acknowledges his predecessors as he creates a heroine who does not merely replace Clarissa, Julie, and Delphine, but assimilates what they offer into her own unique becoming. At the same time, the heroines he draws into Tatiana's world are revivified by the new context in which they now figure. With Tatiana and her books Pushkin reminds us that the evolution of literary characters, like that of language, style, genre, and literary tradition, is to be regarded in terms not of succession, but of perpetual interanimation.

Works Pushkin refers to in the course of *Eugene Onegin*—and the novels Tatiana reads in particular—provide a backdrop against which to evaluate the heroine he himself develops. The difficulties Tatiana must overcome and the potential pitfalls she successfully avoids are more fully appreciated within the literary context in which Pushkin imbeds her. At the same time, the works he alludes to excite in the reader a plethora of expectations that generate a dynamic of their own. In choosing whether to fulfill, delay, or frustrate these expectations, Pushkin expands the possibilities available to him for generating surprise, emphasis, or resolution, and finds also a productive means for highlighting his heroine's complexity and with it his own multilayered artistic platform.

As for Tatiana herself, her identification with Clarissa, Julie, and Delphine signals commendable taste in novels and an equally commendable receptivity to them. Given the circumstances in which she finds herself, Tatiana has chosen well, for central to the stories of these heroines are confrontations with powerful emotions in settings that advocate their complete eradication. Matrimony figures prominently in the lives of Tatiana's heroines, but it is the question of how to deal with intense passion and not the quest for a husband that takes center stage and directs their development and course of action. Struggles with emotions are by no means alien to the male characters in these works, but it is from women that the highest tolls are exacted for surrendering to feeling. If the men represented in these works can choose from a significantly broader range of means to rechannel, dissipate, consummate, or sublimate their desires, women are allowed only to deny their erotic energies, to suppress them, or to retool them into matrimony and maternity. When all else fails, there is always that great stiller of all urges—death. The subsequent discussion will first focus on the role matrimony plays in the stories of Tatiana's three heroines, and then proceed to consider their individual struggles with powerful feelings.

The stories of Tatiana's mother, sister, and nurse have been aptly described as retellings of "the story of a woman's life, repeated from generation to generation and enacting the transition from 'romantic love' to 'married love.'"[36] This common destiny of the women in Tatiana's immediate surroundings is confronted also by the heroines of her novels. The supreme importance marriage must assume in a woman's life remains a constant within these heroines' radically dissimilar settings, and the opinion Harriet Byron expresses in Richardson's *Sir Charles Grandison* accurately characterizes the prevailing sentiment of not only the novels Tatiana reads, but her actual milieu as well:

> I have a very high notion of the marriage-state. I remember what my Uncle once averr'd; That a woman out of wedlock is half useless to the end of her being. How indeed do the duties of a good Wife, of a good Mother, and a worthy Matron, well performed, dignify a woman![37]

In the books Tatiana reads marriage is represented as a rite of passage from which devolves whatever value a woman may ultimately claim in society. Matrimony can ensure social and financial security, or neutralize a multitude of sins. It can signal victory for a woman and her family and is touted as a cure for excessive passion. "In Virgins arrived at Maturity, and rendered mad by Love, Marriage is the most efficacious Remedy," asserts the author of the *Medical Dictionary* which Richardson consulted regularly in the course of his novel writing.[38] The guises marriage may assume are many, but its function as a social or political tool and the moral obligation that it entails are expected to outweigh a woman's individual desire. Where matrimony is concerned, personal inclination is regarded as inappropriate or even downright harmful, and the notion that a woman might choose her husband on the basis of powerful attraction is scarcely countenanced even by female characters in Tatiana's novels. "My mother argues upon the case in a most discouraging manner for all such of our sex as look forward to happiness in marriage with the *man of their choice*," notes Miss Howe in a letter to Miss Clarissa Harlowe.[39]

Whatever the circumstances leading up to the marriage, with its accomplishment a woman's desires are absorbed into selfless dedication to the well-being of her husband, whether he be a profligate who must be taught by the example of his wife's moral rectitude (*Pamela*), or a father figure who edifies the malleable creature he calls wife (*The New Eloise*). "MATRIMONY and LIBERTY—Girlish connexion!" exclaims Miss Grandison in ready acknowledgment of a woman's lot.[40] In matrimony as it is depicted in Tatiana's novels, a woman becomes a helpmeet to her husband's self-realization, and it is from his fulfillment that her own must derive. The dissolution of self demanded by matrimony and vigorously re-

inforced by maternity could only be impeded by the intense self-awareness attendant on individual desire. Accordingly, the "marriage-state"
unequivocally denies the woman's sexuality. Because the representation
of matrimony in Tatiana's novels overlaps with and yet also diverges from
the way it is regarded in the actual world around her, it is instructive to
consider what Tatiana could learn from studying the confrontations of
her three chosen heroines with that question of marriage she too will soon
be forced to confront.

Although Clarissa never marries, she is nonetheless a victim of the institution of matrimony—first by dint of her family's greed-inspired determination to marry her off to a man she finds repugnant and then as an object of the lustful desires of the unspeakable Lovelace, who seeks to bend
her to his will and force her to become his wife. In her attempts to forestall marriage, Clarissa valiantly resists the pressures of her family,
friends, and society, endures a protracted series of adversities, and suffers
extreme physical, emotional, and spiritual anguish. Emblematic of her
moral victory over all the forces that besiege her is the fact that she evades
marriage. The price exacted for this extraordinary victory, however, is
that she dies very soon after achieving it. This she does willingly and in
the most instructive of all possible manners.

Julie too must die at the end of her novel, but her circumstances differ
in significant respects from those of her unfortunate literary predecessor. In
her narrative, marriage functions as a watershed between self-indulgence
and self-sacrifice. Initially Julie is allowed her passion for Saint-Preux,
and their mutual love represents a welcome escape from the artificial conventions and stultifying morals of their society. Yet after Julie's father re-
pays a debt of gratitude to an old friend by bestowing his daughter on
him, Julie is forced to return to those conventions from which she has
strayed with her lover. In this return she is directed by the pontifications
of a paternalistic, wise, and seemingly omniscient spouse who trims and
trains the now fervorless Julie much as he attends to the garden of which
he is so fond. (It is no mere chance that in Rousseau's novel this garden
suggests the need nature has of a firm, guiding hand.) Indeed, Monsieur
Wolmar's systematic edification of Julie is directly parallel to his manage-
ment of her estate which he now owns and seeks to improve. When, despite her husband's and her own best efforts, it proves impossible for Julie
to eradicate her passion for Saint-Preux, her powerful feelings are surrendered to an untimely death.

Like Julie, Delphine too was married to an older, wiser man who
took her as his wife apparently not at the behest of passionate love, but
out of a generous impulse to do her good. Unlike Julie, however, Delphine
is widowed. Her spouse conveniently absent from the scene, de Staël's

heroine is found at the beginning of the novel in enviable circumstances. She is beneficiary of both the social and financial security of a married woman, and yet is able to conduct her life independently of husbandly governance. Her story is nevertheless centered on what her beloved Leonce calls "that ceremony of the dead which men call marriage,"[41] for Delphine unwittingly prepares the way for the espousal of a friend's daughter to the man she herself loves, and whose marriage—precipitated by treacherous machinations of the bride's mother—stands in the way of the fulfillment of their mutually shared ardor. Clustered around Delphine's narrative is an entire constellation of stories that tell of women's entrapments in appalling mismatches and that document the destructiveness of the ironclad conventions of a callous, hypocritical society. The arguments in favor of divorce de Staël advances with these stories uphold the woman's right to a gratifying marital relationship. Delphine's insistence that marriage be regarded as a potential source of a woman's ultimate fulfillment runs counter to the deep-seated conventional expectation that a woman's powerful emotions be surrendered to matrimony. Although Delphine does not achieve this "supreme good," it is here that Tatiana finds a strong argument that a woman's intense feelings be allowed to extend into marriage rather than be replaced by it. De Staël's heroine offers a different way to regard the role of matrimony in a woman's life. "The fact is," Delphine writes to a friend, "a woman's life is over when she does not marry the man she loves."[42]

We can thus recognize that each of Tatiana's three heroines suggests a different approach in the struggle between matrimony and erotic love. Clarissa rejects both sexuality and matrimony. Julie—duty-bound to her father, husband, and children—acquiesces to marriage and attempts, albeit ineffectually, to still her desire, while Delphine launches on a quest for the coincidence of love and marriage. As important as the question of matrimony is in the lives and settings of these women, it is not their desire for a mate but rather their own struggles with intense passion that take center stage in their stories. It would seem that it is precisely these struggles that rivet the now enamored Tatiana to the pages of her books, for she too is absorbed by the newly developing erotic sensibilities that Eugene's appearance has intensified and that the venerable institution of matrimony—as exemplified by her parents' generation —threatens to displace.

Whatever else they may teach, the heroines' stories demonstrate compellingly the extraordinary energy that derives from erotic desire. And yet they argue too that this energy be superseded or rechanneled. Thus Clarissa's heroic resistance to the marriage planned by her parents and the one demanded of her by Lovelace is accompanied by another sort of struggle. Even as she resists these attacks from the outside world, Clarissa wages an internal battle against her own desires—those stirrings that prompted her to take that audacious and dangerous step of entering into an illicit correspondence with Lovelace in the first place and then led her to flee her parents' home with him. Clarissa becomes the object of intense male desire, but admits no desire of her own. It is in fact her categorical denial of her own sexuality that constitutes the "victory" Richardson ultimately allows her.

In the early stages of her development, Clarissa resorts to endless, exasperating "punctilios" in an effort to stifle the erotic sensibilities that she begins to experience but is not prepared to confront. Yet as she gains in strength, maturity, and insight in the course of the ever-greater torments she endures, these punctilios evolve into a genuine moral rectitude.[43] Clarissa averts the terrors attendant on nascent sexuality and on being the object of overpowering male desire by enlisting the energy of her own intense emotions in the cause of maintaining goodness, virtue, and chastity. She does so, moreover, in the face of overwhelming pressures, not the least of which is the ever-present danger that she may succumb not only to Lovelace's superior strength, but to those desires which he threatens to excite within her. Clarissa's fortitude wins her great influence, and everyone in her orbit is much improved by her shining example. The intricate, varied, and—to do the scoundrel justice—imaginative wiles Lovelace employs in his attempts to seduce Clarissa founder on the indefatigable energy with which she defends her virtue. She succeeds in remaining impassive to her would-be seducer, and her chastity—which is to say absence of desire—endures beyond the drug-assisted rape to which Lovelace finally resorts. Certain of her moral righteousness, Clarissa refuses to countenance the socially sanctioned means to restore her honor—marriage to Lovelace. She can thus be credited with attaining a virtuous self-sufficiency as she successfully rechannels her erotic energy without the conventional recourse to matrimony and maternity. Her refusal of male assistance accomplishes something else besides: it counters Lovelace's image of her as the locus of desire and thereby expands in a significant way his capacity to love. Thus, shortly before Clarissa's death, the seemingly incorrigible rake arrives at a momentous insight: "Hence it is that I admire her more than ever; and that my love for her is less *personal*, as I may say, more *intellectual*, than I ever thought it could be to a woman."[44] Lovelace's unfulfilled desire for Clarissa expands beyond itself and draws him out of the narrow confines of the egotistical lust to which he was ever a slave and of which so many women were victims.

Particularly important here are the means by which Clarissa succeeds in holding her own against the inexorable pressures that are brought to bear on her. The first of these means is her inviolable adherence to strict form in every aspect of her life. Those punctilios of the early part of the novel that hint at subservience to social conventions modulate into the genuine strength of personal conviction that is both fostered by and manifested in voluntarily assumed formal constraint. It is her adherence to strict form that determines Clarissa's attitude to her oppressor: "No prudery, no coquetry, no tyranny in my heart, or in my behaviour, to him, that I know of. No affected procrastination. Aiming at nothing but decorum."[45] That scrupulously maintained formality Clarissa employs to keep her tormentor at bay has an effect on Lovelace. In letters that keep his friend abreast of his progress, he complains repeatedly that his various schemes consistently run aground on Clarissa's formality. That Lovelace recognizes the indomitable strength of Clarissa's defense is made clear by the fact that he stakes his hopes for success on circumvention rather than on direct confrontation:

> Could I but have gained access to her in her hours of heedlessness and dishabille (for full dress creates dignity, augments consciousness, and compels distance); we had been familiarized to each other long ago. But keep her up ever so late; meet her ever so early; by breakfast she is dressed for the day; and at her *earliest hour*, as nice as others dressed.[46]

Lovelace goes to great lengths to gain access to Clarissa's private space in an effort to catch her off guard. He resorts to abduction, deceit, coercion, the theft of her letters, and finally to drugs and rape, only to be repulsed at each attempt by his victim's adamant refusal to break with that form in which she contains her emotions, her distress, indeed her entire existence. The forcible violation of her body has no effect on the strict norms of her self-preservation. "The injury I have received from him," she maintains, "is indeed of the highest nature . . . yet, I bless God, it has not tainted my mind, it has not hurt my morals."[47] Clarissa remains untouched by that desire Lovelace threatens to arouse in her.

Even in her preparations for death, Clarissa exhibits an overriding concern with propriety, and not only Lovelace but death itself pales before the power of her decorum. Having prepared her coffin, her last will and testament, and the clothes in which she wishes to be buried, Clarissa complains only of Lovelace's persistent intrusions into that careful formal structure in which she encloses her own death: "He will not let me enter into my Maker's presence with the composure that is required in entering into the drawing room of an earthly prince!"[48] The power of Clarissa's self-mastery is attested to in an outburst of Lovelace who, stricken with anguish at his victim's death, acknowledges the source of his own wickedness: "*Why, why did my mother bring me up to bear no control?*"[49] Although not sufficiently reformed by Clarissa's shining example to assume full responsibility for his actions which he prefers to blame on his mother, Lovelace recognizes both the power of good that derives from self-mastery and the destructiveness that follows in the wake of self-abandon.

As successful as Clarissa is in the art of self-control, she is not yet wholly described by that discipline that governs every facet of her life, for her strictly maintained decorum is balanced by the fluent expressivity of her letters. Clarissa writes a great deal, and she writes well.[50] Her letters map out her emotional and psychological states, reflect her own persona in the making, and afford welcome relief for the pent-up, conflicting emotions she experiences. The act of writing is for her a source of solace, but even more important, of self-affirmation in the face of the many pressures that come to bear on her. At the same time, it is both a much-needed outlet for those very passions Lovelace seeks to excite, and a crucial means for their containment. The restrictions under which she operates—not only those that are forced upon her, but also those that are self-imposed— fuel her need to write, and it is because she can resort to writing that she successfully maintains the self-assertive decorum that constitutes her strongest defense. Clarissa's self-mastery is balanced by the expressivity of her letters. It is here that we find the answer to the question Lovelace poses in exasperated bewilderment at his utter failure to arouse Clarissa's desire: "Can *education* have stronger force in a woman's heart than *nature?*"[51]

Yet although Clarissa's triumph exerts a lasting positive influence on all those around her, her own enjoyment of it is brief. The desire and the marriage she resists against all odds overtake her in the guise of death. She refers to her burial garb as "wedding garments" and as "the *happiest* suit, that ever bridal maiden wore."[52] Repeated references to her funeral arrangements as preparations for a wedding echo and reinforce that very parallel between a woman's marriage and death that is a common trope in the traditional Russian folklore to which Tatiana was exposed in her formative years. Clarissa's erotic, creative, and procreative potentialities are absorbed into death, which replaces the birth of a child for which Lovelace fervently hopes, and conveniently removes the heroine's nineteen-year-old body with its potential to both attract and house erotic desire. Although she deviates but briefly from the woman's common fate and fails to suggest a viable alternative, Clarissa provides Tatiana with a valuable lesson in self-sufficiency, self-mastery, and the power resident in form.

This judicious example is not lost on Tatiana. Although Eugene is no Lovelace any more than Tatiana is a Clarissa, we can observe here in anticipation of the conclusion of Tatiana's story that it is Tatiana's mastery of form in the upper reaches of St. Petersburg society that attracts her own would-be seducer and yet also helps her keep him at bay. We can add too that her rejection of Eugene's advances accomplishes an expansion of his capacity for love that is comparable to the one wrought in Lovelace by Clarissa's rejections. But to say that Tatiana has learned from Clarissa is not to say that her actions are imitative or that she does not progress well beyond Richardson's heroine. For all her strengths and admirable qualities, Clarissa is not an adequate model for Tatiana, who, perhaps sensing this inadequacy, augments her curriculum with the experiences of two additional heroines. Lacking in Clarissa is the ability to countenance those powerful feelings that fuel her writing and sustain her form. Clarissa's unyielding refusal to accord eros a place in her life renders that balance she achieves between self-mastery and self-affirmation so precarious that to maintain it for any significant length of time becomes inconceivable. Her untimely death thus comes as a necessary and welcome relief.

If Clarissa's sexuality is largely denied, Julie's is allowed brief, if fruitless, blossoming. Although Rousseau's heroine is permitted the indulgence of her desire, she lacks the self-sufficiency of her literary predecessor. Both she and her ardent lover remain powerless—she by virtue of being a woman, he because of his inferior social standing. Their impossible situation is not resolved but only exacerbated by Julie's marriage to Wolmar. The moral point of the novel is, in Judith H. McDowell's formulation, "implicitly but forcefully made: if she is carried away by true love, a woman may fall from innocence before she is married without leaving a stain on her character, but after marriage such a lapse would be criminal."[53] Here we may once again observe that for all the differences in the manner of their encoding, the messages of this Western European novel and of the folk custom of Tatiana's Russian milieu coincide, for according to Lotman's account, Russian peasant girls were subject to precisely such a code of ethics as is depicted in Rousseau's novel.[54] After her marriage to Wolmar, Julie is expected to eradicate all vestiges of those passions that Rousseau allowed her before she was wedded. Julie's husband is charged with effecting this desired transformation. Left to her are obedience and submission. As Julie reveres her husband, adores her two children, and enjoys her friendship with Claire, her reeducation appears to be a success. This delusion, however, holds only until the reappearance of Saint-Preux, when it becomes painfully clear that Julie's passion has not in fact been displaced by her husband's coaching, her children's demands, and Claire's solicitude. Julie's story suggests to Tatiana that, contrary to the examples of her immediate surroundings, erotic sensibilities do not necessarily give way to marriage, motherhood, and friendship, and can endure in simultaneity with them to be revived (if disastrously) from within those other commitments. That Tatiana focuses above all not on Julie's marriage, but on the intense desires that marriage proves power-less to quell, is suggested by the reference to Saint-Preux as "the lover of Julie Wolmar" in the catalogue of heroes Tatiana rallies around Eugene. Nabokov notes that Julie's surname was d'Etange, and not Wolmar, when she became the mistress of Saint-Preux, and calls this designation "inex-act."[55] Yet he has perhaps missed the point: of greater import than the un-married Julie's affair with her tutor is her struggle with the passion that persists for him even after she has become Wolmar's wife.

Like Clarissa's before her, Julie's sexual energies are ultimately ab-sorbed into death. When her overwhelming feelings for Saint-Preux can no longer be contained, Rousseau has her succumb to a chill after a heroic leap into turbulent water to save her child, thus allowing her the death of a self-sacrificing mother. In a letter she pens to Saint-Preux on her deathbed, Julie expresses her readiness to part with life, explaining that in her impending death she has found, at last, a cure for her hopeless pas-sion. Like Clarissa, who insists that she has remained pure in spirit even after her body has been violated, Julie emphasizes that she has remained dutiful even though her feelings for Saint-Preux escaped her strict control. In the farewell letter to her beloved she writes:

> My friend, I am making this confession without shame. This sentiment, nourished despite myself, was involuntary; it has cost my innocence noth-ing. Everything which was dependent upon my will was devoted to my duty. If my heart, which was not dependent upon it, was devoted to you, that was my torment and not my crime. I have done what I ought to have done; my virtue remains unblemished, and my love has remained without remorse.[56]

Female eros is represented as tragic and once again—as in the novels Ta-tiana reads, the folktales she hears, and literary works such as *Lenore* to which Pushkin alludes in the course of creating his heroine—leads in-evitably to death.

Julie's story demonstrates to Tatiana both the woman's surrender to desire and the endurance of that desire beyond matrimony. At the same time, she can glean from Julie's records of her experiences that although the longing triggered by love can expand sensibility and the potential for self-realization, the illicit consummation of love does not bring fulfill-ment, but only fans the fires of an ultimately destructive passion. This is taught by Julie's embrace of death as a welcome release from the emotions for her lover that she has failed to still. It is seen too at the very outset of her relations with Saint-Preux, when in the letter she writes immediately upon the consummation of their love, she insists that their surrender to physical desire has irrevocably damaged their relationship. "My remorse is much less for having given too much to love than for having deprived it of its greatest charm," she explains. "We have sought pleasure, and happiness has fled us."[57] Having given in to desire, Julie does not rejoice in gain, but mourns rather what is lost:

> Our enjoyments used to be peaceful and lasting; we now have nothing but fits of passion. This mad joy is more like attacks of frenzy than tender caresses. A pure and lofty flame used to burn in our hearts; now given up to the delusions of our senses, we are nothing but common lovers, sufficiently happy if jealous love still condescends to preside over the pleasures which even the most brutish mortal can enjoy.[58]

The entire letter eloquently champions unfulfilled desire over its gratification and privileges the imagined and the anticipated over the realized. It is significant that Julie's remorse arises not from a moral stance or a fear of social stricture, but from a personal conviction derived from feelings she personally experiences. That the loss Julie describes is indeed irrevocable can be seen from the conclusion of her letter in which she promises, "I shall tell you this evening the means I am inventing for other opportunities to meet."[59] The subsequent events of the novel emphasize that her relationship with Saint-Preux, far from providing a means for self-realization, is ultimately a destructive one.

Significantly, it is in the course of composing her letters and not in the consummation of her love that Julie arrives at self-realization. Saint-Preux regards letter writing as a means for seduction, but also for the expression and the mastery of his emotions: "I moderate my ecstasy by describing it," he explains to Julie at a moment of heightened desire.[60] In her letters, Julie reciprocates Saint-Preux's ardor, but also confronts and analyzes her emotions and actions, delineates her moral position, and defines her self. Julie and Clarissa overlap in the significance that writing assumes in the formation of their characters. Rousseau's heroine, however, loses the self-sufficiency that Richardson's successfully preserves. Julie's is a divided self—torn between duty and desire—that her writing can analyze, but not heal. Her impossible, unfulfilling love only clouds what might have been enjoyment of the happy tranquillity and peace of mind offered by family life. Although in Julie's story desire has been successfully protracted beyond matrimony, its energy fuels what proves to be a life-eroding disharmony within the heroine herself. Tatiana absorbs what Julie has to offer, but the discord between duty and desire that leads Julie to embrace death inspires Pushkin's heroine with the creative energy to find a more satisfying solution.

Delphine, insofar as her place in society is concerned, is the most self-sufficient of Tatiana's three heroines. Yet her story, like Clarissa's and Julie's, is also centered on an uneasy configuration of eros, matrimony, and death. Delphine's exceptional beauty and natural grace are complemented by an independence of mind and spirit that distinguishes her from those around her. Her enlightened upbringing permits her to develop her innate faculties, and rescues her from that "state of the most absurd mediocrity" to which women, in de Staël's observation, had been systematically reduced since the French Revolution.[61] Perfectly at ease in any setting, she acts only in accordance with her inner convictions, heeding little those compunctions of convention that drive the social world around her. Her behavior—whether emotional or intellectual, spontaneous or considered—is governed by a deep-seated morality which she defines in the simplest and most direct of terms: "Morality, which forbids ever causing unhappiness to anyone, stands above all the doubts of heart and reason."[62] It is specifically in this moral climate that de Staël's heroine launches her eloquent defense of a woman's personal independence, integrity, and intellectual capacities.

Delphine's story is propelled by the conflict of her personal desires with the deep-rooted morality she has defined for herself. Set during the French Revolution, the novel focuses not on the momentous political and social upheavals of the time, but on the inner psychological and emotional turmoil of the heroine. Foregrounded are not political events, but the personal affairs of the characters and Delphine's unflagging preoccupation with the well-being of others. The moral imperative according to which Delphine conducts her life remains in full effect despite the fact that Leonce's is a loveless marriage to a woman who is clearly ill suited to him. The heroine's overwhelming desire for Leonce is checked by her horror at the thought of causing his wife to suffer. Regardless of the circumstances under which it was concluded, Leonce's unfortunate wedding to Matilde precludes Delphine's attainment of that one happiness that "society—perhaps even Providence itself—has permitted . . . women: love in marriage."[63] However limiting it may seem to the modern reader, this particular definition of happiness championed a woman's right to marry a man of her own choosing and marked the starting point of de Staël's advocacy for the dissolution of miserable contracts entered into against a woman's will. The moral imperative that governs Delphine's actions provides the necessary context for such advocacy, and de Staël advances her heroine well beyond the notion that is projected in Richardson's novels and played out in Julie's complete submission to her father, that a woman is best *spared* having to choose her own mate. Thus, for example, the words uttered by Harriet Byron (*Sir Charles Grandison*), "But I begin to think that those young women are happiest, whose friends take all the trouble of this sort [i.e., the choice of a mate] upon *them*,"[64] would be unthinkable on Delphine's lips.

Yet Delphine is involved not in deciding whom to marry, but in the wrenching choice between surrender to her love and adherence to her personally held moral convictions. This already intense inner conflict is complicated by the many facets of her love for Leonce that range from all-consuming passion to the profound self-realization and expanded sensibility eros can foster. Thus we recognize in Delphine's letters to Leonce a continuation of both Saint-Preux's impassioned arguments for surrender to desire and Julie's analytical defenses of virtue. The pressures Leonce brings to bear on Delphine exacerbate the heroine's struggle. In the early stages of their relationship, his fanatic preoccupation with public opinion acts as an unwelcome constraint on Delphine's spontaneous but well-grounded actions, and she finds herself torn between her own genuine convictions and Leonce's petty prejudices. In his desperate suit for the resumption of the relations with Delphine that his marriage interrupted, Leonce places great emphasis on Delphine's lack of concern about what others may think or say of her. It is clear that he fails to recognize the moral underpinning that wins her not mere indifference to the tyranny of public opinion, but genuine independence from it.

Delphine's love for Leonce brings not self-realization or fulfillment, but devitalizing inner conflict, and she is ultimately undone by her powerful, contradictory emotions. Her observation apropos Mme. d'Ervins—who is overwhelmed by love for a man far superior to her brutish, egotistical husband—that "Passion turns all our powers against us" is ultimately brought to bear on her own story.[65] The extent to which Delphine's love erodes that exquisite self-sufficiency and independence of spirit she exhibited in the opening of the novel is brought home by her certainty that she cannot survive Leonce. His execution, which she proves powerless to forestall, precipitates her suicide. Whatever course it may take, a woman's intense passion, it would seem, must necessarily lead to death. Delphine's story differs in its outcome from Clarissa's and Julie's only in that de Staël's heroine is allowed to make her own choice between life and death when the impossible triangle of love, marriage, and virtue collapses. Her decision to take her life can be seen as a testament to the power of her emotions, but also to their destructive energy. Torn between her involuntary love and a self-imposed moral imperative, she is in an untenable situation that can be resolved only by death. Delphine's story throws into high relief the fact that Tatiana's response to a similar tension between love and moral convictions is not death-dealing, but ultimately creative and life-affirming.

Because in its rush toward the other, passion threatens to sweep away the boundaries of the self, the question of the indulgence of desire is significantly complicated by repercussions that, as Tatiana's novels show, extend beyond both the subject and the object of love. The tension generated by the desire to indulge passion on the one hand, and the arguments for abstinence on the other, remains, as we have seen, a constant in the stories of the three heroines Tatiana chooses as her models. In the conflict between the fulfillment of desire and its virtuous denial, it falls to the woman to exemplify the latter. In so doing, she prolongs and intensifies that male desire of which she is the object, but is expected to extinguish desire in herself. The heroes of the novels in question operate largely in accordance with their own needs and subscribe to abstract notions of duty or justice in ordering their lives. The actions of female characters, however, are guided primarily by their sensitivity to the effect they may have on others. Thus, for example, Clarissa and Julie remain preoccupied above all else with the impact of what they do on the emotional well-being of their family members—this even after the most barbarous treatment at their hands. Thus too both Julie and Delphine are shown by their respective authors to act not simply at the behest of their own passions, but out of compassion for the men they love. Julie's determination to withstand temptation is ultimately overwhelmed not by the intensity of her own feelings, but by her reluctance to perpetuate those torments of unrequited love that her suitor waxes so long and eloquent in describing. Julie's account of her "fall" is not mere rationalization on her part, but rather an exemplification of prevailing notions about a woman's psychological and emotional constitution: "Perhaps love alone would have saved me; oh, my cousin, it is pity that destroyed me."[66] Julie's subsequent analysis of her surrender to Saint-Preux reveals also her acute discomfort at holding the position of power which she gains with her refusal to submit to his pleas. Along the same lines we see too that in defending her own moral position in the face of Leonce's full-scale attack, Delphine counterbalances the ascendancy that her resistance to his demands wins her with protestations of her dissolution of self in him and with reiterated metaphors of servitude. Her assessments of their situation are permeated with a sense of guilt that attends, paradoxically, her refusal to surrender her own morals to Leonce's demands.

> Leonce wields absolute power over me by right of his mind, his character, and his love. It seems to me that I was made to obey him as much as to worship him; when I am alone, I chide myself for the passion he inspires; but in his presence, my soul spontaneously judges me guilty when I have made him unhappy.[67]

It is when Leonce succeeds in moving her with a vivid display of his suffering that he comes closest to overcoming her scruples. In both *The New Eloise* and *Delphine*, the heroes are overwhelmed by their own feelings. Their heroines, however, are moved by the compassion that the intense passions of the male characters arouse in them. The heroines of each of Tatiana's three novels are reluctant to wield power over others, and their decision-making process bespeaks an acute awareness of and sense of responsibility for the effect their actions might have on others.[68]

From this discussion of Clarissa, Julie, and Delphine we can see that in the novels of Richardson, Rousseau, and de Staël, Tatiana has ample opportunity to study the consequences of admitting into life those powerful feelings she now experiences directly. The stories of these three heroines suggest new points of vantage that broaden Tatiana's perspective, but they offer no ready solutions or livable models. To summarize, Clarissa's sexuality receives only implicit acknowledgment in the energy with which she denies it. Her repudiation of eros and her evasion of matrimony are victories, yet also doomed enterprises. Julie is allowed the recognition and consummation of her erotic love before she is held to the demands of marital fidelity, which Rousseau describes in his *Confessions* as "the root of all social order."[69] Although they must no longer be indulged, Julie's erotic sensibilities endure beyond the marriage and maternity by which they were to have been supplanted. Julie, however, finds no means to engage these sensibilities productively, and the protraction of desire yields disastrous results. Delphine insists that matrimony should neither supplant nor repress a woman's love, but should allow it to flourish, thereby granting her fulfillment rather than self-sacrifice in marriage. Her story, however, documents not such fulfillment, but only desperate struggles with a personal desire that is in harsh discord with her own moral convictions.

The particular lineage of heroines Pushkin establishes for Tatiana neither contains nor determines her. Rather, it highlights the problems entailed in negotiating between abandon and restraint, between personally held convictions and externally imposed demands, between self and others. These are the very problems Tatiana must face and that Pushkin too must confront in both his life and his creative work. As Tatiana moves through *Eugene Onegin* side by side with Pushkin, she charts a course that, although perhaps superficially similar, is in fact qualitatively different from the paths taken by her favorite heroines.

A definitive aspect of Pushkin's own poetic enterprise may be described as the attainment of maximal expressivity from within conditions of maximal constraint—a project in the spirit of Goethe's aphorism, "In der Beschränkung zeigt sich erst der Meister." To a significant extent, Tatiana's story demonstrates the relevance of this poetic principle to the conduct of life by suggesting that the successful way out of impasses such

as those that bring down Clarissa, Julie, and Delphine is the way of poetry. Tatiana's growth in *Eugene Onegin* culminates in her productive engagement of desire operating in conjunction with restrictions—those that
are imposed from outside and those that come from within. Crucial here
are the translation of restraint into self-affirmation, and the idea that desire can be fruitful if it is subjected to appropriate control rather than to
mere suppression or mere satisfaction. Through Tatiana Pushkin shows
that the very tensions that debilitate Clarissa, Julie, and Delphine can be
the source of creative rather than destructive energy. Demonstrated in this
process—as it is also in the tragic fates of Tatiana's heroines—is the fact
that creativity and loss are coterminous, and that the balance to be maintained between self-control and self-surrender is both crucial and precarious.

It is certainly possible to link various aspects of the Tatiana with
whom Pushkin's work culminates to specific qualities exemplified by her
heroines. Thus in Tatiana's rejection of Eugene, we might discern a
Clarissa-like virtue, a Julie-like privileging of duty to her husband over
her powerful feelings for another man, or a Delphinian refusal to win
happiness at the expense of another's suffering. More important than
these individual parallels, however, is the fact of Tatiana's seamless assimilation of what her various heroines offer, as their strengths and victories are reconfigured in the new context of her own becoming. At the end
of her story Tatiana neither dies nor eradicates her love for Eugene, nor
does she surrender her personally held convictions or her private imaginative world. Tatiana, as we will see, does not merely emulate her heroines, she rectifies their failed quests.

The substance of what Tatiana reads is of considerable consequence
in her development; *how* she reads is vital to her characterization. This is
important because novels no less than society suggest ready-made models that threaten the immediacy of life experiences. The individual sensation and spontaneous expression of love are particularly susceptible to in-
terference or inhibition by literary antecedents. Indeed, this problem, at
the heart of which lie the tensions between the reiterated and the unprecedented and between the self-conscious and spontaneous, is explicitly
addressed in the novels Tatiana reads and discussed by the authors who
created them. Thus, for example, Saint-Preux, who is Julie's tutor in
learning before he becomes her tutor in love, curtails his charge's reading
lest books interfere with her natural development. In her preface to *Delphine* de Staël complains that "the expression of true emotion is impeded
by the intrusive memory of insipid writing full of talk about the feelings
of the heart."[70] Receptivity to expressed emotion is similarly threatened
by literary precedent. Thus, for example, in Pushkin's story "The Snow-

storm" ("Metel'") the heroine's immediate reaction to the hero's heartfelt declaration of love is that his words remind her of one of Saint-Preux's letters to Julie.

That preoccupation with the effects of reading should become, like the act of reading itself, a common literary topos is hardly surprising in light of the demonstrative emulations of invented personages that so frequently followed in the wake of popular novels. Readers were known to throw themselves into reenactments of fictional material with a single-mindedness that could, as for example in the instance of imitators of Goethe's Werther, not only dictate what was said or worn, but lead even to suicide. Yet whatever the potential dangers inherent in reading, a return to a "natural state" innocent of imaginative writing such as that advocated by Saint-Preux to Julie was scarcely possible, as the effects of *The New Eloise* itself clearly demonstrated.

The dramatic extent to which novels determined the vocabulary, behavior, and self-definition of the Russian reading public at the end of the eighteenth and the beginning of the nineteenth centuries has been described by V. Sipovskii. "Suicides out of love, and monasteries, and passionate correspondence were in vogue and probably destroyed not a few lives," he observes.[71] Indeed, the danger posed by novels was real enough to prompt one solicitous mother to include in her last will and testament a warning to her daughter against indiscriminate reading.[72] Before Tatiana was even born, literature had so thoroughly permeated Russian society that it asserted its influence—as Pushkin jokingly intimates in *Eugene Onegin*—even over those who read no novels. Thus, as we have seen, the love of Tatiana's mother for "Grandison" is conceived in innocence of Richardson's writings and on the strength of hearsay alone. Even as they offer means to apprehend, structure, and express inchoate emotions, Tatiana's novels carry also the threat of becoming impediments to unmediated apprehension, natural development, and spontaneous expression of precisely those feelings they nurture. In providing a set vocabulary and plot variants of love, they pose a danger no less real than that of Eugene's society to the uninhibited growth of genuine emotion and to the discovery of genuine means for its communication. The interpenetration of life and literature on which Pushkin insists in *Eugene Onegin* acknowledges, indeed highlights, this situation. Again, it is through Tatiana that the means to counteract the potential dangers of reading are demonstrated. Rather than set Tatiana up as a warning, Pushkin makes her an example that shows how reading—her connection to literary precedent—can foster rather than curtail her growth both as an individual and as a unique heroine.

Tatiana, as we observed, is engrossed in her novels not because she seeks to escape her immediate surroundings, or because she cannot distinguish fact from fiction, but because her books foster the development of a part of herself that has found no support in her actual world. The outmodedness of the works she reads functions not merely to underscore her rural backwardness, but more important, to highlight the immediacy of her receptivity. However out-of-date her novels may be in urban society, for Tatiana—whose rural isolation has preserved her from the tyranny of its fashions—they are revelations that catch hold precisely because they resonate with sensations she herself experiences. The new material of the novels is infused with emotions Tatiana knows, and this intersection of the unprecedented with the familiar intensifies her response to the books. Clarissa, Julie, and Delphine do not merely provide Tatiana with a series of literary masks to be donned one after another in order to create an effect or to project a plagiarized identity. Instead, these heroines open new perspectives on life, as Tatiana imbeds their destinies in a personal imaginative space rich with simultaneity.[73] Rather than reenact what is in her books, as do imitators of literary types, Tatiana interacts with her novels and absorbs her heroines into her own world.

Like her creator, who pointedly engages the works of innumerable predecessors in his own, Tatiana goes well beyond mere mimicry. Accordingly, the author/narrator emphasizes the interaction between the "real life" Tatiana and the fictional characters she assimilates:

> Татьяна в тишине лесов
> Одна с опасной книгой бродит,
> Она в ней ищет и находит
> Свой тайный жар, свои мечты,
> Плоды сердечной полноты.
>
> [Dangerous book in hand, she wanders,
> Alone in forest hush and ponders
> To seek and find in it her own
> Mute blaze, her dreams, her heartstrings' tone.][74]
>
> (3:10, ll. 4–8)

Tatiana's reading is described as an empathetic act that gains her new perspectives on self and surroundings. The very books that seemed harmless earlier in Tatiana's story [2:29] are rendered "dangerous" by the new receptivity with which she reads them after she settles her love on Eugene. In the fullness of her own feeling ("serdechnaia polnota") Tatiana's reading is one of recognition and discovery. The importance of her novels lies not only in what they supply, but also in what she herself brings to them. In her capacity of reader she not only draws on the literary text, but helps also to shape its meaning. In so doing she significantly enlarges her own world. The dynamic interplay of discrete psychological and narratological perspectives supplied by her three favorite novels furthers Tatiana's development and precludes the determinism that threatens readers (and writers) who model themselves (or their works) on a single literary precedent.

Yet for all the author/narrator's emphasis on the engagement with which Tatiana reads, and Pushkin's own virtuosic demonstration of how literary precedent can be absorbed creatively, there is a tendency among commentators to represent Tatiana's reading as an intrusion on her individuality, rather than the path to self-knowledge it becomes for her. Thus, to cite but one prominent example, Lotman maintains that "[f]or Tatyana, the traditional norms of plot construction in the novel become a ready-made pattern for comprehending real-life situations. In order to expose the falsity of this (romantic) model of the world, an invented system is constructed. Instead of 'art reproducing life,' 'life reproduces art.'"[75] Such assessments of the effects that Tatiana's reading has on her perception of and response to life overlook the expressly creative quality of her reading and neglect to consider the marked lack of opportunity in her actual setting. Here it is no one-way street that Pushkin represents, and there is no struggle as to what should be reproduced and what should do the reproducing. Life and art are engaged in the dynamic act of reproducing one another, and in the countless mutations to which these reproductions give rise, there transpires the revitalization of both the creative process and the world to which that process responds. Mere replication is superseded by perpetual interanimation.

Tatiana does not simply fancy herself the heroine of the novels she reads. As her letter to Eugene subsequently bears out, she absorbs from them the language of love and the formal conventions on which the communication of the desire she experiences depends. Whatever the literary sources that tutor Tatiana's expressivity and however fictionalized the object of her newly recognized love, her feelings are genuine, and thus enable her to connect with the vastly dissimilar worlds of her heroines.

> Вздыхает, и себе присвоя
> Чужой восторг, чужую грусть,
> В забвеньи шепчет наизусть
> Письмо для милого героя . . . .
>
> [she sighed, and in a trance coopted
> another's joy, another's breast,
> whispered by heart a note addressed
> to the hero that she'd adopted.][76]
> (3:10, ll. 9–12)

It is precisely because the alien ("chuzhoi") delights and sorrows Tatiana finds in her novels intersect with her own emotions that they can be fully assimilated, an assimilation underscored by the gerund "prisvoia" (having made her own). Such intersection of the other with the self fosters a rich swelling of emotion that demands expression and stimulates a creative act—the composition of a letter to her "hero."

3
Tatiana's Letter to Onegin

Where heart, and soul, and sense, in concert move.
                                        Byron, *Don Juan*

Having assimilated what her heroines have to offer specifically in the new context of Eugene's presence in her mind's eye, Tatiana develops a need for something more than a passive, distant, and by now abstract image on which to focus her emotions. That she has grown as an individual under the influence of love and the tutelage of Richardson, Rousseau, and de Staël is evident from the intense need she now experiences for the expression and communication of her feelings. The complete control she can exercise over the selection, orchestration, and direction of events in the space of her imagination must be supplemented with the unpredictability that is vital to her further development and for which she must now turn to her actual surroundings. Having drawn a flesh-and-blood individual into her imaginative realm of literary shades, Tatiana finds that this imaginative space is no longer adequate to contain those emotions that his presence has increased. The creative urge is set into motion and Tatiana rehearses the letter that she will subsequently write to Eugene. The recognition and discovery that characterized her reading remain in full effect as she composes her letter. If the emotions elicited by her novels are described as an intersection of the alien ("chuzhoi") and the familiar ("svoi") (3:10, l. 10), their expression in the creative upsurge Tatiana now experiences is situated at the juncture of oblivion and recollection: "*V zabven'i* shepchet *naizust'* / Pis'mo dlia milogo geroia . . ." (she whispers *in a trance, by heart,* / a letter to the dear hero [3:10, ll. 10–12, my emphasis]).[1] These oral drafts of the letter to Eugene she will shortly write bespeak the onset of inspiration—the moment at which the imagined and the actual intersect.

Between these pregnant mutterings and Tatiana's articulation of her feelings first in the confession to her nurse and then in the letter to Eugene, the author/narrator interjects a series of stanzas in which we can recognize an implicit restatement of the radical dissimilarities of hero and heroine—dissimilarities which, for all Tatiana's sincerity and best efforts, her letter will prove insufficient to bridge. Referred to in stanzas 11 and 12, respectively, are the antithetical literary schools that are aligned with Tatiana and Eugene. Stanza 11 describes the superannuated sentimental tradition that gave rise to those novels that absorb Tatiana, works in which, as the narrator summarizes, vice always met with punishment and virtue with reward ("Vsegda nakazan byl porok, / Dobru dostoinyi byl venok" [3:11, ll. 13–14]). The following stanza is devoted to the then current literary trends that are linked with Eugene's world, trends, as Nabokov reminds us, that were contemporary to Pushkin himself in the 1820s.[2] At this stage, according to the author/narrator's account, admiration of virtue was replaced by an attraction to vice ("porok") clothed in the "gloomy romanticism" ("unylyi romantizm") of Byron and rhymed tellingly with "hopeless egotism" ("beznadezhnyi egoizm"). Adumbrated here is that impending clash of divergent value systems of which Tatiana is innocent when she pens her letter, but which she will subsequently confront when she discovers the annotated texts in Eugene's rural library and then encounters Eugene himself in his native element of Petersburg society.

By foregrounding the dissimilarity between the sentimental-pastoral and the romantic-Byronic schools, these stanzas draw attention to the values projected by any given literary system, and to the moral responsibility entailed in literary endeavor whose consequences, as is demonstrated in *Eugene Onegin*, are so strongly imprinted onto life. Represented here too is the model of a sequential literary unfolding in which one school completely and irrevocably replaces the previous one, a model that Pushkin contests. His own position on this is implied in the subsequent stanza (13), in which the author/narrator undermines the notion of a sequence of literary schools and advocates a productive synchronicity in its place. Here we find the famous announcement of a possible shift of allegiance from poetry to prose:

> Быть можетъ, волею небесъ,
> Я перестану быть поэтомъ,
> Въ меня вселится новый бѣсъ,
> И, Фебовы презрѣвъ угрозы,
> Унижусь до смиренной прозы.

> [Perhaps, my friends, by fate's decree,
> I'll cease one day to be a poet—
> When some new demon seizes me;
> And scorning then Apollo's ire
> To humble prose I'll bend my lyre.]
>   (3:13, ll. 2–6)

These lines—and the last in particular—are often taken to be a statement of Pushkin's literary platform, with little regard for the complexity of the context in which it is imbedded.[3] Such a literal-minded, decontextualized reading forcibly draws these lines into a deterministic scheme in which poetry must be supplanted by prose and the poetic imagination must give way to the sociological sobriety of realism—a scheme to which Pushkin himself does not subscribe and one which he expressly counters in his poetry, his prose, and in his novel-in-verse. This avowal of generic fickleness is a distinct and pointed echo of that great English romantic who is referred to in the immediately preceding stanza of *Eugene Onegin*, and who opens stanza 204 of the first canto of his *Don Juan* with the line, "If ever I should condescend to prose."[4] The author/narrator of *Eugene Onegin* is prepared to describe what he proposes to do in the event that such a transition is accomplished:

Тогда роман на старый лад
Займёт весёлый мой закат.
Не муки тайные злодейства
Я грозно в нем изображу,
Но просто вам перескажу
Преданья русского семейства,
Любви пленительные сны,
Да нравы нашей старины.

[A novel in the older vein
Will claim what happy days remain.
No secret crimes or passions gory
Shall I in grim detail portray,
But simply tell as best I may
A Russian family's age-old story,
A tale of lovers and their lot,
Of ancient customs unforgot.]
(3:13, ll. 7–14)

In his "sunset" years ("zakat"), the poet claims, he will look not ahead to new developments, but back to a tradition that antedated his own literary development. This return to a pre-Byronic literary era is undertaken presumably in an effort to chart an alternative to the path that led to "hopeless egotism"—the moral and aesthetic cul-de-sac into which the romantic movement eventually propelled itself. At the same time however, like Byron's, so too Pushkin's announcements of intent to abandon poetry for prose habitually carry the implication of waning sexual energies, and the postulated return to the moral standards of bygone days is rendered less convincing by the underlying suggestion that such a return would be prompted less by conviction than by an increasing disability to be otherwise than virtuous. To reject recent developments in favor of past tradition is no more desirable than the wholesale rejection of the old in favor of the newer one.

Here it is important to observe that even as the author/narrator advocates a return to those literary traditions of earlier times that he opposes to the contemporary scene, the linearity of both progress and regression is undone by the fact that the last four lines of stanza 13 describe, in fact, not what Pushkin may do once he turns to prose, but precisely what he has just done in the verse of *Eugene Onegin*. The immediately preceding past thus coincides in significant respects with the projected future of his literary trajectory. The mores and morals of earlier days as depicted in his account of the traditional Russian customs perpetuated in the Larin household and their elder daughter's outmoded reading material do not, however, as the reader subsequently discovers, culminate in the happy-wedding-day ending dictated by literary convention. Thus as a hint of what course *Eugene Onegin* may subsequently take, this description proves, in Lotman's observation, to be a "false move" ("lozhnyi khod").[5] With this "false move" Pushkin plays on his reader's expectations and draws particular attention to the amalgamation of the different literary traditions he—together with his heroine—accomplishes within the text of *Eugene Onegin*. The notion that literary development is based on the mere replacement of one thing with another is countered by the synchronicity into which Pushkin's novel-in-verse draws the sentimental, preromantic, and romantic movements, the genres of poetry and prose, and, at this juncture of the text, the projected future and the immediately preceding past. We may observe here that however dissatisfied Pushkin might have been with the moral implications of the Byronic stance, he is in agreement with his English fellow poet, who indicates that a *conjunction* of poetry and prose is to follow his "condescension":

> If ever I should condescend to prose,
> I'll write poetical commandments . . . .
> (1:204, ll. 1–2)[6]

As Leon Stilman notes in connection with *Don Juan* and *Eugene Onegin*, "in both instances the authors show an awareness of producing a nonconventional form resulting from an interplay of conflicting poetics."[7] Although distinctly ironic, Pushkin's author/narrator's emphasis on recollection and retelling in stanzas 13 and 14 goes against the grain of sequence to insist on the constant interrelation of various genres and schools of literature.

Having referred to both the moralistic eighteenth-century sentimental novels that guide his heroine's development and the Byronic "gloomy romanticism" and "hopeless egotism" that inform his hero's stance, the author/narrator launches into a tongue-in-cheek apostrophe to Tatiana in which he bemoans the tragic fate literary convention has in store for her:

> Татьяна, милая Татьяна!
> С тобой теперь я слезы лью;
> Ты в руки модного тирана
> Уж отдала судьбу свою.

> [Tatyana dear, with you I'm weeping:
> for you have, at this early date,
> into a modish tyrant's keeping
> resigned disposal of your fate.][8]
> (3:15, ll. 1–4)

Even as this stanza pokes fun at the literary tradition that activates readers' expectations, its reference to the "modish" tyrant subtly reminds us of how very different Eugene's world is from Tatiana's, while its continuation emphasizes the intensity of Tatiana's emotions:

> Ты негу жизни узнаешь,
> Ты пьешь волшебный яд желаний,
> Тебя преследуют мечты:
> Везде воображаешь ты
> Приюты счастливых свиданий;
> Везде, везде перед тобой
> Твой искуситель роковой.

> ['You learn life's sweetness . . . feel its kiss,
> And drink the draught of love's temptations,
> As phantom daydreams haunt your mind:
> On every side you seem to find
> Retreats for happy assignations;
> While everywhere before your eyes
> Your fateful tempter's figure lies.]
> (3:15, ll. 8–14)

On the strength of her desire and the imaginative faculties it has nurtured, the absent Eugene becomes a constant presence in Tatiana's life. The imaginary auditor to whom she addressed the whispered drafts of her letter is soon found to be inadequate to her needs, and solitude loses its charms. No longer content with a book tucked into her bed, the sleepless Tatiana seeks out human companionship.

She turns first to the person nearest her for comfort—the old, loyal nurse who is a figure familiar to readers as a confidante for frustrated love, be it Phaedra's or that of Shakespeare's Juliet, and who is no stranger either to the Russian literary tradition, or Pushkin's own life and works. Tatiana's nurse is an ideal example of the interpenetration of life and art that lies at the heart of *Eugene Onegin*. Created in the image of the woman Pushkin knew in person, her role in *Eugene Onegin* is best appreciated, as we will see, in the context of her literary predecessors.[9]

If Pushkin, as he wrote in one of his letters, was never bored in the company of his old nurse,[10] his heroine is afforded no relief when she complains to hers of boredom and urges her to speak of bygone days: "Mne skuchno, / Pogovorim o starine" (I'm bored, / Let's talk about old times [3:17, ll. 3–4]). Tatiana's description of the burning desire that torments her as "boredom," although at first glance seemingly less than accurate, suggests that her fantasies can no longer satisfy her growing emotional needs and underscores the dependency of the imagination and of eros on interaction with the actual world. At the same time, Tatiana's profession of "boredom" invites comparison with Eugene's reaction to the evening that precipitated this condition. Far from suggesting any similarity between them, the fact that both hero and heroine should succumb to "boredom" in the aftermath of their first encounter serves only to emphasize the differences between them. The "boredom" that Eugene enacts before Lensky [3:4] and the "boredom" Tatiana confesses to her nurse alert us to the dramatic differences that prevail between hero and heroine and remind us of the gulf between them that has yet to be bridged. Whereas Eugene's "boredom" testifies to a dearth of feelings, Tatiana's attests to a surfeit of emotion. Opposite Eugene's self-conscious refusal to allow himself to be drawn into the Larins' world is the intense receptivity that characterizes Tatiana. Contained in their respective "boredoms" are both Eugene's entrapment in a predetermined role and the freedom of Tatiana's surrender to the emotions he inspires in her. If Eugene disappoints his interlocutor with his demonstrative apathy, Tatiana alarms hers with a display of feeling. Eugene's "boredom" is both cause and effect of his refusal to engage or be engaged in the uncertainties of life and ultimately proves destructive. His verbal jabs at Lensky are a prelude to the actual wound he will subsequently inflict. Tatiana's "boredom"—a sign of her need for expanded possibilities—fosters an upsurge of creativity that finds expression in her letter to Eugene. Eugene's demonstratively de-eroticized reaction that was discussed in the preceding chapter is offset here by the erotically charged condition that drives Tatiana to seek support from her nurse.

Tatiana's attempt to engage her nurse founders on the old woman's inability to recollect the vanished days of her youth and the folklore with which they were infused. The strong erotic undercurrents of those tales "About evil spirits and about maidens" ("Pro zlykh dukhov i pro devits"

[3:17, l. 8]) that the nurse once recounted to Tatiana could now elicit a fuller response from her enamored ward. But these tales have been forgotten, and the nurse can only confess:

А ныне всё мне тёмно, Таня:
Что знала, то забыла. Да,
Пришла худая череда!

[but now my brain is darkened, Tanya:
now I've forgotten all I knew.
A sorry state of things, it's true!][11]
(3:17, ll. 9–11)

The ever-repeated of old has been forgotten, and nothing new has come to take its place.[12] Tatiana's nurse is consigned to the obscurity of a temporal oblivion where there is neither cyclic nor linear time. In an attempt to find relief or encouragement for her own emotions, Tatiana seeks to draw her nurse out of this barren temporal void which can be likened only to lifelessness, and to engage her memories of the "old years," that is to say, the years when the nurse was young.

«Расскажи мне, няня,
Про ваши старые года:
Была ты влюблена тогда?»

["But tell me, nanny,
About the olden days . . . you know,
Were you in love then, long ago?"]
(3:17, ll. 12–14)

The story the nurse tells, however, is not the one Tatiana wants to hear. In response to urgent promptings, the old woman recalls not love, but only a dim past unenlivened by powerful feelings. Her account describes a marriage that apparently antedated sexual maturation and erotically charged love. From her own experience the nurse concludes that matrimony has no place for eros. Indeed, their coincidence strikes her as so inconceivable that she can construe "love" only in terms of an extramarital relationship, noting how violently her mother-in-law would have reacted to the very idea ("A to by sognala so sveta / Menia pokoinitsa svekrov'" [3:18, ll. 3–4]). Far from lending support to Tatiana's emotional state, the nurse's story evokes loveless matrimony and consigns female sexuality to the realm of the unthinkable.

Iurii Lotman has provided valuable sociological background for the story the nurse tells Tatiana and has noted the imprint of these two women's distinct social classes on their discourse on love.[13] Yet for all the class differences he painstakingly documents, the disallowance of female sexuality remains a constant that prevails in both the nurse's and Tatiana's respective social strata, and that is reinforced, as we have seen, in the fictional worlds of her novels as well. Praskov'ia Larina's fantasies about her secondhand Grandison, as we have noted, do not persist very far into the marriage her parents determine for her. Although for now Tatiana is allowed the leisure to peruse her books and to engage in daydreaming, she too, as her mother's story suggests, will be expected to give over her erotic and imaginative sensibilities to the demands of matrimony and prosaic household duties. The tale that the nurse tells is distinguished from the story of Tatiana's mother's marriage only by the vocabulary of the ritualistic sequence of events she outlines: the matchmaker, the paternal blessing, the bride's tears, the lament, the loosening of the maiden's hair, and the singing with which she is accompanied to church.[14] This ever-repeated pattern allows little room for the strong sense of self that powerful emotions excite.

However poignant from the modern reader's point of view, the nurse's story does not speak to her young auditor, who burns with the very desire that is either unknown to or forgotten by its recounter. Appropriately enough, Tatiana interrupts the story just at the moment the nurse enters an alien family ("v sem'iu chuzhuiu") and abandons all hope of love and self-realization. Here we may note parenthetically that in having to leave her self behind when matrimonial ties draw her into a new family, the nurse is denied the opportunity for a fruitful interrelation of the familiar ("svoi") with the alien ("chuzhoi") that we have discussed in connection with Tatiana's entry into the world of her novels (cf. 3:10, ll. 6–7 and 9–10).

There is no help here for Tatiana's plight. The traditional prayers and holy water the nurse deploys to ward off the evil of her "illness" with its accompanying symptoms of nausea, weepiness, and fever cannot offer the relief that Tatiana seeks.[15] Far from dispelling the older woman's solicitude, the confession of love that erupts from Tatiana at this point can only reinforce the nurse's conviction that her charge is seriously ill, and lead her to persist in her attempts to ward off the "malady" of female sexuality. Her own de-eroticized state that prevents her from entering into Tatiana's situation stands out all the more sharply in the context of literary tradition, where a nurse customarily assumes the role of a savvy, willing go-between for eager lovers.[16] In contrast, Tatiana's nurse is not an active agent, but only an unwitting accomplice in Tatiana's love story. It is, we can anticipate here, the nurse's ignorance of love and not her readiness to assist her charge that makes the quick dispatch of Tatiana's letter possible.

In the moonlit *tableau vivant* that concludes stanza 20, an aged nurse whose erotic potentiality is a thing of her forgotten past is seen opposite a youthful charge who urgently seeks recognition of her burgeoning sexuality in a singularly unresponsive world. In the nurse, all the symptoms of the "malady" that afflicts Tatiana have been eradicated. She stands—clad in a long shapeless garment, her hair confined under a scarf—purged of all vestiges, indeed of the very memory, of her sexuality. With her is Tatiana, whose loosened hair and flowing tears betoken the intensity of those very emotions the nurse lacks, and yet also evoke images of the marriage ritual that the nurse has just described. We are reminded that the institution of matrimony threatens Tatiana's own feelings with extinction.

In the face of her nurse's unresponsiveness, Tatiana's assertion of her emotional state is rendered all the more necessary, for she is not prepared to consign her erotic energies to oblivion. Tatiana counters her nurse's conclusion that she is ill ("bol'na") with the rhyme this diagnosis prompts and that more accurately describes her condition. She insists that she is in love ("vliublena"). The threefold repetition of *vliublena* in the space of eight lines suggests Tatiana's growing certainty that she has correctly named her condition. And yet her realization is a disturbing one, and with the increasing conviction that she is in love comes not the ecstasy novels conventionally attach to such discovery, but increasing anxiety. Love threatens to alienate Tatiana still further from an already unsupportive world to leave her stranded in an imaginary realm that can no longer satisfy her and that can develop no further in isolation from the actual world. Hence the "bitterness" ("gorest'") of her second repetition of *vliublena*. Rather than retreat, however, Tatiana reasserts her conviction that she is in love by repeating *vliublena* for a third time. It is precisely the impasse in which Tatiana finds herself that impels her to write Eugene.[17] Onegin is a particularly appropriate addressee for, being neither one with her milieu nor yet purely imaginary, he stands somewhere in between the actual world that discounts her feelings and the imaginary one from which they issue, but which can no longer sustain them. Although on the surface Tatiana's course of action may resemble that of her novelistic heroines, Pushkin goes to some lengths to insist on the profoundly experienced personal need that moves his heroine to take up her pen. However many such letters have come into being before Tatiana's, hers is a genuine, spontaneous, necessary, and thus creative self-expression.

The ten stanzas that separate the account of how it comes to be written from the interpolated text of the letter itself heighten the reader's anticipation and enhance the significance Tatiana's epistle assumes. These stanzas highlight, moreover, both the specific circumstances of the composition of the letter (stanza 21) and the uniqueness of its author. Even a brief look at what guides Tatiana's epistolary enterprise reveals an entire set of distinctly poetical criteria to be in place for its composition. Operating in concert with the powerful frustrated emotions that demand expression are the inspiring moonlight ("Pri vdokhnovitel'noi lune" [3:20, ll. 7–8]), Tatiana's solitude in the quiet of the night, and the distant beloved she approaches in her text. In stanza 21, in which Tatiana conceives the notion to write, the moon and Tatiana's solitude are rhymed twice ("lunu"-"odnu," [ll. 2 and 4]; "odna"-"luna," [ll. 7–8]) to signal the dependency of inspiration on the absence of the object of desire. Everything is in place and Tatiana writes her letter because she is prepared to surrender herself to the inspiration that demands its composition, and not simply because this is how Clarissa, Julie, and Delphine expressed their pent-up feelings. Indeed, at this moment the heroines of her novels are far from Tatiana's thoughts, and she acts spontaneously:

> И в *необдуманном* письме
> Любовь невинной девы дышит.

> [Her guileless maiden love, enshrined
> In *unpremeditated* writing.]
>   (3:21, ll. 11–12, my emphasis)

The spontaneity of Tatiana's decision to write and the immediacy with which her "unpremeditated" letter conveys her emotions reflect the specific and unique situation out of which the letter arises. But this immediacy and spontaneity have been made possible by Tatiana's assimilation of her heroines' expressive vocabulary and by her earlier oral rehearsals of the letter ("V zabven'i shepchet naizust' / Pis'mo dlia milogo geroia" [she whispers in a trance, by heart, / a letter to the dear hero] [3:10, ll. 10–11]). Far from being restrictive or deterministic in any way, it is precisely this assimilation and these rehearsals that enable Tatiana's successful translation of seething emotions into genuine self-expression. Just as Richardson, Rousseau, and de Staël—though outdated in the fashionable world—are for Tatiana fresh revelations that speak to her own condition, so too are the moon that has illuminated the composition of countless lyrics and the erotic desire that has propelled innumerable pens genuinely new sources of inspiration for her. Whatever its literary resonances, Tatiana's letter is no act of schoolgirl plagiarism, but a genuinely creative gesture fostered by intense desire for an absent beloved, made possible by the preparatory work in which she has engaged, and realized on the strength of her responsiveness to inspiration. In evidence here is Tatiana's openness to the unpredictable, her ability to recognize and respond to the moment, and her readiness to take the risk involved in seizing it. The poetic imperative that demands the intersection of unreserved self-surrender with perfect mastery (cf. "V zabven'i shepchet naizust'" [she whispers in a trance, by heart] [3:10, l. 10]) is fulfilled, and Tatiana can begin to write. She surrenders herself freely to the spontaneous expressive act her emotions engender, even as she contains these emotions within the literary form she has assimilated in the course of her reading. Her letter to Eugene is the first of her controlled surrenders. It is balanced at the work's end by the frank admission of love with which she accompanies her rejection of his advances.

The meticulously crafted narrative envelope in which the author/narrator encloses the letter urges powerfully that it be read as a successful text authored by Tatiana herself.[18] The subsequent four stanzas (22–25), in which Tatiana's behavior is contrasted with that of other women the author/narrator has known, champion both the sincerity of her emotions and the appropriateness of the form her self-expression takes. Underscored too is a characteristic of her love that is crucial in her confrontation with Eugene in the concluding chapter of this work: it is a love that remains "pure" because it is unselfconsciously directed toward another, and not intended to promote her self. She does not seek to excite and manipulate emotions to her own ends as do the "cold coquettish beauties" described in stanzas 22 and 23. Far from engaging sexuality in a bid for power, Tatiana knowingly assumes a position of vulnerability.

Tatiana's letter to Eugene, like the letter he writes to her in the final chapter, has neither salutation nor closing. In place of these prominent markers of epistolary intent are descriptive headings ("Pis'mo Tat'iany k Oneginu" and "Pis'mo Onegina k Tat'iane"). Couched neither in Onegin stanzas nor in prose, the letters appear instead in a verse form of uneven stanzas of iambic tetrameter with a free pattern of rhymes. Thus distinguished from both the text into which they are interpolated and conventions of the epistolary genre, the letters take on significance as texts in their own right and invite comparison with one another. The suggestion that we compare the letters is intensified by the symmetry noted by Stilman, who observes that the receipt of each letter is followed by a monologue that constitutes a reply.[19] The prompting is well worth pursuing, for a juxtaposition of Tatiana's and Eugene's letters as texts they themselves have authored permits us to gauge the successes of the heroine and the failings of the hero. The ability to read, write, love, and ultimately also to live are held up in *Eugene Onegin* as correlative, and, as we will see when we consider first Tatiana's letter and later Eugene's, strengths and weaknesses in writing are to be regarded as direct reflections of strengths and weaknesses in character. Although their overlapping formal markers hold these texts in a structural balance within *Eugene Onegin*, this symmetry is rendered precarious by the preferential treatment Pushkin accords his heroine's text. Not only does Pushkin craft a more aesthetically and emotionally satisfying letter on Tatiana's behalf, but he unabashedly privileges it over Eugene's by the framework in which he imbeds it. What might otherwise have been a static symmetry of the letters is disrupted by the pronounced dissimilarity of the circumstances of their composition and their presentation in the text.

If in chapter 8 of *Onegin* the letter Eugene writes to Tatiana is given verbatim and introduced with no further ado than "Vot vam pis'mo ego toch' v toch'" (Here is his letter word for word [8:32, l. 14]), Tatiana's letter to him is prefaced by the rapturous author/narrator's insistence on the distance between the inspired and inspiring French original currently in his possession and the "incomplete, feeble translation" ("Nepolnyi, slabyi perevod" [3:31, l. 11]) with which he supplies his reader. The narrator makes enough of the inadequacy of his translation—comparing it to a pale rendering of a vivid painting and a clumsily executed piece of music—to suggest that his decision to assume the role of translator rather than transmitter of Tatiana's letter is of some significance. Certainly there is more than "encyclopedic" accuracy at stake in having Tatiana pen her letter in French, the preferred language in her milieu, particularly since Onegin writes his letter in the humble idiom of their native soil.[20]

Viazemskii describes Pushkin's discomfiture at the prospect of writing on his heroine's behalf a letter whose language would adequately and plausibly convey her feminine sensibilities: "The author said that for a long time he could not decide how to make Tatiana write without infringing on her female personality and verisimilitude of style."[21] The notion of a "translation" was hit upon, according to Viazemskii, as a felicitous solution to this dilemma, relieving the anxiety of authorship Pushkin experienced in connection with feminine writing.[22] Keenly aware of the extent to which the manner of writing is bound up with the emotional and psychological makeup of any individual, Pushkin hesitated to invent the language in which his heroine might choose to express her innermost feelings. His hesitation reflects the respect he held for Tatiana's autonomy and suggests too his recognition of the complexity and inscrutability of the feminine—not in the abstract, mystical sense with which the romantics imbued it, but in a concrete and specific acknowledgment of a woman's otherness as it would be reflected in language. His concern could only be intensified by the fact that such a language did not, in fact, yet exist, for if male writers had at least begun to render into Russian the language of love they learned from their Gallic tutors (Rousseau in particular), women of Pushkin's class were still expressing themselves almost exclusively in French.[23]

Recalling briefly the authors of Tatiana's novels helps us appreciate both the task Pushkin confronted and the recognition he accorded feminine otherness.[24] Richardson, who met with rebuke from Dr. Johnson for exhibiting a marked preference for female society over that of other males, could pass his time in what an early biographer described as a "flower garden of ladies,"[25] absorbing their manner of self-expression before recreating their language in his novels. Rousseau, the tutor of men and women alike in the grammar of love, did not concern himself with the uniquely feminine, and regarded women's "charms" as mere ornaments to his own ideals. "I imagined," he noted in his *Confessions*, apropos *The New Eloise*, "love and friendship, the two ideals of my heart, in the most ravishing of forms, and took delight in adorning them with all the charms of the sex I had always adored."[26] De Staël's heroines—no longer projections of male notions about women—accomplished epistolary revelations of the feminine in a language that, although dictated in part by Rousseau, was distinctly their own. Pushkin, however, was being called upon to invent not only a mode of self-expression particular to his heroine, but the very idiom in which it could be couched. His reticence is well motivated, for in Tatiana's letter he was faced with devising a language that would, in accordance with his project, render feminine sensibilities every bit as genuine as the heroine he had set out to create.[27]

Implicit in Pushkin's masking of his authorship of Tatiana's letter is the suggestion that a woman be allowed to find her own language and to write for herself. Significantly, it is their language and not women themselves that Pushkin was reluctant to characterize. Indeed, like the authors of Tatiana's novels, he too, it seems, was prepared to define women exclusively in terms of their passions: "Les femmes n'ont pas de caractére, elles ont des passions dans leur jeunesse; et voilà pourquoi il est si facile de les peindre," he wrote in a letter shortly after completing this chapter (3) of *Eugene Onegin*.[28] Thus the same author/narrator who thinks nothing of penetrating Tatiana's unconscious to provide a vivid account of her dream is given pause by the thought of shaping the language that would adequately express her own intense, personal feelings.

The respect Pushkin accords Tatiana's language distinguishes her and makes her a highly appropriate model not only for future heroines, but, more important, for women writers. This is all the more significant in light of Greenleaf's penetrating observation that "the whole protracted translation scene has permitted Pushkin to . . . represent his own process of creation in almost seamless mimetic disguise."[29] As will be discussed in the epilogue to this study, both Karolina Pavlova and Marina Tsvetaeva mark their connectedness to the Russian poetic tradition over which Pushkin presided by aligning themselves with his privileged heroine. Such alignment is particularly encouraging for writing women, for in designating himself as the translator of Tatiana's letter, Pushkin's author/narrator places himself in the role of an apprentice of feminine writing rather than its master. The assumption of this role highlights Tatiana's autonomy in authoring her own text. Her letter becomes a model that fosters the author/narrator's own assimilation of alien sensibilities and tutors him in the idiom into which he transcribes them. To appreciate the significance of translation in this context, we have only to recall the "translations" that Bürger's *Lenore* underwent (to cite but one example conveniently close at hand). The complex cultural, stylistic, linguistic, and psychological negotiations that are involved in the various Russian renderings of this work are themselves part and parcel of the literary process which is both stimulated and enriched in the course of those intersections of the alien and the familiar that translations accomplish. The turbulent debates that were set off by the various renderings of *Lenore* gauge the significance such negotiations were accorded in the evolution of Russian literature in Pushkin's time.[30]

The author/narrator's insistence on his "translation" draws particular attention to the language of the letter. Yet for all his protestations of inadequacy, the translation is a "mystification"[31] for the fact remains that there is no extant trace of a French original behind the Russian version.[32] With Tatiana's letter Pushkin emerges, as his contemporaries were quick to recognize, "in the role of reformer: he does not reproduce the norms of the "ideal" language of a Russian noblewoman, but creates them."[33] Accordingly, contemporary reviewers marveled that Russian women had not adopted Tatiana's idiom upon reading her letter[34] and turned to Pushkin himself with those questions his author/narrator directs to Tatiana:

> Кто ей внушал и эту нежность,
> И слов любезную небрежность?
> Кто ей внушал умильный вздор,
> Безумный сердца разговор
> И увлекательный, и вредный?
> Я не могу понять.

> [Who taught her then this soft surrender,
> This careless gift for waxing tender,
> This touching whimsy free of art,
> This raving discourse of the heart—
> Enchanting, yet so fraught with trouble?
> I'll never know.]

(3:31, ll. 5–10)

Bocharov observes that the letter Tatiana writes is itself a translation of her own powerful emotions into the idiom she absorbed from her epistolary novels. Thus in the absence of an actual French text underlying the author/narrator's Russian version,[35] he convincingly postulates another sort of "original" for the letter: "Pushkin's translation then is not a translation of the French text of a provincial miss in love, not a translation of this 'verisimilar' reality whose sign is the assumed letter 'in French,' but a 'translation' of profound reality, of Tatyana's 'heart.'"[36]

Here we must note another translation that often goes without notice. Tatiana's letter is translated not only from French into Russian, but like Eugene's letter undergoes the transformation of what was presumably the prose of the original into Pushkin's own poetry. It is not difficult to imagine that Pushkin, who first sketched Tatiana's letter in prose,[37] might have hesitated to distinguish the interpolated letters too dramatically from the remainder of his text. Yet the freely rhymed iambic tetrameter that is to count for prose in the context of the more structured Onegin stanza is neither Tatiana's nor Eugene's, but Pushkin's own. The success of the letters *as poetic texts* thus remains in his control.[38] Here Pushkin finds another opportunity to privilege Tatiana's letter over Eugene's for, bluntly stated, his heroine's letter is couched in noticeably better poetry than his hero's. In meter, syntax, pacing, tonality, and expressive range Eugene's letter pales before the more varied and yet also more coherent text ascribed to Tatiana. The poetical strength of Tatiana's letter vouches for its sincerity and originality, even as the poetical weakness of Eugene's epistle undermines its emotional vitality and credibility. Even if the fact that these letters are written in verse is overlooked, the reader cannot but fall under the sway of their poetry.

As successful as this stratagem is in privileging his beloved heroine, it is not one Pushkin would have his reader notice, for he is intent on preserving the illusion that she develops autonomously. Tatiana's serene alienation from those around her, her silent contemplation of her surroundings, and the readiness with which she absorbs Eugene and the events of her novels into her animated private sphere point to a central feature of Pushkin's characterization of his heroine—she is self-creating. We can observe here that the author/narrator, who repeatedly draws attention to how he manipulates the narrative, represents his characters as already formed well before their appearance in the text—shaped, as we are to believe, by outside forces and not by the author/narrator himself.[39] Thus, Onegin is the product of his fashion-driven society, Lensky of German idealist aesthetics, Olga of jaded novelistic conventions, and Tatiana's mother and nurse of prevailing social norms. Only Tatiana is and remains for the duration of the work a complex, developing character whose continual formation draws together a broad range of influences.

Having exempted his heroine from the type of predetermination of character to which the other major figures are subjected, Pushkin allows

Tatiana to create herself, and it is precisely because she demonstrates how she becomes that he can attach his own ideas about literary process to her development. Thus, as we have seen, Tatiana is represented not only as the product of Pushkin's own ability to assimilate and respond to a variety of literary schools, but as a reader in her own right, who singles out her literary models on the basis of her own (rather than only her author's) personal preference. Because the letter she writes to Eugene is a crucial step in the process of Tatiana's self-creation, it is especially important that the author/narrator absent himself from its composition, and we are well advised to heed Bocharov, who argues in connection with the posited original of Tatiana's letter that "Pushkin does assume the fiction of this text and it is a 'fact' of the artistic reality which must be taken into consideration."[40]

That Tatiana's literary debut should be an epistolary one is highly appropriate, not only because this is the form with which she is most familiar, but also because the peculiarities of the genre are particularly well suited to describe her present condition and to further her self-awareness. The epistolary form, as we have had the opportunity to observe in connection with Tatiana's novels, is highly conducive to the process of self-realization. Author and narrator are absent from the field of vision, and the immediacy of the act of writing foregrounds the emotional state of the imputed author whose social standing, education, expressive range, and psychological makeup are revealed in how she writes. Less important than any given event are those emotions that propel the composition of the letter and color what is being described.

Because letters successfully bridge an entire series of antinomies that we have already recognized in *Eugene Onegin*, Tatiana's development and Pushkin's project are well served by the interpolation of this "document" into the text. As the letter bridges the inner and the outer worlds, the imaginative and the actual spheres inhabited by its writer interpenetrate. Those powerful emotions that demand expression dictate the language of the letter and find containment within the form it provides. At work within a letter is a complex dynamic between an interdependent author and addressee. The writer of the letter projects a persona that is somehow suitable to both self and the addressee and at the same time shapes the addressee to whom that persona writes. Writer and addressee are thus interrelated within the textual bounds of an individual letter whether or not it receives a reply. Thus, for example, we see that in her letter Tatiana not only projects a created self, but also invents the Eugene—or possible Eugenes—with whom she interacts in the space of her letter. Once sent, a letter spans the private and public spheres to convey personal feelings to the outside world, and to elicit a response. We can recall here that having been read by its addressee, a letter was habitually passed on to other readers to be copied, circulated, or used as a model by other would-be writers. Thus Tatiana's letter (or a copy of it) has come into the possession of the author/narrator who enters it into the public domain of *Eugene Onegin*.

The epistolary genre also raises interesting questions that are important to *Onegin's* larger design about the role of creativity and originality in the process of self-expression. Even when purporting to convey intensely personal emotions, letters were not necessarily the product of their signators. Thus, for example, Vigel' observes in his memoirs that Russian love letters "were sooner copied than composed."[41] In order to recognize that the custom of copying letters extended well beyond Russia and the billet-doux, we have only to recall that Richardson wrote his best-selling epistolary novel *Pamela* in between working on his *Familiar Letters on Important Occasions*, a book of sample business and personal letters. In this sense the epistolary genre vigorously eroded the boundaries not only between public and private, but also between personal and cultural. There was nothing unseemly in couching one's sentiments in another's words. Indeed, the copying of preexisting models served as an effective means to learn the craft and stimulate the emotions necessary to the composition of a letter. Thus, for example, Germann from Pushkin's "Pikovaia dama" ("Queen of Spades") advances from the calculated copying out of love letters to their inspired (albeit duplicitous) composition. The search for an extant document suitable for the expression of personal feelings involves both recognition—that important catalyst of empathy that we have noted in connection with Tatiana's reading—and the interaction of the "alien" with the "familiar" that fosters growth. In electing to compose her own letter to Eugene rather than select an emotionally charged text from one of her novels, Tatiana demonstrates that she has fully assimilated the language of the novels and does not, therefore, need to resort to wholesale borrowing for her own self-expression.

In the process of writing her letter to Eugene, Tatiana gives the expressive, the seductive, and the creative powers of language their full due. Richard Gregg's designation of Tatiana as "an exceptionally unreliable witness"[42] in connection with her speech to Eugene in chapter 8 holds also in connection with her letter, for here too Tatiana's account does not "square with the facts."[43] Indeed, it is not the facts that are of primary concern here, and it would be highly improbable for Tatiana to suddenly fall in with that actual world from which she is alienated to produce an objective letter of "fact." "If," as Pushkin wrote in a letter to Viazemskii (29 November 1824) in regard to Tatiana's letter, "the sense is not quite precise, there is more truth in the letter—the letter of a woman—and, on top of that, a seventeen-year-old one—and on top of *that* a woman in love."[44] The letter does not purport to be an objective account of what has transpired in Tatiana's life—actual or imaginative. Rather, as Pushkin's references to the epistolary genre and to the gender, age, and emotional state of its ostensible writer indicate, it is an expressive gesture that idiosyncratically amalgamates what transpired in Tatiana's surroundings, what transpired in her epistolary novels, and what transpired in that emotional/imaginative sphere into which both the actual and the novelistic have been absorbed. As such the letter provides the reader with an opportunity to observe how Tatiana makes sense of her emotional experiences and to evaluate the means she engages to describe them. The "imprecisions" of the letter signal a veracity of a different order that overlaps but does not coincide with that of the actual world. A unique expression of the directly and the empathetically experienced, Tatiana's letter is a creative act. Tatiana draws on the literary material that she has assimilated and on her own emotional experiences to shape the persona who pens the letter, its addressee, and the text they can both inhabit. If her reading included both recognition and discovery, her writing is both expression and exploration. Her letter is the culmination of her development up to this point in *Eugene Onegin*. It documents her growth thus far and demarcates a stage that is crucial for her subsequent evolution into the Princess N who rejects Eugene's advances.

Considerable scholarly energy has been devoted to discussing the extent of Tatiana's indebtedness to a broad array of literary texts. Her reading provides an important underpinning to her own text, and it is appropriate that reference be made to the discernible effects of what she reads on what she writes. Yet to make too much of the reliance of the letter on other works is to lose sight of the singularity of both its author and the message she conveys. Thus, for example, Belinskii's particularly harsh assessment of Tatiana's dependency on her novels emphatically denies both her strength as a reader and her correlative capacity to write—qualities that are crucial to her characterization. Tatiana, as Belinskii maintains, "would be able neither to understand nor express her own sensations if she did not resort to the impressions left on her mind by the bad and good novels she read with no understanding or discrimination."[45] (We have noted already Tatiana's commendable choice of Clarissa, Julie, and Delphine from among the many heroines she encountered in her readings and have discussed too the empathy with which she reads.) In Nabokov's commentary, the number of texts that are rallied around Tatiana's letter grows disproportionately large. Thus, to Sipovskii's catalogue of the resonance of an entire series of Julie's (*The New Eloise*) letters in Tatiana's epistle,[46] Nabokov appends his own list of literary works that includes de

Krüdner's *Valerie*, Constant's *Adolphe*, Viazemskii's *First Snow*, Chénier's *Les amours* (no. 9), Byron's *The Bride of Abydos*, an 1819 elegy of Marceline Desbordes-Valmore, Racine's *Phèdre*, Vincent Campenon in *Almanach des Muses*, and Jane Austen's *Mansfield Park*.[47] Beyond implicitly denying Tatiana's letter any singularity and demonstrating his own erudition, Nabokov's list accomplishes little. It is not likely that even a mature poet like Pushkin would undertake to juggle such a formidable number of literary allusions in the space of some seventy-nine lines, and still less likely that he should have his beloved heroine attempt to do so. Indeed, Tatiana herself has never read the majority of the works listed by Nabokov. John Garrard suggests that it is the letter Byron's Julia writes to Don Juan that serves as a model for Tatiana's epistle rather than Julie's correspondence with Saint-Preux.[48] Pushkin's interest in Byron's work is well documented, and Garrard's comparison of Tatiana to Julia is supported by a letter in which Pushkin writes, "esli uzh sravnivat' 'Onegina' s 'Don Zhuanom', to razve v odnom otnoshenii: kto milee i prelestnee (gracieuse), Tatiana ili Iuliia?" (If 'Onegin' and 'Don Juan' are to be compared, then only perhaps in one respect: who is sweeter and more charming (gracieuse), Tatiana or Julia?).[49] The comparison, as Garrard demonstrates, can indeed be a fruitful one, and yet in connection with Tatiana's letter, it is not plausible to speak of a dependency on the one Julia writes, for such a borrowing would appear to run contrary to Pushkin's intent. Having gone to some pains to establish Tatiana's autonomy in the text of *Eugene Onegin* in general and in the authoring of this letter in particular, Pushkin is unlikely to have let the letter show signs of indebtedness to a poet whose writings Tatiana has not yet discovered. The similarities between Julia's letter to Don Juan (1:192–97) and the one penned by Tatiana to Eugene are perhaps better explained by the fact that they share a common source, for both hark back to Rousseau.[50] This context highlights a crucial difference between Julia and Tatiana, for if in *Don Juan* it is Byron who draws on Rousseau to create the letter of a heroine who cannot have read *The New Eloise*, in *Eugene Onegin* Tatiana herself reads Rousseau and demonstrates her thorough assimilation of his idiom. Pushkin may well feel confident in suggesting a contest between Byron's privileged heroine[51] and his own, for the autonomy he grants Tatiana sets her well above her competitor.

Overwhelmed by love, Tatiana aligns herself appropriately with a literary tradition in which feelings are the driving force of all that transpires. The expressive means this tradition affords her accord well with those emotions it in fact helped to shape. In relying on Rousseau to tutor her in the language of love, Tatiana joins the select company of an entire gallery of preeminent Western European writers who similarly appren-

ticed themselves to this influential grammarian of the heart. Sipovskii reminds us that Rousseau was, and remained for quite some time, the don
of "the science of tender passion" in literary Europe, among whose many
students were no lesser literary figures than Goethe, Chateaubriand, and
de Staël.[52] Pushkin himself was credited with knowing much of *La nouvelle Héloïse* by heart, and this particular novel is included in the libraries
of several of his characters in recognition of its literary influence and popular appeal.

Tatiana's letter to Eugene bears the unmistakable effects of the sentimental novels she has been reading. Expressed in it we find a readiness to
suffer love silently, the instant recognition of the beloved, fated love that
precludes future matrimonial contentment, regret that they have met, yet
also insistence on the inevitability of the meeting which is determined by
destiny and foreseen in her dreams. At the same time, however, the letter
Tatiana composes reflects self-knowledge and an awareness of the options available to her—leavened with imagination and integrated into a
seamless whole. The sincerity and heartfelt urgency of her letter bespeak
a surrender to the moment of inspiration and a fluency in the idiom that
derives from her earnest reading and her earlier rehearsals of the letter. It
is telling that Pushkin's contemporaries, who sensed something of Saint-
Preux in Onegin's letter, received Tatiana's as an inspired, sincere, and
original composition.[53] That her letter, far from being merely derivative,
emerges as an analogue to the creative process as it is revealed in *Eugene
Onegin* itself, can be seen from the direct applicability of what Leon Stilman writes about Pushkin's novel-in-verse to the composition of Tatiana's
letter:

> The saturation of *Eugene Onegin* with literary materials, the particular pal-
> pability in it of the phenomenon of literature does not, of course, exclude in
> the least the ties of the work with reality, just as the effects on *Eugene
> Onegin* of various literary sources does not exclude its profound artistic
> originality.[54]

Tatiana does not adapt her own experience of life to the precepts of
the sentimental school. Rather, she adapts the formal markers and expressive gestures of that school to serve her own needs. In this regard, Tatiana acts as a corrective to Lensky's undeviating adherence to the tenets
of German idealism, tenets that even before they lead him to a needless
death, absorb in advance all facets of his life, his love, his potential for development, and his creativity (see, e.g., "On pel poblekshii zhizni tsvet, /
Bez malogo v os'mnadtsat' let" [He sang life's bloom gone pale and sere—
/ He'd almost reached his eighteenth year] [2:10, ll. 13–14]). Tatiana's
openness to change, her readiness to assume risk, and her interrelation of

her inner imaginative life with the outside world are foregrounded in the writing of her letter. On the strength of these qualities that define a genuinely creative being, Tatiana provides a positive counterexample to Lensky, whose rehearsal of a single predetermined program closes down possibility for growth.

Tatiana's freedom of movement within and beyond the literary tradition that shapes her development demands that we go beyond Sipovskii's catalogue—thorough and convincing as it is—of textual similarities between Julie d'Etange's letters to Saint-Preux and what Tatiana writes to Eugene. Although Pushkin does not show us how Tatiana writes, it is safe to assume that she does not comb the pages of her Rousseau for spicy bits to include in her own epistle. Tatiana's "borrowings" constitute a unique compendium of expressive gestures culled from her reading by the selective memory of the heart that chooses only what is appropriate to her condition. It is important to recognize too that Tatiana draws freely not only on Julie's letters, but on those of Saint-Preux as well. Indeed, the very fact that it is she who initiates the correspondence dramatically distinguishes her from the heroines in her novels.[55] That Tatiana writes the first letter, that she does so out of a surfeit of emotion for which there is no socially acceptable outlet, and that this action would be condemned in the worlds both of her novels and of her society, testify to an emotional intensity that her novels admit only in male characters. Tatiana's letter thus demonstrates that the desire that urges her to put pen to paper is every bit as intense as Saint-Preux's. Unlike Julie, who is moved by the eloquent pleas of her tutor to write out of compassion for him, Tatiana writes at the behest of her own powerful feelings—feelings that she makes no attempt to disguise, but is prepared to admit as frankly as do the male characters in the novels she reads.

Even as Tatiana's initiation of illicit correspondence with a man she scarcely knows manifests the intensity of her frustrated emotions, the act of writing the letter itself balances expressivity and containment. (This balance is evident also in her final speech to Eugene.) Tatiana's letter is inspired by a complex simultaneity of the absent object of her desire, of her frustrated attempt to gain support for her intense emotions, of a need to interact with the surrounding world, and of her longing for the adventure of the unpredictable. The letter is, as Emerson summarizes, "covert, confessional, maximally risk-laden."[56]

Pushkin's insistence on Tatiana's autonomy, the personal choice of literary models that he allows her, and his emphasis on her inspired state as outlined above, argue for the significance of Tatiana's authorship. Accordingly, the subsequent discussion of her letter will follow the lead of Diana L. Burgin, whose insightful analysis accords Tatiana recognition as an author in her own right.[57] The focus is on Tatiana's incorporation of the material at her disposal into her own emotional field, whence it is translated into her text. Tatiana's capacity to convey personal, deeply experienced emotion by means of a given form aligns her with all creative writers. The meaningful structuring of her feelings, the judicious, original use of the language of her novels, and the urgency of the message it records argue strongly against Belinskii's assertion that in writing her letter "the poor girl did not know what she was doing."[58] On the strength of the emotional intensity of the present in which she writes, Tatiana reshapes her past and projects future possibility. With the composition of her letter, she also gives shape to those frustrated desires that have led her to write.

The various drafts to which Pushkin subjected especially the first part of Tatiana's letter show a steady movement away from the expression of powerful feelings to their containment and redirection. Interjections, exclamations, and direct confessions of love were dropped, and the text was relieved of the verbal and emotional excesses that were characteristic of the novels Tatiana read. This distinct muting of the vocabulary of amorous excitability is accompanied by another significant departure from epistolary convention. We have noted already that the author/narrator distances himself from the authorship of the letter by claiming it is a translation. In the particular context of the epistolary genre, however, where no author or narrator interferes with the illusion of unmediated self-expressions of the individual characters, this proffered "translation" must be perceived as intrusive. Thus the distinct alignment of Tatiana's literary debut with her epistolary novels is accompanied by an equally strong movement away from their generic conventions. Here is another instance of that intersection of invention and tradition that lies at the heart of creativity and that fosters the unfolding of literary process. Just as Tatiana draws the material of her novels into a context that gives it new meaning, so too does Pushkin recontextualize a literary tradition that takes on new function and new life in his work.

We do not see Tatiana's first meeting with Eugene, and we are barred also from observing her write to him. Once the stage for the composition of the letter has been set with Tatiana's failed attempt to communicate with her nurse, the completion of the letter follows immediately, with no time allowed for the process of its composition. Privileging the preparation and aftermath of the letter just as he also privileged the preparation and aftermath of Tatiana's meeting with the hero, the author/narrator denies immediate access to the event of its writing, leaving the reader with only a flood of moonlight in which to invest a Tatiana of his own imagination.

Whatever else she may have learned from her novels, Pushkin's heroine has clearly grasped the significance of writing itself, and as Burgin persuasively argues, her letter "has literary intentionality apart from the context of spontaneous confession to which it pretends to belong."[59] This point is well taken, for Pushkin, as we have seen, has carefully documented the stages of his heroine's progress toward inspired authorship and has distanced himself from the composition of the letter. In considering Tatiana's letter as a literary text in its own right, we gain the opportunity to examine the notions about the creative process and the definition of the muse Pushkin's heroine implicitly advances on his behalf.

The letter falls into three sections of unequal length. In the first thirty lines Tatiana takes stock of her situation and describes her setting. The central part of her letter (45 lines) opens into her private world that is so rarely glimpsed in the course of *Onegin*. Here her literary models lend that very language that excited Tatiana's emotions to the project of their direction. Even as she gives herself over to the inspiration that propels her letter, Tatiana assesses her own situation and considers the options open to her. Recorded here is her clear-sighted awareness of the cause and of the possible consequences of her letter. The four agitated lines with which she concludes mark Tatiana's return from a private, imaginative sphere to her actual surroundings. They evince an anxiety of authorship, and yet show no inclination on Tatiana's part to retreat from the consequences of having undertaken the risky business of writing. Thus the large middle section that is devoted to Tatiana's imaginative emotional world is framed by an opening and closing that are rooted in actuality.[60] The transitions between actual and imaginative are articulated both grammatically and stylistically. To the actual world of the opening and concluding sections belong the formal "you," a fairly straightforward, literal use of language, reference to social convention, and relatively simple syntax. The central section in which Tatiana charts her inner world is marked by the "thou" of her address, metaphoric language, and greater syntactic complexity. Addressed in the framing sections is an actual man; addressed in the central part is a source of inspiration. Read in this light, Tatiana's account of what has transpired in her life does in fact square with what the author/narrator has already described, and yet also moves beyond it into an interpretive field guided by the imagination.

There is no trace of coyness in Tatiana's writing, and the complete absence of coquetry in the Princess N is prefigured already in the forthright directness of this letter which opens with the announcement, "Ia k vam pishu—chego zhe bole?" (I am writing you—what more?). A proclamation that replaces the earlier variants "Liubliu—dovol'no—vse izvestno" and "Ia vas liubliu chego zhe bole" (I love—that's enough—all is known, I love you what more [*PSS* 6:314]), this statement reflects Tatiana's awareness of the import of writing and insists not on her emotions themselves, but on the fact that she is acting on them. The "I" with which she boldly opens and which she insistently reiterates no fewer than seventeen times in her letter bespeaks both the self-assertive emotional intensity she seeks to convey and the responsibility she is prepared to assume in so doing. For Tatiana the phrase "I write" is not merely a euphemism for "I love" dictated by maidenly modesty, but a powerful conflation of her desire with the act of writing Eugene—hence the "what more can I say?" that immediately follows. Tatiana knows what she is doing and does not pretend otherwise.

As she writes, Tatiana shapes an addressee whom she immediately engages in her self-creation, and yet whom she also acknowledges as an unknown quantity that introduces an element of risk—but also of possibility—into her enterprise. Tatiana realizes the potential for self-affirmation vested in the act of writing, but understands too that her letter invests Eugene with power over her ("Teper', ia znaiu, v vashei vole / Menia prezren'em nakazat'" [ll. 4–5]).[61] Within the compass of her own text (as in the compass of her imagination), Tatiana can shape her projected addressee at will; but although she can anticipate possible responses and urge desirable ones in the world in which this text will be received, she can neither determine nor control the way the recipient of her letter will read and respond to her bold initiative. At this stage Tatiana seeks not dialogue, but possibility.

Aware of the risk she incurs, Tatiana considers also what has prompted her to take this step. She explains to Eugene (and to herself) that it was his absence that made silence impossible. The "shame" of her self-revelation might have been avoided or concealed, she claims, if even so much as an occasional glimpse of him had been vouchsafed her. Tatiana resorts to this letter to create an alternative to the actual presence of the object of her desire. This is an essentially poetic project. Yet because she writes a letter and not a poem, her text has a literal function that coexists with its metaphoric one. In the absence of direct contact with Eugene, Tatiana creates a text within whose abstract space a metaphorical meeting with him is accomplished. At the same time, the concrete form of the letter opens the possibility for interaction with him in the actual world as well.

Although the addressee who emerges in Tatiana's letter is dependent largely on the sketchiness of her acquaintance with the flesh-and-blood Onegin, it is clear that at this juncture Tatiana is in need of Eugene as an autonomous creature, as an unpredictable other and not as pure invention on her part. The insistent opposition of "I" and "you" throughout the letter is indicative of Tatiana's attempt to distinguish Eugene from herself, which is to say, to disassociate him from the shades of her imaginary realm. This is precisely why she insists on her need to see *him* rather than the image in her mind's eye, to hear *his* speeches rather than those she could invent on his behalf, and to find in him an actual auditor for what she herself says (ll. 13–15).

At the same time, the imbalance in the relationship she invents here suggests that it is above all in his capacity as nurturer of her imagination rather than as potential suitor or husband that Eugene interests her. That Tatiana should thus order her priorities is scarcely surprising, for inasmuch as Pushkin has excised all vestiges of powerful feeling from her surrounding world, in her experience the erotic is aligned exclusively with the imaginative sphere. Tatiana seeks no dialogue with Eugene. Neither is she concerned with how he might regard her. It is she who would see him, hear (not "listen to") his "speeches" ("rechi"), and briefly address (not "respond to") him.

> Сначала я молчать хотела;
> Поверьте: моего стыда
> Вы не узнали б никогда,
> Когда б надежду я имела
> Хоть редко, хоть в неделю раз
> В деревне нашей видеть вас,
> Чтоб только слышать ваши речи,
> Вам слово молвить, и потом
> Все думать, думать об одном
> И день и ночь до новой встречи.

> [I first tried silence and evasion;
> Believe me, you'd have never learned
> My secret shame, had I discerned
> The slightest hope that on occasion—
> But once a week—I'd see your face,
> Behold you at our country place,
> Might hear you speak a friendly greeting,
> Could say a word to you; and then,
> Could dream both day and night again
> Of but one thing, till our next meeting.]
> (ll. 8–17)

Tatiana seeks occasional brief contacts that would suffice to fuel her thoughts, as she puts it, "ob odnom" (about one [person, thing, or act]). In this vague prepositional phrase we recognize a perfect rhyme with the "o tom" (about that [person, thing, or act]) on which Tatiana centered those rapturous involuntary ruminations that were called forth earlier by her meeting with Eugene (3:7, l. 4). It is telling that Pushkin replaced the more concrete "Vse razmyshliat' ob vas odnom" (To think of you alone) of an earlier draft (*PSS* 6:3115) with this less specific phrase, for in so doing he expanded his heroine's thoughts beyond the particular man who is to receive the letter. Looking ahead, we can observe here that the configuration of "o tom" and "ob odnom" is joined at the end of *Eugene Onegin* by the "drugomu" (to some one/thing else) of Tatiana's final speech to Eugene. Although Eugene is at the center of the "o tom" we considered earlier and the "ob odnom" of her letter, these designations expand beyond him to indicate an erotically charged creative space of the imagination. The "drugomu" (other) to which Tatiana avows constancy in her final speech to Eugene similarly refers, as I will argue, to more than her husband.

Eugene, however, does not appear as a regular visitor in the Larins' home, and Tatiana, astute reader of signs that she is, sees in the very absence that forces her to write him a possible point of intersection with her hero: "No govoriat, vy neliudim; / V glushi, v derevne vse vam skuchno" (They say that you are unsociable / You are bored in the wilds, in the country [ll. 18–19]). Whether from her own observations on the day of his visit or from gossipy neighbors, Tatiana has learned two of her hero's distinctive features—unsociability and boredom. Significantly, these are characteristics that Tatiana apparently shares with Eugene. Her alienation from family and friends is one of her defining characteristics, and this reference to Eugene's boredom echoes the boredom in terms of which she described her own emotional state to her nurse (3:18, l. 3). It is on the strength of these shared features, as she believes, that Eugene will be able to understand her as no one else in her setting does. Because she has not yet gained access to Eugene's revealing library, she cannot know that the causes and consequences of her addressee's unsociability and boredom differ dramatically from her own and that the designations "unsociable" and "bored" carry very different meanings in the disparate contexts of their respective worlds.

Yet Tatiana is also alive to the differences between the world in which she has grown up and the one Eugene has recently left to come to the country. However alienated she may feel from her own milieu, she recognizes that it is in its context that Eugene must perceive her. Accordingly, as the "we" she opposes here to the "you" of Eugene indicates, she identifies herself with the rural world that, as she acknowledges, cannot but seem lackluster beside the glitter of the capital from which Eugene hails: "A my . . . nichem my ne blestim, / Khot' vam i rady prostodushno" (We lack, I know, a worldly tone, / But still, we welcome you with feeling [ll. 20–21]). Having noted an apparent similarity in their characters, Tatiana now regards her setting from Eugene's point of view, demonstrating in this small detail the perceptual flexibility that makes her more "rounded" and distinguishes her from the other characters in *Eugene Onegin*, who are defined by the single perspective they have on life.

Inasmuch as it is precisely Eugene's otherness that attracts her with its promise of new possibility and the chance to deviate from the single plotline recognized in her milieu, the difference between Eugene and herself is important for Tatiana. Indeed, we can recognize here that Tatiana establishes from the outset that critical intersection of the familiar (his alienation and boredom) with the unfamiliar (his urban origin) upon which growth and productivity depend. Had Eugene not appeared on the scene, she explains, no new alternatives would have presented themselves to her. In lieu of the emotional and imaginative growth that she experiences as a consequence of having met him and that she is now loath to relinquish, she might have followed the conventional course of subduing her feelings to enter into amicable matrimony and benevolent motherhood:

> Зачем вы посетили нас?
> В глуши забытого селенья,
> Я никогда не знала б вас,
> Не знала б горького мученья.
> Души неопытной волненья
> Смирив со временем (как знать?),
> По сердцу я нашла бы друга,
> Была бы верная супруга
> И добродетельная мать.

> [Why did you ever come to call?
> In our remote and sleepy borough,
> Not having known of you at all,
> I would be spared this bitter sorrow.
> I might in time—who knows, tomorrow—
> Have stilled the soul's young urge and strife,
> Have let my heart seek out another;
> I would have been a loving mother,
> And a devoted, faithful wife.][62]

(ll. 22–30)

Here we see that Tatiana's assessment coincides in important particulars with the information provided earlier by the author/narrator. Her account reflects a clear awareness that the development of her erotic sensibilities ("Dushi neopytnoi volnen'ia" [l. 26]) antedated Eugene's appearance, and that his entry into her life did not trigger her emotions, but rather provided them with an object. Tatiana acknowledges too that with

Eugene's appearance those feelings grew too strong to be tamed and that they, as she now believes, demand an unconventional life's course. This intensity in an otherwise staid and uneventful setting means a great deal to Tatiana. The distinctly Rousseauesque tone and diction she adopts here ("Ne znala b gor'kogo muchen'ia, / Dushi neopytnoi volnen'ia," [I would not know this bitter suffering / The agitation of an inexperienced soul] [ll. 25–26]), does not conceal her sober awareness of the limited options open to her. Indeed, even as the resonance of *The New Eloise* at this point in her letter serves to communicate her feelings, it acts also as a reminder of the inescapability of the woman's traditional role. The meager alternatives Tatiana describes—either frustrated desire or staid, desexualized matrimony—are those already familiar to her from her own reading and from the stories of her mother and nurse. It was these very options, as we have seen, that found graphic representation in the *tableau vivant* that concluded Tatiana's failed attempt to communicate with her nurse. Tatiana does not relinquish the possibility of clinging to "the agitation of an inexperienced soul" (she appends a "who knows?" ["kak znat'"] here), but she does acknowledge that had she not met Eugene, she would most certainly have followed in her mother's footsteps (ll. 26–30).

Crucial here is Tatiana's alignment of the object of desire with the potential for generating new possibility. With heightened emotion she avows—and this is the first exclamation to appear in her letter—"Drugoi! . . . Net, nikomu na svete / Ne otdala by serdtsa ia!" (Another! No! In all creation / There's no one else whom I'd adore [ll. 31–32]). This vehement assertion is sooner a rejection of the common lot offered by her surroundings and a dedication to those feelings that point beyond it than an expression of love for Eugene himself. The significance that his otherness takes on for Tatiana catapults the emphatically punctuated "Drugoi! . . ." (other) into the privileged position of opening the longest, most impassioned, and most metaphorical section of her letter—the section in which she naively but earnestly explores the broad possibilities offered by the imagination as an alternative to the narrow scope of the actual.

Tatiana's satisfaction with only occasional glimpses of Eugene, her separation of herself from his partially actual, partially invented image, her need only to see and hear rather than interact with him that are described in the opening section all point to the fact (whether she is conscious of it or not) that as she writes Eugene, Tatiana is creating her own muse. Arriving at the main part of her letter, she demonstrates her command of the idiom that she has assimilated from her literary models and that now—in the section of the letter that appears most derivative stylistically—is used to affirm her dedication to the creative imagination. The heightened emotional tone of this section signals a shift from the actual world that provided the impetus for writing to an imaginative space in which Eugene is not a flesh-and-blood male, but a source of creative possibility. Driving Tatiana's subsequent discussion is not a preoccupation with whether Eugene will seduce or marry her, but rather the question of whether or not he will continue in his present role of invigorating her imagination.

As Tatiana insists on the inevitability of Eugene's appearance in her life, emphasizes the fatedness of her love, and concludes by surrendering to this powerful, unknown entity, the questions arise as to how she can grant so much to a man she knows so little, and why she would seek to evade one deterministic fate only to subordinate herself to another seemingly fixed one. Here Tatiana's replacement of the formal "you" with an intimate "thou" is particularly important. Common in French epistolary novels, such transitions conventionally signal heightened emotion and intimacy. Between 1824 and 1830, as Krystyna Pomorska notes, Pushkin himself wrote four works in which pronominal shifts play a central role.[63] In his lyric "Thou and You" ("Ty i vy" [1828]), where it is most pronounced, the shift from the formal to the intimate suggests strong feelings escaping grammatical control. In Tatiana's letter, however, this transition is the consequence of neither blind adherence to literary convention nor an inability to contain her feelings. It is rather a sign that branching off from the "you" of the actual man who began as her addressee is the "thou" who animates her imagination. Burgin has given particular attention to the identity of this "thou" and has provided discussion that is valuable to our understanding of both Tatiana's letter and the heroine herself. "Because it is a literary convention," she writes, "Larina's thou somehow desexes her and undercuts the intimacy of her message to Onegin *as himself*. It also reinforces the idea that the risk she is taking is the risk of *writing* and implies that the *thou*, unlike Onegin, *is* familiar to her."[64] Tatiana's "thou" emerges, in other words, as an addressee of her own making who, in contradistinction to his real-life prototype, is as "quintessentially poetic" as is Tatiana herself. In Burgin's incisive summary, "the *you* and the *thou* appear to be different addressees. . . . The *you* is the real Onegin, recalcitrant and bored lover. And who is the *thou*? As the reason for her writing and her dear, writer's fantasy, he appears to be her Muse. Tatiana writes her Muse into the text, the text he inspires. . . ."[65] Read as an address to the poetic muse to whom Tatiana responds, but whom she also shapes in the process of writing her letter, the central section moves beyond literary convention and social impropriety to map Tatiana's creative world. To recognize a male muse in the "thou" of Tatiana's letter is to understand its most impassioned section in a new light. Used to embody inspiration, rather than communicate with an earthly beloved, the familiar idiom of sentimental novels takes on expanded significance, and the stylistic marker "thou," which in her novels suggests physical intimacy, propels Tatiana's letter out of the physical world into the disembodied creative one. A borrowed medium becomes Tatiana's own as she dedicates herself to an imaginative realm over which a Eugene of her invention presides. In place of an account of what actually transpired that is distorted by the combined effects of heightened emotion and literary borrowings, we recognize an insightful metaphoric exposition of her own development into the creative being who authors this text.

In this context, her fated dedication to her addressee ("To volia neba: ia tvoia" [It is the will of heaven: I am yours] [l. 34]) emerges as Tatiana's description of that heightened receptivity that operates in conjunction with her desire. The "inevitability" of her meeting with Eugene, and the assertion that she loved him even before he appeared ("Nezrimyi, ty mne byl uzh mil" [Unseen you were already dear to me] [l. 40]), describe a longing whose very intensity ensures that it will find an object for itself. This account accords with the author/narrator's explanations, "Pora prishla, ona vliubilas'" (The time came and she fell in love [3:8, l. 6]), and "Davno serdechnoe tomlen'e / Tesnilo ei malduiu grud'; / Dusha zhdala . . . kogo-nibud'" (Long since had the heart's languishment / constrained her youthful bosom; / her soul waited—for somebody [3:7, ll. 12–14]). As Tatiana describes it, her meeting with Eugene endows with retroactive significance those tumultuous emotions for which an object was so fervently desired. Accordingly, her life emerges as a pledge of their fated meeting (ll. 35–36).

Tatiana's assessment of her heightened emotional state demonstrates a flexibility in temporal perception that is particularly remarkable in the context of the fixed vantage point from which all the other characters in *Eugene Onegin*—with the notable exception of the author/narrator—regard their surrounding world. In Tatiana's account of her relation to the man who modulates into her muse, time undergoes a dramatic expansion which then intersects with an equally dramatic temporal compression. Finding her emotions too overwhelming to be contained within the span of time in which she actually experienced them, Tatiana perceives them spilling over into the broad expanse of fate and destiny. At the same time, she condenses her "recognition" of Eugene into a single intense instant ("Ty chut' voshel, ia v mig uznala" [Scarce had you entered, instantly I knew you] [l. 44]) that retroactively lends significance to everything that has thus far transpired in her life and promises also to give meaning to her future.

Just as her outdated novels kindled her emotions and were in turn made fresh by them, so now too on the strength of Tatiana's powerful feelings a jaded rake is transformed into a muse—a source of inspiration and creativity. What is more, that jaded rake-cum-muse is himself destined, as we will see, to be revivified by this transformation. Once again, as in the case of her novel-inspired fantasies about Eugene, the question of whether the addressee of Tatiana's letter coincides with the actual man is beside the point. Crucial is the fact that, as Nabokov observes in passing, "the two images, fiction and reality, fuse,"[66] for it is precisely out of such fusions that poetic muses are born. Tatiana considers her presentiments of Eugene's appearance—the visions of him, his glance, his voice (ll. 39–41)—and determines that these arose not in a dream ("net, eto byl ne son!" [l. 43]), but in that creative state between dreaming and waking, between the "son" (dream) and the "on" (he) with which it is rhymed. Tatiana's discovery of her muse follows her recognition of Eugene, and it is significant that both the discovery and the recognition transpire not during their undescribed meeting, but in a letter which emerges from a creative, nocturnal interstice between dream and actuality.[67] In place of the account of Tatiana's first meeting with Eugene viewed from the outside that the author/narrator would have provided, the reader receives Tatiana's description of the event viewed from within. Indeed, it is her abstract meeting with Eugene within the text that she herself creates and not their actual encounter that is privileged in Pushkin's text.

We have seen already that the interrelation of the actual with the imagined is represented in *Eugene Onegin* as a vital source of creativity that operates in conjunction with the interrelation of the familiar and the new. As we read Tatiana's lines

И в это самое мгновенье
Не ты ли! милое виденье,
В прозрачной темноте мелькнул.

[And at this very moment
was it not you, dear vision,
that slipped through the transparent darkness.][68]
(ll. 52–54)

we are reminded that just such intersections inform Pushkin's own muse-making, for a year later these very lines resonate delicately but distinctly in his "K***"—Ia pomniu chudnoe mgnoven'e ("To ***"—I Remember the Wonderous Moment [July 1825]),[69] a lyric that describes the appearance and effects of the muse Pushkin discerns in Anna Petrovna Kern.[70]

As Tatiana's muse takes shape in this portion of her letter, expressions of desire are counterbalanced by beatific imagery that hints at what is perhaps sublimation through the process of writing. Eugene is dear to her (l. 40) and whispers words of promise (l. 57), she languishes under his gaze (l. 41), is first stupefied and then aflame upon recognizing him (l. 45). The erotic implications of these images are absorbed into beneficence and selflessness, while her surrender to him is described as willed by heaven (l. 34) and motivated by a need for protection—from what, Tatiana does not specify (ll. 38 and 67). Her addressee is purportedly sent by God (l. 37) as a guardian angel of sorts (l. 38), and it is his voice she hears when she ministers to the poor (l. 49), or resorts to prayer to quell the tumultuous longing in her soul (ll. 50–51).

Here we may consider what Tatiana seeks protection from when she presents herself as a supplicant to Eugene:

> Но так и быть! Судьбу мою
> Отныне я тебе вручаю,
> Перед тобою слезы лью,
> Твоей защиты умоляю . . . .
>
> [But so be it! My fate
> henceforth I place into your hands,
> before you I shed tears,
> for your defense I plead.][71]
>
> (ll. 64–7)

Sipovskii notes a literary precedent for Tatiana's professed need for Eugene's guardianship and takes it for a sign that she is not speaking for herself, but simply assuming the role of Rousseau's Julie who similarly, but seemingly with better cause, called on Saint-Preux's honor, urging him to defend her from his own passions.[72] Remarking that "Tat'jana is not in need of defense from Onegin's passions," Kelley similarly considers Tatiana's pleas for protection as a motif causelessly imported from her sentimental novels into her letter.[73] Yet even though her vocabulary coincides with Julie's, Tatiana is indeed speaking for herself here. Although she does not in fact need to be protected from Eugene's advances, she has good cause to seek protection from her own passions which have, after all, prompted her to write a letter to a man she scarcely knows. It is worth recalling here that however threatening the attacks from male suitors, it was the fear of being overcome by her own desire that loomed large in the minds of many a sentimental heroine, and this fear surfaces now also in Tatiana.

We have already considered Clarissa's struggles to contain the arousal that threatened to erupt in response to Lovelace's advances. (Here we may add parenthetically that the drugs that assisted Lovelace dulled Clarissa's senses and thus protected her from infection by passion.) Another striking example culled from Tatiana's reading list is Charlotte, heroine of Goethe's *Die Leiden des jungen Werthers* (*Sorrows of Young Werther*), who is prepared to let Werther commit suicide out of fear not of his emotions, but of the reciprocal passion he arouses in her. After she is overcome by desire for Werther, Charlotte (who long befriended him in full knowledge that he was passionately in love with her) makes no attempt to dissuade her husband from letting Werther borrow the gun with which he shoots himself—this although she realizes that he is overwrought and in no condition to be trusted with firearms. To elaborate on this example, we can observe that Emilia Galotti, heroine of Lessing's eponymous tragedy which is found on Werther's desk after his suicide, chooses to stab herself not out of fear of possible rape by her abductor, but specifically out of fear that she might involuntarily respond to his advances. Stepping briefly outside of Tatiana's own reading list to include a text to which the author/narrator refers, we can add that it is her own uncontrollable desire that undoes Bürger's Lenore, and not the advances of a male. Given these literary precedents, Tatiana has good cause to fear the emotions to which she is now responding, for desire, as we have already discussed in connection with Tatiana's favorite novels and will briefly touch on in speaking of Russian folk rituals, is time and time again represented as leading women to death. Far from a casual parroting of her heroines' words, Tatiana's solicitation of Eugene's protection signals acknowledgment of her own desire, an awareness of the risk it leads her to take, and her wish to ensure that her own powerful feelings, be protracted and yet not allowed to destroy her. Here the vulnerability she readily assumes in writing her letter is significantly intensified and foregrounded.

Tatiana's attempts to align the feelings Eugene inspires in her with virtue and good deeds are perhaps signs of maidenly modesty on her part, but they are also signs of apprehension. Tatiana's novels make it clear that not the least among the dangers entailed in surrendering to powerful emotion is that desire, which lies beyond the sway of moral considerations, can be stimulated by good or evil. Tatiana's question as to whether her addressee is her guardian angel or her treacherous tempter (ll. 58–59) is not simply an attempt to determine whether Eugene will turn out to be a Grandison (heroic guardian of female virtue) or a Lovelace (its unconscionable destroyer).[74] It is a sign of her understanding that attraction does not distinguish between these polar opposites. For all their patent dissimilarities, the wicked Lovelace and the noble Grandison are identical in their irresistible appeal, for the epitome of vice is every bit as attractive to women as the epitome of virtue.[75] Tatiana recognizes that although here in her letter Eugene can remain in the aura of her own virtue, it is not at all certain that this will remain the case in that unknown into which she allows his image to guide her. There is also the concern that the emotions Eugene has aroused in her can be just as readily channeled into destructive behavior as into the beneficence she describes in her letter or the creativity she demonstrates in composing it. Thus, for example, to draw once again on Richardson, we can observe that both the heinous deeds perpetrated by Lovelace and the countless acts of good stored up to Grandison's credit are fueled by one and the same force—the sexual energy that underlies their exceptional dynamism and attractiveness. Tatiana's risk is thus twofold, for as she surrenders to her powerful feelings by writing to Eugene, she knows neither what sort of man has aroused her passions, nor whether her emotional response will lead to creativity or destructivity. She calls on Onegin to resolve her doubts ("Moi somnen'ia razreshi" [l. 60]).

Because desire and creative potential are projected as being correlative in Tatiana's development and particularly in her letter, we can recognize the implication that surrender to the creative urge is a business no less risky than surrender to the promptings of love. Not only the consequences of the creative act, but also its inspiration is uncertain and mysterious—alternately described by artists as a God-sent gift or a daemonic curse. Like the person who loves, the person who writes an unsolicited letter to an unknown love object, or, for that matter, a poem, must be prepared to assume both the risk and the responsibility of surrendering to inspiration. This Tatiana is prepared to do. The question that concerns her now is neither whether Onegin is a Lovelace or a Grandison, nor whether her own emotions will lead her to a good end or a bad one, but the more burning issue that both eager lover and inspired poet must confront: Is the love/inspiration to which she surrenders in fact genuine? Acknowledging her lack of experience, Tatiana admits her uncertainty in this regard: "Byt' mozhet eto vse pustoe, / Obman neopytnoi dushi!" (Perhaps, 'tis nonsense all, / An inexperienced soul's delusion! [ll. 61–62]). Yet Tatiana does not share the fear the author/narrator expressed earlier that she will "perish" at Eugene's hands ("*Pogibnesh'*, milaia" [You will *perish*, my dear] [3:15, l. 5, my emphasis]). Her concern is that she not "perish" in the silence of stifled sexuality and creativity:

> Вообрази: я здесь одна,
> Никто меня не понимает,
> Рассудок мой изнемогает,
> И молча *гибнуть* я должна.

> [Imagine: I am here alone,
> none understands me,
> my reason is breaking down,
> and, silent, I must *perish*.][76]
> (ll. 68–71)

Burgin sees the difference between the "you" and the "thou" clearly
defined here: "Without the *you* Tatiana Dmitrievna believes she will eventually find another man and become a faithful wife and mother. Without
the *thou*, who supersedes Onegin or another in her heart, the novice
writer fears a worse fate: alone and misunderstood, she will 'perish in silence,' unable to tell her story."[77]

In full awareness of the risk she is taking, Tatiana makes no attempt
to mitigate her vulnerability and places herself in the power of the man
whom she has made both the object of her desire and her muse. However
uncertain, this alternative is surely preferable to the stifled feelings and silence to which she is otherwise doomed. She is prepared to brave the consequences of her love and her letter as, having responded to Onegin the
muse, she now puts herself at the mercy of Onegin the man and the
reader. Whether or not Eugene is willing or able to respond to her complex needs remains to be seen. As Tatiana construes it, her addressee will
either enliven her hopes or put an end to her fantasies:

> Я жду тебя: единым взором
> Надежды сердца оживи,
> Иль сон тяжелый перерви,
> Увы, заслуженным укором!
>
> [I'm waiting for you: with a single look
> revive my heart's hopes,
> or interrupt the heavy dream,
> alas, with a deserved rebuke!][78]
>
> (ll. 72–75)

Of primary concern to her here is whether Eugene will continue in the
role of muse to fuel the creative energy that derives from desire. The two
possible responses she suggests to her addressee engage two very different
vehicles to convey one and the same tenor. Although at first glance
"heart's hopes" on the one hand and "heavy dream" on the other seem
little more than a conventional description of love as a source of both ecstasy and torment, the meaning is, in fact, more complex. The four lines
that convey her options are so ordered that the antithetical vehicles occur
side by side, framed by Eugene's postulated responses. This achieves a
powerful condensation: in the absence of Eugene's encouraging glance
Tatiana's emotions are transformed immediately from "heart's hopes"
into a "heavy dream." Accordingly, his reproaches would not cause the
unpleasant dream, but instead free the dreamer from its effects. Formu-
lated here is not the simple question of whether Eugene will encourage or
reject her, but the more urgent one of whether he will continue to animate
her imagination with the longing his silent presence would inspire, or

whether he will effect her "awakening" and return both Tatiana and the image of him she has created to the narrow space of the actual world where her gesture warrants reproof. Of paramount concern for Tatiana, then, is not whether Eugene's response will be honorable or dishonorable, but something more serious: whether Eugene will turn out to be a man or a muse. The risk Tatiana assumes is indeed high, for in entrusting her fate to her addressee she stakes not simply her maidenhood but her entire imaginative domain, leaving it in Eugene's power to decide her fate not only as a woman but as a creative being. Influenced perhaps by the folk custom of augury, Tatiana is prepared to read her entire destiny in the single sign she expects from Onegin.[79] Should he offer encouragement, she can persist in her allegiance to that inner realm that nurtures her emotions and offsets the insufficiencies of her surrounding world. In the event of his reproof, she pledges to surrender those feelings that fuel her creativity, presumably to pursue the life course like her mother's that she described in the beginning of her letter (ll. 26–30). In the event of the awakening that would follow on his reproach, Eugene's powerful effects on her will be undone, and it will be as if she had never met him. Thus Eugene must either live up to the image of the addressee Tatiana has shaped in her letter, or close down her imaginative world and thus also exclude himself from it.

Worth noting here is not only the extravagant significance Tatiana is prepared to accord Eugene's response, but also the signs she suggests as carriers of such import. Having just expressed her own dismay at having to perish in silence ("I molcha gibnut' ia dolzhna"), she construes her addressee's ideal response as a speechless one. Tatiana seeks only a gaze ("vzor") from Eugene. As we have noted already in discussing the opening section of the letter, she wants no dialogue with Eugene but only the possibility his presence inspires, and this explains why she does not appear to entertain in the text of her letter the obvious possibility that it could initiate a correspondence between them.[80] She asks only that Eugene's silent image fuel her "hopes," that is, those unfulfilled desires that give rise to creative activity. In this regard Tatiana's letter can be seen as a test of Eugene's suitability for her project. Although from the perspective of the surrounding world Tatiana's letter places her in Eugene's power, from the vantage point of her imaginative realm, it serves as a trial that will determine whether he is a man or a muse. In this sense, Eugene is being tested as a reader, for whether or not he will continue in the role she projects for him is largely dependent on how he reads Tatiana's message. If he reads her letter as an admission of physical desire, he will respond with the reproach she justly deserves in the mundane context or, alternately, with an attempt to seduce her. If, however, he understands the letter to be a sign of her intense need for something beyond what her immediate surroundings have to offer, and recognizes it as a creative impulse, then he will prove to be a muse.

This "trial by letter" is a severe one, and the unsuspecting Eugene, who little resembles its addressee, can scarcely be expected to fulfill Tatiana's exorbitant expectations. He responds neither with the encouraging look she hoped for nor with the "ukor" (reproach) she feared, but with its perfect anagram "urok" (lesson). Eugene's answer to Tatiana's letter will be considered in the following chapter. Here we will digress briefly to expand the context in which to compare heroine and hero in preparation for our later discussion of the first actual meeting between them that the reader witnesses.

In the course of *Eugene Onegin* the art of reading, the art of writing, and the capacity to experience intense emotion are closely interrelated. Tatiana's success and Eugene's failure in these spheres of human activity (we are speaking here only of his development thus far in the text) are correlative, and the source of Onegin's weakness in all three areas is immediately apparent in the context of Tatiana's strength in them. Tatiana's emotions, her reading, and her writing, as we have seen, are closely interrelated within her synchronous, creative inner world. For Eugene, these vital manifestations of human emotional and creative potential remain, according to the account provided by the author/narrator, merely disconnected, frivolous pastimes, undertaken out of boredom rather than personal need. Missing from Eugene's constitution is Tatiana's capacity to absorb and that ability to empathize that draws the inner and the outer worlds, the self and the other, the past, present, and future into productive interanimation. External stimuli glance off his polished social carapace, and the masks and personae he dons form an impenetrable boundary between his outer and inner selves. His undeveloped private world can neither inform nor be informed by his surroundings, and he is left with an impoverished repertoire of responses to life. It is precisely because Eugene remains disengaged from self and others that eros is trivialized and the women he flirts with and seduces one after the other stand no chance of stimulating either deep, lasting feelings or creative activity. He remains uninspired, and finds no particular reason to invest requisite energy in the writing that he casually undertakes when he has tired of amorous pursuits:

> Хотел писать—но труд упорный
> Ему был тошен; ничего
> Не вышло из пера его . . . .

[And tried to write. But art's exaction
Of steady labor made him ill,
And nothing issued from his quill.]
(1:43, ll. 9–11)

Failing to produce anything of his own, he turns next to the writings of others, but fares no better in this attempt :

Уселся он—с похвальной целью
Себе присвоить ум чужой,
Он рядом книг уставил полку,
Читал, читал—а всё без толку.

[A laudable temptation pricked him
To make what others thought his own.
In scores of books, arrayed on shelving,
He read and read—in vain all delving.][81]
(1:44, ll. 3–6)

In using the same verb—*prisvoit'* (to make one's own)—in his description of both Eugene's and Tatiana's reading, Pushkin underscores how very differently his hero and heroine relate to their books. Tatiana's emotions are heightened and her imagination is stimulated by the outmoded books she draws into the new context of her own world, while Eugene can only yawn as his eyes glide over the pages of the most recent writings. Eugene takes up reading with the pragmatic intent of appropriating the ideas of others ("Sebe prisvoit' um chuzhoi" [To make what others thought his own] [1:44, l. 4])—only to fail in the attempt. Tatiana, who reads avidly and with no premeditated purpose simply because her books speak to her, succeeds in assimilating the broad emotional spectrum of their characters: "i sebe prisvoia / Chuzhoi vostorg, chuzhuiu grust'" (and having made her own someone else's delight, someone else's sorrow [3:10, ll. 9–10]). Eugene's reading is a cerebral activity; Tatiana reads with the heart. That necessary intersection of "the familiar" and the "alien" ("svoi"— "chuzhoi") that Tatiana accomplishes remains unrealized by Eugene, who is left none the better for his books.

Eugene's disadvantage derives not only from his failures in the areas of love, writing, and reading, but also from the sequence in which he undertakes these activities. Thus, according to the author/narrator, he abandons his recreation with members of the opposite sex in order to take a stab at writing, which he then abandons to try reading. Tatiana, on the other hand, progresses from reading to love and writing, moving between the world of the imagination and the actual one. More important, these activities do not merely succeed one another, but are instead interrelated. Onegin assumes one superficial attitude after another and displays great agility in hypocrisy, dissimulation, and appearances—all with the purpose of producing an effect on others, but remaining unaffected himself (1:10). Opposed to this public role-playing are Tatiana's introspective tranquillity, her lack of interest in outward appearances, undemonstrative day-to-day behavior, and receptivity. If Eugene is to be transformed into the being Tatiana addresses in her letter, his inner world must be opened so that a reintegration of what he has isolated from the wholeness of life can be accomplished. Although it becomes an important step in that direction, Tatiana's letter cannot by itself effect this desired transformation.

Even this brief juxtaposition of hero and heroine reflects the premises of imagination and creativity that Pushkin projects in Tatiana's story and in the composition of her letter in particular. These are to be found not in the novelty Eugene pursues, but rather in the interrelationships of existing things, for it is only in the act of interconnecting that meaning can be found. There may be nothing absolutely new under the sun, but the possibilities of combining and recombining what that sun shines on are virtually inexhaustible, and it is in the process of ceaseless recombinations that life and art transpire. Pushkin devoted an important passage to precisely this notion in his 1836 review "Ob obiazannostiakh cheloveka. Sochinenie Sil'vio Pelliko" ("On the Responsibilities of Man. A Work by Silvio Pellico") where he wrote:

> *Это уж не ново, это было уж сказано*—вот одно из самых обыкновенных обвинений критики. Но всё уже было сказано, все понятия выражены и повторены в течение столетий: что ж из этого следует? Что дух человеческий уже ничего нового не производит? Нет, не станем на него клеветать: разум неистощим в *соображении* понятий, как язык неистощим в *соединении* слов. Все слова находятся в лексиконе; но книги, поминутно появляющиеся, не суть повторение лексикона. *Мысль* отдельно никогда ничего нового не представляет; *мысли же* могут быть разнообразны до бесконечности. (*PSS* 12:100)

> [*This is not new, this has been said before*—this is one of the most common accusations leveled by critics. But everything has already been said, all concepts expressed and repeated in the course of centuries: so what follows from this? That the human spirit no longer produces anything new? No, let us not slander it: the intellect is inexhaustible in its grasp, just as language is inexhaustible in its combination of words. All words are in the dictionary; but the books that are constantly appearing are not repetitions of the dictionary. A *thought* in isolation will never represent anything new; *thoughts* however can be varied endlessly.]

Thus, to return to Tatiana's letter, her engagement of the idiom of an eighteenth-century French epistolary novel in an address to a muse that she has shaped from an actual man she barely knows, but to whom she attaches her love, gives rise to a text that demonstrates its author's poetic capacity to negotiate between the imagined and the actual, the abstract and the concrete, the metaphoric and the literal, and the self and the other.

Here we can pause briefly to extrapolate from Tatiana's letter the function that a muse fulfills, for later we will see Tatiana herself emerge in this role vis-à-vis first the author/narrator and then Eugene. Whatever the psychological, emotional, and metaphorical functions she or he may carry, in the context we are considering here the muse embodies those intersections of the imagined and the actual and of the familiar and the new that invigorate life and art. Genuine creativity cannot remain exclusively in the space of the imagination any more than it can flourish if confined exclusively to the actual world. For a creative act to transpire, the imagined must be drawn into the space of uncertainty and possibility offered by an actual world that has itself been enlarged by the entry of the imaginative. The muse is an emblem of this realm of possibility.

Tatiana, who remains at all times open to change, projects an entire complex of functions onto her addressee, even as she herself assumes a variety of roles that include submissive sentimental heroine, assertive initiator of illicit correspondence, charitable worker of good deeds, seducer and seduced. At the same time she is also an author who, although uncertain as to the sources and consequences of the act of writing, is prepared both to risk writing and to assume responsibility for it. In her conclusion, she considers the letter she has just written from Eugene's perspective. Thus, as Burgin describes, "At the end of the 'Letter' Tatiana Dmitrievna turns her attention from her addressee to herself and becomes a would-be reader of her own text."[82]

As she considers the dependency of her text on her addressee, Tatiana succumbs briefly to anxiety of authorship ("Konchaiu, strashno perechest'" [I close! I dread to read this over] [l. 76]). This anxiety is twofold, connected first with the possible consequences of her surrender to the inspiration that moved her to write and second with the surrender of her text to its reader. Who can tell what thoughts and actions her own letter might inspire once it is enveloped in the alien context her addressee will supply. Yet for all the shame and fear she feels ("Stydom i strakhom zamiraiu" [I'm faint with shame and fear] [l. 77]), Tatiana does not back away from what she has written, and her closing rings with a determination that verges on defiance: "No mne porukoi vasha chest' / I smelo ei sebia vveriaiu" (But to me your honor is a pledge, / and boldly I entrust myself to it [ll. 78–79]).

It is easy to describe Tatiana as flitting in and out of fantasy as she reads her novels, peoples her solitary walks with their heroes, assumes the roles of their heroines, and then writes a letter steeped in sentimental sensibilities to an addressee of her own design. Thus, for example, Nabokov observes, "The letter is finished; it has been written automatically, in a trance, and now as reality asserts itself again she becomes aware that it is addressed by the real Tatiana to the real Eugene."[83] There is a tendency among some commentators to speak with disapproval of Tatiana's sallies into the imaginative realm and to construe her imagination as an impediment to her understanding of life. Thus, for example, Kelley writes of Tatiana that "her struggle will be to live in the real world, not in the world of her imagination."[84] Yet the suggestion that the imaginative and the actual be kept separate denies the energy Tatiana derives from their interaction and is, moreover, contrary to the intent of both *Eugene Onegin* and Pushkin's own thinking about his art.

Tatiana, as her letter demonstrates, depends on the concrete particulars of her surrounding world to fuel her imagination and consequently regards her surroundings from a perspective that has been significantly broadened by her excursions into fantasy. The imagination provides her with a way to court the unknown, and the alternative ways of construing existence it opens create the possibility to reshape destiny. Imagination offers not merely escape, but a welcome expansion of the narrow compass of her milieu and its conventional responses to life. Thus, for example, while her family and friends see in Eugene only an eligible male, Tatiana herself finds in him a source of emotional and creative energy. As the flesh-and-blood neighbor modulates first into the object of her desire and then into her muse, what he may or may not be in the actual world pales before the effect he has on the subsequent course of her life. For however fanciful we find Tatiana's meditations on what Eugene's appearance in her world means to her, the fact remains that her love for him and the expectation of an unusual life's course prompt her refusals of the eligible young males in her own surroundings and set off the series of events that lead her to the upper reaches of St. Petersburg society as the Princess N. Meticulous as Eugene may be in calculating the effect he has on others and as painstakingly as he crafts his personae, Tatiana's reading of him advances him well beyond the limits of his own intentions. It takes perceptual faculties made flexible by the exercise of the imagination to recognize the insufficiency of any one perspective to illuminate the richness of existence. The multiple roles Tatiana assigns Onegin signal not confusion of fact and fancy, but rather Tatiana's responsiveness to the complexities of life. The questions that she must now confront (and which will be answered in chapter 8 of *Onegin*) are not whether she can learn to distinguish fact from fiction, but whether she can translate the principles that govern creativity into the conduct of her own life, and—

more difficult still—whether on the strength of so doing she can bring the actual Eugene into closer alignment with the addressee of her letter.

As we move out of the text of Tatiana's letter we suddenly realize that our perusal of what was introduced as its "weak translation" has returned us to the time of the composition of the original, for even though the author/narrator has been carrying the letter around with him lo these many years, and even though in his narration he proclaimed the letter written and folded up a full ten stanzas before providing his rendition of the text, we now find ourselves at the very moment of its completion. Its translator, the ubiquitous author/narrator who delights in intruding on the narrative, has completely faded away and we are now alone with the Tatiana who has just finished writing her letter to Eugene. Original and translation meld into one creative impulse to recall from the author/narrator's past into our present the inspiration that both fueled Tatiana's letter and was captured in it. Demonstrated here is that, like any genuine poetic text, Tatiana's letter has the capacity to prolong indefinitely the moment of its own coming-into-being. Not only the actual text that the admiring author/narrator carries around in his pocket, but that ephemeral moment of inspiration that dictated its writing remains potentially ever-present, retrievable through the act of translation whether into other idioms or into the various worlds of other readers.

As the moon that inspired and illuminated the composition of Tatiana's letter gives way to a new day, it emerges that she has been up all night. Allowing even for a late start and the brevity of northern summer nights, it would appear that, although there is no mention of anything so prosaic as drafts, Tatiana's spontaneous letter has taken some time to complete. Considerable time has also apparently been devoted to her contemplation of the consequences of writing the letter, but the Tatiana we see before us, as Pushkin's artful framing of her letter underscores, remains outside of passing time in a protensive creative present into which the reader too is drawn. Here in the privacy of her room Tatiana gives herself over to signs of heightened emotion that she never allows herself to reveal in public. Her trembling hand, parched tongue, bowed head, exposed shoulder recall conventional depictions of young women in the aftermath of nocturnal trysts in a graphic reaffirmation of that coincidence of love and the act of writing with which Tatiana's letter opened. Insensible to the many familiar signs of dawning day, a time when she is customarily most alive to her surroundings, Tatiana remains immersed in the creative nocturnal space that she entered on the strength of her inspiration and made her own with the writing of her letter.

Bringing in the morning tea, Tatiana's unsuspecting nurse finds no trace of that affliction that moved her to prayer on behalf of her ward the night before. She regards Tatiana's glowing cheeks as a sign that she has found relief from her malady, as indeed she has. Yet though Tatiana has channeled her frustrated emotions into writing, her letter must still find its addressee, for without its receipt by a reader her text remains unfulfilled. After an awkward exchange with the faithful nurse who has been rendered uncomprehending by the thoroughness of her own desexualization, the letter is dispatched at last.

The intense longing that prompted its composition now escalates into intense anticipation that subsumes everything that transpires around her, as the unfortunate Tatiana is forced to endure a consequence she has not foreseen. Eugene grants her neither the gaze nor the reproof she suggested as possible replies, but quite simply nothing at all. Tatiana's urgency is absorbed into his indifference, her anxious waiting into his leisure. In the absence of a response from Eugene, for Tatiana there is nothing, and two days pass in the space of a mere two lines of text that stress this nothingness: "No den' protek, i net otveta, / Drugoi nastal: vse net kak net" (But the day passed, and no answer, / Another dawned: still nothing, nothing [3:36, ll. 1–2]). These nothing-bringing days are filled with waiting and foster an unprecedented self-consciousness in Tatiana. The mere mention of her addressee's name throws her into a highly uncharacteristic fit of blushes and tremblings, while Lensky's innocent remark about the mail that has detained his friend rings in her ears like an "angry reproof" ("zloi ukor") reminiscent of the one she anticipates from Onegin. With the writing and dispatch of her letter Tatiana has fallen from the innocent state of unselfconsciousness. This is as it should be, for this stage of her development demands interaction with the surrounding world, and thus also the awareness of herself in it. It was precisely this demand, as we have noted, that attracted her to Eugene in the first place and that determined that the letter be not only written, but also sent to him. Crucial for Tatiana's development is the fact that her own inner world is highly developed before she enters into this self-conscious interaction with her surroundings, for, as we have observed, Eugene's preoccupation with what the surrounding world makes of him antedates and thus impedes his development of an inner being.

Tatiana's anticipation grows, and when Eugene appears at last, her first impulse is to flee. The rapid enumeration of familiar landmarks that stream past her field of vision conveys the swiftness with which she absents herself from the long-awaited meeting with him. The courtyard, garden, bridges, meadow, avenue, lake, copse, flower beds, and stream are quickly passed. Spatial expansion, operating in concert with temporal condensation, lends Tatiana's precipitous flight a dreamlike quality that conveys her agitated emotions at the prospect of confronting the recipient of her letter. (Indeed, the emotionally charged atmosphere and scenery we encounter here are soon to resurface in her dream.) Tatiana's headlong flight is not brought up by the end of the stanza that describes it (38), and she finds herself on the other side of a stanzaic boundary before her collapse on a bench terminates her swift progress ("I zadykha-ias', na skam'iu / Upala . . ."). This particularly strong articulation of the verb "fell" conveys the weight of her drop to the bench and the stillness that ensues, and intimates also, perhaps, a fall from Edenic innocence. A long pause is demanded at this point by the ellipsis that follows the verb "fell," by the fact that the continuation of this line is dropped one line lower, and by the fact that "fell" ("upala") both completes a sentence begun in the preceding stanza, and rhymes with its lines 9 and 12 ("obezhala"-"perelomala"-"upala"). With this emphatically articulated cessation of flight, the focus shifts from Tatiana's surroundings to her tormented heart that "Harbors a vague dream of hope" ("Khranit nadezhdy temnyi son" [3:39, l. 4]), a description that conflates the positive and the negative responses she suggested in her letter: "Nadezhdy serdtsa ozhivi" (Revive my heart's hopes [l. 73]) and "Il' son tiazhelyi perervi" (Or interrupt the heavy dream [l. 74]).

What it is that Tatiana hopes for as she sits breathless on her bench is by no means clear, just as the motivations for her flight remain distinctly ambiguous. The embarrassed Tatiana may well have thought to evade an encounter with Eugene, but it is possible too that she flees not her addressee, but the public space of the drawing room in order to secure privacy for their meeting. Even as she exhibits dread at encountering Eugene, Tatiana shows also distinct signs of arousal as she listens intently for his approach: "Ona drozhit i zharom pyshet, / I zhdet: neidet li?" (She trembles and glows hotly, / and waits: does he not come? [3:39, ll. 5–6]).[85] It is clear that she needs time to collect herself and possible too that she seeks to prolong that intense anticipation and uncertainty that will be brought to an end once the meeting is accomplished. Yet whatever her concerns, the meeting cannot be postponed indefinitely.

The time of her waiting is filled with the local berry pickers' obligatory singing that is intended to prevent their fulfillment of desire for the ripe fruit they must gather but not eat. Balancing the European novels that inform Tatiana's letter is the "folk song" that provides the immediate context for Eugene's impending response to it. Like Tatiana's and Eugene's letters, this song is marked as an interpolation into the text, but deviates metrically from the letters, constituting, as Nabokov observes, "the only noniambic set of verses in *Eugene Onegin*."[86] Although it was composed by Pushkin himself, its trochaic trimeter, diction, and imagery lend the song a convincing folk quality.[87] The text Tatiana hears replaces one of an earlier draft that told of a woman forsaken by her beloved for the comely women in a distant land. In it the woman who is denied the freedom of movement granted her beloved can only wait passively in the hope that he might return to her. Yet rather than invoke the passivity of a woman's role and the theme of abandonment at this point in Tatiana's story, Pushkin opts for a song in which women assume an active role. Although the demand that they sing is an imposed constraint intended to prevent them from eating the fruit they pick, the song itself describes unconstrained behavior. In it the berry pickers mischievously recount how they will use their song to lure an unsuspecting lad into their territory, only to flee at his approach and pelt him with their luscious, freshly gathered, forbidden fruit in punishment for his audacious entry into the forbidden precinct of their maidenly pastimes. The alternating attraction and repulsion of the male by these young women accords with Tatiana's own ambivalent feelings about her impending meeting with the man who has been reached by the "song" of her letter, and whose approach she has just fled. Yet stronger than this superficial parallel to Tatiana's present predicament is the telling contrast the song provides to what has already transpired. The girls' taunting of the lad, their flight from him, and the "punishment" they inflict describe an erotically charged game and not a serious commitment. Their playfulness is both charming and seductive, but it bespeaks both the insincerity of the words used to attract their "victim" and a refusal to accept responsibility for the effect of these words. This song thus provides a folk version of the flirtations with which St. Petersburg coquettes lure men into their nets (cf., e.g., "Vernee v seti zavedet" [3:25, l. 7]) that the author/narrator described by way of defending Tatiana's decision to write Eugene.[88] The insincere enticements held out by urban ladies and peasant girls frame the text of Tatiana's letter, highlighting the heartfelt sincerity of her address to Eugene.

Tatiana's inattentiveness to the song signals her preoccupation with Eugene, but also its irrelevance to her situation. Concentrating now on containing the visible signs of her emotions, she succeeds only in intensifying them further. If in the song the berry pickers disperse gaily at the approach of their male victim, Tatiana remains immobile, described by the author/narrator with images of helpless victimization. She is the fluttering moth held captive by a mischievous schoolboy (3:40, ll. 9–11) and the small, trembling hare at which a hunter's rifle is aimed (3:40, ll. 12–14). Although this imagery harks back to the author/narrator's earlier mock despair that his heroine has placed herself in the hands of a "modish tyrant" ("modnyi tiran" [3:15, l. 3]) and must now perish ("Pogibnesh', milaia" [3:15, l. 5]), it is more significant as a comment on Tatiana's present condition vis-à-vis Eugene than as an indication of her future. Not only are hero and heroine far from evenly matched, but what is for Tatiana a situation of considerable import is for Eugene—as for the Petersburg coquettes and the rural berry pickers—merely sport.

Just as Tatiana collects herself and rises from the bench, Eugene looms ominously before her. His eyes flash, either because Tatiana in her agitation thus imagines them, or because he is trying to create an effect, but not because he is overcome with emotion. Tatiana is met not with the singular "vzor" (gaze) she had envisioned in her letter, but with a plurality of "vzory" (gazes) that undo her efforts at self-composure and set her aflame ("I kak ognem obozhzhena" [3:41, l. 7]). She stops before Eugene. And here the story stops as well.

In charting her destiny in her letter Tatiana both asserts and surrenders, both reveals and conceals herself. At the same time she both maintains control over her idiom and courts the risks and uncertainties entailed in her enterprise. An outdated form becomes the vehicle for spontaneous self-expression, and figurative language dramatically expands the significance of actual events and situations, opening the limited literal world into a creative sphere where sexuality blossoms into creativity and a man emerges as a muse.

Yet the letter also reveals its author's limitations, for Tatiana has read her addressee incorrectly and the Eugene she projects is still very much her own ("svoi"). Although her books have helped her to come to terms with her self and have fostered her individual development, they have done nothing to promote her understanding of Eugene, whose world remains apart from the one she knows. If her hero is no Grandison, as we are assured by the author/narrator ("No nash geroi, kto b ni byl on, / Uzh verno byl ne Grandison [3:10, ll. 13–14]), neither is he a Lovelace. The hero who now plays opposite Tatiana is neither good nor wicked; he is indifferent. He eludes the alternatives she frames in her letter, not intentionally, but simply because there is no point of intersection between his and Tatiana's dissimilar worlds.

Tatiana has yet to augment the by now familiar worlds of her rural milieu and her novels with the new ones of Eugene's books and his urban setting. We can say that it is precisely the impending collision of her world with that of her hero that constitutes the next stage in Tatiana's development and rescues her from a sterile, Lensky-like aloofness from conflicting constructs. The subsequent unfolding of Pushkin's heroine can be described in terms of a collision of the invented addressee of her letter and its recipient. Initially the actual Eugene she comes to know displaces the muse, and bereft of his inspiring presence, Tatiana agrees to marry. By the work's end, however, she succeeds, as we will see, in drawing the actual Eugene *and* the Eugene of her imaginative space into a productive simultaneity. It is precisely her capacity to do so that holds out promise for Eugene's eventual regeneration.

At this juncture, however, Tatiana's reading of Eugene is still incomplete, and she cannot yet bridge their disparate worlds. The success of her letter as a literary text, however, is indisputable, for Pushkin has done much to ensure that this be so. Indeed, it is hard to imagine an interpolated document more privileged than Tatiana's letter, and harder still to understand how Pushkin manages to keep the bold textual signs of his partiality from obtruding on his heroine's text. Thus, to recapitulate briefly the strategies that enhance his heroine's letter, Pushkin insists on Tatiana's autonomous authorship by maintaining the fiction of the author/narrator's "weak translation"; he frames the sincerity of her emotions and their expression in the coy games of Petersburg coquettes and peasant girls; he crafts a complex temporal frame in which the inspired spontaneity of Tatiana's letter is protracted to endure beyond the moment of its inception into the time of our reading; and he couches the letter, moreover, in verse that is distinctly superior to that of the one Eugene subsequently writes. Tatiana, although sincere in her own assumption of epistolary risk, is in the context of Pushkin's text at no risk at all, for her loving author has so stacked the deck in her (literary) favor that she cannot but prosper.

4
Aftermath

The worlds beyond this world's perplexing waste
Had more of her existence, for in her
There was a depth of feeling to embrace . . .
                        Byron, *Don Juan*

Those readers who were enchanted by Tatiana's letter could not but be disappointed by what seemed Eugene's unforgivable lack of emotional responsiveness to its sincerity and charm. The severity of reproaches leveled against the unfortunate Onegin prompted Belinskii's defense of the hero who, in that critic's judicious estimation, "had a perfect right, without fearing the stern judgment of critics, not to fall in love with the girl Tatyana."[1] What Belinskii construes as Eugene's "perfect right" not to fall in love is in fact an urgent demand of the text itself. Pushkin decided against an earlier plan to have Tatiana's letter reawaken Eugene's dormant feelings, for at this point in the work mutual love between heroine and hero is neither feasible nor desirable.

Tatiana, as suggested in the previous chapter, invents the Eugene to whom she writes, and the recipient of her letter differs markedly from its addressee. Left exhausted in the wake of a long series of meaningless liaisons, Eugene is dissatisfied, and yet unprepared to venture beyond the limits of his predictable world. He can scarcely fall in love upon reading Tatiana's letter, for at this stage in his development he is incapable of serious attachment. Gained with the postponement of Eugene's emotional response to Tatiana is the opportunity to enlarge on the causes and consequences of his predicament. The expectation that he fall in love with Tatiana is imported into the text by readers who anticipate a love story and who, together with the author/narrator, are moved by the letter and smitten by the heroine who composed it. The frustration of this expectation sensitizes the reader to Tatiana's strengths and to Eugene's weaknesses—this with the purpose not of discrediting the hero, but rather of highlighting the potentially destructive features of his constitution for which Tatiana suggests an antidote.

This chapter focuses on the disparity between Tatiana's and Eugene's respective worlds and constitutions—specifically as it is highlighted by their meeting in the aftermath of the heroine's letter. We will begin with an evaluation of Eugene's response to Tatiana that focuses on the actual text of his speech, and will then consider what bearing the opening stanzas of chapter 4 have on the meaning of his words. This will prepare us to consider the ramifications of those particular features that mark Eugene as a negative counterexample to Tatiana. If we acknowledge the disadvantages Pushkin has imposed on the hero and recall too the advantages he has granted his heroine, we can better appreciate that, however unsatisfying it may seem, Eugene's response is the very best that can be expected. Just how good this "very best" is remains to be seen, for if we assure the harshest of Eugene's critics that he is not so bad, we must also insist to those who laud his honorable behavior toward Tatiana that neither is he so very good. Eugene, as we will see, emerges as neither a Lovelace nor a Grandison but as a limited hero in whose indifference lie the seeds of destruction.

The author/narrator's interruption of the story at the crucial and long-awaited moment of Tatiana's encounter with Eugene—the first the reader is allowed to witness—serves naturally to prolong and intensify the anticipation of the hero's response to the letter. Here Pushkin takes the opportunity to foreground the conventions of narrative to which his reader might be expected to surrender in the course of perusing the text and whose illusion he as author can dispel at any moment. More important, the delay in the story which returns now to document Eugene's receipt of Tatiana's letter leaves the reader time to appreciate the three distinct contexts in which the letter is regarded. We have considered the particular conditions under which it is written, what its writing means to Tatiana herself, and the risk involved in the dispatch of the letter into the unknown world of its addressee. The world in which this letter is received is described in stanzas 7 and 8 which, in the absence of stanzas 1–6, begin the fourth chapter of *Eugene Onegin*.[2] Foregrounded here is the fact that Eugene's world does not intersect with Tatiana's, and thus that his reading of her letter must accordingly differ markedly from her own. The context in which Eugene receives the letter is, moreover, as different from that in which the reader of *Eugene Onegin* finds it as it is from the one in which Tatiana wrote it, for the hero remains outside the sway of those textual privileges that the author/narrator accords the letter. Indeed, Tatiana, Eugene, and the reader of *Onegin* regard the letter in contexts so dissimilar that we might well speak of three different texts when we consider the effects of what Tatiana has written. Along the same lines, Eugene's reply conveys to Tatiana and to Pushkin's reader disparate messages that do not entirely coincide with one another or with what he himself intends. Thus we undertake our evaluation of Eugene's speech to Tatiana in the awareness that her letter signifies in three contexts provided by the distinct worlds of the heroine, of the hero, and of the larger text in which they are imbedded. It is important to be aware of these contextual differences.

Even as the textual privileging of Tatiana's letter significantly enhances the receptivity of Pushkin's reader to it, Eugene's capacity to appreciate its merits is pointedly undermined. To begin with, he is necessarily limited by those correlative weaknesses we have noted already in the areas of loving, writing, and reading. He is impeded further by the fact that Tatiana's world remains alien to him, and further still by the fact that the letter he peruses is perforce removed from that highly advantageous situation it enjoys in Pushkin's text. Thus Eugene, who knows nothing of the inspired state in which it was written, presumably reads the prose French original of the letter rather than Pushkin's poetical Russian rendering, and remains untouched by the fuss the author/narrator makes over the inadequacy of his translation. Nor is the text Eugene receives tellingly framed by that glaring insincerity of manipulative noblewomen and peasant girls which throws Tatiana's vulnerable forthrightness into high relief. Under these circumstances Eugene can scarcely be expected to be as moved by Tatiana's letter as is the reader of *Eugene Onegin*. Indeed, as far as Eugene is concerned, the letter is but the opening move of just such an erotically charged contest as those to which the author/narrator contrasts Tatiana's behavior. It is this view that dictates his reply.

The author/narrator, who apprised the reader in some detail of Tatiana's oral rehearsals of her letter and her preparation for its writing, makes no mention of whether Eugene's monologue—quoted in full in stanzas 12–16—was prepared in advance of his meeting with Tatiana, or erupted spontaneously when he met her in the garden. Its palpably self-conscious rhetoric and logical inconsistencies suggest however that Eugene selects his vocabulary—like perhaps also the "flashing looks" that precede its delivery—from a stock of ready-made responses. His "ukor"-cum-"urok" (reproach-cum-lesson) is distinguished from the direct speech he has been heard to utter thus far in *Eugene Onegin* by its elevated tone and embellished language—features that stand out with particular prominence against the pronounced simplicity of tone and diction that marks the return of the author/narrator in stanza 17. The artificiality of the address is indicated also, as Vinogradov has observed, by the fact that both Eugene's speech and Pushkin's prose sketch of it contain markedly more Gallicisms than do Tatiana's purportedly French letter and its drafts.[3] At the same time the didactic quality of the "sermon" removes it from that category of spontaneous self-expressive communication into which Tatiana's letter falls.

Because, like Tatiana's letter, what became Eugene's speech was initially set down in prose jottings, Nabokov plausibly speculates that Pushkin had originally thought to have his hero answer by post.[4] The oral response that appeared instead spares Eugene the more lasting commitment of words to paper for which he is not yet ready and highlights the imbalance between the letter and his reply to it. Whereas Tatiana evokes an abstract addressee who expands well beyond the actual Eugene, Onegin confronts a concrete addressee whom he has undervalued.

Although Eugene does not grasp the import of Tatiana's letter, his monologue does suggest an (albeit imperfect) adoption of its vocabulary and an adjustment of his own persona to the one he thinks he sees projected in it. Thus, for example, he echoes the motifs of sincerity and destiny, and, despite his alleged surrender to Tatiana's judgment ("Sebia na sud vam otdaiu" [Unto your judgment I commit myself] [4:12, l. 14]),[5] readily assumes the power Tatiana has vested in him to determine her fate. Framed by an introductory and a concluding stanza (12 and 16) that emphasize not so much Tatiana's virtues themselves as Eugene's own purported ability to appreciate them, the three middle stanzas of his speech (13–15) are devoted to the topic of matrimony. Eugene's monologue indicates that he has read Tatiana's letter with the conventional assumption that she must have marriage on her mind. Whether or not he has read Richardson, Eugene assumes the role of a Grandison who is nobly prepared to protect a woman from her own passions, and who only hints darkly at the Lovelacian possibility he has rejected: "Ne vsiakoi vas, kak ia, poimet / K bede neopytnost' vedet" (For few will understand you so, / And innocence can lead to woe [16, ll. 13–14]). Although Eugene's course of action is commendable, the very fact that he reduces the broad range of possible responses to Tatiana's letter to the limited choice between matrimony and seduction removes in advance the chance to provide her with the expansion of possibility that she so earnestly seeks. Far from generating new options, Eugene's reply only reinforces those painfully inadequate alternatives offered by Tatiana's milieu and by the novels she has read that she either surrender her intense emotions to matrimony or be undone by them. In light of Eugene's narrow reading of the letter, his assurance that he understands Tatiana is ironic, while his injunction that she learn to exercise self-control takes on a hypocritical cast when we recall his earlier self-indulgence and the current absence of intense feelings that would demand restraint.

Even as Eugene's stern opening statement echoes the beginning of Ta-

tiana's letter, it closes down that broad imaginative spectrum into which
Tatiana's letter opened and roots Tatiana's expansive gesture in the
specifics of the here and now. "You wrote to me," he establishes, and follows with the admonition, "Do not deny it" ("vy ko mne pisali / Ne ot-
piraites'"[4:12, ll. 3–4]). These words set the tone of the speech. Reflected
in it is Eugene's assumption that Tatiana is behaving like one of the coy
Petersburg coquettes of his acquaintace and his own determination to retain the upper hand.

Eugene admits that Tatiana's letter has moved him. The vocabulary
that follows this admission, however, derives from the sphere of economics, where all exchanges are considered exclusively in terms of loss or
gain, a world where Tatiana's readiness to stake all on an exceptionally
dubious venture can have no place.[6] Eugene's gracious acknowledgment
of her forthrightness is undermined by his promises to "repay" her with
a similarly "artless" admission ("Ia za nee vam *otplachu* / Priznan'em
takzhe *bez iskusstva*" [Let me *repay* you with a vow / As *artless* as the one
you tendered] [4:12, ll. 11–12, my emphasis]).[7] This calculation contrasts
sharply with Tatiana's spontaneous letter, particularly if we recall that
what is for Tatiana a serious risk is for Eugene a safe transaction.

His claim to perceive and respond in kind to the artlessness of Tatiana's letter reflects Eugene's association of the imagination with duplic-
ity, a position that, as we have already had the opportunity to observe in
connection with Tatiana's reading, is contrary to the verity of the creative-
imaginative spirit that Pushkin has his heroine champion. The sermon that
follows is indeed devoid of specific literary allusions.[8] Yet, as we quickly
recognize, this does not make it more true than Tatiana's letter. Just as Tatiana's engagement of literary models in her writing did not preclude the
sincerity of her own self-expression, neither does the absence of particular
references in Eugene's speech ensure that his communication is genuine.
Indeed, the very promise that he will speak "bez iskusstva" (without art)
signals a self-consciousness that must interfere with uninhibited self-expression. Tatiana, who in the author/narrator's words, "loves without art"
("liubit bez iskusstva" [3:24, l. 5]), expresses herself unselfconsciously,
drawing on the vocabulary of her novels not because she has no vocabulary of her own, but because with its complete assimilation it has, in fact,
become hers. It emerges from the juxtaposition of her letter with Eugene's
speech that art and veracity are interdependent, while mendacity creeps in
just where there is no art. Tatiana's ability to absorb art artlessly and seamlessly into her own life and thus to imbue her chosen form with genuine
meaning is contrasted with Eugene's inability to productively engage literature *or* life—an inability that leaves him stranded in the barren void of
mere form where there can be neither self nor other.

Despite Eugene's protestation that he is "confessing" to Tatiana and throwing himself on her mercy, it is clear that he is "repaying" her in currency of lesser value than the sterling of her letter. Eugene has little at stake as he responds to her confession of love with his "confession" of an unworthiness that serves only to secure his own position. His meeting with Tatiana entails neither social nor emotional risk. The author/narrator points out in stanza 17 that given the freer customs of the countryside his tête-à-tête with Tatiana places him under no obligation. As for Eugene's emotions—they have been stilled by habit and are just now in little danger of being agitated. The resistance to dialogue we noted in Tatiana's letter was prompted by a need for greater openness than actual discourse would allow. By contrast, Eugene's insistence that his speech completes their exchange indicates his unwillingness to enter into a relationship which he construes as yet another of those highly predictable games of love that no longer have the power to excite him but for which he neither knows nor seeks an alternative. His appointment of Tatiana as the "judge" of his "confessions" could not be easier, for the vulnerability remains entirely on her side.

Having made his preparatory remarks, Eugene launches into the core of his argument—an elaborate account of his own disinclination, indeed unfitness, for matrimony. If earlier Eugene assured Lensky that he would choose Tatiana if he were a poet, here he insists that he would certainly choose her if he thought of marrying. That he has no intention of taking such a step is accounted for by the inconsistent explanations that he is not prepared to assume the *restrictions* of the married state ("Kogda by zhizn' domashnim krugom / Ia ogranichit' zakhotel" [Had I in any way desired / To bind with family ties my life] [4:13, ll. 1–2]) and yet also that marriage is a *desirable* fate that has been denied him ("priiatnyi zhrebii" [pleasant lot] [4:13, l. 4]). However chivalrous Eugene's insistence that it is marriage itself and not Tatiana that he finds unattractive, the announcement of his own decision to forgo matrimony can only underscore that while he can choose an alternative life's course, for Tatiana marriage remains the only viable option. (At the end of *Eugene Onegin* this situation is inverted, and we find opposite Tatiana, who is both married and yet also genuinely free, a Eugene who is neither married nor free.)

Bent on proving his unsuitability for marriage, Eugene parades before Tatiana a series of personality traits that guarantees an insufferable conjugal life with him. Foregrounded against his inability to empathize with Tatiana is Eugene's clear, accurate assessment of his own shortcomings—shortcomings that are both cause and consequence of his inability to get beyond himself to accomplish the intersection of the familiar ("svoi") and the alien ("chuzhoi") that advances Tatiana's development. So frank is his admission of his various failings that were we not aware of the dim view Pushkin took of the confessional mode, we might be inclined to praise Eugene for his candor.[9] Yet Eugene describes his character flaws with a complacency that eschews both responsibility and the possibility for change. Depicting them as somehow fated, he parades his shortcomings before his silent auditor and in so doing assumes a superior stance opposite her.

The picture Eugene paints seems as accurate as it is bleak. His exposé reflects a commendable awareness of those very features that we have already recognized as central to his characterization: his need for ever-new stimuli and the correlative incapacity for deep, sustained engagement. Unbeknownst to Eugene, his observation that habit will drive away his love ("Ia, skol'ko ni liubil by vas, / Privyknuv, razliubliu totchas" [However much I loved you, dear, / Once used to you . . . I'd cease, I fear] [4:14, ll. 7–8]) coincides with the situation that Tatiana has observed in her own milieu and that she herself seeks to avoid.

It is telling that in this part of his speech Eugene assumes that while his own love for Tatiana is doomed to quick, inevitable extinction even in his full appreciation of her merits, hers is certain to endure even in full awareness of his weaknesses and in spite of the callous behavior toward her that he foretells. Here we recognize that Eugene's projections of the disastrous relationship ahead sound suspiciously like generalizations abstracted from the story of that influential literary precursor of Childe Harold, Benjamin Constant's Adolphe, whose character is determined by a paralyzing self-consciousness that interferes cruelly with his emotional development, leeches him of vitality, and leaves him hopelessly trapped in the narrow confines between his divided selves. Adolphe's tormented relationship with the unfortunate Ellénore (who is modeled on Germaine de Staël) appears to have supplied Eugene with a vague plot for the prognostications Eugene now unfolds before Tatiana.[10] In such generalized appropriation of literary precedent there is indeed no art.

By way of conclusion, Eugene contrasts his own world-weariness with Tatiana's youthful naiveté. Offering her fraternal affection, he emphasizes—just as he had in his conversation with Lensky after his first meeting with Tatiana—his own imperviousness to eros. He goes on, moreover, to assure Tatiana that her love for him will not last. If (in her letter) Tatiana evoked the heavens to describe her unwavering dedication to Eugene ("To volia neba: ia tvoia" [It is the will of heaven: I am yours] [l. 34]), Eugene resorts to those very heavens to insist that her fancies are ephemeral and fated to change many times over. (He does not seem troubled by the fact that this particular assessment contradicts that unswerving constancy he has just described in his gloomy forecast of a marriage in which his own love vanishes while Tatiana's persists.) Focusing on the irreconcilable differences that keep them apart, Eugene insists on the impossibility of recapturing the vivacity of his own youth: "Mechtam i godam net vozvrata; / Ne obnovliu dushi moei" (There is no return for dreams and years; / I will not renew my soul [4:16, ll. 1–2]). For Tatiana, he presages an entire series of changing fancies, a prediction based on his own experiences and one that discounts the depth of her emotions:

> *Сменит* не раз младая дева
> Мечтами легкие мечты;
> Так деревцо свои листы
> *Меняет* с каждою весною.

> [a youthful maid more than once will *exchange*
> for dreams light dreams;
> a sapling thus its leaves
> *changes* with every spring.][11]
> (4:16, ll. 8–9, my emphasis)

It would seem that in thus contrasting himself with Tatiana, Eugene distinguishes implicitly between the sequential linearity of his own world and the cyclicity of repeated return that predominates in Tatiana's milieu. Although he appropriately applies to Tatiana a metaphor drawn from her rural setting, it is telling that he evokes this vernal image not to suggest renewal, but to emphasize the replacement of one set of leaves/loves with another.[12] As the sapling becomes for him simply another exponent of sequence, we recognize the extent to which this temporal construct limits his conceptual field, for to regard the tree in terms of a mere succession of leaves is no more fruitful than to construe its verdure as the mere repetition of the same leaves year after year. In comparing Tatiana to a young tree that puts out new leaves each spring Eugene has inadvertently hit upon an image that, if better understood, offers a positive alternative to the inadequacies of both unalloyed linearity and unalloyed cyclicity and that encapsulates the ideal of new yet lasting, lasting yet new. The growing sapling exemplifies the natural vitality that derives specifically from change working in concert with continuity, but the significance of this humble image remains unappreciated by the hero who evokes it.

Upon Eugene's completion of his sermon to Tatiana, the author/narrator praises the nobility of his response. On the basis of his speech alone, this nobility can be readily granted him. In the context of the stanzas that introduce it, however, the "genuine nobility of soul" ("Dushi priamoe blagorodstvo") with which the author/narrator credits the hero appears to derive not from a resolute moral stance, but from mere disinclination to engage in what has become for him a tediously predictable sport. Here we recognize that immoral modern hero who, according to the author/narrator's earlier description (3:11–12), has replaced the sensitive, intelligent, and virtuous hero of earlier days—a new hero whose vices are flaunted and who is prepared to live by moral standards of a bygone era only after he is too exhausted to do otherwise.[13] It is precisely in this context that the epigraph of the chapter, "La morale est dans la nature des choses," takes effect.

The cynical notions expressed in stanzas 7 and 8, which convey Eugene's thoughts on the subject of love, are translated into the text of *Eugene Onegin* from a letter Pushkin wrote his brother in September–October 1822, and in which he made the following observation: "Je vous observerai seulement, que moins on aime une femme et plus on est sûr de l'avoir. Mais cette jouissance est digne d'un vieux sapajou du 18 siècle" (*PSS* 13:50).[14] Todd notes that "[t]he passage from letter to verse novel is difficult to chart and includes many excursions by Pushkin into other works and forms." He plausibly describes the ideas in question as a "stylization" of Byron and Constant, whose accounts of society were corroborated by Pushkin's own experiences.[15] The bearing of this passage on Eugene's response to Tatiana's letter is of considerable consequence. In the text of *Eugene Onegin* these thoughts are ascribed directly to Eugene and augmented by three further stanzas in which the author/narrator recapitulates the development that informed these views. Although the author/narrator purports to provide a precise record of Eugene's thoughts ("Tak tochno dumal moi Evgenii" [Precisely thus my Eugene thought] [4:9, l. 1]), they are presented not as quoted material, but as reported speech. Moreover, the reader does not learn that these thoughts are ostensibly Eugene's until the ninth stanza, that is, only after having taken them to be the author/narrator's own observations. The distinction between the hero and author/narrator is thus blurred, and it appears that Eugene is not the original author of the generalized "philosophy of love" that is advanced here, but only one of its many subscribers. In earlier drafts Pushkin had Eugene himself supply much of the information that was ultimately provided by the author/narrator. The question of who is to convey which information is indicative of the problem Pushkin confronts when he finds it necessary to acquaint the reader with the hero's thoughts on love—a context necessary for evaluating his speech to Tatiana—and yet to do this without giving him a degree of insight, self-awareness, and consciousness of the forces that shaped his development that would be inconsistent with his development thus far in the story.

Eugene's thoughts on strategies of amorous conquest reveal him to be a fitting partner for those coquettes the author/narrator describes in chapter 3. The indifference he touts as a certain means to secure a woman's attachment echoes distinctly one of the tactics favored by the flirtatious women described earlier, and repeats too the image of the net that must ensnare the less skillful of the players:[16]

> Чем меньше женщину мы любим,
> Тем легче нравимся мы ей,
> И тем ее вернее губим
> Средь обольстительных сетей.

> [With womankind, the less we love them,
> the easier they become to charm,
> the tighter we can stretch above them
> enticing nets to do them harm.][17]
>
> (4:7, ll. 1–4)

The amorous games in which Eugene habitually engages are described throughout *Eugene Onegin* in terms of victory, conquest, surrender, defeat, and entrapment. The players—male and female alike—guardedly seek to manipulate the "antagonist" or "prey" into a vulnerable position in order to assert their own supremacy. (In the chaste relationship between Olga and Vladimir, this contest is transferred to a chessboard [4:26].) Victory hinges on retaining control, which is to say, on remaining unsmitten by love, and, in the case of the woman, of successfully resisting the consummation of desire (this regardless of whether it is her opponent's desire or her own). The carefully planned behavior and maneuvers of the participants leave little room for the spontaneous or unforeseen and thus drastically curtail the possible course of events and outcomes. The closely guarded self of each participant is denied its own expressivity even as admission of otherness is barred. The fresh, direct, and intense emotions Tatiana experiences and seeks to convey in her letter have no place in this world, where feelings are absorbed into self-conscious calculation of how to gain a desired end and where showing signs of vulnerability is tantamount to defeat. Indeed, Eugene's past experience teaches that victory is certain only in the absence of emotional involvement. The lust-driven Lovelacian debauchery described here, tellingly, as an outmoded fashion has been replaced with strategic moves that, in the absence of desire and uncertainty, grow tedious with repetition.[18] Because he construes the choices open to him in terms of *either* control *or* surrender, Eugene cannot achieve that productive reconciliation of antinomies that the controlled surrender of Tatiana's letter exemplifies.

The context provided by Eugene's thoughts on love calls into question his "honorable" behavior at this stage in his relations with Tatiana, for the speech that ostensibly removes the threat of seduction projects at the same time that very absence of reciprocal ardor that purportedly guarantees the woman's ensnarement and downfall. Thus a strong suspicion arises that Tatiana is saved from "perishing" not by his "honor" but by her own innocence and trust in language that lead her to accept his words at face value and to react to them accordingly.

The description of Eugene that the author/narrator supplies immediately after the account of the hero's thoughts on amorous pursuits reveals the sources of those cynical views and reinforces the image of an oversatiated hero who, to borrow from Byron, "has squandered his whole summer while 'twas May." A thumbnail sketch of the hero's early youth reveals him to have been the victim of unbridled passions, whose energies in the absence of control, were eventually dissipated by habit and dissimulation:

> Он в первой юности своей
> Был жертвой бурных заблуждений
> И необузданных страстей.
> Привычкой жизни избалован,
> Одним навремя очарован,
> Разочарованный другим.

> [Who in his youth had known the sway
> Of those tempestuous delusions,
> Unbridled passions' helpless prey.
> Life's soothing custom once implanted,
> He now was by one thing enchanted,
> Now disenchanted by the next.][19]
>   (4:9, ll. 2–7)

The information provided here adds nothing new to what has already been said of Eugene in the opening chapter of *Onegin*. The biographical material reproduced here reemphasizes the dissimilarities that prevail between hero and heroine and draws attention to the context in which Eugene and his speech to Tatiana are to be considered. In the absence of restraint, Eugene's capacity to experience intense emotions has been blunted. Conversely, the dearth of powerful feelings leaves his self-mastery unexercised. Blighted by apathy, he goes through the motions of a codified ritual that has lost its significance and that leaves him as indifferent to success as to failure. In the ominous intersection of uncontrolled passions with surrender to habit we discern the formula for destroying creative potential, indeed life itself:

> Вот, как убил он восемь лет,
> Утратя жизни лучший цвет.

[And so he killed eight years of youth
And lost life's very bloom, in truth.]
(4:9, ll. 13–4)

In the absence of the productive conjoining of self-surrender with self-control, Eugene has already metaphorically killed the best years of his own life and will shortly realize this metaphor by shooting Lensky.

Although he did not allow Eugene to fall in love with Tatiana upon receiving her letter, Pushkin did grant his hero a moment of feeling in response to it. He underscores thereby the powerful effect of Tatiana's letter without, however, crediting Eugene with a capacity to read and feel in excess of what he is capable of at this point in his development. Although Tatiana's letter cannot accomplish the hero's emotional regeneration, his susceptibility to its candor must be regarded as a positive sign. Indeed, if the author/narrator's account is to be believed, Eugene's immediate reaction deviates significantly both from that "philosophy of love" that he professes in the opening of chapter 4 and from the sermon he subsequently delivers to Tatiana. The detached appraisal of the predictable course of events he envisions gives way spontaneously and unexpectedly before the fresh sincerity of Tatiana's letter. Hence the "But" with which stanza IX opens:

Но, получив посланье Тани,
Онегин живо тронут был:
Язык девических мечтаний
В нем думы роем возмутил;
И вспомнил он Татьяны милой
И бледный цвет, и вид унылый;
И в сладостный безгрешный сон
Душою погрузился он.

[But having read Tatyana's letter,
Onegin was profoundly stirred:
The tongue of maiden dreams besought him,
Sent fancies swarming, would be heard;
Tatyana's image rose before him
And, wan and sad, seemed to implore him;
A dream of sinless, sweet delight
Engrossed his spirit at the sight.][20]
(4:11, ll. 1–8)

The letter moves Eugene to private behavior that is at odds with his public persona, as he envisions Tatiana in his mind's eye, sinks into innocent reverie, and "perhaps," as the author/narrator cautiously qualifies, even surrenders himself briefly to long-forgotten ardor. For one significant moment, Tatiana's letter interrupts Eugene's linear progress and prompts him to recollection that permits him to reconnect with a vital part of himself that his ruthless forward drive has left behind. However fleeting, the vision granted Eugene is of considerable importance, for in it we glimpse the potential for regeneration Tatiana offers him.

Two things in particular deserve emphasis in connection with Eugene's private reaction to the letter: that he is moved specifically by the *language* of Tatiana's "maidenly fantasies" and that this language activates his own imagination, prompting him to recollect the young woman he has recently met. Tatiana's letter stimulates Eugene's neglected inner world and disrupts his habitual mode of thinking. Unlike the sleep of complete indifference ("Spokoino doma zasypaet" [Calmly falls asleep at home] [4:10, l. 1]) of the preceding stanza that describes a Eugene who remains unaffected by the amorous games he halfheartedly pursues, the "sweet, sinless sleep/dream ['son']"(4:10, l. 12) in which he immerses himself here is suggestive of engaged imaginative faculties that take him beyond the shallow liaisons of which he has wearied. However briefly, Tatiana's letter effects Eugene's return to that very springtime of his life that he pronounces irretrievably lost in his speech to her.

Yet the public persona of the here-and-now is quick to reassert itself. Ushered in by a second "but" that returns us to Eugene's habitual point of vantage, this persona extinguishes the fleeting image of the pallid Tatiana from his mind's eye, leaving before him a young woman whom he regards in accordance with the anesthetic code that dictates his response. Eugene's sermon to Tatiana shows that the positive effects of her letter are quickly absorbed into those predictable patterns of behavior according to which he orders his life. In it he resorts to the ready-made language provided by his "philosophy of love" with little concern for the specific circumstances at hand. The Eugene who addresses Tatiana is far removed from those reveries that her letter initially stimulated. From his speech she cannot know of that brief stirring of feelings and imagination that brought Eugene—if ever so slightly—closer to the world which she herself inhabits, even as she knows nothing of that world that dictates his response to her.

The author/narrator prefaces his record of the hero's words with the explanation that Eugene did not wish to deceive the trusting, innocent Tatiana:

Но обмануть он не хотел
Доверчивость души невинной.

[But he resolved not to betray
A trusting spirit's pure surrender . . .]²¹
(4:11, ll. 11–12)

Yet what has already been revealed of Eugene's thoughts on the subject of love undermines this motivation for his behavior by suggesting that playing roles from a limited repertoire is the only form of interaction he knows. That he should be bored by the predictability of the patterns of behavior he reenacts is very much to his credit. That he seeks no alternative to them reveals the extent to which he is trapped in convention. Indeed, any attempt on his part to assess his situation must inevitably be subverted by his assumed persona. Because this persona remains disassociated from his self, Eugene remains incapable of interaction with others. The self-deception that underlies this behavior is both cause and consequence of atrophied imaginative faculties—those very faculties that foster the empathy necessary to the success of all human relations and of love and creativity in particular. Eugene cannot adequately respond to Tatiana because he remains out of touch with himself and because he can imagine no world beyond the limited one by which he is himself defined. His problem is not that he fails to fall in love with Tatiana, but that in his present circumstances he is incapable of falling in love at all.

It should be emphasized here that the predictability that leaches Eugene of his life's energies is paired with deception. Here we recognize a corollary to the unpredictability that Pushkin regards as necessary to genuine vivacity and creativity and that he has Tatiana court with her letter. Eugene's concerted pursuit of new conquests has led paradoxically to mere repetition that stalks his world of sequential linearity as relentlessly as it does the cyclical one of Tatiana's milieu. He too is trapped in endlessly repeated patterns of behavior that have ceased to carry meaning and mired in that deceptiveness which habitually consorts with predictability. We can add here that the predictability of Lensky's actions—predetermined as they are by the ready-made model according to which he regulates his life and art—makes him even in his unwavering attachment to Olga no less a self-deceived deceiver than the fickle Eugene who pursues an entire succession of women. The very real threat posed by determining in advance one set of norms according to which to conduct life, art, or anything else for that matter is graphically demonstrated in Onegin's emotional moribundity and in Lensky's pointless death. By contrast, Tatiana champions the truth and the genuine freedom that Pushkin connects with the imagination—a force that ever subverts conventional norms and expectations by engaging the unpredictable to sustain its momentum.

Tatiana listens in breathless silence to Eugene's exposition of his unsuitability for matrimony and his assurance of the insignificance of her feelings for him. The tears she evoked in her letter ("Pered toboiu slezy l'iu" [I shed tears before you] [l. 66]) to refer metaphorically to the free expression of her feelings for Eugene are now rendered literal by his response, which she understands as a prohibition of any further communication with him. Tatiana cries openly, as we recall, when she confesses her love to her nurse (3:20, l. 9), and, as in that scene, so here too her overflowing eyes betoken emotions too powerful to be contained and not an attempt to move her interlocutor. That Tatiana's weeping is self-expressive and not conventionally manipulative is lost on Eugene, who knows only those generalized "tears" from that glossary of gestures calculated to produce a particular effect ("Ugrozy, / Molen'ia, kliatvy, mnimyi strakh, / Zapiski na shesti listakh, / Obmany, spletni, kol'tsy, *slezy*," [Entreaties, vows, pretended fears, / Betrayals, gossip, rings, and *tears*, / With notes that run to seven pages] [4:8, ll. 9–12, my emphasis]).

For all the author/narrator's professed delight in Eugene's honorable behavior (4:18), the hero's response is clearly inadequate to Tatiana's letter. It is also profoundly and unavoidably disappointing for the heroine whose expectations it falls so painfully short of meeting. Tatiana's letter has failed to find *her* addressee, as indeed it must, for the hero she invented did not intersect with the prototype she addressed. If completely disassociated from the here-and-now, the muse cannot endure. For Tatiana the speech signals closure—that awakening from "heavy dreams" that she describes in her letter and that returns her to a mundane world, gone from which is that hero/muse who recedes before her stern lecturer. From Eugene's response that focuses on matrimony and refuses to countenance the depth of her emotions, Tatiana can glean only that, although he puts a very different complexion on her behavior, he does not come much closer to understanding her than did her old nurse. His unbridled amorous pursuits have rendered him unreceptive to Tatiana's needs no less effectively than did the rigid restrictions to which the nurse's sexuality succumbed. (It is not for nothing that both scenes are set next to the bench.) As after her frustrating tête-à-tête with her nurse, so now too in the aftermath of her meeting with Eugene, Tatiana experiences an intensification of desire. Her emotional energy contrasts sharply with the detached coolness of Eugene's thoughts on love. Although the heightening of her feelings is correctly anticipated by Eugene's "philosophy of love," Tatiana deviates from the prediction that, having been repulsed, she will intensify her efforts to win his attentions. (This is what Eugene does in the final chapter of *Onegin*.) Accepting his speech at face value, she neither seeks audience with him nor writes him any more letters. The symptoms of her desire—sleeplessness, listlessness, and an even more pronounced disinterest in her surroundings—are soon remarked by inquisitive neighbors who readily suggest matrimony as the cure for her "ailment." The attitude toward love and marriage projected in the outmoded novels Tatiana has read, as we are reminded here once again, remains in full effect in her actual world.

The subsequent account of Vladimir's cliché-ridden courtship of

Olga throws into high relief that alienation that has always characterized Tatiana. Here the difference between her sister's bloom and her own pallor is intensified with the juxtaposition of a Tatiana made even paler by unfulfilled longing with a rosier-than-ever sister who is steeped in shallow contentment. Lensky's avowed surrender to Olga and her passive acceptance of his professions of love bespeak a relationship as predictable and unremarkable as the scribbles in a young lady's album that are described in stanzas 28 and 29 as a generic analogue for their courtship. Omitted from the reading aloud of edifying novels with which Lensky regales his beloved are all passages that might prove "dangerous to a maiden's heart" ("opasnye dlia serdtsa dev" [4:26, l. 7]), as we see Olga's suitor assume the paternal duty of censor that Tatiana's father neglected to fulfill in connection with her "dangerous" reading. Lensky only blushes as he judiciously excises anything that threatens arousal of that chaste, abstract, and unchanging ideal he insists on seeing in Olga—that very image that prompts Eugene's earlier reference to her as a Van Dyck Madonna. Vladimir's desexualization of Olga precludes the intersection of an abstract ideal with an actual woman that is necessary for the emergence of a lasting muse. If Eugene's relations with the opposite sex focus exclusively on flesh-and-blood women, Vladimir's love for Olga is represented as a complete abdication to a disembodied ideal—one that in actual life translates into an infantilized woman and that in literature translates into cliché. Whatever else we may say of Eugene's disappointing sermon, it rescues Tatiana from following in Lensky's footsteps by undermining her idealized image of him. In this sense, Eugene is, unbeknownst to himself, a true hero.

The chapter concludes with a reflection on the sterile, illusory control Eugene seeks to maintain over the events of his life and provides an additional context in which to consider his speech to Tatiana and his subsequent relations with her.

> Но жалок тот, кто всё предвидит,
> Чья не кружится голова,
> Кто все движенья, все слова
> В их переводе ненавидит,
> Чье сердце опыт остудил
> И забываться запретил!

> [but pitiful is he who foresees all,
> who's never dizzy,
> who all movements, all words
> in their translation hates,
> whose heart experience has chilled
> and has forbidden to be lost in dreams!][22]
>
> (4:51, ll. 9–14)

The conduct of life according to a predetermined pattern establishes a predictability from which an illusory sense of control can be derived, but only at the expense of the possibilities that are shut down in order to achieve it. Thus, for example, the hostility to "translations" referred to in this passage indicates a fear of metaphor, indeed of any recontextualization which necessarily involves transferring a gesture—be it linguistic, literary, social, or personal—into new terrain, where its effects expand beyond the immediate sphere of the original. In this sense, the dynamic nature of translation is opposed to the stasis of mere replication. This situation is well illustrated by the energetic debates over the various renderings of Bürger's *Lenore* that we touched on earlier, by the hypothetical translation of the letter from Tatiana's French prose into Pushkin's Russian poetry, and by the delivery of Tatiana's letter into the new context of Eugene's world. The potentially fruitful imprecision that is entailed in the act of translation lends it that vivacious element of risk that Pushkin prizes so highly.

The relevance of these general observations to the creative process is unmistakable. At the opposite end of the spectrum stands Eugene, who in order to be able to foresee the future has severely curtailed it. To admit new possibility is to threaten his narrow but comforting "clairvoyance." It is telling that in conveying Eugene's thoughts and words, the author/narrator tends to emphasize the precision with which he does so (e.g., "Tak tochno dumal moi Evgenii" [Exactly thus my Eugene thought] and "Vot vam pis'mo ego toch' v toch'" [Here you have his letter word for word]), for this exactitude is informed by the hero's own preference for safe repetition over risk-laden translation. Eugene believes himself to be in command when he has, in fact, blocked out a wide range of possible experiences. Although understandably bored with the reenactment of predictable gestures, he is not prepared to relinquish the illusory sense of control that he derives from this predictability. Accordingly, life for Eugene retains no more significance than a game of whist, which is, as Lotman observes, "a mercantile game and not one of chance" ("kommercheskaia, a ne azartnaia igra").[23] That he is compared to an indifferent guest who comes only to play this particular game ("whist" is italicized in the text) underscores Eugene's express avoidance of risk.

In this context we can briefly look ahead to note that Onegin's acceptance of the duel to which Lensky later challenges him may seem at first glance a way of breaking out of this predictable world. Yet though he stakes life itself, the risk he ventures is cushioned in the ritualistic gestures of dueling etiquette and is undertaken, moreover, not at his own initiative, but because he first fails to predict the consequences of his behav-

ior toward Olga, then finds himself unable to deviate from established social norms that demand a particular response to the challenge whatever
his private feelings may be. Eugene may well hate translations, for it is just
when he feels confident manipulating Olga's, Vladimir's, and Tatiana's
emotions at the name day festivities that he in fact misjudges the effects
of his behavior. Failing to recognize that, translated into Lensky's world,
his flirtation with Olga takes on far greater significance than he himself
ascribes to it, Eugene fails also to gauge Vladimir's reaction—a reaction
that is fully predictable within the idealist scheme Lensky has adopted for
himself and that dictates that he and Onegin must now assume those familiar antinomic roles of savior versus seducer. Yet although Eugene does
not foresee Lensky's challenge,[24] his reply to it is determined well in advance of the event by a code that dictates his acceptance regardless of the
particular circumstances at hand. As in his response to Tatiana's letter, so
now again, the public persona overrides Eugene's private reaction with
which it is out of joint ("no Evgenii / Naedine s svoei dushoi / Byl nedo-
volen sam soboi" [but Eugene / alone remaining with his soul, / felt ill-
contented with himself] [6:9, ll. 12–14]).

We can observe here that for all the time these erstwhile friends have
spent together, each has maintained a distinct world in which the other
has effected no change. The intersection of "svoi" (the familiar) and
"chuzhoi" (the alien) has not been accomplished in the course of their relations. For all the dissimilarities that prevail between Onegin and Lensky
(e.g., "Volna i kamen' / Stikhi i proza, led i plamen' / Ne stol' razlichny
mezh soboi" [Wave and stone / Verse and prose, ice and flame, / Were not
so different from one another] [2:13, ll. 5–7]), idealist and cynic alike succumb to a code of behavior that is, as each recognizes, distinctly at odds
with the given situation and contrary to their personal inclinations. Eugene's untoward invitation of a servant to act as his second is but an
empty gesture of defiance that does nothing to alter the consequences of
his submission to the dictates of social norms and the fear of public opinion.[25]

Clayton has perceptively noted that Onegin "is defined, not in terms
of what he is, but rather in terms of what he is not, or more precisely in
terms of the activities he avoids," and Eugene's response to Tatiana falls
easily into the category of "non-service" that Clayton postulates to describe the hero.[26] It is not simply, as Lotman, for example, sees it, that in
responding to Tatiana's letter Eugene "comported himself not according
to the laws of literature, but according to the norms and regulations, according to which a worthy person of Pushkin's circle conducted his
life."[27] Indeed, Pushkin intentionally subverts the opposition between life

and literature throughout *Eugene Onegin*.[28] The "hopeless egotism" that stands in the way of Eugene's self-realization, of his intercourse with the surrounding world, and of his formulation of an adequate response to Tatiana has too much in common with Benjamin Constant's Adolphe and Byron's Childe Harold to be deemed exempt from the sway of literature. At the same time, Tatiana, as we have seen, assimilates the worlds of her heroines too perfectly into her own actual experience to be defined entirely by the sentimental novels she reads. It would seem rather that the collision Pushkin orchestrates here is not between life and literature, but between different modes—modes that span the actual and the imaginative—of perceiving experience, structuring it, and endowing it with meaning. Here it is a question not simply of what codes are in effect—and we have spoken already of the noncoincidence of Eugene's and Tatiana's and of Eugene's and Vladimir's. The real question is whether the individual remains fixed by rigid adherence to a given code, or is able to move freely within it, allowing for its expansion and maintaining its flexibility by readily assimilating new stimuli and admitting new perspectives. The Eugene who seeks to control is in fact himself determined by the narrow limits of a ready-made code. At the same time, the Vladimir who seeks to surrender himself wholly to his ideals is inflexibly contained by them. Tatiana remains free because she successfully and continually interrelates a variety of codes in the constant evolution of her own. We need not stretch far to see the direct applicability of these observations both to the creation of an individual poetic text and to the evolution of the larger process of literature.

In this context it is significant that Tatiana is characterized by a disinclination to exercise control over others that is manifested already in her girlhood days by her complete lack of interest in dolls:

> Охоты властвовать примета,
> С послушной куклою дитя
> Приготовляется, шутя,
> К приличию—закону света,
> И важно повторяет ей
> Уроки маминьки своей.

> [Mark how the world compels submission:
> The little girl with docile doll
> Prepares in play for protocol,
> For every social admonition;
> And to her doll, without demur,
> Repeats what mama taught to her.]
> (2:26, ll. 9–14)

Tatiana neither dominates nor repeats. She has no interest in manipulating the dolls she later encounters in urban society any more than those of her girlhood years. Her freedom derives from her readiness to acknowledge, indeed to seek out, otherness that lies refreshingly beyond what she knows or controls, and that she can continually assimilate into her own world with unprecedented, incalculable results. Her openness and preparedness to take chances are ultimately as creatively life-affirming as Eugene's closedness and illusory control are destructively life-negating. Here we recall again the quintessentially Pushkinian theme that drives, for example, "The Queen of Spades" and *Mozart and Salieri* with their warnings of the grave consequences of refusing to relinquish control and of seeking to circumvent that element of risk that is vitally and equally necessary to life and art. This is a theme to which Pushkin returned time and time again with ever less sympathy for the would-be manipulator. As Andrei Siniavskii notes, "Pushkin relates in dozens of variations how opponents of fate are brought to their knees, how despite all ruses and intrigues fate triumphs over man, mixing up his cards or surreptitiously throwing in a surprise."[29]

In the juxtaposition of Tatiana's letter and Eugene's response to it, the hero's calculated behavior emerges as a negative counterexample to the spontaneity and intensity that characterize the heroine. Yet Tatiana is also the more vulnerable of the two. Indeed, there is no contest here, as is underscored by the imagery that appears just before Eugene's speech where Tatiana is the captured moth in a careless boy's hand and the cornered rabbit on whom the hunter's rifle is trained. It is presumably this very vulnerability that initially stirs long-forgotten feelings in Eugene. Yet inasmuch as it falls outside of and thus challenges his predictable world, Tatiana's vulnerability is disconcerting, even threatening to him. We cannot overlook the fact that his "honorable" sermonizing affords Eugene the opportunity to reestablish his control in the face of what is clearly an unexpected move on Tatiana's part. To the various functions Eugene's speech fulfills we add that it reasserts his own code of behavior and bars the otherness of Tatiana's world from penetrating his own. (Indeed, precisely this aspect of his behavior toward Tatiana comes to the fore at the name day festivities, which are discussed in the following chapter of this study.)

In the aftermath of Eugene's response to her letter, Tatiana is left once again confronting the unresolved problem of how to deal with her surfeit of emotion. She has just weathered the collision of that ideal addressee she projected in her letter—one who, as she hoped, would open new worlds to her—with the flesh-and-blood Eugene, who effectively rejects not only Tatiana herself, but also that broad imaginative space of possibility that he was to replenish and sustain. To the highly unsatisfactory options suggested by the all-too-placid lives of her parents and the excessively turbulent emotional experiences of her favorite heroines, Eugene adds only the even less appealing set of alternatives of either a wretched married life with him or a sequence of trivial attachments. In this context the fortune-telling in which Tatiana next engages must be considered as a continued quest for expanded possibility.

5
Tatiana's Dream

But the thoughts we cannot bridle
Force their way without the will . . .
      Byron, "Fare Thee Well"

Fueled by frustrated desire, Tatiana's need for more than her surroundings offer, her longing for the unknown with which to enlarge her familiar world now takes her into the uncertain realm of the supernatural—a
realm in which possibility emerges in the myriad potential meanings that
are seen to reside in ordinary signs. Like her early interest in folktales, Tatiana's participation in fortune-telling rituals is frequently invoked as a
sign of an innate "Russianness" that is counterposed to her imperfect
knowledge of her native tongue and absorption in Western European
novels. Pushkin's own well-documented interest in Russian folklore is
very much in evidence as he enters a detailed account of traditional soothsaying rituals into his text. Indeed, the accuracy of the information he
supplies here has prompted O. N. Grechina to refer to *Eugene Onegin* as
an "encyclopedia of Russian ethnography and folklore of the 1820s."[1]
Pushkin's preoccupation with Russian national identity and particularly
its expression in a developing literary tradition is clearly in evidence in the
record of folk custom we find at this juncture in the text. Like all the oppositions Pushkin sets up in his novel-in-verse, however, the distinction
between Russian and European cultural phenomena—like the distinctions between literature and folklore and literature and life—is eroded by
the dynamic interrelation into which these apparent antipodes are insistently drawn. Thus we can observe that the references to Zhukovskii's
Svetlana in chapter 5 where Tatiana's divinations are described (in the
epigraph and in stanza 10) draw particular attention to the absorption of
the Russian folk idiom into literature. These references serve also as a
convenient reminder of the potent effects of the German preromantics
(whose ethos Zhukovskii was instrumental in introducing to Russia) on
the burgeoning Russian interest in folklore and questions of national and
literary identity. Underlying the "Russianness" evoked in this chapter of

Eugene Onegin, we find also a distinctly European dynamic that has been translated into Russian circumstances.

Tatiana's wholehearted response to English and French novels of sentiment cannot extinguish the folk idiom she absorbed from her nurse any more than the fortune-telling rituals in which she now engages can efface the effects of the novels she has read. At this point in her story Tatiana is described as being in her own element in the Russian winter.[2] Yet we must not lose sight of the fact that she was just as engrossed by her estival European novel reading as she now is in her hibernal Russian fortune-telling. Tatiana is not hemmed in by the opposition of Russian and European, but continues to profit from the interrelation of this antinomial pair.

Here we can observe that even as Pushkin's evocations of *Svetlana* suggest a literary precedent for Tatiana's "folksy" behavior, the function his heroine's fortune-telling games assume in his text departs markedly from literary convention. This situation is summed up by Kelley:

> Contrary to the expected use of prophetic games in literature, the narrator of *Eugene Onegin* never returns to the outcomes of any of these games in such a way as to suggest that they may have come true or that they were misleading. Nor is there any evidence in the novel that Tat'jana ever reflected on her later experiences as having been foretold by these fortune-telling games.[3]

This singular lack of interest in the effects of the various rituals does not necessarily suggest that Tatiana has failed in her efforts, as Kelley goes on to maintain. It can instead be regarded as Pushkin's insistent redirection of attention away from specific consequences of the fortune-telling and toward the expanded possibilities for apprehending the surrounding world that the rituals themselves suggest. In the absence of Tatiana's response to the auguries, their possible import remains in suspension, and the emphasis thus falls on the openness of the meanings that might be derived from them. The fact that Tatiana's immediate reaction to the results of the rituals in which she takes part goes similarly without notice suggests that a replenishment of possibilities and not a specific outcome is at stake here: Tatiana seeks not to secure a knowable future but to escape the limits of the options available to her. The rituals of divination find their way into the text of *Eugene Onegin* not simply because Pushkin wants to familiarize his readers with quaint ethnographic details or provide local color, but because these rituals contribute to the contextual complexity of his work and draw particular attention to the *process of reading signs*.

Tatiana's early preference for fearful tales over childish pastimes[4] now manifests itself as her susceptibility to the seductiveness of terror:

Что ж? Тайну прелесть находила
И в самом ужасе она.

[Yet—fear itself she found presented
a hidden beauty in the end.]⁵

(5:7, ll. 1–2)

This particular description of Tatiana fits in Pushkin's oeuvre, as Chizhevskii has observed,⁶ between the assertion in his 1820 lyric "Mne boi znakom" ("Battle Is Familiar to Me") and the lines from Val'singam's song in *Pir vo vremia chumy* (*Feast in Time of the Plague* [1830]):

Перед собой кто смерти не видал,
Тот полного веселья не вкушал.

[He who has not seen death,
Has not partaken fully of mirth.]

(*PSS*, 2:128)

Всё, всё, что гибелью грозит,
Для сердца смертного таит
Неизъяснимы наслажденья—
Бессмертья, может быть залог!

[All that threatens with destruction,
Harbors for the mortal heart
Ineffable pleasures—
A pledge of immortality perhaps!]

(*PSS*, 7:180)

Here we can also recall other great Pushkinian risk takers: the Pretender from *Boris Godunov* who, unlike Boris whom he seeks to depose, is attracted at least as much by the risk of his enterprise as by the prospect of attaining the throne, and Don Guan from *Kamennyi gost'* (*The Stone Guest* [1830]) who is perhaps of all Pushkin's heroes most addicted to the seductive pleasures of danger.

That the extolment of risk should resonate in the characterization of Tatiana just as she is about to begin her divinations suggests that it is not so much her *narodnost'* (national character) as her liberating readiness to take chances that is at issue here. Indeed, this extolment balances the warnings Pushkin issues against those futile and ultimately limiting attempts to remain always in control that we have noted already in connection with Eugene. Here, as we recognize, is a major theme that Pushkin was to explore in many variations and with ever-increasing intensity—one that although perhaps veiled by the love story is as crucial to *Eugene Onegin* as it is, for example, to *Mozart and Salieri*, "Vystrel"

(The Shot), and *Egipetskie nochi* (*Egyptian Nights*). In the opposition—around which each of these works is built—of the desire to control and the freedom from such desire, Pushkin explores those precarious negotiations between self-mastery and self-abandon that define the creative process—be it of love, of art, or of life.

Tatiana is not deterred by the element of danger. She is inspired by it. Her participation in rituals of divination bespeaks her engagement of chance in an attempt to escape the complacency of her surrounding world. Grechina perceptively notes that Tatiana treats the folk rituals not as "an ossified form, but rather a key facilitating access to mysterious powers."[7] As she stakes her future on a series of disconnected signs (a bit of wax, the song being sung as her ring is drawn out of a bowl of water, the name of a casual passerby) we recognize that this is the closest she can come to the gambling—be it with cards or with dueling pistols—in which men engage. Although ostensibly an attempt to determine the future, the fortune-telling serves more importantly as a means to introduce new variables into an all too easily decipherable existence. With the aid of supernatural forces, conventional boundaries are crossed and conventional relationships disrupted. Engaged is a potential-expanding lack of fixity that is guaranteed by the indeterminacy of the signs and by the inadequacy of the information gleaned from the various rituals—information that is either too vague (e.g., "misfortune") or too particular (e.g., the given name of the future spouse) to be of much value in charting one's life.

We have seen already that the imaginative landscape of the novels Tatiana read and the language they supplied for the recognition and expression of her nascent sexuality nurtured not only flesh-and-blood desires, but also the creative urge into which these desires are absorbed. Tatiana's receptivity to her novels and her assimilation of their worlds into her own are indicative, as we have argued, of the creative potency with which Pushkin invests his beloved heroine. The various folk beliefs which he now introduces highlight another aspect of the creative mind which is prepared to recognize in commonplace signs—dreams, cards, a cat, the moon, a shooting star, a dark monk, or a rabbit crossing the road (5:5–6)—their capacity to point beyond conventional referents, indeed well beyond the actual, literal world to a figurative one that coexists with it. There is nothing exceptional in the list of superstitions to which Tatiana subscribes, except perhaps the notable fact that these were beliefs Pushkin himself shared with his heroine. Unlike Eugene, who purports to foresee everything, and who, resisting all "translation," prefers to assign unequivocal meaning to signs, Tatiana, like her creator, is prepared to chance the possibilities afforded by translations of signs from the confines of a literal world into an unbounded realm of symbolic potentiality. Here the folk imagination vividly demonstrates the transformation of everyday objects into supernatural indicators that pry open, if ever so slightly, the otherwise tightly closed door of the here-and-now.

Fortune-telling demands the dissolution of conventional links between signs and their referents. The consequent instability of meaning—the locus of the supernatural—opens the possibility for startling and thus also potentially revelatory reconfigurations. As the risk of the figurative is undertaken, literal meaning is left behind, and the richly uncertain symbolic, metaphoric power of language is engaged in a radical transformation of the everyday. For Tatiana the rituals suggest another way to construe the surrounding world and her place in it. She scrutinizes familiar signs for expanded meaning in rituals that may be described as fostering yet another type of intersection between the "svoi" (familiar) and the "chuzhoi" (alien). Although fortune-telling presumably suggests various means for glimpsing a destiny that is already in place, the time of divination creates the overpowering sensation that the future is just then being created. It is as if the sign that falls to a person's lot determines what the future will bring and not the other way around. Out of this confusion of cause and effect there emerges the sense of having some part in shaping what the future is to be, while in the active interpretation of the sign, a measure of self-creation is admitted into the destiny of the individual. Originating in the distant past, the rituals are engaged to shape present contingencies into intimations of the future. Both cyclic and linear conceptions of time thus give way before the confluence of past, present, and future that transpires in the process of divination.

Like the superannuated novels Tatiana reads with such earnestness, so too the endlessly repeated rituals to which she resorts are invigorated by the intensity of her need, even as they, in turn, contribute to the expansion of her world. Tatiana is described as taking joy in the recurring signs of winter and in subscribing to age-old superstitions. Her divinations, however, are distinguished from the less than inspired peeps into their mistresses' futures which are undertaken by the maidservants, who year after year arrive at one and the same fortune:

Служанки со всего двора
Про барышен своих гадали
И им сулили каждый год
Мужьев военных и поход.

[The servant maids would guess the fate
Of both young girls with superstition;
Each year they promised, as before,
Two soldier husbands and a war.]
(5:4, ll. 11–14)

Here we can observe that divination can go no further than the imaginative (and grammatical) capacities of the fortune-teller. In their reading of portents, the servant girls fail to get beyond that one rather unoriginal possibility that, tellingly, turns out to be the clichéd Olga's lot. Tatiana's superstitiousness and her intense response to omens (6:5–7)—characteristics she shares with Pushkin himself—signal not only her Russian roots, but also, and doubtless more important, her well-developed imagination and receptivity that act in concert with heightened desire to distinguish her reenactment of the folk rituals from uninspired repetition.

Grechina notes that Pushkin gives a precise account of Tatiana's participation in three distinct categories of what are "increasingly mysterious and frightful types of augury." These types are the group songs, the solitary nocturnal auguries, and, finally, the most dangerous—the calling up of a prophetic dream, an activity that "gives evil forces access to humans."[8] Delineated here is a steady intensification of vulnerability as Tatiana engages an ever-greater range of powers, variables, and uncertainties within an ever more private space. Each ritual marks an increase in the breadth of the *chuzhoi* (alien) and the depth of the *svoi* (familiar) that Tatiana dares to bring together. The axes that are drawn into this intersection are increasingly far-flung.

Whatever they reveal of the Russian folk tradition, the various divination rituals in which Tatiana participates provide distinctly different perspectives on the fluidity of meaning any given sign or configuration of signs can assume. Highlighted here are both the process itself by which meaning is derived and those forces that affect its derivation. That Tatiana does not arrive at a particular meaning for the bit of molten wax to which she links her future in the first divination (5:8, ll. 1–4) focuses our attention on the interpretive possibilities that open when this shard of realia is regarded as an indicator of something beyond itself and the everyday in which it commonly signifies. In the second ritual, songs that have been repeated from time immemorial come to be portents of the future, as their literal meaning is subsumed by a figurative one. In this divination each song has an assigned meaning. Required of the participants is the acceptance of an eerie, incongruous grafting of symbolic significance onto the given text. Thus the song that falls to Tatiana's lot tells of riches but signifies loss or, more specifically, as we learn from the note Pushkin appends, death. Small wonder then that, as the author/narrator relates, another song is dearer to maidens' hearts—the one that tells of cats and presages marriage.

As Pushkin describes it here, this particular folk ritual, like the novels Tatiana has read, suggests only the alternatives of death or marriage—alternatives that tend moreover unsettlingly toward synonymity both in the novels and in the folk idiom, where weddings are commonly described in funerary terms. In her determination to get beyond these options, Tatiana turns to another ritual, but the mirror she holds over her shoulder that frosty night reflects only a solitary moon. Once again Pushkin leaves without record Tatiana's reaction to the omen she encounters. Its possible meanings remain unexplained and continue to radiate in a fullness of engaging ambiguity. In the absence of specific indications as to how this sign is to be regarded, the reader too is drawn to consider and directly experience those contextual forces that exert their pull on any given sign. There is perhaps a touch of the supernatural here as Tatiana, who trains her mirror on a crescent ("mesiats"), sees the reflection of a full moon ("luna")—that very moon, in fact, that shed its light on the composition of her letter to Eugene, yet also the one to which Eugene disparagingly compared Olga's bland visage ("Kak eta glupaia luna" [Like this stupid moon] [3:5, l. 11]). If the reader were to regard the moon in Tatiana's mirror as a portent of her future, would it indicate the creative energy born of heightened desire as exemplified in the letter, or predict the surrender of creative potential to a conventional marriage of the sort on which Olga is preparing to embark? What the moon portends—if indeed it portends anything at all—is suggested by its possible links with details in the text that precedes it and can be determined only with the subsequent unfolding of Tatiana's story, a story which, as we will see, ultimately spans the two seemingly incompatible "meanings" that have been suggested for the moon image in the text thus far.

In the next ritual Tatiana asks a passerby his name—an action that, as Pushkin notes, is believed to supply the augurer with the name of her intended. Once in possession of that name, the augurer is left with a sign to which a referent has yet to be attached. It is obvious, after all, that the same name can belong to very dissimilar people and that to know the name of the intended is not yet to know the intended himself. Pushkin's drafts of this passage suggest that he devoted considerable attention to selecting the name Tatiana would hear in response to her question. They reveal that after considering Miron, Khariton, and Paramon, he settled on Agafon (PSS 6:385 and 603). Like the others in the list of options, this too is a peasant name that, as Lotman has observed, must surely clash with Tatiana's romantic expectations.[9] "Agafon" can neither stimulate her imagination, nor provide a viable option in Tatiana's actual life. Although class distinctions are temporarily blurred in the enactments of the various fortune-telling rituals, Tatiana's brief sally into folk custom cannot permanently efface social boundaries. Her marriage to an "Agafon" remains unthinkable. Yet however briefly and tentatively, the augury has contradicted conventional expectations with its suggestion of this incongruous union. We can observe, moreover, that whatever the sociological unlikelihood of Tatiana's appearing before the altar on the arm of an "Agafon," this improbable pairing has already transpired onomastically. It is precisely where his heroine is named (2:24, l. 1) that Pushkin introduces a footnote in which he lists "Agafon" among those euphonious Greek names that—like the name "Tatiana"— are current in Russia only among the common folk (*PSS* 6:192). Class distinctions may hold their bearers apart, but the names themselves are well suited for conjoining. It is the referent to which "Tatiana" has been attached that disrupts their mutual compatibility.

The folk divinations in which Tatiana has taken part thus far highlight different aspects of the productive lack of fixity in the various signs that are encountered. Thus, to summarize, the molten wax ritual illustrates the extent to which meaning rests in the eye of the perceiver who contemplates the sign and whose fate is thus directly linked to her own powers of the imagination. The song ritual draws attention to the vast difference between the literal and the symbolic meanings that the words of the songs comprise simultaneously. The equivocal moon points to the contextual forces that exert their effect on the derivation of meaning from any particular sign, while the name Agafon underscores the propensity of the sign to indicate many different referents. Demonstrated in all these rituals is the readiness with which any sign lends itself to symbolic usage and provides thereby a means for eluding the conventional, prosaic norms of the day-to-day. Significant too is that the portent of the future lies not in the sign itself, but rather in the reading to which it is subjected. The destiny of the individual is thus bound up with her adeptness at associative, analogical thinking that imbues the random signs made available by the actual world with far-reaching significance. The potential effects of the soothsaying also deserve notice. Anticipation of the fulfillment of the omen as it has been read colors the way subsequent events in the auguring individual's life are construed, even as those events exert a retroactive effect on how the omens might be understood. Thus augury draws the past, present, and future of the individual's story into a mutual interdependency that undermines that very causality that the rituals of divination appear to invoke.

Yet whatever the fortune-telling rituals may suggest to us about broader questions of signification, and for all Tatiana's receptivity to their possible import, she cannot be satisfied with the scant material they have yielded up. Persisting in her search for more gratifying signs according to which to shape her future, Tatiana now undertakes the most risk-laden of the rituals—the dream augury. Common among traditional Yuletide fortune-telling activities, this particular form of divination is intended, as Grechina notes, "not simply to discover the future, but also to assist in its realization."[10] Here protection—whether sacred or magical—must be relinquished, leaving the augurer vulnerable to those potentially danger-ous forces she invokes.[11] It is evident that Pushkin was well versed in the vocabulary of such rituals. Indeed, not only his interest in folk belief, but also his own superstitiousness is well documented. Here we can note too that in ascribing significance to dreams, the Russian folk tradition inter-sects with European culture of Pushkin's time, and that he, "like many creative artists of his generation in Europe, believed that dreams might be prophetic."[12] The specific references to the bathhouse and to Tatiana's re-moval of her belt (5:10) indicate that his heroine is about to engage in a venturesome ritual, for the bathhouse has no protective icons to shield the augurer from the forces she summons, while the undoing of the knot of the belt similarly leaves her open to their effects.[13] According to custom, the participation of an older, experienced woman in such undertakings is obligatory,[14] and Tatiana is guided by her nurse whose otherwise deficient memory has apparently retained this ancient ritual. Here the very need for more than is immediately available that prompts her epistolary sally into the unknown is translated into the folk idiom, which her nurse un-derstands. Having failed to assume the role of active intermediary be-tween Tatiana and Eugene, she now undertakes the mediation of her ward's contact with supernatural forces.

Just as Tatiana was not deterred from writing to Eugene by the awareness that her letter could reach a Grandison or a Lovelace, so too does she now readily engage the unknown forces of what might be good or evil. Her ritual-evoked dream leads into that perilous realm of the su-pernatural—a realm where disassociated meanings hover, waiting for the augurer's summons in order to attach themselves to unexpected signs. The unconscious, which plays a significant role in the reading of the enig-matic signs that are yielded up by auguries, is in evidence particularly in Tatiana's dream. In this sense, her fortune-telling is indeed an affirmation of an unknown that she herself helps to shape.

Even as Tatiana's participation in the auguries draws attention to the indeterminacy of signs, the text of *Eugene Onegin* suggests to its readers a variety of codes (e.g., folkloristic, literary, literal) that can be engaged—with varying results—in attempts to arrive both at what the rituals might mean for Tatiana and at their function within Pushkin's work. It is with this background that the reader now joins Tatiana in confronting a dream in which myriad symbols carouse riotously in defiance of unequivocal meaning. The complexity of these symbols is significantly compounded by the various contexts and multiple codes that have been suggested for their decoding. The many possible readings of the dream jostle elbows, occasionally overlap, and inevitably deny primacy to one another.

Tatiana's dream stands at what was to have been the compositional center of *Eugene Onegin*, which Pushkin had initially envisioned as a nine-chapter work. As such, Grechina observes, it occupies a place analogous to that of Zemfira's song in *Tsigany* (*The Gypsies*).[15] But if in that work the song carries a fairly distinct, readily discernible message—that Zemfira has tired of her possessive paramour and now challenges his attempt to control her—Tatiana's dream, which comes at a crucial point in her development, proffers a baffling complex of possible meanings that remain both elusive and irreducible. If the information yielded up by the other rituals of divination is too scant to be of any particular use, Tatiana's dream offers a surfeit of potential meaning. At the "geometrical center" of Pushkin's novel-in-verse, the illusion of order conventionally imparted to the universe and the language that describes it are—like the protective knot of Tatiana's belt—undone, and Tatiana departs from the world as we know it. The bridge that she crosses in her dream with ursine assistance translates her into a symbolic and metaphoric realm where the literal recedes to reveal virtually illimitable possibilities for meaning, but also the very real threat of chaos. Tatiana's engagement in the dream augury makes explicit not only her latent fears and desires, but also the extraordinary potency vested in figurative language and her own willingness to explore the new, unsettling realm it reveals to her. We have considered already Eugene's inability to escape the narrow confines of a world whose inadequacy he senses but whose limits he cannot bring himself to traverse. Tatiana, by contrast, is prepared to embark on a ritual that leads her into other worlds. The alacrity with which she crosses the torrent in her dream is indicative of the readiness with which she effects the various border crossings we have already considered and those we have yet to discuss—between life and literature, European and Russian, rural and urban, and the actual and the imagined.

Tatiana's dream, which Richard Gregg has aptly described as "an embarrassment of exegetic riches,"[16] has provided fertile ground for testing the critical and imaginative faculties of countless readers. Indeed, Michael Katz has called it "the most complicated and written-about dream in Russian literature."[17] Its signs are many and complex, its function in the text invitingly open to interpretation, and its intertextuality enticing. The dream ensures a rich yield for any number of textual strategies, and it is precisely the polyvalence of Tatiana's nocturnal vision rather than any particular meaning that might be coaxed from it that is crucial here. Not a specific message, but the potential of the dream to signify luxuriates before the reader, for Pushkin has crafted a fruitful confusion of possibilities that defies all attempts at reduction.

It is important not to lose sight of the fact that Pushkin deliberately imbeds Tatiana's dream in the strategic context of the fortune-telling activities. Tatiana does not simply have a dream, she conjures it up herself in a ritual that is expected not simply to disclose her future, but to allow for her own active participation in shaping it.[18] If the early stages of Tatiana's sexual awareness were aligned with the imaginative worlds of the books she read and the novel-oriented reveries they inspired, her heightened erotic desire leads to the very fountainhead of the imagination—a perplexing world where signs are divorced from their conventional referents to suggest uncanny opportunities for new interrelations. In the face of this complexity, the importance of assigning a particular meaning to either the dream or its constituent parts recedes, and the emphasis falls squarely on the functions the dream assumes in the text.

The dream works simultaneously on a variety of levels around which the subsequent discussion will revolve. A heady blend of psychology, folklore, and literature, it is, as commentators concur, a masterful representation of Tatiana's emotional state. (It is here in the space of the heroine's unconscious that critics acknowledge the sexuality that is generally skirted in discussions of her conscious world.) Even as the dream reflects Tatiana's inner turmoil, it also attests to her concerted effort to direct her own future toward expanded possibility. This very stroke that permits Pushkin to underscore his heroine's flexibility provides him also with an opportunity to sport with those of his audience who bring a conventional grammar of reading to his text—a grammar that Tatiana's dream renders hopelessly inadequate. At the same time, specifically in the context of the romantics' alignment of dreams with creative activity, Tatiana's dream emerges as a window on a distinctly poetical space where conventional boundaries are displaced and conventional relationships disrupted by newly generated associative energy.

The divination rituals in which Tatiana has participated thus far underscore the propensity of any given sign to comprehend simultaneously a broad range of figurative meanings and to carry virtually illimitable associative potential. In Tatiana's dream, the openness generated by these possibilities is increased still further by the different contexts in which its images might be considered. Thus we can read the dream within the larger contexts of *Eugene Onegin*, of dreams in works by Pushkin (e.g., *Ruslan i Liudmila*, "Metel'," *Boris Godunov, Kapitanskaia dochka*), of dreams in other literary works, particularly those referred to in *Eugene Onegin* (e.g. the dreams of Clarissa, Werther, and Svetlana), and of dreams as they are construed in the folk tradition. There are, to be sure, significant points of intersection among the distinct perspectives that these various contexts offer, but it remains true that each promotes a different reading, none of which can be singled out as definitive or exhaustive.

Like the graphics of M. C. Escher, Tatiana's dream palpitates with conflicting possibilities that highlight the dynamic generated by the tensions between them. Even the indications of the role it assumes in Tatiana's story are pointedly equivocal. The dream occupies a central place in the narrative structure of *Eugene Onegin*. And yet the injunction of the epigraph from *Svetlana*, "O ne znai sikh strashnykh snov, / Ty moia Svetlana (Oh, never know these frightful dreams, / My dear Svetlana!"), seems to cast doubt on the relevance of the dream to the heroine's story, for Svetlana's nocturnal vision exerts no lasting effect on her waking hours. The epigraph suggests that Tatiana should, like Zhukovskii's heroine, simply wake up from her frightful dream into a happy reality from which all vestiges of those horrors attendant on female sexuality are expunged by conventional matrimony. Read from the perspective of the recent events in Tatiana's story, the dream appears as a forceful rendering of the heroine's psychological state and heightened desire, while the unfolding of subsequent events—Lensky's death by Onegin's hand and Tatiana's marriage in particular—retroactively endows the dream with prophetic significance.

In Tatiana's ritual-invoked dream, points of reference remain too fluid to provide any grounding, and conventional notions of cause and effect are continually thrown into disarray. Thus, for example, we can observe that because Tatiana's name day celebration is an annual event, there is every reason to suggest that the dream is not a prediction of the upcoming festivities, but rather the translation of images from what is for Tatiana an already familiar event—one that, as she knows, is shortly to be repeated—into the dream state. A similar instability between cause and effect is noted by W. F. Ryan and Faith Wigzell, who point out that, inasmuch as Tatiana "habitually took to bed with her" Martin Zadeka's dream book, it can easily "be thought to be the source of, rather than the key to her dreams."[19]

Jakobson has observed that in *Eugene Onegin* "[e]ach of Pushkin's images is so elastically polysemantic and manifests such an amazing assimilatory capacity that it easily fits into the most varied contexts."[20] On the strength of this quality, as Jakobson goes on to describe, the text sustains a broad range of essentially incompatible readings. This very quality, we can elaborate further, is concentrated with particular intensity in Tatiana's dream, where the determinacy of fate itself is undone by the protean nature of the signs that signal it. In this regard the dream can be regarded as an extreme posing of the question—implicit in the indeterminacy of *Onegin* itself—as to how a text is to be read. The dissolution of fixed relationships in favor of new connections and lines of contrast is a vital source of poetic energy. For this energy to remain engaged, however, it is crucial that readers be prevented from reimposing those very boundaries that the text destabilizes. The openness to unconventional possibilities that is cause and consequence of creative writing must inform creative reading as well.

That this particular challenge be concentrated in a dream is highly appropriate. A characteristic peculiar to dreams—one that is shared also by the poetic text—is that the signs operating within them derive their significance from the dynamic interrelationships into which they are drawn and thus can neither be assigned one fixed meaning or function, nor contemplated in isolation from their text. Accordingly, how the symbolic world of the dream is *not* to be approached is demonstrated in Tatiana's quickly abandoned attempt to attach unequivocal referents to individual signs singled out from her dream. The futility of her recourse to Martin Zadeka's dream book is as much a warning to Pushkin's would-be interpreters as a sign of his heroine's bewilderment. Not surprisingly, little is to be gleaned from the disconnected series of "meanings" Tatiana's dream book yields up for the random, decontextualized signs she isolates for explication. As in the other divinatory rituals in which she participates, so too in her dream, the particular "answers" that might be attached to the indicators through which supernatural communications are made pale before the vast possibilities for signification that are suggested. Indeed, the very notion of the "supernatural" as it functions in Pushkin's text can be regarded as an analogue for just such promising uncertainty.

If the dream insists on fluidity of meaning, so too does it underscore the syncretism which is crucial to Tatiana's characterization. Accordingly, Todd observes that "Tatiana's dream shows most completely the range of her cultural resources"[21] and goes on to say that "[i]n this chaotic dream world Tatiana blends the images and patterns of her sentimental readings, her folk heritage, and her social situations as Pushkin has established them earlier in the novel."[22] Concentrated in the dream are those influences that prove crucial to Tatiana's development, and it is here that the question of how these influences might be productively interrelated becomes more pressing:

> The English epistolary novels (2:29), the book for interpreting dreams (5:23), and the mirror for folklore fortune-telling (5:10) that crowd Tatiana's bed give no answers to her fears and desires. They are, rather, emblematic of the cultural elements from which, as she matures, she will assemble and make sense of her life.[23]

Todd's point is well taken, and we have only to shift his focus slightly to recognize that, confronted with the text of Tatiana's dream, the reader of *Eugene Onegin* joins the augurer in an attempt to integrate the enigmatic, often conflicting possibilities suggested by its signs into something resembling a convincing whole.

Here we arrive at a feature of Pushkin's writing elucidated by Caryl Emerson in connection with *Eugene Onegin*, *Boris Godunov*, and particularly "The Queen of Spades," namely, Pushkin's parodying of readers who are determined to reduce the complexity of his works to a comfortable norm. "What is parodied," Emerson notes in her discussion, "is the reader's search for a system or a key, and in this search, the more numerous the partial hints and tantalizing fragments provided by the author, the more challenging and irresistible the search becomes."[24] The warning inherent in such parody is directly applicable to the reading of all literary texts, indeed of life itself, and thus pertinent, as Emerson remarks, to *Eugene Onegin* as well.[25] The element of reader parody described by Emerson is concentrated with particular energy in Tatiana's dream, for in it Pushkin achieves a maximal indeterminacy while yet creating the distinct impression that it harbors a particular, undisclosed meaning. In this respect, Emerson's penetrating observation apropos "The Queen of Spades" is very much to the point: "Pushkin provides us not with a code, and not with chaos, but precisely with the *fragments* of codes, codes that tantalize but do not quite add up."[26]

It is precisely in this carefully crafted quality of "not quite adding up" that we perceive a glimmer of that chaos which, like the potentially dangerous supernatural invoked in Tatiana's dream augury, is engaged in the course of the creative process. Even as Pushkin thumbs his nose at those readers who cannot resist their inclination for reductive analyses of his text, in Tatiana's dream he also reveals essential features of the poetic enterprise. The dream takes Tatiana into a realm that is aligned with sexuality, with the subconscious, and with poetic creativity. Both Ralph Matlaw and Michael Katz rightly warn against linking Pushkin's notion of dreams too closely with the "higher state" or "true state of waking" that the romantics were inclined to see in them, for the mystical aspect of dreams was indeed "essentially foreign" to him.[27] Heightened in Tatiana's dreamworld is the power of figurative language which, as in the other fortune-telling rituals in which she engages, transforms commonplace signs into mysterious indicators of an enticing elsewhere. In this regard the opening statement of G. H. von Schubert's *Die Symbolik des Traumes*, the romantics' "guidebook" to dreams as Chizhevskii refers to it, is very much to the point: "Im Traume . . . scheint die Seele eine ganz andere Sprache zu sprechen" (In dreams . . . the soul seems to speak an entirely different language).[28] The dream language Schubert goes on to describe, to draw on Katz's summary, "is made up of images, objects, and persons connected by laws of association fundamentally different from those governing our conscious lives."[29] Precisely this quality is fore-grounded in Tatiana's dream, and it is on the strength of its associative potentiality and not on mystical grounds that Pushkin relates the dream-world to the poetic.

In dreams, as in poetry, conventional boundaries and relationships are displaced in favor of new, often seemingly improbable connections—connections whose possibilities go largely unremarked in waking or un-poetical hours. In place of a one-to-one correspondence between sign and referent, we encounter a complex, resonant simultaneity of various pos-sibilities resident in each emblem. Thus, for example, the point is not whether the ursine figure in Tatiana's dream stands for Onegin or for the spouse looming in her future, but that this creature, who bears little out-ward resemblance to either gentleman, can be linked more or less plausi-bly with either or with both, and yet remain open to the possibility of still other connections. The impulse to realize associative potential is stimu-lated by the text and draws the reader into direct participation in its recre-ation. Thus to Katz's observation that "[d]reams in Pushkin's works con-stitute a special metaphorical language, different from that used by the fictional characters in their conscious waking states,"[30] we might add that dreams—and Tatiana's in particular—destabilize language in much the same way that Pushkin destabilizes notions of genre, national identity, and cultural phenomena in the course of *Eugene Onegin*.

That such destabilization, which lies at the heart of creative activity, is, like Tatiana's dream augury, a risky enterprise is graphically demon-strated in her dream. Having traversed a barren, moonlit, wintry land-scape, assisted willy-nilly by a helpful but frightening anthropomor-phized bear, Tatiana finds herself on the threshold of a boisterous assemblage of priapic creatures headed by Eugene. The powerful erotic undercurrents in the dream as a whole and particularly in the account of the pandemonium over which Onegin presides in his remote cabin in the woods have received considerable scholarly attention.[31] Of interest to us here is that in charting Tatiana's development Pushkin interrelates his heroine's sexuality with her imagination. As they were also for Pushkin himself, her erotic energies are linked directly to the creative impulse. It is therefore important to consider the bizarre creatures carousing with Onegin for what they suggest to us about the dangers inherent in the cre-ative process. These are creatures of a chaos that manifests itself not sim-ply in their unruly behavior—this Eugene apparently has the power to contain—but in the unsettling incongruity of the parts of which they are assembled.

Grechina situates Tatiana's dream in the fairy tale tradition in which, as she explains, the fantastic derives from unprecedented combinations of recognizable but irreconcilable parts.[32] Lotman, in his discussion of the creatures who carouse with Onegin, similarly focuses on the "conjoining of unconjoinable details and objects," which he connects with representations of evil forces in both medieval iconography and romantic literature.[33] As in other aspects of *Eugene Onegin*, so here too, the folkloristic is virtually indistinguishable from the literary, and Lotman has good cause to speak of the "dual nature" of the dream imagery which derives from both.[34] Indeed, the prodigious variety of works—pictorial, literary, and folk—that have been cited by commentators as exemplifying strange unions like those of the creatures in Tatiana's dream take us into uncanny worlds created by artists as dissimilar as Bosch, Murillo, Callot, Goethe (via de Staël's retelling of the *Walpurgisnacht* from *Faust* in her *De l'Allemagne*), Chulkov, and the anonymous creators of the cheap popular Russian prints known as *lubki*.[35] We can add too that Nabokov suggests an autobiographical underpinning for the dream imagery in which he discerns the aftermath of an Arzamas gathering: "An echo of these dinners, the skeleton of the goose and the remains of its crimson coif will be found in Tatiana's dream."[36] Of interest to us here, however, is not which source or sources might have affected Pushkin's drawing of Eugene's bizarre and boisterous cohorts (his own sketches grace the margins of his manuscript), but rather the prevalence of peculiar graftings of incongruous constituent parts in representations of worlds that are beyond the pale of the everyday.

In the introductory remarks that precede his account of the fortune-telling rituals, the author/narrator notes the tendency of nature itself to conjoin seemingly contradictory elements within its creations:

> Так нас природа сотворила,
> К противуречию склонна.
>
> [For nature—fond of contradictions—
> Has so designed the human heart.]
> (5:7, ll. 3–4)

This is, of course, precisely what Pushkin himself does as he sets out to conjoin life with literature and the Russian folk idiom with the Western European literary tradition within a work that amalgamates two disparate genres. It is also what he does as he creates a novelistic heroine who is also his poetic muse, and who holds in simultaneity the precepts of divergent schools of literature, and the antinomial constructs of rural-urban, Russian-European, folk-gentry, natural-civilized. Yet in Tatiana's dream we observe the same principle giving rise to ghoulish figures—creatures with horns and dog's faces, witches with goat beards, hybrids of crane and cat, and red-capped skulls on goose necks. These bizarre figments of Tatiana's dream serve as a graphic reminder—one much needed given the grace with which Pushkin accomplishes his own impossible graftings in *Eugene Onegin*—that such enterprises are not without their dangers. Thus, for example, the "poetry and prose" and the "ice and flame" of Onegin and Lensky are brought together with ultimately tragic results. Even as he effects unprecedented unions, the poet must be prepared to forestall the chaos and potential destructivity that threaten such risk-laden adventures.

That the risk entailed is a quintessentially poetical one becomes clear when we recognize something that has gone without notice in considerations of Tatiana's dream, namely, that the "conjoining of the unconjoinable" that Lotman distinguishes in Onegin's cohorts is the provenance of figurative language—of the symbolic, metaphoric world of the poetic imagination that, like the rituals of divination that precede the dream, draws together hitherto unwed signs and referents. In this context, the disturbing visual stimuli and the cacophony surrounding them remind us that the very material of his art draws the poet perilously close to chaos. Tatiana's vulnerability as she engages supernatural forces in the ritual of dream divination emerges here as an analogue for the vulnerability of the poet who must engage the figurative potentiality of language.

In this regard, reference to Bosch is particularly appropriate, not simply because his paintings are populated with beings who are, like those in Tatiana's dream, composed of incongruent parts, but more important because the bizarre creatures he depicts are neither grotesque flights of fancy nor attempts to represent daemonic beings, but rather the pictorial realizations of common figures of speech.[37] Indeed, Tatiana's dream harbors concrete vestiges of this very dynamic. Thus, as Grechina notes, the real-life suitors who materialize later in Tatiana's story suggest the fantastic revelers in her dream, in which Tatiana's neighbors Buianov, Petushkov, and Pykhtin—Mssrs. "Brawler," "Roosterson," and "Panter" (the last of whom connects metonymically to the panting bear) appeared as realizations of their names. This link to her dream is reinforced by the figurative "petty devil" in the turn of phrase "melkim besom rassypaias" with which the narrator characterizes the efforts of the last of these suitors (7:26).[38]

Represented in Tatiana's dream, as in Bosch's works, is a realm of chaos that is situated between literal and figurative meaning—a realm that the poet repeatedly traverses and that he must ultimately span in his writings. The venture is a far from certain one, and those who, like Eugene, are wary of relinquishing control may well experience discomfort in the face of the instability threatened by such "translation," which presupposes inscrutable codes beyond their own familiar ones, and includes, moreover, perilous crossings into the wilds of figurative language. In Tatiana's readiness to chance just such uncertainty with her augury by dream, we recognize a characteristic feature of Pushkin himself—one that he has bestowed on his heroine and that distinguishes her from the unventuresome hero opposite whom she plays.

Here it is instructive to consider briefly the contrast that Eugene provides. If the Onegin of chapter 4 demonstrates the negative consequences of the desire for excessive control, the weird creatures of Tatiana's dream warn of the chaos appurtenant to abandon. It is not by chance that in the dream these two extremes, which have figured already in Eugene's characterization, are drawn together. The scene of revelers that Tatiana observes in her dream suggests only the alternatives of chaos or its subjugation. There is no room here for the controlled surrender or for those sallies into uncertainty that are demanded by the creative act. Eugene, who is in control, can subdue and even banish the progeny of chaos. He cannot, however, transfigure it. For all its implicit sexuality, the scene is a barren one. Whatever it reveals of that frustrated desire that has given rise to the dream, it speaks also of the need for mediation between control and abandon, and between form and its transcendence.

The openness of meaning generated by the dream suggests vast potential, but also the threat of meaninglessness. Yet, whatever its perils, under proper guidance, this indeterminacy opens a path to creative freedom even within the bounds of apparent determinism. However restrictive the surrounding world, this freedom can be preserved as long as the potential vested in the fluid relation between signs and their referents continues to be recognized and deployed, and as long as the potential for ever new connections continues to be realized. Pushkin never loses sight of the dangers involved in the approximation to chaos that this dynamic demands, but neither does he forget the threat of stasis that sets in when a safer distance from the brink is maintained. It is in the tension between order and chaos that he situates his own art—a crucial tension that he explores with particular urgency in the great *poema Mednyi vsadnik* (*The Bronze Horseman*).

By investing Tatiana's dream with a surfeit of distinct and yet incompatible clues for its decoding, Pushkin thumbs his nose at those readers who persist in searching for a key to unlock its "meaning." At the same time, however, with this very dream he affords us a glimpse into his *Hexenküche* of a poetic workshop. And what of Tatiana's frustrated desires? Here too an analogy suggests itself. Even as inspiration leads the artist toward those strange conjoinings of the dissimilar from which creative momentum derives, so too does desire effect that two-backed beast of incongruous coupling on which procreation depends.

Just as upon completing her letter to Onegin, Tatiana fails to notice the dawn ("Ona zari ne zamechaet" [3:33, l. 1]), so does she now, in the wake of her dream, remain insensible to the entrance of her rosy, Aurora-like sister ("No ta sestry ne zamechaet" [5:22, l. 1]). Intimated with this parallel is a correspondence between Tatiana's composition of the letter and her engagement in the dream augury. Tatiana's preoccupation with Eugene, as we have seen, fosters the growth of her imaginative faculties, intensifies her desire and leads her to assume risk. Just as the addressee of her letter did not coincide with that actual Eugene who was its recipient, so too is the Eugene of her dream distinct from the actual man who recently sermonized before her. (Indeed, he is no more the actual Eugene than the bear is an actual bear.) When her sister asks her who appeared in her dream, Tatiana makes no reply, but persists in her efforts to make sense of what she has seen.

Tatiana's method is rudimentary, and the alphabetical list of entries she consults in her dream book can do little to enlighten her.[39] The attempt to find an unequivocal meaning for each image that appears in her dream is as naive as it is antipoetical, and Tatiana soon abandons it. She is not one of the readers parodied by Pushkin's text. Her strong sense of the inadequacy of the dream book is correlative with her innate sense of the inadequacy of her surrounding world and parallel to her dissatisfaction with Eugene's response to her letter. Michael Katz suggests that inasmuch as Tatiana fails in her attempt to decipher her dream, her "soul" and her perception of Onegin are revealed "only to the reader and not to Tatyana's conscious self."[40] Just what objective knowledge Tatiana might have derived from her dream, however, remains unclear. Whatever her nocturnal vision reveals of Tatiana's subconscious to her readers, for her it represents the consequence not of a search for answers, but of what is ultimately a richly rewarded quest for something beyond those mundane contingencies that she finds so inadequate. To say that Tatiana failed in her naive attempt to decode her dream is not to say that she remains unaffected by it. Even as it lures readers deep into the poetical realm of analogical thinking, Tatiana's dream yields up for the heroine a future that is enticingly open in its incomprehensibility. Thus, as Matlaw has observed, "the dream itself provides an impetus for her to undertake the long journey towards discovery that is the culmination of Pushkin's novel."[41]

Indeed, though Tatiana can derive no concrete information from the various symbols of her dream, its dynamics provide her with a lesson that proves crucial to her subsequent development. We have seen that from the novels she reads, Tatiana assimilates an idiom that enables her self-expression and the creation of an inspiring addressee in the image of the man she has just met. The folk rituals of divination which culminate in her dream augment what Tatiana has gleaned from the novels with a demonstration of the capacity of the ordinary to point to the extraordinary. As such, the rituals both suggest and reinforce a possibility that is subsequently brought to fruition in Tatiana's story: the muselike Eugene, whom she composed on that inspired moonlit night as she penned her letter and whom she continues to ponder with increasing intensity, need not be displaced by the actual man who, although he little resembles her ideal, can nevertheless continue to indicate it. If there is any reassurance to be found in the fortune-telling activities, it is not in possible "answers," but in the capacity displayed by signs to indicate vast reaches of signification beyond themselves. The limited options open to Tatiana in the actual world are expanded dramatically in the coterminous world of the imagination—that very world, in fact, that provided Pushkin himself with the means to rise above the ignominious constraints to which he was constantly being subjected.

In light of the author/narrator's emphasis on Tatiana's attraction to danger and on the risk inherent in the enactment of this particular ritual of divination, the dream conveys the intensity with which Tatiana wants Eugene to be more than that disappointing sermonizer who materialized in response to her letter. The "son tiazhelyi" (heavy dream) to which Tatiana refers in her letter (l. 74), and which has surely been interrupted by Eugene's speech, gives way to the dream she herself conjures up. The enigmatic image of Eugene that appears to her in this dream—an image that is both "dear and terrifying" ("i mil i strashen")—must be particularly enticing for Tatiana. In this sense the dream, for all its densely priapic imagery, is not simply an indicator of unsatisfied erotic desire, but also itself the satisfaction of Tatiana's need to enlarge the scope of the day-to-day and to find a Eugene who is out of the ordinary. Indeed, the uneasy stirrings of guilt she experiences after Onegin kills Lensky in the duel may well stem not only from the fact that she continues to love the assassin of her would-be brother-in-law, but also from the fact that it is *she* who, discontented with Eugene in his guise as her frosty lecturer, conjured up his daemonic side and thus participated in shaping this tragic future.

The Eugene whom Tatiana now contemplates is a multifaceted creature whose various guises are scarcely more coherent than the assembled parts of his fantastic fellow revelers in her dream. He is the hero of her readings and the muse who inspired her writing. He is also the actual man who cut short her daydreams with his sermon, only to reappear in an erotically charged, symbolic dream to claim her as his own with the disturbing neuter possessive pronoun "moe" (5:20, l. 1). It is in this bewildering context that Tatiana's third actual meeting with Eugene takes place.

Tatiana's second encounter with Eugene, in the wake of her letter, was preceded by intense anticipation. His appearance at her name day celebration, however, catches her unawares. That Eugene is naturally among those invited to the festivities is something Tatiana surely must have known together with the reader who has been apprised of the fact in 4:49. Yet Tatiana, it seems, has taken Eugene at his word, and what she understood to be his unequivocal rejection of her advances is apparently enough to convince her that he will not accept the invitation.

In the motley crowd of guests who swarm to the celebration, in the din and overall excitement it generates, we recognize a benign echo of the daemonic carousing in Tatiana's dream. Whether or not Tatiana is sensible of this similarity remains undisclosed. It is clear, however, from her reaction to Eugene's appearance that the dream has intensified the very desire that fed it. The emotional turmoil his arrival elicits is described in frankly sexual terms reminiscent of her dream. At the same time, however, the reference to a pale, morning moon harks back to Tatiana's completion of her letter, while the hunted fawn reminds us of the hunted rabbit to which she was compared as she awaited Eugene's response to her letter (3:40, ll 12–14):

> Сажают прямо против Тани.
> И. утренней луны бледней
> И трепетней гонимой лани.
> Она темнеющих очей
> Не подымает: пышет бурно
> В ней страстный жар: ей душно, дурно.

> [Just facing Tanya's where they're sitting;
> and paler than the moon at dawn,
> she lowers darkened eyes, unwitting,
> and trembles like a hunted fawn.
> From violent passions fast pulsating
> she's nearly swooned, she's suffocating.][42]
>
> (5:30, ll. 1–6)

This multifaceted description of Tatiana's reaction recalls three significant points of contact with Eugene: the letter, his reply to it, and her dream of him. In the context of these subtly evoked "meetings" we can recognize the uniqueness of the present one, for, although hero and heroine remain at cross-purposes, this encounter marks the first time that we witness them interacting with one another in the actual world. The import of the conventionally privileged "first meeting," it will be recalled, was discounted, and it remained undescribed. The second transpired between Tatiana and the hero *she* wrought in the abstract space of her letter. The third—a monologue delivered to a silent auditor abstracted by Eugene into an impersonal audience—appeared to close down rather than to foster communication between them, while the dream encounter took place in an elsewhere well beyond the actual world.

In the absence of any references to Tatiana's anticipation of another meeting, it comes as a surprise to her and to Pushkin's reader when Onegin bursts onto the scene in the midst of the revelry and the middle of a stanza (29). Caught off guard, Tatiana is nearly overwhelmed by emotion when Eugene is seated directly opposite her. Accustomed to shielding her inner self from public scrutiny, she now too, although on the verge of tears and fainting, neither cries nor loses consciousness, but retains her place at the table and continues to preside over both the festivities and her own turbulent feelings. The source of her self-control is spelled out with a vigorous directness: "No volia i rassudka vlast' / Prevozmogli" (but will, and reason's strong constraint, / prevailed [5:30, ll. 11–12]).[43] This brief but forceful explanation highlights the positive counterexample Tatiana provides to Eugene. While his youth was marked first by surrender to unbridled passion and then by the adjustment of his emotions to shallow societal norms that sapped their vigor, Tatiana is shown to resort to her own powers of will and reason to rule (*not* suppress) the feelings that well up inside her upon Eugene's appearance. The words *volia* (will) and *rassudok* (reason) resonate with tremendous significance in Pushkin's lexicon in connection with the act of governance—whether of individual self or of state. Their conjunction is the source of genuine liberty—personal and political—and the responsibility on which it is founded. It is precisely with this victory of will and reason over her seething, conflicting emotions that Tatiana comes into her own.

Eugene, who has taken no interest in the pie that deflects the guests' attention from the agitated Tatiana at this point, remarks both the brief eruption of her feelings and her successful containment of them. Long accustomed to the controlled deployment of feigned emotions—the common currency in his circle—Eugene, as the author/narrator informs us here, can experience only irritation at the sight of tears and swoons. Yet it is just when Tatiana succeeds in holding back her tears and arresting her faint—indeed, just when she adheres to that very injunction with which he concluded his sermon to her, "Uchites' vlastvovat' soboiu" (Learn to control yourself)[44]—that Eugene is overcome with irritation and, in what appears to be a displaced gesture, determines to wreak vengeance on the unsuspecting Vladimir. Lensky is, to be sure, responsible for bringing Eugene to this large gathering, having assured him that only the immediate family would be present (4:49), but this generally unquestioned motivation does not account fully for Eugene's subsequent behavior. At this point the narrator seems to forget about Tatiana. Yet whatever the focus of the narrator's attention, it is not likely that Tatiana would remain oblivious to Eugene's actions nor that Eugene would lose sight of the effect they have on Tatiana. Particularly in light of the fact that his thoughts of vengeance are triggered specifically by the self-mastery Eugene observes her achieve, we can recognize that his behavior is calculated not only to upset Lensky, but also to disconcert Tatiana.

Certainly her behavior is disconcerting to him. Eugene may well be disturbed by his own incapacity to experience reciprocal emotions similar in intensity to Tatiana's. The blushing, tremulous woman before him can only remind him of that youth which, as he explained in his speech to her, he no longer hopes to recapture. Yet perhaps more to the point here is that Tatiana's behavior has deviated from the single script Eugene knows and anticipates. To begin with, she did not renew her efforts to win his attention after he rejected her, as his "philosophy of love" predicted she would. (Indeed, we can speculate here that it may well be this very noncompliance on Tatiana's part that prompts him first to inquire after her [4:48] and then to attend her name day celebration.) Upon his arrival he observes a similar deviation from the behavior he anticipates as Tatiana reveals her strong feelings for him, but neither loses control in the face of his sudden appearance, nor uses this opportunity to try to "ensnare" him.

Onegin contents himself with composing epigrams at the expense of those assembled around the table, while the narrator, like the guests he describes, becomes too absorbed in the comestibles to pay any heed to Tatiana. Indeed, the hero's thirst for revenge is all but forgotten in the midst of the descriptions of the food and drink enjoyed by the revelers. As the guests, in turn, offer their congratulations to Tatiana, Eugene bestows upon her a silent bow and a tender gaze that can only arouse those hopes that are soon to be dashed by the attention he lavishes on Olga:

> Он молча поклонился ей;
> Но как-то взор его очей
> Был чудно нежен. Оттого ли,
> Что он и вправду тронут был,
> Иль он, кокетствуя, шалил,
> Невольно ль, иль из доброй воли,
> Но взор сей нежность изъявил:
> Он сердце Тани оживил.

> [He bowed to her in silence, grave . . .
> But somehow just the look he gave
> Was wondrous tender. If asserting
> Some feeling for Tatyana's lot,

> Or if, unconsciously or not,
> He'd only teased her with some flirting,
> His look was still a tender dart:
> It reawakened Tanya's heart.]
>   (5:34, ll. 7–14)

The ambiguity of the look, which perplexes the narrator and disarms the unsuspecting Tatiana, suggests Eugene's ambivalence as he confronts a young, inexperienced provincial girl whose actions he, with all his worldly experience, has failed to anticipate. Tatiana's unsettling departure from the conventional norms that determine his own discourse with the surrounding world poses a threat and a challenge to Eugene. Potentially liberating, this departure undermines that sense of control he values so highly. Eugene need not be in love with Tatiana to recognize that she is not like the other women he has known. It becomes increasingly clear that interaction with her would not take the all too familiar course he envisioned, but would be an unpredictable venture. He stands briefly on the threshold of risk, only to retreat to the safety of those conventions he has mastered. Although purportedly designed to infuriate Vladimir, his "revenge" is clearly directed no less—indeed, perhaps more—at the woman to whose challenge he did not rise than at his ostensible victim whose more conventional challenge is soon accepted. The narrator's account of the remainder of the evening focuses exclusively on the attention Eugene lavishes on Olga and the jealousy it inspires in Vladimir, and the chapter culminates with the departure of a seething Lensky, who is determined to duel with Onegin. Vladimir's "poetic" formulation of the circumstances recalls those signs of destiny offered by the rituals of divination with which the chapter opened:

> Две пули—больше ничего—
> Вдруг разрешат судьбу его.

> [A brace of pistols and a shot
> Shall instantly decide his lot.]
>   (5:45, 13–14)

Here, however, metaphorical potential is destined for grim realization, for Lensky's fate is, in fact, decided by two bullets (5:45, ll. 13–14).

Tatiana's reaction to the trying evening remains unrecorded until the following chapter. Yet it takes no great powers of the imagination to sense the anguish she must have experienced when Eugene followed the tender gaze that aroused her hopes with obvious signs of preference for Olga. Nor can we overlook the fact that the self-conscious Eugene could scarcely remain oblivious to the effect his behavior would have on Tatiana. Indeed, the dissatisfaction with himself that he experiences the fol-

lowing day is couched in terms that apply to his behavior not only toward
Lensky, but toward Tatiana as well:

> Во первых, он уж был не прав,
> Что над любовью робкои, нежнои
> Так подшутил вечор небрежно.

> [last night he'd erred in making fun,
> so heartless and so detrimental,
> of love so timorous and gentle.]⁴⁵
> (6:10, ll. 4–6)

When the name day feast comes to an end, Tatiana, finding herself
alone at last, sits in a window, where, illuminated by the moon, she takes
stock of her emotions and attempts to make sense of Eugene's ambivalent
behavior. Her very perplexity is to her credit and distinguishes her from
the impetuous Lensky, who must pay with his life for his overhasty assessment of Olga's actions as female perfidy. In this sense we can say that
he dies a victim, not so much to Onegin's spleen or Olga's fickleness, as
to his own inability to recognize that the signs he confronts can carry
meanings that do not necessarily coincide with those of his own predetermined system. Even when disabused of the notion of any serious interest in Onegin on Olga's part, Lensky remains within the limits of his
adopted tenets and casts Eugene in the role of an evil seducer who must
be prevented from destroying the maiden's now-rehabilitated purity. If
Eugene's participation in the duel is dictated by a preestablished social
code, Vladimir's is dictated by idealistic notions that remain divorced
from actuality. It is clear that someone who remains fixed within an abstract, predetermined world and fails to interrelate the imaginary with the
actual could never develop into a full-fledged poet. J. Thomas Shaw observes that Lensky "dies as a poet because he lacks the potentiality for poetic maturity."⁴⁶ The very weakness that curtails Lensky's poetic development leads him also to an untimely death.

Onegin considers signs to be carriers of false meaning. Lensky regards them as carriers of unequivocal meaning, and there is ultimately little difference between these seemingly distinct but equally erroneous
views. It is only Tatiana who is alive to the polyvalence of signs. Yet although vital, this awareness makes her present situation all the more
difficult. Baffled by the inexplicable incongruity of Eugene's tender gaze
and his subsequent behavior no less than by her enigmatic dream, Tatiana
falls back on familiar terms in her attempt to dispel her perplexity. Eugene's tactics mystify her, and it is this mystery that holds her in the thrall
of love for him. Convinced he cannot bring her happiness, Tatiana prepares to perish at his hands:

«Погибну», Таня говорит,
«Но гибель от него любезна.
Я не ропщу: зачем роптать?
Не может он мне счастья дать».

["I'll die," she whispers to the dawn,
("But death from him is sweet compassion.
Why murmur vainly? He can't give
The happiness for which I live.")]

[6:3, ll. 11–14]

This admittedly naive profession of devotion, which Lotman calls "coarse stereotyping" ("zhestkie stereotipy") dictated by Tatiana's romantic and folkloric tendencies,[47] can be seen as a retreat that parallels Eugene's from an incomprehensible situation into familiar territory. Failing to make sense of one another, hero and heroine withdraw—each to a separate world.

Significantly, it is not a direct encounter with Eugene, but one mediated by the books in his library, that provides Tatiana with a bridge to his alien world. In the course of a solitary ramble through the countryside, Tatiana happens on Eugene's deserted estate, much as Germann of "The Queen of Spades" was to wander through Petersburg only to find himself unexpectedly before the home of the countess who held the secret of the three cards.[48] Clearly Tatiana is in the grip of the conflicting signs she is left to contemplate in the wake of Eugene's departure. His contradictory behavior at her name day festivities and the duel in which he kills Olga's unfortunate suitor in seeming fulfillment of Tatiana's own dream have intensified her need to make sense of him. At the same time, her emotions are significantly complicated by the jealousy, heightened desire, and guilt that attach themselves to her love for the enigmatic Eugene.

The confluence of heightened desire and heightened creativity we observed already in connection with Tatiana's letter to Eugene is once again evoked as she approaches his library. That Tatiana arrives at Eugene's manor house on a moonlit evening connects the reading on which she is about to embark with the moonlit writing that was dictated by her frustrated emotions in chapter 3. Like the writing of her letter earlier, so now her reading is noted twice as being undertaken in solitude: "Chtob knizhki zdes' odnoi chitat'" (To read books here alone [7:20, l. 14]) and "Ostalas' nakonets odna" (Was finally left alone [7:21, l. 140]). And, like her writing earlier, so too her reading is preceded by tears which we so seldom see Tatiana shed. The moonlight, the solitude, and the tears highlight the intensely personal, emotionally charged nature of the reading in which she is about to engage.

Tatiana now enters Eugene's own setting, which augments those in which she actually saw him and those she has created for him in her imagination. That the living space of a character reflects his or her inner world is a literary commonplace, and guided by his housekeeper, Tatiana now intently studies Eugene's home and the objects with which he surrounded himself for clues to his mysterious personality. Her pulse may well quicken as she gains access to Eugene's rooms, for both in *Clarissa* and in *The New Eloise*, entry into private space—accomplished first by means of illicit correspondence and then *in corpora*—is a prelude to physical intimacy between hero and heroine. That it is Tatiana who writes the first letter and that it is she who now enters Eugene's rooms marks a significant departure from the novels she has read, for in them the penetration of private chambers, like the initiation of illicit correspondence, is an exclusively male prerogative.

In the rooms the housekeeper shows Tatiana, the reader recognizes the statuette of Napoleon and the portrait of Lord Byron. For Tatiana, however, these signs of Eugene's derivative romantic egotism have no meaning. In tacit acknowledgment of the formative influence of her own reading, she turns to Eugene's books in an attempt to make sense of him, and it is through this imaginative medium rather than his actual world that she comes to know him. That Eugene himself is no reader was noted earlier in the text (1:44), and is reiterated here (7:22, ll. 1–2). We have observed already that Pushkin represents the capacities to read, to write, and to love as correlative and that the abilities to read, write and enter into meaningful relationships are expressly denied Eugene from the very start (1:43, ll. 7–11). Accordingly, Pushkin's earlier plan to provide Tatiana with Eugene's private journal gave way to her discovery of his annotated books. The solution is a felicitous one inasmuch as it highlights Tatiana's reading ability without granting the hero a self-expressivity that is inconsistent with his characterization thus far.

Pushkin, who made direct reference to the specific works that proved crucial to his heroine's development, is deliberately vague when it comes to describing the contents of Eugene's library.[49] Whereas Tatiana, as we have seen, is accorded a particular, carefully crafted literary genealogy that is ostensibly shaped by her own tastes and emotional needs, Eugene is loosely connected with a jumble of fashionable literary texts that depict contemporary man and suggest a generalized model of behavior. With each of his four drafts of this section, Pushkin's catalogue of Eugene's books grew shorter and less specific, until in the end there remained only a reference to Byron and "two or three novels" of the period:

> Певца Гяура и Жуана,
> Да с ним еще два-три романа,
> В которых отразился век,

И современный человек
Изображен довольно верно
С его безнравственной душой,
Себялюбивой и сухой,
Мечтанью преданной безмерно,
С его озлобленным умом,
Кипящим в действии пустом.

[The bard of Juan and the Giaour,
And some few novels done with power,
In which our age is well displayed
And modern man himself portrayed
With something of his true complexion—
With his immoral soul disclosed,
His arid vanity exposed,
His endless bent for deep reflection,
His cold, embittered mind that seems
To waste itself in empty schemes.]
(7:22, ll. 5–14)

The focus here is not on individuated works or characters, but on a literary type that originates with the eponymous hero of Benjamin Constant's *Adolphe* and culminates with Byron's Don Juan and Giaour—disillusioned heroes who both reflected and perpetuated what quickly became both in literature and in life a morally and aesthetically impoverished ethos. Pushkin first eliminated references to books which would, in Gibian's observation, "have given but a slight and misleading glimpse of Onegin's character,"[50] and then went on to excise even the more apt references to *Melmoth, René,* and *Adolphe*. Although removed from the final version of *Eugene Onegin,* reference to this last work was to resurface in Pushkin's note "O perevode romana B. Konstana *Adol'f*" ("On the Translation of B. Constant's *Adolphe*") which appeared, unsigned, in the January 1830 issue of the *Literary Gazette (Literaturnaia gazeta)*. In this announcement of the imminent publication of Petr Viazemskii's Russian rendition of the work, Pushkin quotes lines 8–14 of the passage from *Eugene Onegin* cited above when he refers to this influential French work as being among the *"two or three novels"* (Pushkin's emphasis) that reflect the times and contemporary man.

In Eugene's library of books that promote egotism and feed not love (as did her own books) but amour-propre, Tatiana once again exercises her virtuosic reading skills and demonstrates that exceptional receptivity that is her defining feature. That these books, as the narrator explains, open another world for her ("I ei otkrylsia mir inoi" [7:21, l. 14]) is no hyperbole, for documented in them she finds a moral stance and an emotional and psychological condition that she has never before encountered in either her day-to-day life or her reading. The literal journey Eugene undertakes after his duel with Lensky is paralleled by Tatiana's figurative one through the newly discovered world of Onegin's books. Her reading is not the casual browsing for a fashionable role model that Eugene's appears to have been, nor yet a passage from place to place in the attempt to evade responsibility in the actual world. It is an intensely pursued personal quest to understand the man she loves. Tatiana reads from within.

If the books she discovers in Eugene's library suggest his sources, the signs of Eugene's private responses to the texts reveal to the discerning Tatiana the contours of his very soul:

> Везде Онегина душа
> Себя невольно выражает
> То кратким словом, то крестом,
> То вопросительным крючком.
>
> [And on those pages everywhere
> She found Onegin's soul reflected—
> In crosses or a jotted note,
> Or in the question mark he wrote.]
>   (7:23, ll. 11–14)

The fashionable literary school that supplied Eugene's models of behavior received criticism in the third chapter of *Eugene Onegin*, where it appeared as a negative counterexample to the earlier literary period to which the books in Tatiana's library belonged:

> А нынче все умы в тумане,
> Мораль на нас наводит сон,
> Порок любезен—и в романе,
> И там уж торжествует он.
>
> [But now our minds have grown inactive,
> We're put to sleep by talk of "sin";
> Our novels too make vice attractive,
> And even there it seems to win.]
>   (3:12, ll. 1–4)

But it is not only Eugene's reading material that is suspect. It is also how he engages it in the conduct of his own life that comes under attack. Eugene's public reenactment of his readings stands as a negative counterexample to Tatiana's private, empathetic response to novels that provided her with an idiom for self-expression. It is precisely because Tatiana is herself a consummate reader who allows for the fruitful interpenetration of life and literature that she not only penetrates the new worlds of the texts themselves, but succeeds in reconstructing the reader who has left his marks on them. With this reconstruction comes the suspicion that Eugene is but an unwitting parody of those enervated romantic heroes she finds in his fashionable books:

Чудак печальный и опасный,
Созданье ада иль небес,
Сей ангел, сей надменный бес,
Что ж он? Ужели подражанье,
Ничтожный призрак, иль еще
Москвич в Гарольдовом плаще,
Чужих причуд истолкованье,
Слов модных полный лексикон? . . .
Уж не пародия ли он?

[A strangely bleak and reckless creature,
Issue of Heaven or of Hell,
Proud demon, angel—who can tell?
Perhaps he is all imitation,
An idle phantom or, poor joke,
A Muscovite in Harold's cloak,
An alien whim's interpretation,
Compound of every faddish pose . . . ?
A parody, perhaps . . . who knows?][51]
(7:24, ll. 6–14)

Tatiana is quick to perceive the connection between Eugene's self-stylization and his books. Whatever the sentimental sensibilities that informed her fantasies, they do not prevent her from reassessing the man who gave rise to the hero/muse of her imagination. That very "rassudok" (reason) that enabled her self-mastery at her name day celebration is apparently engaged also in Tatiana's emotionally charged reading. Though Tatiana loses a great deal with this solution of what is now called a "riddle" ("zagadka" [7:25, l. 1]) rather than a mystery, she does not delude herself or shy away from reevaluating her erroneous notions about Eugene. Her muse and the possibility she vested in him recede as she considers Eugene's past behavior from the new vantage point his library has provided. (It is also against this literary background that Tatiana assesses Eugene's demonstrative professions of love in the final chapter of the work.) For all the urgency with which she peruses Eugene's books and studies the laconic signs of his response to them, she retains sufficient distance on both the novels in question and their annotator to perceive those two distinct planes on whose simultaneity parody depends. The implications of Tatiana's achievement are elegantly summarized by George Gibian:

In the poem [*Eugene Onegin*] the works of Byron and other romantics reveal to one character how another character has destroyed his own identity by becoming a living pseudo-Byronic shadow. A derivative and unreal creature, Onegin is the verdict passed by Pushkin on the whole romantic generation which included Byron himself.[52]

The source of Tatiana's success in this regard is to be found in the quality of her relation to the imagination in general and to literary texts in particular. Todd regards Tatiana's reading of Eugene's books as a step in a maturation process which he construes in terms of an increasing separation of life from literature:

Tatiana understands from observing Eugene that life can be a reflection of literary stereotypes, something she could not understand when she was unconsciously following them herself. Her new approach to the relationship of literature and life is a mature one, for she is now aware that such imitation is not a matter of mere reproduction, but can be distorted by parody or inappropriate in its context . . . .[53]

Yet while we can agree with Todd that Tatiana recognizes the parodic distortion of literature in Eugene's behavior, the notion that she herself unconsciously mimics literary stereotypes does not, as we have suggested earlier, square with the author/narrator's accounts of her reading and composition of the letter. The ability to integrate the actual world with that of the imagination remains a constant in Pushkin's characterization of Tatiana and serves as a counterexample to the other characters, who fail in precisely this respect. Tatiana does not merely mimic what she reads as does Eugene; she *translates* it into her own world, and this root metaphor of translation champions the intersection of the familiar and the new on which Pushkin predicates creative momentum. The *quality* of Tatiana's reading—characterized by her openness to the texts and by the grace with which she absorbs them into her own life—remains unchanged whether she is reading Richardson or Byron. The central opposition is to be found not between her earlier reading and that in which she now engages in Eugene's library, but rather between the *way* she and Eugene relate to their books. Revealed to Tatiana, and to Pushkin's reader, are not only Eugene's literary sources, but, above all, the weakness of his interaction with his books. It is precisely what Todd calls "mere reproduction"—something of which Tatiana is not guilty—that gives rise to Eugene's involuntarily parodic behavior, as he decontextualizes and indiscriminately appropriates the features not of a particular character, but of a generalized literary type. Eugene remains trapped in the accoutrements of the modern hero and exemplifies a wasting relationship between life and literature that is distinctly unlike Tatiana's perfect assimilation of her reading material. Contrasted to Eugene's unreflecting approximation, is Tatiana's creative absorption.

Here it is necessary to observe that commentators generally dismiss Tatiana's earlier reading as marking a stage in her development that is superseded when, with the help of Eugene's more recent books, she penetrates his world. Yet the novels in her own library must not be forgotten. Tatiana is quick to understand Eugene from his books not because she has matured beyond confusing life with literature, but precisely because her own earlier reading affords her a context in which she can evaluate Eugene's. Indeed, the fact that she is privy to a larger literary framework of which Eugene is ignorant gains her considerable advantage over him as a reader.

It is important to note that Tatiana's reading of discovery in Eugene's library is at the same time a reading of recognition, for opposite the new heroes she now encounters are heroines whose roles have remained essentially unchanged and who are therefore already familiar to her. We are alerted to this circumstance by a passage from Pushkin's *Novel in Letters* to which we alluded earlier. In that work Liza makes an observation apropos eighteenth-century epistolary novels that is directly relevant to our present discussion:

> Чтение Ричардс.<она> дало мне повод к размышлениям. Какая ужасная разница между идеалами бабушек и внучек. Что есть общего между Ловласом и Адольфом? между тем роль женщин не изменяется; Кларисса, за исключением церемонных приседаний, всё же походит на героиню новейших романов. (*PSS* 8:47–48)

> [Reading Richardson has given me cause for contemplation. What a frightful difference there is between the ideals of grandmothers and their granddaughters. What do Lovelace and Adolphe have in common? the role of women, meanwhile, remains unchanged. Clarissa, her formal curtsies aside, still resembles the heroines of the latest novels.]

This passage serves as a convenient reminder of a crucial element that has gone unheeded in discussions of Tatiana's study of Eugene's books. Even as it shatters the image of the hero she has cast opposite herself, the reading in which she now engages reaffirms that very identity she has, with the help of her novels, shaped for herself. It is only Eugene and not Tatiana who must undergo substantial reevaluation in light of what she now reads. Indeed, if Constant's *Adolphe* is one of the books Eugene read and annotated—and we have every reason to believe it is—Tatiana finds in Eugene's library a fictional representation of one of her favorite authors. Whether or not she realizes that Ellénore, who plays opposite Adolphe, is based on Germaine de Staël, Tatiana would see in her, as she would also in the women in Byron's works, a heroine of the type she herself identified with when she read Richardson, Rousseau, and de Staël. The necessary intersection of the familiar ("svoi") and the alien ("chuzhoi") is once again in place. Against the *cantus firmus* of the role assigned women, Tatiana assesses Eugene and the new departure of the heroes on whom he styles himself. Within this context shaped by the continuity of literary heroines and the discontinuity of literary heroes, she comes to understand that although Eugene is neither a Lovelace nor a Grandison, neither is he a hero who can be counted on to assist in the expansion of her limited world.

Here it is not difficult to recognize that the statement on reading implicit in the juxtaposition of the way Tatiana and Eugene relate to books is directly relevant to writing as well. The momentum of literary process, Pushkin indicates, is ensured by the productive assimilation and expansion of extant idioms, and not by mere imitation. Thus, for example, while Eugene's heedless mimicry of Adolphe leads to a dead end, Viazemskii's translation of *Adolphe* fosters the assimilation of a foreign idiom that expands the Russian literary language and opens a new world for Russian letters.[54] David Bethea has argued persuasively that Pushkin was

> one of the first Russian writers to make the tradition conscious of itself as both European *and* other and to teach it to borrow and rework prior sources—often ones that were foreign and therefore in the reading public's eye privileged.[55]

Indeed Pushkin's own interest in Viazemskii's translation project attests to the importance he ascribed to such borrowings. In his "On the Translation of B. Constant's *Adolphe*," Pushkin writes of his anticipation of the forthcoming Russian rendering of the French work:

> С нетерпением ожидаем появления сей книги. Любопытно видеть, каким образом опытное и живое перо кн. Вяземского победило трудность метафизического языка, всегда стройного, светского, часто вдохновенного. *В сем отношении перевод будет истинным созданием и важным событием в истории нашей литературы.* (PSS 11:87, my emphasis)

> [With impatience we await the appearance of this book. It is curious to see how the experienced, lively pen of Prince Viazemskii conquered the difficulty of metaphysical language that is always balanced, urbane, often inspired. In this regard *the translation will be a genuine creative act and an important event in the history of our literature.*][56]

That Pushkin recognized translation as a creative act must be kept in mind in any assessment of the way Tatiana relates to her books, for her incorporation of their idioms into her own personal development directly parallels the incorporation Pushkin observed and encouraged of the European literary idiom into a developing Russian literary tradition.

In the continuation of the passage from *A Novel in Letters* cited above, Liza speculates on why men's roles in novels underwent such great alteration while women's remained constant:

> Потому ли, что [способы] нравиться в мужчине зависят от моды, от минутого мнения . . . а в женщинах—они основаны на чувстве и природе, которые вечны. (*PSS*, 8:48)

> [Can this be because in a man the means to please depend on fashion, on fleeting opinion . . . while in women they are based on feeling and nature which are eternal.]

Central to Liza's observation is that very issue of negotiating between tradition and invention that is enacted as Tatiana develops both as a heroine and as a reflection of Pushkin's thinking about his art. Here we can step back to observe that the rapid change which gives rise to emotionally impoverished heroes like Adolphe, Childe Harold, and Eugene is clearly no alternative to the repetition that yields up commonplaces like Olga. The E and O Tatiana traced with her finger on a misty window pane as she eagerly awaited Eugene's response to her letter could well suggest Eugene and Olga to Pushkin's reader, for both characters emerge as copies of exhausted literary originals and are in this regard ideally suited to one another—elective affinities. It is worth noting here that Olga—whom the author/narrator styles as a no longer viable literary cliché—bears no resemblance to the heroines Tatiana encounters first in her own library and then in Eugene's. Their constancy, which, like Tatiana's own, argues for continuity in the face of a fashion-driven world, is of a distinctly different order from mere replication that must always be unwittingly unfaithful like Olga or unwittingly parodic like Eugene.

At the heart of Tatiana's own constancy, as we will elaborate in the following chapter, is the fact that she neither shies away from what the actual world reveals, nor abandons the imaginary. Neither here in the privacy of his secluded and now-abandoned estate, nor later in the dazzling public sphere of St. Petersburg society where he takes every opportunity to display his attraction to her, does Tatiana delude herself concerning Eugene's character as it is now revealed to her. Crucial to her subsequent development is whether the actual Eugene as she has come to know him and the hero/muse she once saw in him can be made to coexist. We may briefly anticipate the unfolding of events by noting that in the concluding chapter of Pushkin's work, Eugene must similarly confront and learn to reconcile two seemingly incompatible guises of Tatiana, when the callow rural girl he once knew unexpectedly appears before him as the Princess N. For Tatiana the breaking away of the actual man from the ideal she herself created is a major impetus for the growth and development of her inner world. The "you" ("vy") of Eugene and the "thou" ("ty") of the male muse that we considered in Tatiana's letter already suggested the possibility that the distinct identities of Eugene as man and as muse can coexist. By the end of her story, Tatiana comes to appreciate more fully that although she is disillusioned in the flesh-and-blood Eugene, he can still sustain the muse who flashes on her inward eye and is detachable from the flesh-and-blood man. The distance between the actual world and that of the imagination as Tatiana experiences them in the course of her development causes not rupture, but an increasing tension that generates a creative energy that is as vital to the conduct of life as it is to the perpetuation of literature. Tatiana's encounters with Eugene and with books teach her that the world of the imagination possesses a reality of its own, a reality that must continually interact with the actual, but that need not give way before it. Indeed, it is precisely the reverberations of the collision of the man she imagined and the one she now comes to know that rescue Tatiana from the touching, perhaps comical, but ultimately sterile irreality like Lensky's whose failure is emblematized by his obliviousness to the discrepancy between the ideal he projects onto his beloved and the beloved herself.

By allowing literary experience to augment that of life, Tatiana learns considerably more about Eugene than she could have through actual encounters. Meanwhile, in the actual world which recedes before the imaginative one she enters in Eugene's library, Tatiana's steadfast rejection of suitor after suitor cannot forestall indefinitely that husband who must inevitably figure in a woman's fate. Even as Tatiana pursues the reading that reveals the limitations of the man she took for a muse, her mother makes plans to take her to Moscow where she might be married off. Tatiana, who has always loved winter, now lives in dread of this harbinger of her debut on the Muscovite bride market. The vast possibility suggested by the hibernian rituals of divination described in chapter 5 is closed down as that symbolic space gives way to the acquisition of a husband in an adamantly literal world.

The account of Tatiana's sojourn in Moscow serves as a transition between the familiar Russian countryside she reluctantly leaves behind and the glittering new world of the European capital over which she subsequently presides. Viazemskii found that Pushkin's description of Moscow in chapter 7 of *Onegin* did not "live up to his talent."[57] Yet Pushkin's primary concern, it seems, was not to depict Moscow society as, for example, Griboedov had done in his brilliant *Woe from Wit (Gore ot uma)*, with which this passage is often compared.[58] The setting he creates at this juncture of *Eugene Onegin* serves primarily as a backdrop against which to highlight his beloved heroine's uniqueness and put her to the test in a stultifying social environment.

Like Zhukovskii's Svetlana, Tatiana awakens to find herself between the formlessness of the sexual energies manifested in her dream and an artificial set of social norms that threaten to annihilate those energies. With the move to Moscow, Tatiana's problem of how to preserve her powerful feelings from extinction without being undone by them is translated from the imaginative worlds of her novels and auguries into her public life. Tatiana's situation is particularly difficult, for she must endure her social Muscovite ordeal having lost two mainstays of her private world: her hero/muse has been dethroned and she is deprived of the natural setting in which she nurtured his image as an emblem of possibility. Even as Tatiana finds both her actual world and that of her imagination curtailed, she is forced inexorably toward the state of matrimony which she has successfully resisted thus far. The physical features of her new setting make palpable that narrowing of possibility that comes with the anticipated replacement of an imaginary companion with a flesh-and-blood husband. Crowding buildings cut off that expansive view she once commanded from the window of her country home, and the incessant bustle of endless social engagements encroaches on the blissful solitude that sustained her inner world.

Perhaps most striking in the context of these changes is the extent to which Tatiana remains unimpressed by the new setting in which she finds herself. The seductive novelty of her situation and the liveliness of her urban setting fail to obscure the losses she has suffered in moving from her rural refuge. Although touched by the affectionate solicitude of her relatives, Tatiana remains singularly unmoved by the whirlwind of activities into which she is swept and unresponsive to the throngs of people she meets. Her aloofness is a sign not of her resistance to change, but of her dissatisfaction with the merely apparent variety she encounters in her new environment. The account of Tatiana's sojourn in Moscow is couched in the kindly tone the author/narrator used to describe his heroine's rural Russian setting. Indeed, for all their outward dissimilarities, these distinct settings have much in common. In the reactions of kinfolk and friends to Tatiana, we quickly recognize those very inadequacies that were reflected in her rural milieu. Distinctions between habit and novelty, advanced age and youth, rural and urban society collapse in the fulsome predictability that continues to stalk the members of Tatiana's supporting cast. Upon seeing her, those of the older generation recollect a past that mercilessly highlights the unrealized promise of their youthful emotions. The ailing

Princess Alina briefly recalls her "Grandison"—the object of youthful passions that neither she nor the object of her desire has sustained. ("Grandison," as we learn, has just married off his son [7:41, ll. 9–14].) The other elderly friends and relations look past the Tatiana now before them to the child she once was. The swift passage of time that is documented by her changed appearance has left them unaltered:

> Но в них не видно перемены:
> Всё в них на старый образец.
>
> [In *them*, though, nothing ever alters;
> The same old patterns still are met.]
> (7:45, ll. 1–2)

They remain in a past that holds out no promise of future change. Counterposed to the static invariance of the older generation is the younger generation's fashion-driven quest for constant change, which we recognize at once as but a prelude to the ossification that is destined to follow.

Though they lack Eugene's extensive experience in matters of love, the girls who befriend Tatiana have already adopted a vocabulary that aligns them unmistakably with his world. Their emotional experiences are construed in terms of "victories," while in their expectation of Tatiana's "repayment" ("otplata") for the secrets they disclose with her own "confessions" ("priznan'ia" [7:47, ll. 5–6]) we perceive a distinct echo of the speech with which Eugene promises to "repay" ("otplatit'") Tatiana for her "confessions" to him ("priznan'ia" [4:12, ll. 5 and 11]). Her new-found friends' rapidly changing affections are consistent with Eugene's account of the inconstancy of girls' fancies. It is these young women, so unlike Tatiana, who fall in readily with the predetermined course of events that he has come to expect. Here is a world whose predictability offers that seductive sense of control that Eugene is not prepared to relinquish and that Tatiana is not prepared to assume.

She cannot relate to her new acquaintances' idle talk of love, while her attempts to participate actively in the social gatherings she attends are doomed to failure by the lack of content and emotion in the "disjointed" ("bessviaznyi"), "petty" ("poshlyi"), and "barren" ("besplodnoi") chatter around her (7:48). It is tellingly the poet Viazemskii who appears on the scene as a character in Pushkin's work to engage Tatiana and to rescue her from this predicament. This apparently lighthearted introduction of a personal friend into the text is, in fact, significant, for it is given to the poet to suggest an alternative to the equally unsatisfying worlds of shapeless, solitary dreams and vacuous social forms.

Here we arrive at the climax of that marriage plot which holds little interest for the heroine herself but which draws tight the oppositions be-

tween the actual and the imagined, the public and the private, and between social demands and personal needs. At the Russian Assembly of
Nobility Tatiana, unbeknownst to herself, scores an unlooked-for "victory" by attracting the attention of an eligible male. She remains obliv-
ous to the "conquest" in question, for she has retreated from the chaos of
her actual setting, which, as Chizhevskii has noted, is comparable to that
of her dream.[59] The "dream" into which she now retreats ("No Tania
tochno kak vo sne" [But Tania seems to be in a dream] [7:47, l. 8]) marks
Tatiana's flight from the certain wedlock that looms in her immediate future to the tranquillity of the humble countryside of her past, where her
creative imagination could yet prevail over the contingencies of the mundane and where her companion was not a husband, but a hero/muse of
endless possibility:

> Татьяна смотрит и не видит,
> Волненье света ненавидит;
> Ей душно здесь . . . она мечтой
> Стремится к жизни полевой,
> В деревню, к бедным поселянам,
> В уединенный уголок,
> Где льется светлый ручеек,
> К своим цветам, к своим романам
> И в сумрак липовых аллей,
> Туда, где *он* являлся ей.

> [Tatyana looks with eyes unseeing
> And loathes this world with all her being;
> She's stifled here . . . and in her mind
> Calls up the life she left behind—
> The countryside, poor village neighbours,
> A distant and secluded nook
> Beside a limpid flowing brook,
> Her flowers, novels, daily labours . . .
> The linden shaded walk and fir
> Where *he* always appeared to her.][60]
>   (7:53, ll. 5–14)

The imperfective verb that in the original signals "*his*" repeated appearances indicates that she is contemplating not the flesh-and-blood Eugene
whom she has actually seen only three times (and only once in an outdoor
setting) but rather the inspiring muse to whom he gave rise and who accompanied her on her rambles. As Tatiana retreats from a painfully limiting here-and-now to the time and space of a past in which her possibilities had not yet been closed down, the defenses of her imagination seem
particularly frail and ineffectual. However understandable in her present

circumstances, the escapism to which she resorts can have no relevance to the responsible conduct of life that she must now confront; nor can it constitute an adequate representation of the poetic principle that Tatiana must yet fully become. The hard truth remains that neither an actual husband nor the potential one of her dreams and auguries can—in isolation—adequately fulfill her needs.

Here it is fitting to recall the epigraph for this chapter (7) of *Onegin* that Pushkin takes from Griboedov's *Woe from Wit*:

> Гоненье на Москву! что значит видеть свет!
>   Где ж лучше?
>   Где нас нет.

> [Attacking Moscow! This is what comes from seeing the world!
>   Where is it better, then?
>   Where we are not.][61]

Well suited to describe the dissatisfaction that prompts Onegin to undertake his travels, this ironic passage is less obviously but equally appropriate to Tatiana's figurative departure from the intolerable situation in which she finds herself at the assembly. That Tatiana's figurative voyage is no more successful than Eugene's literal one is signaled by the "victory" with which the author/narrator congratulates her in the final stanza, for this is clearly a victory of the actual world whose demands have yet to be reconciled with those of the imagination to which Tatiana ineffectually resorts. It is to this reconciliation that Pushkin devotes the final chapter of his novel-in-verse.

6
Tatiana's Glory

And if it dares enough, 'twere hard
If passion met not some reward.
                    Byron, *The Giaour*

It is unhappily your disposition to consider what you *have* as worthless—
what you have *lost* as invaluable. But remember that you believed yourself
most miserable when I was yours.
                    Lady Byron to Lord Byron

Completed in chapter 8 of *Eugene Onegin* are the structural symmetries
that both express and contain the dynamics of Pushkin's work. Thus the
letter Eugene writes to Tatiana in this chapter balances the one she wrote
him in chapter 3, while her concluding speech to him complements the
one with which he responded to her letter in chapter 4. Yet just as the mirror image of any molecular structure marks a radical qualitative difference (cumin and cyanide are mirror images), so too does the mirror
Pushkin now holds up to the earlier portion of his work reflect the profound qualitative difference of this final chapter. The context in which Eugene's letter and Tatiana's speech appear has been transfigured by the
identification of the heroine with the author's muse, and the structural
symmetry Pushkin accomplishes emerges not as a static construct housing the balanced stories of hero and heroine, but as "that superior disequi-
librium without which we cannot conceive lyricism."[1] Urged here is the
application of poetic criteria to the governance of life, and the imagination is brought into productive interdependency with the actual world.
Pushkin uses characteristics of a novelistic heroine to create a poetical
muse and the vocabulary of the quotidian to define the poetic imperative.
Tatiana's stance is integrally related to the precepts of poetry itself, and
her story is a double one—a story of her life in the world and a correlative story of her life as a poetic principle.

It is presumably the "conquest" with which Pushkin ends chapter 7
that has led to Tatiana's marriage, and the provincial heroine appears in
chapter 8 as the Princess N who presides with great dignity over the *haut
monde* of St. Petersburg. The author/narrator makes much of Eugene's in-

credulity at the extent of Tatiana's transformation: "No i sledov Tat'iany prezhnei / Ne mog Onegin obresti" (Not even a trace of the former Tatiana / Could Onegin secure [8:19, l. 6]), "Uzhel' ta samaia Tat'iana?" (Can it be the same Tatiana? [8:20, l. 1]), "Kak izmenilasia Tat'iana" (How Tatiana has changed [8:28, l. 1]). That many of Pushkin's readers should share Eugene's wonder at coming upon Tatiana in the role of Princess N is not surprising, for there is no description of the courtship and marriage that account for this sudden transformation.

This lacuna in her story is emblematic of the heroine's own unconventional lack of interest in the pursuit of "conquests." Tatiana is not ruled, as we have seen, by the commonplace imperatives of securing a husband, wealth, and social standing. Like the omission of her first meeting with Eugene, so too the omission of her courtship and marriage urges the reader past these mainstays of conventional narrative to focus instead on Tatiana's inner development and the poetic mission she fulfills on behalf of her creator. From this perspective it is not the omitted courtship and marriage, but Tatiana's dream—the dark hour of her soul and of the author's creative process—that constitutes the necessary step toward the lucidity that heroine and text attain in this final chapter. The change crucial to the text itself is to be found not in the transformation of Tatiana into "Princess N," but rather in the expansion of context that occurs when what the reader has taken for a novelistic heroine is presented as a hypostasis of the poet's muse, and Tatiana emerges as both the source of the poet's inspiration and its consequence.

In a series of metamorphoses that are unmistakably related to Pushkin's own creative biography, the muse whose story opens chapter 8 appears as a frolicsome bacchante in the midst of revelers, a solicitous companion in the poet's solitude, a Lenore galloping with him through a craggy, moonlit Caucasian landscape, the guide who urges him to hearken to the ceaseless sounds of the sea, an uncivilized dweller among nomadic tribes, and finally as the "young lady" ("baryshnia") in whom we recognize Tatiana:

> И вот она в саду моем
> Явилась барышней уездной,
> С печальной думою в очах,
> С французской книжкою в руках.
>
> [And in my garden she appeared—
> A country miss—contemplative,
> With mournful air and brooding glance,
> And in her hands a French romance.]
> (8:5, ll. 11–14)

The Princess N is next in the series of transformations of Pushkin's own muse, and this metamorphosis must naturally eclipse the duly omitted marriage that explains only Tatiana's meteoric rise in society, and not what she means to the poet himself.

From Pushkin's account we can establish definitive features of his muse that enrich our assessment of Tatiana. Foremost among these is the readiness with which she adapts to the poet's rapidly changing circumstances. The various guises in which she appears are not arbitrary changes of costume, but necessary transformations that bespeak acute responsiveness and demonstrate a perfect assimilation of a wide variety of distinct worlds. Manifested in this capacity for change is the muse's unfailing constancy to the ever-changing poet. For his part, the poet unfailingly recognizes—whatever her semblance—the muse who inspires and is herself inspired by his creative journeys. Linked firmly to tradition (mentioned are Derzhavin's blessing and Bürger/Zhukovskii's Lenore), and yet also uniquely the poet's own, the muse accomplishes the intersection of the collective and the individual, the repeated and the new, the lasting and the ephemeral, the cultivated and the natural, and it is not by chance that she engages the poet in fleeting cosmopolitan festivity and yet draws him also to solitary contemplation of the endlessly repeating waves of the sea.

Lotman has persuasively argued that in this history of his muse Pushkin projects a new conceptualization of his poetic evolution that supersedes the earlier ones to which the passage alludes. One of these superseded conceptualizations, Lotman suggests, finds expression in the poem "Demon" (1823), where the poet traces a progression from naive lucidity to tormenting doubt, and finally to profound indifference. A second, closely related model for Pushkin's evolution comprises, according to Lotman, the triad "first, pure days," "delusion," "rebirth" which is first delineated in the 1819 poem "Vozrozhdenie" (Rebirth) and then repeated with variations throughout the 1820s.[2] Indeed, J. Thomas Shaw discerns this triad already in the lyric "Demon," where the explicit accounts of enchantment and disenchantment are joined by a mature reenchantment that is implied in the very fact that the poem came into being. Shaw, who compares the persona of "The Demon" and the author/narrator of *Onegin*, describes their shared stance as "that of one who has gone through a stage of youthful perceptivity and enchantment, followed by a stage of disenchantment, followed by a third stage (the implied present tense of narrating the novel) of mature reenchantment."[3]

According to Lotman the opening of the final *Onegin* chapter replaces Pushkin's "purely psychological triad" with a

history of his Muse and a succession of creative periods, of the reading public, of life's circumstances that constitute a single evolution. In place of "fall" and "rebirth" there is a unified logic of development.[4]

Analogous to the poet's own growth is that of his heroine, and the "unified logic of development" that Lotman perceptively discerns is projected in her development. We can add here that it falls to Tatiana not simply to suggest an alternative to Pushkin's earlier conceptualizations of poetic development, but to provide, moreover, an inspiring, life-affirming antidote to that spirit of negation that rules Pushkin's various "demons," among whom are the hero of *Eugene Onegin* and that very demon who threatens the poet who created him. If in his "Demon," as Pushkin explained in his 1825 sketch about the poem ("O stikhotvorenii 'Demon'"), he sought to embody the spirit of negation which Goethe rightly designated as the "eternal enemy of humankind" ("vechnogo vraga chelovechestva" [*PSS* 11:30]), he now engages Tatiana to translate the sources of that negation into a productive tension whose energy can propel the creative acts of poetry and of life. Tatiana thus appears in *Eugene Onegin* not simply as a counterexample to Eugene, but as the positive dynamic that promises both to revivify the hero and to preserve his creator from deadly and deadening negativity. Thus the Princess N, who presides in splendid natural grace over the *haut monde* of St. Petersburg, is introduced against the unlikely confluence of two distinct contexts: the history of the poet as the history of his muse, and the history of the poet as the history of his hero. In Tatiana Pushkin finds a heroine and a muse who has the power to reopen possibilities both within the text and in his own creative biography.

It emerges here that the real tension is not between Russia and Europe, the countryside and the city, tradition and novelty, and ultimately not even between duty and desire, but between two areas of human experience that subsume these apparent antitheses that the text evokes. Pushkin positions Tatiana between the Scylla and Charybdis of formless individual desire and empty social form, and, because his heroine means so very much to him, he stacks the odds heavily against her that her success in steering beyond this impossible choice may emerge in greater glory.

Tatiana, as Pushkin recognizes, cannot remain in her fantasies any more than the poet and his muse can remain among the freewheeling gypsies, for jettisoned with the restrictive norms of society are also those expressive means that civilization makes available. The price for remaining apart from the civilized world is not one the poet can afford. "I pozabyla rech' bogov / Dlia skudnykh, strannykh iazykov" (she lost the language of the gods / for the bleak tongue of boorish clods [8:5, ll. 7–8]),[5] he writes of the muse who, fleeing societal restraints, wanders happily with a gypsy tribe. Yet neither can those nomads be forgotten. Their freedom of movement—without which the imagination grows dull and the language of the gods tarnished—must also be preserved. It is no mere accident that, as Leslie O'Bell reminds us, "Chapter III of *Onegin*, 'Baryšnja' (The Young Lady), was written in alternation with *The Gypsies*."[6] For Pushkin the free and noble savage must ultimately be replaced with a still nobler free creature of civilization. In the final chapter of *Onegin*, Tatiana must negotiate between the unbounded realm of the imagination and an exacting social world.

It is against the backdrop of this vast poetical vista that Tatiana's strengths and the failings from which she promises to rescue Eugene are to be considered, for Pushkin's alignment of his heroine with his muse urges us to consider those essential poetic qualities that Tatiana's story translates into the social domain. With the author/narrator's introduction of his muse into Petersburg society, we observe her modulation into Princess N and recognize the relevance of aesthetic norms to the conduct of life. Unabashed by the new circumstances in which she finds herself, the muse takes up the position not of direct participant, but of keen observer of the activity around her. Significantly, she enjoys the disordered, noisy bustle of the crowded event—the flickering dresses, the fragments of conversation, and the mixture of ranks and ages—but takes pleasure also in the underlying sense of order:

> Ей нравится порядок стройный
> Олигархических бесед,
> И холод гордости спокойной,
> И эта смесь чинов и лет.

> [She likes the stately disposition
> Of oligarchic colloquies,
> Their chilly pride in high positions,
> The mix of years and ranks she sees.]
>   (8:7, ll. 1–4)

The muse savors, in other words, that very conjunction of dynamic disarray with careful structure that Pushkin was to extol in his much-anthologized description of St. Petersburg in *Mednyi vsadnik* (*The Bronze Horseman* [1833]), a work that focuses explicitly on those perilous tensions between order and chaos that obtain in both the creative act and the work that it accomplishes.

It is immediately on the heels of Tatiana's double metamorphosis into muse and Princess N that Eugene returns—after his sojourn in the country and his travels—to the world in which his formative years were spent. The arbitrary series of fashionable masks he might assume contrasts sharply with the preceding account of the necessary transformations of the author's muse. If the muse can be always new and yet always familiar to her poet, Eugene remains neither a known nor yet an unknown quantity:

Скажите, чем он возвратился?
Что нам представит он пока?
Чем ныне явится? Мельмонтом,
Космополитом, патриотом,
Гарольдом, квакером, ханжой,
Иль маской щегольнет иной.

[In what new guise is he returning?
What role does he intend to fill?
Childe Harold? Melmoth for a while?
Cosmopolite? A Slavophile?
A Quaker? Bigot?—might one ask?
Or will he sport some other mask?]
(8:8, ll. 3–8)

Here the dissimilarity between hero and heroine is dramatically heightened, and the love story takes a particularly unpromising turn. If Eugene is distinguished from the author/narrator's muse by the qualitative difference in their respective transformations, his contrast to the heroine is emphasized with the author/narrator's inventory of what is missing from their respective constitutions. Clearly the absence of both externally imposed and voluntarily assumed constraints has done nothing for the hero:

Убив на поединке друга,
Дожив *без* цели, *без* трудов
До двадцати шести годов,
Томясь в *бездействии* досуга
Без службы, *без* жены, *без* дел,
Ничем заняться не умел.

[When he had killed his friend and neighbor—
Now twenty-six, still vague of aim,
Void of employment—he became
A martyr to his leisure's labor:
No service, business, or wife
To occupy his empty life.][7]
(8:12, ll. 9–14, my emphasis on "bez" [without])

Here we can observe parenthetically that Pushkin chose "ne umel" (was not able to, did not know how) rather than the equally fitting (metrically and acoustically) "ne khotel" (did not want to). Emphasized with this choice is the absence of volition and self-assertiveness on Eugene's part. His is not a rebellion against the surrounding world, but merely the incapacity to relate to it.

If Eugene is described as lacking those things that might give his life meaning, Tatiana's representation accentuates the absence of those very characteristics that have led Eugene into this cul-de-sac. Opposed to the jumble of "withouts" that signal Eugene's shortcomings is the well-ordered series of "withouts" that aver her preeminence.

> Она была нетороплива,
> Не холодна, не говорлива,
> *Без* взора наглого для всех,
> *Без* притязаний на успех,
> *Без* этих маленьких ужимок,
> *Без* подражательных затей . . .
> Всё тихо, просто было в ней,

> [She isn't hurried or obtrusive,
> Is neither cold nor too effusive;
> She casts no brazen glance around
> And makes no effort to astound
> Or use those sorts of affectation
> And artifice that ladies share—
> But shows a simple, quiet air.]
>   (8:14, ll., 5–11, my emphasis)

Another series of carefully chosen "withouts" marks the distinctly positive effects of this absence of affectation on the assembly of guests Tatiana entertains in her home :

> Перед хозяйкой легкий вздор
> Сверкал *без* глупого жеманства,
> И прерывал его меж тем
> Разумный толк *без* пошлых тем,
> *Без* вечных истин, *без* педанства.

> [But, with this hostess, it is light,
> Gay nonsense, free of priggish preening,
> Or, grave at times, is never brought
> To fatuous themes or hallowed thought,
> But brims with undidactic meaning.][8]
>   (8:23, ll. 8–12)

Eugene has fallen short of arriving at that freedom which, as he described earlier in his sermon to Tatiana, he intended to secure by eschewing marriage. Opposite him stands Tatiana, who, having reluctantly assumed the bonds of matrimony and accepted the exacting formal demands of the upper reaches of society, has attained that genuine liberty which is unavailable to the hero who has spent his life avoiding commitments.

There is no mere mimicry, let alone unwitting parody, in Tatiana's behavior. She has perfectly assimilated the dicta of her new circumstances, and it is precisely this assimilation that wins her freedom of movement. Because Tatiana, like her creator, brings her own content to preexisting forms, she is enabled rather than determined by them, and can thus function freely within their constraints. Goethe's famous pronouncement, "In der Beschränkung zeigt sich erst der Meister," whose applicability to Pushkin himself we have already noted, is perfectly illustrated by her comportment. The author/narrator's emphasis on his inability to render *"du comme il faut"* and "vulgar" into Russian when he describes his heroine draws attention to the perfection with which Tatiana herself has been translated into her new surroundings.

In marked contradistinction to the poet who knows his muse in all her various guises, Eugene proves incapable of recognizing Tatiana in the Princess N. There is a distinct resonance here of Pushkin's "Ia pomniu chudnoe mgnoven'e" ("I Remember the Wondrous Moment"). In that lyric, it will be recalled, the persona describes three stages in his own life: (1) his perception of the flesh-and-blood Anna Petrovna Kern as a muse whose image endures well beyond their fleeting encounter; (2) his disremembrance of the muse in a whirl of social activity and the consequent barrenness of his existence; and (3) the second recognition of the muse that follows immediately upon the reawakening of the persona's soul ("Dushe nastalo probuzhden'e: / I vot opiat' iavilas' ty"[The awakening of the soul came: / And now you appeared again] [*PSS* 2:358]). We have already noted an echo of this particular lyric in the inspired letter Tatiana addressed to her Eugene-muse. Here its reverberations highlight the torpor of Eugene's soul and the absence of inspiration in his life as, upon his return to Petersburg, he fails to recognize not only the potential muse in Tatiana, but Tatiana herself. The repetitions of "without" ("bez") we noted in the characterization of the newly returned Eugene evoke the fivefold "bez" that describes the persona of Pushkin's lyric, who has forgotten his muse: "Bez bozhestva, bez vdokhnoven'ia, / Bez slez, bez zhizni, bez liubvi" (Without divinity, without inspiration, / Without tears, without life, without love [*PSS* 2:358]). The vague sense of familiarity that prompts Eugene to train his lorgnette "Na tu, chei vid napomnil smutno / Emu zabytye cherty" (At her, whose appearance dimly reminded him / Of the features he had forgotten [8:17, ll. 6–7]) is reminiscent of the lyric to Kern. Here, however, images of poetical inspiration are reduced to barren, mundane terms. Thus the "chudnoe mgnoven'e" (wondrous moment) and "mimoletnoe viden'e" (fleeting vision) of "I Remember" become the "pominutno" (every moment) of the repeated gazes the perplexed Eugene casts at the Princess N.

The focus is clearly on the absence of inspiration, and yet Tatiana's continued presence and the resonance of "I Remember" suggest the possibility that Eugene may yet awaken and learn to distinguish the muse he has thus far been unable to perceive in Tatiana. The author/narrator has already done as much in the opening of this chapter, and Eugene must follow suit. We have seen already that both Tatiana's individual Bildung and the unfolding of the text in which she appears are heavily dependent on the conjoining of heretofore unconjoined elements and on the intersection of the familiar and the alien. We can therefore recognize the potential value of the demand now placed on Eugene to reconcile the two distinct guises of Tatiana. For this to become possible, Eugene, as we will see, has to return to the time and place of his first meeting with her to endow that "wondrous moment" with retroactive significance. At issue here is not whether Tatiana and Eugene will become lovers, but whether they can become sources of inspiration for one another.

Here it is important to remember that this is Tatiana's first meeting with Eugene since the hero-muse she saw in him receded before the mere parody that the marginalia in his books revealed to her. For all the difference in outward appearances, hero and heroine find themselves in situations that mirror one another. Eugene must reconcile two seemingly incompatible guises of Tatiana, while she must realign her vanished muse with the man who now appears before her.

The difficulty Eugene experiences identifying the girl he once knew with the princess he now meets signals not only his failings, but also the remarkable success of Tatiana's translation from rural backwater to the urban limelight. Eugene, who cannot conceive of such a translation, must resort to a relative to establish the identity of the extraordinary woman who has captured his attention. The prince to whom he applies for information responds not with the indicated woman's name, but with the startling information: "Zhena moia" (My wife [8:17, l. 14]). The possessive pronoun and marital status that are used to identify Tatiana suggest that her earlier fears of losing her self to marriage were not unfounded. Even as this attractive woman is presented as forbidden fruit to Eugene, the question arises as to whether her dazzling social success has been purchased at the price of the emotional and imaginative vivacity she had been determined to preserve. Crucial here is not how Tatiana attained her lofty position, but whether her innate sense of the inadequacy of the immediately surrounding world has been sacrificed to it. It remains to be seen whether her imperturbable unresponsiveness to Eugene is the product of self-mastery or the consequence of mere satisfaction.

Earlier Eugene was disconcerted by Tatiana's failure to act in accordance with his expectations. Now her unforeseeable transformation and perfect self-command confound him. Only the dreamworld, where incompatibles are readily conjoined, suggests a possible explanation: "il' eto son?" (or is this a dream? [8:20, l. 10]). The new Tatiana disturbs his peace of mind, haunts his sleep, and elicits emotional symptoms that leave the author/narrator at a loss: "Dosada? suetnost'? il' vnov' / Zabota iunosti—liubov'?" (Vexation? Vanity, or now anew / Youth's bother, love [8:21, ll. 13–14]). Whatever his emotions, the tongue-tied, gloomy ("ugriumyi"), and awkward ("nelovkii") Eugene is described by a twice-noted obstinacy that contrasts sharply with Tatiana's exquisite flexibility:

Голова
Его полна *упрямой* думои.
Упрямо смотрит он: она
Сидит покойна и вольна.

[His head
is lost in *obstinate* reflection;
and *obstinate* his look. But she
sits imperturbable and free.]⁹
(8:22, ll. 11–14, my emphasis)

The author/narrator's observation that Eugene is preoccupied with Tatiana *alone* emphasizes not only the intensity of the hero's absorption but also his exclusive focus on her present image which he regards as distinct from the girl he knew in the country.

Но мой Онегин вечер целый
Татьяной занят был *одной*,
Не этой девочкой несмелой,
Влюбленной, бедной и простой,
Но равнодушною княгиней,
Но непреступною богиней
Роскошной, царственной Невы.

[But my Eugene all evening heeded
Tatyana . . . *only her alone*:
But not the timid maid who'd pleaded,
That poor enamoured girl he'd known—
But this cool princess so resplendent,
This distant goddess so transcendent,
Who ruled the queenly Neva's shores.]
(8:27, ll. 1–7, my emphasis)

The naive, infatuated girl who paid little heed to the social norms that govern his life has been eclipsed by the indifferent, unapproachable woman who has mastered them.

The narrator's renewed attempts to describe the emotions that the Princess N inspires in the hero yield up conflicting assessments that only intensify the uncertainty as to whether Eugene desires forbidden fruit (27, ll. 9–14) or is transformed by the sudden onset of innocent love (30, ll. 1–2). Either alternative is possible, and it is not clear whether the hero himself knows what course his feelings might take. The unexpected meeting with a miraculously transformed Tatiana once again jars his complacency and, like her letter and the events of the name day celebration, issues a challenge to his predictable world. Yet whatever course his feelings might have taken, Eugene falls back on that familiar code that construes love in terms of conquest. In so doing he resists acknowledging the new possibilities Tatiana's uniqueness suggests. His behavior is dictated not so much by his heart as by his habits, and his rehearsal of conventional public gestures inhibits the blossoming of his emotions. The dogged pursuit, endless small services, and unmistakable symptoms of a debilitating malaise are a display that does not guarantee content. These efforts have no visible effect on Tatiana, and Eugene's borrowed, stubbornly applied, and ineffectual gestures stand out against the freedom of movement she retains within the regulations of her exacting role. As in her girlhood, so now too Tatiana remains free from the desire to manipulate—a desire that, as we must note here, is highly inappropriate in a muse. Opposed to the "Svobodno doma prinimaet" (Freely receives him at home [8:31, l. 3]) that describes her is the "A on *upriam*, otstat' ne khochet" (While he is *obstinate* and does not want to leave her alone [8:32, l. 5]) that characterizes Eugene's behavior. The strong resonance of Byron's *Don Juan* in the author/narrator's description of the social gathering at which Eugene sets his sights on the Princess acts as a subtle reminder of the literary type Eugene unwittingly and weakly parodies.[10]

Having exhausted to no avail the arsenal of amorous gestures at his disposal, Eugene resorts in desperation to letter writing. His letter to Tatiana, as Blagoi notes, "established a perfect symmetry in relation to the development of the basic love story of the novel."[11] Indeed, it was apparently the urge toward this symmetry that prompted Pushkin to compose this letter after the remainder of his novel-in-verse was already complete. Dated 5 October 1831 in the manuscript, Eugene's letter, like Tatiana's, is treated as a document interpolated into the text of *Eugene Onegin* and similarly departs from the Onegin stanza to suggest the prose in which it is presumably couched. Although it echoes both Tatiana's letter and the literary sources from which she derived its idiom, Eugene's letter differs essentially—as a mirror image must—from the epistle which it structurally balances. The symmetrical positioning of these two texts serves above all to highlight the differences between the letters themselves and the characters who penned them. Eugene's public show of ardor that culminates in the dispatch of a stream of letters stands out sharply from Tatiana's inspired, private attempt to find expression for her feelings.

We have already considered in chapter 3 the extent to which the author/narrator privileges Tatiana's letter even as he subjects Eugene's to calculated disadvantages. Here we can add that the author/narrator's lack of enthusiasm for the fruits of Eugene's pen appears to be shared by the hero himself. Even before Eugene's letter is cited, it is undermined by his lack of faith in its effectiveness, belying the passion it ostensibly conveys:

> Он пишет страстное посланье.
> Хоть толку мало вообще
> Он в письмах видел не вотще.

> [He writes her an impassioned message;
> Though by and large he had small use
> For letters (not without excuse).][12]
> (8:32, ll. 9–11)

This attitude toward the epistolary genre contrasts sharply with the momentous significance Tatiana ascribes to writing in the opening line of her letter: "Ia k vam pishu—chego zhe bole?" (I am writing you—what more?) and underscores that Eugene's missive is a controlled deployment of amorous tactics and not the necessary, risk-laden gesture that Tatiana's was. Even as he nears completion of his letter, Eugene remains unconvinced of its expressive possibilities and continues to complain about the lack of means at his disposal to convey his feelings to Tatiana. Thus in the very process of composing his letter, he resorts to what can only be regarded as an inappropriate conditional: "Vse, vse chto vyrazit' *by mog*" (All, all I *could* express [l. 52, my emphasis]).

The Princess N now before Eugene appears to fit comfortably within the familiar social norms that the earlier Tatiana disconcertingly disregarded. Dismissing the image of the Tatiana he once knew to concentrate exclusively on the guise in which she now appears before him, Eugene launches on what would seem to be a predictable course of action in the pursuit not simply of another conquest, but of a reaffirmation of that code whose adequacy she has thrown into doubt. If the addressee of Tatiana's letter is greater than the man to whom it is delivered, the addressee of Eugene's falls painfully short of embracing the complexity of the woman to whom it is directed.

The author/narrator's lackluster introduction, "Vot vam pis'mo ego toch' v toch'" (Here is his letter word for word [8:32, l. 14]), excludes the hero from the positive domain of translation, which Pushkin aligns, as we have seen, expressly with growth and creativity. In fact, like the passage that introduces his reply to Tatiana's epistle, Eugene's letter brings no new information to Pushkin's text, but serves instead to reiterate familiar flaws in the hero's constitution within the immediate context of Tatiana's accomplishments. Implicit in his letter is an unequivocal answer to the question of whether Eugene's travels have changed him in any significant way. In light of Pushkin's marked privileging of synchronicity over sequential linearity throughout *Eugene Onegin*, it is hardly likely that his hero's travels from place to place would have cured what ails him any more than those "waters" now recommended to him could ease his present malaise. A close look at the text of his letter suggests that there is in fact no substantial difference between the orator who refused Tatiana and the writer who would now woo her.

Indeed, the very words with which Eugene opens conspire with the author/narrator's tepid introduction to reveal a hero who has remained essentially unchanged. The assertion "Predvizhu vse" (I foresee everything [l. 1]) announces that he is determined to adhere to the limited set of possibilities offered by his own code rather than to seek out and risk new ones. The narrow future he purports to foresee as he undertakes to write contrasts sharply with the expansion of possibility that Tatiana sought both with her own letter and with the rituals of divination in which she took part. That very need to assert his control that culminated in Onegin's duel with Lensky has clearly persisted beyond his travels, and Eugene's journey appears to have had no more effect on him than the peregrinations of Don Juan and Childe Harold had on Byron's heroes. The edifying benefits that protagonists of *Bildungsromane* traditionally derived from travels cannot be reaped by the exhausted romantic hero whose egocentricity precludes the requisite responsivity to the new worlds that open before him. Eugene is, moreover, driven to undertake his travels not by a desire for something beyond what he already knows, but by the need to evade the grim evidence of the insufficiency, indeed destructivity, of his stubborn adherence to a single, ultimately ineffectual code. It would seem that Pushkin had good reason to omit the account of his hero's travels from his novel-in-verse. There were, of course, the possible political ramifications that have been noted by commentators. But there were also the considerations that Pushkin was not prepared to condone such flight from responsibility and that his hero was ill prepared to benefit from change of scenery.

Eugene's letter reflects his continued efforts to avoid confronting the inadequacy of the way he relates to both self and surrounding world. In

the brief account of his relations with Tatiana that he includes in his letter, Eugene attempts both to vindicate his behavior and to avoid assuming responsibility for it. By crediting himself with discerning in Tatiana
what he calls a "spark of tenderness" and claiming that he did not dare
believe it, he undercuts the intensity of Tatiana's fully revealed feelings
even as he exaggerates his own fleeting emotional impulse, which he
quickly smothered in a conventional response. Rather than consider the
circumstances that led to his duel with Lensky and acknowledge his role
in it, Eugene attaches his friend's death to the dictates of a vaguely invoked
fate. He includes Lensky's death—together with the unwillingness to surrender his individual freedom to the bonds of matrimony he described already in his speech to Tatiana—in the list of causes for his purportedly reluctant parting from her: "Eshche odno nas razluchilo . . . / Neschastnoi
zhertvoi Lensky pal . . ." (One thing more separated us . . . / An unfortunate victim Lensky fell . . . [ll. 15–16]). If the ellipses in Tatiana's letter
suggest a surfeit of emotion and indicate the erotic, creative space into
which her letter opens, the ellipses in Eugene's are the visible signs of his
evasion of answerability and in this sense constitute an orthographic analogue of the actual flight to which he resorted. Eugene's suggestion that,
like Lensky, he too fell prey to forces beyond his control takes on a distinctly ironic cast when we recall that the duel was precipitated largely by
his own attempt to reassert control over a situation that had slipped beyond predictable norms.

Here Eugene arrives at a quintessentially Pushkinian formula:

> Я думал: вольность и покой
> Замена счастью. Боже мой!
> Как я ошибся, как наказан . . . .
>
> [I thought: in freedom, peace of mind,
> A substitute for happiness I'd find.
> How wrong I've been! And how tormented!]
>   (ll. 20–22)

Pushkin's own endorsement of this motto spanned his poetic career from
the 1817 ode "Vol'nost'" ("Freedom") to the 1835 lyric "Pora, moi drug,
pora"("It's Time, My Friend, It's Time") with its assertion, "Na svete
schast'ia net, no est' pokoi i volia"(There is no happiness on earth, but
there is tranquillity and freedom [*PSS* 3:330]). Eugene, who senses that
something is amiss, is mistaken not, as he believes, in his designation of
"freedom and tranquillity" as viable alternatives to happiness, but in the
notion that this is an accurate assessment of his present condition. It is
clear that the alienation he describes—"Chuzhoi dlia vsekh, nichem ne
sviazan" (Alien to all and bound by nothing [l. 19])—is not to be confused

with liberty, which in Pushkin's view depends on the responsible integration of social demands and individual needs and on voluntary self-mastery rather than the exercise of control over others. Not Eugene, but Tatiana is "tranquil and free" ["pokoina i vol'na" [8:22, l. 14]). Here is a preferable alternative to the "habit" suggested as a possible replacement for happiness in chapter 2 "Privychka svyshe nam dana: / Zamena schastiiu ona" (Habit is given us from above / It is a substitute for happiness [2:31, ll. 13–14]).

The opportunity for occasional meetings with the object of her love that Tatiana deemed sufficient to sustain her feeling are not enough to satisfy Eugene, who wants nothing less than her guaranteed presence (ll. 23–30). But the real awkwardness of the passage lies in the fact that the "blazhenstvo" (bliss) of watching, hearing, and admiring her that he claims to miss is already available to Eugene, for he sees Tatiana frequently and loses no opportunity to press his attentions on her. His plaint "I ia lishen togo" (And I am denied this) in reference to a series of wants that have, in fact, been satisfied attests to a discrepancy between what he writes and what actually transpires. We observe here not the fruitful workings of metaphor that convey one sense in terms of another, but a disjunctive, potentially destructive engagement of language for manipulation rather than self-expressivity.

Tatiana's assimilation of a literary idiom that furthered her imaginative and emotional development fostered, as we have seen, the controlled surrender of her letter. Eugene's epistle, in contrast, bears no signs of such assimilation. The phrases he unreflectively adopts have lost their significance not only because they have borne excessive repetition, but also because he uses them with no heed for the contexts which originally gave them meaning and because he invests them with no content of his own. Thus, as Lotman observes, although Tatiana and Eugene resort to similar formulations in their letters, "the meaning and function of these formulae differ profoundly in their usage." Eugene's letter abounds not with specific literary reminiscences evoked by directly experienced emotion, but with a series of phrases that remain disconnected both from the contexts that enlivened them and from his own emotional experience. His borrowings—unlike Tatiana's—can serve neither to intensify nor to adequately express his feelings.[13]

Lotman has argued persuasively that this crucial difference in the idioms of their respective letters is accentuated by Pushkin's decision to pass over the realistic detail that Eugene, like Tatiana before him, was more likely to have written his letter in French than in Russian. A consequence of this decision, Lotman notes, is that in Onegin's letter the common formulae cease to be connected with a *particular* text, and become facts of general usage. Thus, for example, it would be possible to indicate tens of "sources" for the phrase "sweet habit" (*douce habitude*). In fact, however, this expression has already been severed from all of them. But it is precisely because Onegin uses these expressions without stopping to consider where they came from, because these expressions in themselves mean nothing to him, that they are closely linked with his actual biography.[14]

Eugene's connection to his literary sources is significantly weaker than Tatiana's and fosters neither truer self-expression nor enhanced persuasiveness.

As weak as Eugene's ties are to literature, his connection to the actual world is scarcely more compelling, and it appears that his own experiences have brought him no closer to understanding Tatiana. The empathy on the strength of which the familiar ("svoi") and the alien ("chuzhoi") can be interrelated is nowhere in evidence. His letter reveals that he is reacting not to Tatiana herself, but to the new guise in which she appears, for though he has been told that they are one and the same, he has not yet connected the Princess N with the Tatiana he knew in the countryside. Eugene's letter is not a reply to Tatiana's, but the initiation of a correspondence with the new woman now before him. That he addresses an immediate present that remains disassociated from the past manifests itself with particular clarity in his attempt to win the sympathy of his addressee:

> Когда б вы знали, как ужасно
> Томиться жаждою любви,
> Пылать—и разумом всечасно
> Смирять волнение в крови.
>
> [But if you knew the anguish in it:
> To thirst with love in every part,
> To burn—and with the mind each minute,
> To calm the tumult in one's heart.]
>
> (ll. 45–48)

Yet Tatiana, as Eugene apparently fails to recognize, knows only too well the anguish of precisely such unhappy circumstances. Indeed, it was just such a situation that prompted her to write him. She knows too, as Eugene might have realized, what it means to feign indifference and to retain composure in trying social circumstances, for this is what he made her do at her name day celebration. The futility of his attempt to master his feelings that Eugene notes in the concluding quatrain of his letter

("No tak i byt': ia sam sebe / Protivit'sia ne v silakh bole" [But let it be: against myself / I've not the strength to struggle further] [ll. 57–58]) suggests an attempt at self-restraint of which there has been little evidence, for his pursuit of Tatiana is both dogged and demonstrative. The possibilities afforded by writing that were so fully realized by Tatiana are not in effect in Eugene's letter.

When she first met Eugene, it was his inaccessibility and mystery that led Tatiana to assume the risk of initiating an illicit correspondence with him, and this risk, in turn, contributed to the urgency of her letter and the emotions that dictated it. In the beginning of his letter to her, Eugene suggests the venturesome nature of his enterprise, claiming that the revelation of his feelings makes him vulnerable to Tatiana's scorn and malicious mirth. Yet however real, this "danger" is distinctly incommensurate with the one Tatiana braved, and its very mention can only trivialize Eugene's undertaking. Both the letter Tatiana writes to Eugene and those she receives from him threaten her with ruin that would bring him only enviable social notice. For his part, Eugene might fear a bruised ego, but even this apparent danger is significantly minimized by the fact that his letter is not a disclosure of private feelings. Well before he writes he makes a public spectacle of his ardor, and what he refers to as his "sad secret" ("pechal'naia taina") can scarcely have escaped Tatiana's notice, or, for that matter, anyone else's. If Tatiana has thus far refrained from "malicious mirth" at his expense, there is no particular reason to expect it now. Indeed, by predicting such a response, Eugene mitigates in advance its possible effects.

The lines with which Eugene closes vigorously reinforce the disparity between hero and heroine and the letters they write. Although Eugene seems to echo the importance Tatiana ascribed to her own letter and her awareness of the risk she incurred in writing it, this apparent similarity only underscores once again how very much more Tatiana has at stake than he:

Всё решено: я в вашей воле,
И предаюсь моей судьбе.

[The die is cast: I'm in your power,
And I surrender to my fate.]
(ll. 59–60)

Like the series of conventional gestures that precede it, Eugene's professed capitulation to Tatiana's will is intended above all to bring about her surrender. The profound difference between the symmetrically positioned letters is summarized by Lotman, who notes that the distance between what Eugene writes and what he intends sharply distinguishes his letter from Tatiana's, where no such discrepancy is in evidence, and where "as in poetry, expression is at one and the same time also content."[15] Whether or not Eugene adheres to facts in his letter (and we have already seen that in her letter Tatiana does not) is less significant than the marked absence of that inner, emotionally dictated logic that propels Tatiana's letter and lends it coherence and credibility. The formulaic expressions to which Eugene resorts fail to add up to a convincing whole, and their assemblage remains as awkward as that of his fantastical cohorts in Tatiana's dream.

That the two letters carry different meanings to their respective authors is evident. In contrast to Tatiana's intense anticipation of an exceptional, unspecified consequence is Eugene's acute impatience to gain a particular end. In place of the expectation-filled days that followed the delivery of Tatiana's single *billet doux*, we find here Eugene's swift dispatch of letter after letter:

Ответа нет. Он вновь посланье.
Второму, третьему письму
Ответа нет.

[No answer comes. Another letter
he sends, a second, then a third.
No answer comes.][16]
(8:33, ll. 1–3)

The assurance that no reply is forthcoming is equally swift, for Tatiana remains impervious to Eugene's writing. Divorced from genuine expressivity, Eugene's language remains sterile and ineffectual, devoid of seductive power. For Tatiana, his letters can only reaffirm his fall from muse to unwitting parody. Accordingly she is not inspired to invest his letters with her own emotional content. (This, we may observe parenthetically, is the downfall of the unfortunate Liza in "The Queen of Spades," who succumbs to the calculating Germann's letters because she fills both the epistles and their enigmatic author with her own feelings.) Tatiana is better prepared to resist epistolary seduction. She appears to struggle to contain not enflamed ardor, but the indignation Eugene's letters arouse in her (8:33). Her comportment is impeccable, and yet the very success of her impassivity to Eugene suggests that perhaps something has been lost, for the extraordinary receptivity and responsiveness that have been her defining features are no longer in evidence. The reader is left to wonder whether her emotional energy has been sacrificed to formal exactitude.

Tatiana's impassivity holds out little promise for Eugene's attempt to seduce her. It does, however, provide a crucial impetus to his development as it forces him out of a frustrating immediate present to return to a time and place in which their union might have been possible. His ardent display having failed to elicit the anticipated response, Eugene retreats from the code that Tatiana has yet again showed to be inadequate and enters a brooding but beneficial solitude. Sequestering himself in his study, he embarks on a course of reading that is indiscriminate ("Stal vnov' chitat' on bez razbora" [He began to read anew with no distinctions] [8:35, l. 1]) yet also suggestive of an enhanced receptivity ("Ne otvergaia nichego" [Rejecting nothing] [8:35, l. 8]). In place of the abridged list of books Tatiana discovers in the library of Eugene's abandoned country estate, we find here a list of no fewer than ten authors who fall into his purview (8:35, ll. 2–6). The collection of volumes appears to be a random one, and attempts to find method in Eugene's reading have remained less than convincing.[17] Indeed the expressly disorganized nature of his approach suggests a positive relaxation of that very need for control and predictability that we have seen consistently inhibiting his growth. Particularly significant is the absence of fashionable works from Eugene's new reading list, which consists entirely of seventeenth- and eighteenth-century authors, for this plunge into a bygone literary era is correlative with the recollections of his own past that now absorb Pushkin's modish hero. Eugene's excursion into a literary yesteryear that antedates those literary heroes he is doomed to parody coincides with his return to the juncture in his own biography that precedes his thralldom to "khandra" (spleen) (8:34, ll. 11–14).

Just beyond the lines of the books he takes up, Eugene reads his own past:

Мечты, желания, печали
Теснились в душу глубоко.
Он меж печатными строками
Читал духовными глазами
Другие строки. В них-то он
Был совершенно углублен.

[desires and dreams and griefs were breeding
and swarming in his inmost soul.
Between the lines of text as printed,
his mind's eye focused on the hinted
purport of other lines; intense
was his absorption in their sense.][18]

(8:36, ll. 3–8)

Eugene reenters a time and place in which the disappointing here-and-now in which he is mired has not yet been fixed and winters in the space of a recollected past which he regards with open "spiritual eyes" ("dukhovnymi glazami" [8:36, l. 6]). He returns, in other words, to both a literary and a personal point of departure from which a new course might presumably be charted to avoid both the romantic and the personal cul-de-sac in which he now finds himself. It is this metaphoric voyage into his own past and not his actual travels that offers Eugene the possibility for renewal.

Tellingly, the author/narrator no longer associates Eugene with the risk-free game of whist as he had in 4:10, where the hero's desire to retain control over the events in his life was foregrounded. Here the metaphor is, refreshingly, a game of chance that signals Eugene's entry into the associative—and therefore unpredictable—space of the "Imagination:"[19]

> А перед ним Воображенье
> Свой пестрый мечет фараон.
>
> [While in his mind Imagination
> Dealt out her motley faro pack.]
>   (8:37, ll. 3–4)

Nabokov's insightful commentary on stanzas 36 and 37, where Eugene's private world is described, alerts us to the dramatic change that transpires with his retreat from the public eye:

> The wording may fool one at first, for it seems a routine display of formulas to which *Eugene Onegin* has accustomed us—"dreams," and "desires," and "legends," and the usual epithets "secret," "forgotten," and so forth. Yet very soon the inner eye and the inner ear begin to distinguish other colors and sounds. The elements are the old ones but their combination results in a marvelous transmutation of meaning.[20]

As familiar formulae are invested with new meaning in Eugene's ruminations, that very shortcoming we have considered in his letter is rectified. With this rectification comes hope, for if the exhausted phraseology of bygone days can be resuscitated with a healthy infusion of new content, might not the jaded hero himself respond to analogous treatment? The "bezumstvo"—(madness [8:34, l. 6]) of Eugene's pursuit of Princess N recedes before a recollected past that may yet lend itself to new significance. This is a disordered space of old customs, dreams, prophecies, fairy tales, and the letters of young maidens—a space, in short, defined by those very features that shape Tatiana's development, and one, moreover, that the author/narrator himself intends to revisit, as he suggests in his plans for future literary activity (3:13–14).

In the dreamlike state that envelops Eugene, his newly awakened imagination is aligned expressly with the workings of memory, which, like poetry itself, figures somewhere in the space between the distinct, but equally self-absorbed, tyrannical domains of thought and emotion ("I postepenno v usyplen'e / I chuvstv i dum vpadaet on [And gradually both his thoughts and feelings are lulled] [8:37, ll. 1–2]). The images that Eugene now contemplates come neither from direct perception of the actual world nor yet from the psychological depths of the dreamworld, but arise instead from the creative space between them—a space where imagination and memory rule jointly. As his life passes before his mind's eye— Lensky dead in the snow, multitudes of petty, cowardly enemies and slanderers, unfaithful women, despised comrades—its motley images are dominated by one recurring vision: "To sel'skii dom—i u okna / Sidit *ona* . . . i vse ona! . . ." (or else a country house, and by the window / sits *she* . . . and ever *she*! [8:37, ll. 13–14]). No longer signs of a refusal to confront the consequences of his actions as they had been in his letter to Tatiana, the ellipses now signal a transition from the actual world to the space of the imagination. In this newly discovered world a protensive past endures in the present, and it is this synchronicity that permits him to recognize the muse who earlier escaped his notice but who now appears as a revivifying counterbalance to the friend who continues to lie lifeless in the snow. As J. Douglas Clayton observes, "We may say that in Eight, for the first time, the character 'Onegin' has a content."[21] This content is love for Tatiana and remorse for Lensky's death, which become possible only once he has retrieved his past.

The absent Tatiana approximates the role of muse and becomes his "*ona*" *(she),* counterpart to the "*on*" *(he)* that he had been for her. But just as Eugene draws tantalizingly close to the verge of madness or of poetry, the author/narrator abruptly pulls him up short:

—и у окна
Сидит *она* . . . и всё она! . . .
XXXVIII
Он так привык теряться в этом,
Что чуть с ума не своротил,
Или не сделался поэтом.

[A rustic house—and who would be
Framed in the window? . . . Who but She!
XXXVIII
Absorbed and wrapped in this employment,
He was about to lose his mind,
Or else turn poet.][22]
(8:37, l. 13–8:38, l. 3)

Though undoubtedly ironic, the subsequent explanation for his failure to become madman or poet is of substance. Eugene, as the author/narrator describes, does not master the form—the "mechanism of Russian verse"—that could presumably help him to express, order, and thus also to understand the emotional consequences of his disordered musings. Nor has he succeeded in either breaking away from vacuous models or bringing new content to them. Reverting yet again to a ready-made role, Eugene comes to *seem* like a poet but not to *be* one:

> Как походил он на поэта,
> Когда в углу сидел один,
> И перед ним пылал камин,
> И он мурлыкал: *Benedetta*
> Иль *Idol mio* и ронял
> В огонь то туфлю, то журнал.

> [He looked the poet so completely
> When by the hearth he'd sit alone
> And *Benedetta* he'd intone
> Or sometimes *Idol mio* sweetly—
> While on the flames he'd drop unseen
> His slipper or his magazine!]
> (8:38, ll. 9–14)

Here is a mirror image of that controlled surrender that Tatiana exemplifies in her letter (and will demonstrate again in her speech to the hero), for Eugene remains too undisciplined and yet also too constrained to succeed. His retrieval of his past presents him with the inescapable image of his slain friend, but provides also the potentially regenerative image of *her*. This marks a pivotal stage, but his development is not yet complete. Accordingly, the concluding couplet of this stanza (8:38) which leaves him shy of poetry and madness closes with the rhyme pair "i ronial–to zhurnal" that comes acoustically close to "ideal," but, like Eugene, falls just short of arriving at it.[23]

The world Eugene fled has yet to be reconciled with the recently rediscovered past to which he was driven by the Princess N's impassivity. In particular, the two seemingly incompatible images of Tatiana must be reintegrated. Eugene's precipitous return to her suggests that though neither madman nor poet, he experiences a promising upsurge of feeling that neither his exile nor social decorum can contain. The urgency of these feelings hurls him across a stanzaic boundary in a graphic suggestion that he is breaking out of those norms that have up to now fully contained him.

It is not that Eugene has changed, but that he has arrived at a point at which change becomes possible. Indeed, discussion of whether or not Eugene is transformed, be it by his travels or by his love for Tatiana, bypass the more urgent question of whether a space of possibility might yet be pried open for this jaded, overdetermined hero. At stake here is the *potential* for change. Whether or not this potential finds realization is projected tantalizingly beyond the boundary of the text. We can speculate that it is the strong sense of the hero's renewed possibility that may well have prompted Caryl Emerson to suggest that the remainder of the work be read as the product of Eugene's imagination rather than as a record of events as they occur in the story.[24] Emerson's new reading places a productive emphasis on the crucial but largely overlooked emotional and imaginative energy that Eugene derives from his hibernal, solitary excursion into his own past. Whether or not we consider the conclusion of *Onegin* a product of Eugene's imagination (I take the more conventional position), it is important to recognize, as Emerson does, that the hero has now reached an auspicious stage that holds out considerable promise for his subsequent development. Of interest here are the particular circumstances that permit Eugene to draw his own past into the present and thus to reconcile not only the double image of Tatiana that he confronts, but also his own divided self.

With extraordinary speed "the incorrigible eccentric" ("neispravlennyi chudak" [8:40, l. 4]) arrives at the home of Princess N, and, making his way through the empty house, comes upon Tatiana in her boudoir. Tatiana's toilette is not yet complete, and Eugene surprises her as she sits shedding tears over a letter—presumably one of his own.

Eugene's swift passage through St. Petersburg, his unimpeded progress through the house, and his easy attainment of Tatiana's private chambers have, as Emerson summarizes, "been interpreted variously as dreamlike activity, fairy tale logic, or the narrator's irony."[25] At the same time we recognize here a literary topos familiar to us—as it would also be to Tatiana—from Richardson's *Clarissa* and Rousseau's *The New Eloise*. In the idiom of these eighteenth-century epistolary novels that exerted a formative influence on Tatiana, transgression of the firmly drawn boundary between the public and the private leads inevitably to the slippery slope of moral transgression. Thus, as we have seen in our discussion of Tatiana's reading, Clarissa's valiant struggle to protect herself from Lovelace is centered on barring his access to her chambers and frustrating his attempts to surprise her before her toilette is complete. In Rousseau's novel, Saint-Preux's entry into Julie's private rooms is a prelude to their sexual intimacy. (We recognize an inversion of this topos earlier in *Onegin* when the narrator underscores the asexuality of Olga and Vladimir's relationship by referring to their *chaste* meetings in Olga's room.) With Eugene's entry into Tatiana's boudoir and the state of undress and heightened emotions in which he surprises her, the stage is set for the consummation of their love.

We can recall here that this familiar topos found its way into a number of Pushkin's works, where he plays with the conventional expectations it generates and moves beyond its strictly moral implications to explore also its broader psychological possibilities. Whatever its permutations, however, one constant remains: the penetration of private space uncovers the individual concealed beneath a publicly assumed role. Thus, as we have seen, Tatiana's exploration of Eugene's living quarters and library yields up crucial insights into the hero's character. In Pushkin's story "Baryshnia krest'ianka" ("Mistress into Maid"), Aleksei discovers the true identity of the woman he loves when he surprises her alone at home divested of her publicly sported disguises and reading one of his letters. In "The Queen of Spades" Germann similarly attains with exceptional ease the bedchamber of the Countess, where he observes the now morbid rather than erotic shedding of her public guise.

Inasmuch as the poet's art is dependent precisely on negotiations between the public and the private that are highlighted by this particular topos, Tatiana's response to Eugene's sudden appearance in her room is of paramount importance not only to the plot of *Eugene Onegin*, but also to the defense of poetry Pushkin advances in this work. Introduced at this juncture of the text, the topos has two notable effects. Even as it creates an overriding expectation that hero and heroine will be united, it throws into high relief the grace with which Tatiana negotiates between her public role and her private self. Tatiana's exemplary self-mastery in Petersburg society is complemented in the private sphere Eugene now enters by an equally admirable self-disclosure. Revealed to him are those signs of emotion he sought in vain to elicit from her earlier, and it is in this intimate, unguarded moment that he recognizes in the forbidding Princess N the "Tania" he once knew:

> О, кто б немых ее страданий
> В сей быстрый миг не прочитал!
> Кто прежней Тани, бедной Тани
> Теперь в княгине б не узнал!

> [In that brief instant then, who couldn't
> Have read her tortured heart at last!
> And in the princess then, who wouldn't
> Have known poor Tanya from the past!]
> (8:41, ll. 1–4)

The affectionate diminutive of Tatiana's name is used here to refer specifically to the love-stricken rural girl Eugene recollects in the course of his hibernation, in contradistinction to the impassive Princess N he has recently met. This particular form of the heroine's name is used also by

Tatiana's fond Muscovite relations, who persist in recalling the girl they once knew when they see the changed young woman before them. In her speech to Eugene, Tatiana similarly adopts this designation to distinguish between her actual and her recollected selves. For Eugene, the callow girl and sophisticated princess, the remembered and the actual, the past and the present are now brought together by the Tatiana before him. Crucial here is the fact that the image of the austere Princess does not recede before the recuperated image of "Tania," and that Eugene succeeds in holding the remembered past and the actual present in a simultaneity that counters the barren sequential linearity that has thus far determined his life.

Eugene's reconciliation of the recollected "Tania" with the actual "Princess N" enables him to "read" Tatiana with the empathy any good reader should bring to a work. For her part, Tatiana immediately connects what is written in Eugene's features with the torments of love that she has herself experienced. Her immediate response to Eugene's abrupt intrusion is highly unconventional. She is neither surprised nor angered ("Bez udivleniia, bez gneva" [8:41, l. 9]), and the mute, impassioned pleading of Eugene's gaze leads her not into his arms, but into her own past. Even as Eugene unexpectedly recognizes "Tania" in the Princess N, so too does his sudden appearance induce the Princess N to recuperate her former self:

> Его больной, угасший взор,
> Моляций вид, немой укор,
> Ей внятно всё. *Простая дева,*
> *С мечтами, сердцем прежних дней*
> *Теперь опять воскресла в ней.*
>
> [His stricken, sick, extinguished eyes,
> Imploring aspect, mute replies—
> She saw it all. In desolation,
> *The simple girl he'd known before,*
> *Who'd dreamt and loved, was born once more.*]
>   (8:41, ll. 10–14, my emphasis)

Suddenly Eugene is once again Tatiana's muse. Like the "thou"-muse of "I Remember the Wondrous Moment," he reappears before Tatiana to return to life a past that has been obscured by her present circumstances.

The question offered by the author/narrator, "O chem teper' ee mechtan'e?" (Of what are her reveries now? [8:42, l. 5]), directs us beyond the passionate man at Tatiana's feet to the space of her ruminations, as she retreats from a present that offers the fulfillment of desire to a recollected past of unrealized possibility. Correlative with this choice of potential over realization and of the recollected over the actual is Tatiana's translation of her intense emotions into self-expressivity rather than physical gratification—a choice that stands out forcefully against the expectation of consummated love that is generated in this scene.

If we consider closely the text of Tatiana's final speech and the circumstances in which it is delivered, we find that it is considerably more complex and far-reaching than the self-sacrificial avowal of matrimonial duty it is conventionally made out to be. In it Tatiana's organization of experience draws the conditions of reality into an essentially poetic framework, and the precepts of her moral stance are integrally related to those of poetry itself. From what Tatiana says, we understand that the long silence that precedes her response to Eugene ("Prokhodit dolgoe molchan'e" [8:42, l. 6]) marks not an inner struggle between duty and desire, but a profoundly enabling contemplation of a former self. Tatiana's present circumstances are vividly illuminated by the past that is involuntarily called forth by Eugene's sudden appearance. Her recollections are analogous to Eugene's immediately preceding retreat from his fugitive, time-bound social existence into a past where possibility had not yet been closed down. Tatiana similarly returns to the countryside where Eugene appeared to her in an aura of potentiality—a time that preceded his fall from muse to man and her own marriage. The recollection of her past within the context of her drastically altered present draws together the Eugene of her reveries with the flesh-and-blood man who now kneels before her and gives rise to a multiple consciousness out of which spring Tatiana's glory, the potential for Eugene's regeneration, and Pushkin's defense of poetry. Tatiana's speech is neither the punishment nor the revenge that some commentators hold it to be. It is a vital, self-expressive act in the course of which she recognizes her lost muse and finds sustenance both for the intense feelings of her younger days and for her mastery over them. Like her letter, Tatiana's speech is a controlled surrender. Even as it crowns Tatiana's story, its recapitulation of the poetic imperative points the way to a poetic becoming that unfolds in concert with the demands of an actual world.

Significant here is Todd's note that Tatiana achieves social success in Petersburg because she imposes "what her age considered an aesthetic order upon reality."[26] The success of the famous speech she delivers to Eugene may be described in terms of a similar imposition of aesthetic order upon a recollected past that is juxtaposed with her present circumstances. Thus the girl Eugene once spurned arises alongside the princess he now courts, the solitude of the drowsy Russian countryside is set next to the glittering capital where she is a social success, and the inspiring muse rejoins the disappointing man, making it possible for Tatiana's own reconciliation of "Tania" and the Princess N. With this reintegration of past and present, she springs free of the baleful inadequacies of both mere cyclicity and mere linearity. The interaction of two temporal frameworks—the time of the events and the time of their recollection—reopens a realm of possibility to which she swears allegiance.

Richard Gregg has recorded his doubts concerning the veracity of the information Tatiana conveys in her speech, which does not, as he puts it, "square with the facts" and is accordingly to be regarded as the "rhetoric of pathos" of this "exceedingly unreliable witness."[27] There can indeed be little doubt that Tatiana's speech is no objective documentation of actual events any more than was her letter to Eugene. Tatiana's recollection of her younger years is by no means to be equated with her actual sojourn in them.

A perfect hybrid of the actual and the imagined, memory freely draws past events into combination with the present and even the projected future, thereby exceeding any simple tense. Memory, in Siniavskii's description, "leads us again and again to traces of the past and through them reconstructs life in its lasting presence."[28] Because memory is enabled—not merely determined—by past experiences, it fosters recreation with emphasis on "creation." It is neither mere inventory, nor pure invention, but rather "one form of the imagination . . . of which a nobler version is poetry."[29] For memory, time is no arrow, but a two-way thoroughfare, and we recognize at once that even as Tatiana's evaluation of her present condition is shaped by her recollection of past events, so too does that past she recollects bear unmistakable signs of an open present. Thus we see, for example, that the Russian nanny who was still living in the time Tatiana recalls is dead and buried in the recreated scene (8:46, ll. 12–14).

The preference Tatiana expresses for the humble surroundings of her formative years over her present glamorous setting is generally construed as her vote for the natural rural Russian world over the artificial, cosmopolitan urban capital. As Richard Gregg elegantly summarizes,

> few "truths" about Tat'jana have been repeated more often or accorded greater significance than that she despises the false glamour of the cosmopolitan *haut monde* into which her loveless marriage has thrust her and longs to return to the bucolic tranquillity of Larino.[30]

Gregg goes on to remind readers that for Tatiana life in the country was no more perfect than her present world is odious. This is indeed the case, but it would seem that Tatiana's "unreliability" on this score signals not the "dubiety" for which Gregg argues, but rather a verity of a different order.

Tatiana's preference for rural life, it will be recalled, found clear articulation in the author/narrator's account of her reaction to the Moscow rout where she was brought to find a husband (7:53, ll. 5–14). In her speech to Onegin, however, we discover considerably more than the mere reiteration of those sentiments, for the context in which they are uttered has changed, and with it the import of Tatiana's words. It is no longer the author/narrator speaking on her behalf, but Tatiana herself who expresses her partiality for the countryside. Her evaluation comes, moreover, not from the perspective of a timid, inexperienced, and discomfited outsider who would naturally prefer to be in familiar terrain, but from a lofty position in society where she is both successful and perfectly at ease. The ascendancy Tatiana accords her rural experience in her speech to Eugene manifests not her preference for Russian countryside over European capital, but rather her longing for a past in which her future appeared more open than the one she contemplates from her present vantage point. Retrieved with this past are features we recognize as having played a crucial role in the concurrent development of Tatiana's sexuality and her faculties of the creative imagination: nature, solitude, her books, and that wondrous moment in which the man who became her muse appeared to her. Tatiana does not seek an actual return. The countryside where her formative years were passed becomes for her not a concrete point of destination, but rather a point of departure for a reassessment of her present situation—a reassessment on the strength of which she moves beyond the contingencies of the here-and-now.

We have seen already that from girlhood on Tatiana's actual setting has always been tangential to her privately nurtured inner world, and we recognize that even the tremendous social advantages that are now hers have not displaced her allegiance to what is not immediately available. The difference here is that, believing her muse to be lost and her future to be fixed by her marriage, Tatiana returns to an earlier time in which her own destiny was yet open. With the exclamation "A schast'e bylo tak vozmozhno, / Tak blizko!" (And happiness was so possible, / So near! [8:47, ll. 1–2]), Tatiana evokes not an actual opportunity that has been missed, but rather that stimulating sense of possibility that enlivened her early years. With a few brief strokes she fills in a part of her story that the author/narrator neglected to supply—the courtship and marriage that we now see not as they occurred, but as Tatiana reconstructs them:

> Но судьба моя
> Уж решена. Неосторожно,
> Быть может поступила я:
> Меня с слезами заклинаний
> Молила мать; для бедной Тани
> Все были жребии равны . . .
> Я вышла замуж.

[But now my fate
Has been decreed. I may have merely
Been reckless when I failed to wait;
But mother with her lamentation
Implored me, and in resignation
(All futures seemed alike in woe)
I married . . .]

(8:47, ll. 2–8)

In describing her capitulation to her mother's pleas as perhaps " reckless," Tatiana acknowledges the irrevocability of her decision. In the indifference which, according to her account, prompted her decision we recognize Tatiana's resignation to social demands that she no longer had the wherewithal to evade. Abandoned by her muse and pressed to marry by a lachrymose mother, Tatiana could well consider her options irredeemably closed down. Now, in the presence of the amorous Eugene, it might seem that her marriage is perhaps less determinate. And yet Tatiana turns toward a past where she met with no encouragement from Eugene, rather than remain in the present in which he offers his love, because she knows instinctively that a liaison with him could perhaps vary but by no means undo the fate she describes as having been sealed with her marriage.[31]

Tatiana does not delude herself with mirages of possibility where there are, in fact, none. Even as the accomplished Princess N does not displace the callow "Tania" for Eugene, so too does the image of the unfeeling sermonizer persist for Tatiana in the face of the ardent professor of love Eugene has become. Any apparent transformation the characters have undergone is to be evaluated in the context of their former selves, for, as Pushkin has demonstrated with the account of his muse that opens this chapter, beneath any surface change we must seek also a deeper, inviolable continuity. Tatiana does not shy away from the possibility that Eugene's amorous public pursuits are motivated by the change in her own circumstance rather than by a change in Eugene himself. Soberly, she judges against him.

Tatiana may well take a dim view of Eugene's behavior toward her, for she is fully cognizant of the fact that she is now more than ever at risk and stands to lose more than he (8:44). As at her name day celebration, so too in Petersburg society it falls to her to exercise self-control in the face of Eugene's irresponsible behavior. Given her present circumstances it is that very self-restraint Eugene advocated in his sermon and not his extravagant displays of feeling that would attest to his genuine love for her. Tatiana's reproach is a stern one: "Kak s vashim serdtsem i umom / Byt' chuvstva melkogo rabom?" (With your heart and mind, / How can you be the slave of trivial feeling [8:45, ll. 13–14]). Yet the reproof is also generous, for it acknowledges in Eugene that very quality of heart and mind with which she is herself endowed. As in her younger days, so now too, Tatiana sees more in Eugene than is immediately apparent. Like the guests we have seen becoming better in her presence (8:23, ll. 8–14), Eugene too stands to improve in the aura of Tatiana's high expectations. If earlier Tatiana was not possessed of the means to forestall Lensky's death to which Eugene's misguided actions led, here her impeccable behavior permits her to avert the potentially disastrous consequences of yielding to Eugene's importunate demands.

The transition from the past tense of "I ia liubila vas" (And I loved you [8:43, l. 3]) to the present tense with which her speech culminates ("Ia vas liubliu" [I love you] [8:47, l. 12]) signals that Tatiana's reintegration of her past and present is now complete. With this completion comes the realization that her love for Eugene, like her memories of the Russian countryside, and perhaps even like that "younger" self to which she refers earlier in her speech (8:43, ll. 1–2), need not recede before the present but can be made to endure within it. The paradise thus regained is the possibility of her past with which she imbues her circumscribed present world. That very realm that Tatiana indicates with her seemingly less than accurate assertion, "A schast'e bylo tak vozmozhno, / Tak blizko ..." (And happiness was so possible, / So near [8:47, ll. 1–2]), is now renewed in her present circumstances.

It is no mere coincidence that this intimation follows directly on the heels of Tatiana's remembrance of the setting in which a flesh-and-blood man became—on the strength of her frustrated love—a muse. Brought into collision in the double consciousness of Tatiana's recollections are the "thou" and the "you," the addressee of her letter and its recipient, the Eugene of her past and the one now before her. In this particular context, the decision Tatiana faces is no longer between two men—her own husband and Eugene—or even between marital duty and personal gratification. The Eugene who was both the source and the consequence of her inspired romantic reveries has returned to stand alongside the man who now seeks to secure her attentions, and it is between them that Tatiana must choose. She can either dedicate herself to the fragile realm of possibility that she has just recaptured, or satisfy and thus dispel the longing that creates this possibility. The moral choice between husband and lover is subsumed by the larger poetical one that Tatiana faces between man and muse, between the consummation of desire and its protraction, between an unattainable ideal and an available man. Here Pushkin's heroine is at the height of her role in *Eugene Onegin*, which, in Stephanie Sandler's felicitous formulation, is "both a text of renunciation and a text of continuing attraction."[32] If Tatiana's position vis-à-vis Eugene is the more vulnerable, so is it also the one heavier with responsibility. Divested of the accouterments of her public image and particularly susceptible emotionally, Tatiana, as we have observed, has far more to lose than he (8:44). Yet in a way that he could scarcely have imagined when he penned his letter to her, Eugene's fate is indeed in Tatiana's hands, for it now falls to her to act either as the unattainable muse who will sustain his recently revived emotions or as the woman who will satisfy them and thus dissipate their potential energies.

As in her letter, the insistent reiteration of "I"—prevalent throughout the speech and heard no fewer than six times in its last seven lines—signals both the increased awareness that comes with self-expressivity and the acknowledgment of responsibility that lends authority to her words.[33] Like her letter, Tatiana's speech is a journey of revelation and discovery that marks her self-formative progress. It reestablishes the continuity between "Tania" and the Princess N and between her muse and the would-be seducer who is its prototype. Poised between the creative potentiality of unfulfilled desire and the sealed fate of consummation, Tatiana concludes with what are perhaps the most oft quoted lines in Russian literature: "No ia drugomu otdana; / Ia budu vek emu verna" (But I am given to another; / I will be true to him forever [8:47, ll. 13–14]).[34]

The possible sources of Tatiana's concluding statement have received scholarly attention, the fruits of which are conveniently summarized by Todd:

> These lines, it has been established, are adapted from a song found among the folk, thought in Pushkin's time to have been written by Peter I, and translated into French by Pushkin's uncle . . . Tatiana could have read the song in M. D. Chulkov's collection of various songs, in A. S. Shishkov's collected works (1824), or in an old issue of the *Mercure de France* (1803), or else she could have heard it from her nurse. It is at once representative of the wealth and syncretic nature of Russian culture and of Tatiana's ability to draw on that culture to create and understand her life.[35]

Whatever their origin, the moral stance these famous lines presuppose was widely promoted both in the folk and in the literary traditions. Here our immediate concern, however, is not the source of these unoriginal words, but the significance with which Tatiana infuses them as she translates a commonplace into the unique circumstances of her life. The "drugoi" (other) for which Tatiana opts here has always been understood to refer unequivocally to the husband she has wed offstage, and the marital fidelity her words ostensibly signal has received widespread enthusiastic praise (with only some dissenting murmurs against her apparent inability to break with convention to follow the dictates of her heart).[36] The resulting picture is the comforting commonplace—one that has, I maintain, no place in Pushkin's text—of a woman's selfless surrender of her own desires to the institution of matrimony and a paternalistic husband who tames her passions. It is a situation, in short, whose vivid depiction in Rousseau's *The New Eloise* we have considered already. In order to intensify the sacrificial quality of what they construed to be Tatiana's exemplary gesture, some commentators (notably Dostoevsky) went so far as to make her husband older, fatter, and less virile than is warranted by Pushkin's text. The circumstances in which Pushkin places his beloved heroine, however, are very different, and ironically it is not Tatiana who falls back on the models suggested by the novels she reads, but those readers who emphasize her dependency on them.[37]

Readers have traditionally assumed that the man who catapults Pushkin's reticent heroine into the public eye and a Cinderella-like story is indeed that "fat general" whose attention she unwittingly captured at the Moscow rout (7:54). To stare fixedly at a young girl, however, is not yet to wed her, and Pushkin, characteristically, has left us with strong likelihood, but not absolute certainty on this score.[38] Whoever he may be, and whatever his girth, Tatiana's husband has at the very least to be commended for his discriminating choice of partner. Although now justifiably proud of his wife's social success, it was clearly not for this that Prince N married an unsophisticated girl of scant means and no connections who failed to attract much attention at the time of her Moscow debut. Independent of those appearances to which Eugene remains enslaved,[39] the Prince proved capable of appreciating Tatiana in the guise of an "uezdnaia baryshnia" (country miss) no less than in the radiant figure of Princess N that she becomes. In this, as in his many accomplishments, he is surely the better man. Indeed, far from marrying Tatiana off to an inadequate individual, Pushkin gives her a husband who has everything that he himself lacked—an enviable social position, a brilliant military career, wealth, the love of the court, and finally, the discrimination to choose an exceptional heroine-muse as his wife.[40] Having thus provided for her, Pushkin proceeds to bestow on his beloved heroine the one gift that is truly his own to give, and Tatiana comes into her glory not in the conventional novelistic role of wife to a distinguished man, but as the fulfillment of a poetic ideal.

And this is why—although Tatiana's husband is surely worthy of her fidelity—it is not specifically to him that she refers in the renowned pronouncement with which she leaves Eugene and the pages of Pushkin's novel-in-verse. Her final words do not simply complete her story. They convey a poetic potency that extends well beyond the bounds of the text, for beyond their commonly accepted meaning we can discern another content. In light of Mme. Larina's insistence on her daughter's wedding, "otdana" is generally construed to mean "given away." Yet "otdana" also means "devoted, dedicated to." At the same time, the "other" that commands Tatiana's constancy is not simply her husband, but also the "other," recollected Eugene who is juxtaposed with the man now before her. We have noted already that Tatiana's references to Eugene repeatedly indicate not the man himself, but a broader, erotically charged imaginative space into which he is absorbed. Thus, it will be recalled, after her first meeting with him, Tatiana "Nevol'no dumala o *tom*" (Involuntarily thought about that [person/thing/act] [3:7, l. 4]), while in her letter she expressed the desire "Vse dumat', dumat' ob *odnom*" (To think and think about that one [person/thing/act] [l. 16]). As in her letter, so too in her speech, Tatiana addresses a Eugene who does not coincide with himself, and the "drugomu" expands to refer not only to some*one*, but also to some*thing* else.[41] Tatiana refuses Eugene even as she admits her love for him because she has dedicated herself to that "other" that lies beyond the confines of her here-and-now. The very words that purportedly convey an essentially novelistic expression of marital fidelity put into effect two vital, interrelated poetic imperatives: that desire be prolonged rather than fulfilled, and that the realm of the imagination take precedence over the actual world. The "other" to which Tatiana dedicates herself derives from and confirms what is not immediately present, something that here in the final chapter of *Onegin* she aligns with the Russian countryside and that in the opening chapter her creator refers to as "his African sky" ("pod nebom Afrike moei" [1:50, l. 11]). Seen in this light, Tatiana's fidelity to her husband emerges as a side effect of her far-reaching allegiance to the creative imagination.

Thus Tatiana's speech champions the exquisite appropriateness of poetic ideals to the ethical demands of well-lived everyday life, for Tatiana succeeds in remaining true to her husband, in finding a means to sustain the creative energy of unfulfilled desire that she has seen consistently dulled by marital contentment and habit, and in fulfilling her poet's mission. We can note parenthetically that Pushkin, with his own rakish past and impending marriage to the beauty Natalia Goncharova in mind, might well have been anxious to promote the cause of marital fidelity, as Clayton has suggested.[42] But he must have been at least as anxious about preserving the erotic energy that fueled his creativity from marital contentment. Even as she remains a loyal spouse, Tatiana remains also a quintessentially creative and inspiring being.

Tatiana recognizes and readily assumes on behalf of both herself and Eugene the cost exacted for the protraction of possibility. Out of the painfully inadequate, merely apparent choices offered by the rural and urban worlds as Pushkin represents them in the opening chapters of this work, Tatiana derives a creative energy that enlivens her perfectly mastered social form and promises to revitalize Eugene. The starry-eyed girl who wrote him is now a clear-sighted woman who has derived her clarity of vision not from a transferal of allegiance from the imaginative to the actual or from the humble rural to the dazzling urban, or from personal needs to social demands, but specifically from the interrelation of these seemingly irreconcilable antipodes.

What is perhaps most extraordinary about the ending of *Eugene Onegin* is that there are no losers. Tatiana's allegiance to the imagination is not driven by failure in the actual world but coexists with her glamorous success in it. She makes no sacrifice here, for neither her place in St. Petersburg society nor her private imaginative world need be surrendered. Nor is it at Eugene's expense that Tatiana preserves both her marriage and the poetic ideal with which Pushkin entrusts her. Her rejection of him is neither revenge nor a bid for power, but an important step toward the regeneration for which he has been prepared by the repeated challenges of her unconventional behavior. We have seen already that Tatiana's earlier refusal to respond to Eugene's professions of ardor led him to a recollected past when she might have been his, to the countryside where he first met her, to books, to "*her.*" Now by confessing her love for him even as she rejects his advances, Tatiana completes her modulation into muse—both flesh-and-blood woman and unattainable ideal—who draws him toward that space of possibility that is opened by mutual unrequited love.

With the avowal of love for Eugene that is coupled with her firm refusal of his attentions, Tatiana asseverates her unequivocal allegiance to a creative imaginative sphere where he is her muse, and in so doing unerringly supplies also the criteria necessary for the resuscitation of the jaded hero. This choice engages the creative energies of eros and leaves moral and social obligations unviolated. Reflected in the climactic confluence of questions of individual, social, moral, and poetical demands with which *Eugene Onegin* ends, we see the import and the verity of Pushkin's observation that "poetry is above morality."[43]

Having come to the end of Tatiana's and Eugene's stories, we can appreciate the significance of "Fare Thee Well" from which Pushkin drew the epigraph for this final chapter of *Onegin*. Written on 17 March 1816, in the wake of Lady Byron's departure, Byron's lyric is pertinent to the conclusion of *Eugene Onegin,* for both the poem itself and the well-known circumstances of its composition throw into high relief what Tatiana has accomplished in her speech to Eugene. This is not the place to enlarge on either Lord and Lady Byron's unfortunate marriage or on their troubled parting. Whichever of the partners in the dissolution of this uneasy union may command our sympathies, the fact remains that the loss of his wife triggered in Byron the expression of emotions that had not been in evidence while she was yet with him, but which, upon her suing for separation, overflowed into poetry liberally watered with tears. (The tear-stained manuscript of this poem has excited considerable commentary.) Byron's exquisite lyric emerges entirely out of a reinvented past that arises in the face of irreparable present loss. The power with which the desperate need for reconciliation is expressed derives specifically from the underlying certainty of its impossibility, for the poem is written in complete awareness that reconciliation would banish the very emotion that now makes reunion so fervently desired. The loss of his wife generates in Byron powerful feelings that reshape the past as he searches for a space in which this impossible union might yet be accomplished. It is in his poem that Byron finds this space of possibility—this in the full knowledge that only the fulfillment of the overpowering longing he expresses in "Fare Thee Well" can close it down. Tatiana's reply to Eugene bespeaks her intuitive comprehension and acceptance of the poetic imperative of loss and sustained desire that fuels Byron's "Fare Thee Well." Unlike that poet, however, she exacts no victims.

In considering the final encounter of the heroine and hero of Pushkin's work, Walter Vickery observes,

> This whole incident is not so much a defeat for Onegin or a victory for Tatiana; it involves rather the vain hope of a second chance, and the grim certainty that there are no second chances.[44]

Vickery is right to forgo describing the final encounter of Pushkin's hero and heroine in terms of victory and defeat, but the "grim certainty" he describes is neither as certain nor as grim in *Eugene Onegin* as it is, for example, in *Kamennyi gost'* (*The Stone Guest*) whose Don Guan, as Leon Stilman reminds us, Onegin meets chronologically.[45] Tatiana recognizes that the past can be returned only in the imagination and not in the actual world where attempts to recapture lost opportunity must necessarily destroy it. Unlike the unfortunate Anna and Guan of *The Stone Guest*, Pushkin's Tatiana and Eugene are taken beyond a second chance at fulfillment to a quintessentially poetic space of unending possibility.

The continuity Tatiana's speech establishes between her dissimilar past and present manifests the enduring qualities that underlie the apparent transformations of the muse—whether that muse be Pushkin's own, the one Tatiana discerns in Eugene, or the one she herself becomes for him. By no means does this muse-making signal a disregard for the demands of the actual world, for these demands are fully and consciously met. The consummate success of Tatiana's speech leaves little room for speculation on the "unfinishedness" of *Eugene Onegin*, for a more perfect ending can scarcely be imagined. Tatiana's crowning choice of the "other" which she ever privileged over the here-and-now is right both morally and poetically. The physical involvement of hero and heroine is superseded by a relationship in which each fulfills a more profound need for the other. That love be consummated is a novelistic expectation. *Eugene Onegin* is a defense of poetry—a genre, as Pushkin demonstrates, into which the novel can be absorbed. Pushkin leaves his hero and heroine not locked in embrace, but free to come into their own and to savor that moment of opening that Eugene ever feared and that Tatiana ever courted but believed to have been lost. Stanley Mitchell has observed that on the strength of the poetry she successfully retains, Tatiana emerges "as a culmination rather than a new beginning,"[46] but she is really both, for the genuine muse, like the living, sentient being, remains always in the process of becoming—a manifestation of the human preoccupation with what is permanent in passing time. Reconciled in Tatiana's changeability and firmness of principle, in her emergence as muse and in her story of matrimonial fidelity, and finally in her mastery of form and capacity for intense emotion are precisely those antithetical qualities that are evoked metaphorically earlier in *Eugene Onegin* to distinguish the two unlikely friends who fail tragically in their attempt to coexist: "Volna i kamen', / Stikhi i proza, led i plamen'" (Wave and stone, / Poetry and prose, ice and flame" [2:13, ll. 5–6]). Surely this is the happiest of all possible endings.

Epilogue

But then the fact's a fact—and 'tis the part
Of a true poet to escape from fiction
Whene'er he can; for there is little art
In leaving verse more free from the restriction
Of truth than prose . . .

>   Byron, *Don Juan*

'There is a tide in the affairs of men,
   Which, taken at the flood,'—you know the rest,
There is a tide in the affairs of women,
   Which, taken at the flood, leads—God knows where . . .

>   Byron, *Don Juan*

Any reading of *Eugene Onegin*—and the possibilities are endless—is well served by T. S. Eliot's dictum that "when we are considering poetry we must consider it primarily as poetry and not another thing." That the place of this genre in his own creative biography and in society at large preoccupied Pushkin as he began his novel-in-verse is revealed in the bitter "Razgovor knigoprodavtsa s poetom" ("Conversation of a Bookseller with a Poet" [26 September 1824, *PSS* 2:290–94]) which introduced the first chapter of *Eugene Onegin* in its two separate publications in 1825 and 1829. This poem centers on a perverse realization of Pushkin's root metaphor that designated poetic inspiration as the source of transcendent freedom. In it, the poet confronts the demands of a starkly literal world that offers to transform pages of verse into stacks of bills that purchase a distinctly unmetaphysical "freedom" from day-to-day cares. The poet's situation in the pragmatic world represented in "Conversation" is an untenable one, for under the circumstances Pushkin describes, the very practice of his art amounts to its betrayal. Transcriptions of the creative experience find no resonance in the unimaginative "they" who are opposed to the poet and for whom the divinely inspired is merely comical. "Blazhen kto molcha byl poet" (Blessed is he who was a poet in silence [l. 68]). The freedom the poet now claims is the freedom from writing verse (l. 167). Having heard out the bookseller's mercantile arguments, he

212

agrees to accept in exchange for his manuscript the "freedom" that in this "iron age" is identified with gold. This acceptance is uttered with icy hauteur in a line of prose.

Caryl Emerson has observed that Pushkin's "own life provided ample evidence that a collapse of freedom, a sudden and apparently unwelcome constraint, could trigger the most marvelous creativity."[1] The bookseller's demands represent just such an "unwelcome constraint," and it is the "most marvelous creativity" of *Eugene Onegin* that constitutes Pushkin's real response and not the prosaic acquiescence that ends "Conversation." Pushkin had no intention of surrendering his poetic ideals—however underappreciated they might be—or of merely grousing at their trivialization by an uncomprehending public. According to Lotman, "[t]he law of art is the increase of possible choices,"[2] and with *Eugene Onegin* Pushkin set out to create new choices where there appeared to be none, for only thus, to borrow from Emerson, "could the poet transfigure that by which he was himself transfixed."[3] His novel-in-verse is just such a transfiguration.

The extraordinary receptivity, syncretism, and creative energy that characterize Pushkin's activity in the heady literary process of early-nineteenth-century Russia are concentrated in *Onegin* to defend not only poetry, but a poetical way of being. Sustained by the muse he creates for himself, Pushkin resolutely presses beyond the reach of that demon whose intonation is distinctly perceptible in the chilling prose that concludes "Conversation." By the end of his novel-in-verse the impasse depicted in that poem is transcended, and negation is averted. The publications of the complete *Onegin* of 1833 and 1837 are no longer prefaced by "Conversation."

Boris Gasparov writes that Pushkin's

> living ties with the stylistic, generic, and psychological system of a past age in combination with the turbulent innovative aspirations of [his] contemporaneous epoch, gave rise to a unique creative phenomenon, whose irrepeatable qualities permitted his creative work to become one of the most powerful creative impulses in the history of Russian culture.[4]

Nowhere is this extraordinary energy more in evidence that in *Onegin*. With consummate grace Pushkin orchestrates what is apparently dissonant material into a fresh, new, liberating whole. Incompatible lexical and semantic units, stylistic elements, points of view, literary schools, and genres conspire to reproduce the dynamic motley of life itself. The *joie de vivre* of *Onegin* derives specifically from the success with which Pushkin not only forestalls the courted threat of chaos, but brings unprecedented order and wholeness to his newly created world. The source of this success is the distinctly poetical conjunction of strict, rational form with the emotional, associative freedom of the imagination. Life's prosy disarray and the unfreedoms it imposes are contained and transcended in verse. This is the poet's answer to "booksellers" of every sort—an answer that rises well above the trivial pragmatism of the merchant who can no more "repay" the poet for his work than Eugene's speech can "repay" Tatiana for her letter.

We have seen in the course of this study that Tatiana's role in the poetic enterprise of *Eugene Onegin* is animating and crucial. To draw on David Bethea's elegant formulation, "her way of *interacting* with the world, of developing her imaginative potential in a context full of real risk and real constraint, is the embodiment of *inspiring* behavior."[5] We must now touch on possible explanations for the general neglect of this aspect of Pushkin's heroine. This epilogue will open with a speculation on why the poetical slipped away and conclude by way of counterexample with a brief look at two important instances of its recognition: Karolina Pavlova's and Marina Tsvetaeva's incorporation of Tatiana into their own poetic self-presentations.

The primary stumbling blocks to a fuller appreciation of Tatiana and thus also of *Onegin* can be roughly designated as "genre and gender," for Pushkin's poetical heroine was emulated by novelists rather than poets, and what was construed as the self-sacrificial marital fidelity with which *Onegin* ended was allowed to obscure the poetic imperative that guided the heroine's development in Pushkin's work. Whatever the earnestness and meticulously crafted irrefutability of Pushkin's defense of poetry in *Eugene Onegin*, that very prose in which the poet yielded to the bookseller was soon to predominate on the Russian literary scene, and the creative impulse of his novel-in-verse was absorbed into the development of the prose novel. The younger generation of Russian romantics—Bestuzhev and Ryleev in particular—sought in vain the Byronic hero beyond whom Pushkin had already grown. Failing to recognize in Onegin Pushkin's warning of the dead end to which the egocentric romantic hero must come, they saw in Eugene only a disappointing counterpart to Childe Harold. The potential vested in Tatiana for the regeneration of the hero remained similarly unremarked, for readers tended to fall back on those very conventions that Pushkin actively destabilized in his text—particularly when it came to filling the telling lacunae in Tatiana's story. The significance of the omissions themselves was overlooked. The unique heroine, whose development ran parallel to the poet's own and in whose co-creation Pushkin urged his readers to participate, was relegated to that invariant feminine role of the self-sacrificing woman whose autonomous existence was surrendered to the man she wed. Pushkin's new heroine and the poetic message she was to convey were overwhelmed by convention.

At the same time the tendency to construe literary development in terms of sequence made *Onegin* seem a transitional work that conveniently connected the Golden Age of Russian poetry with the great tradition of the Russian novel. Overlooked here was the fact that this work does considerably more than merely bridge the poetry of the romantics and the subsequent prose of the naturalist school, for *Eugene Onegin* acts above all as a corrective both to the excesses of romantic denigration of the day-to-day world and to what became the realists' intolerance of the imagination. For Pushkin, as for any true poet, poetry is not only a genre, but also the wherewithal to see life steadily and see it whole. Ultimately, *Eugene Onegin* argues for a synchronous approach to literary development, for if poetry can inform life, surely it can inform prose. In the prevalent sequential model of literary history, however, Pushkin's defense of poetry was construed as preparation for its abandonment. Tatiana's quintessentially poetical space was swallowed up by social-minded, realistic prose of which Pushkin's work was alleged to be a harbinger.

To the habits of the individual reader and the course of Russian literary history we must add also Pushkin's own contribution to the undervaluation of the poetical import of *Eugene Onegin* and of Tatiana's significance in carrying it through. The reference in the final chapter of *Eugene Onegin* to the "magic crystal" reminds us that Pushkin cast his author/narrator in the role of a conjurer who—if the illusion he creates is to be granted the status of reality—must produce great flurries of activity to draw the public eye away from what he is really about. The novelistic gestures of *Eugene Onegin* are just such a flurry of activity intended in part to distract attention from the poetical movements of Pushkin's practiced hand. The characteristics of the novelistic heroine with which Pushkin endows Tatiana deflect attention from the exponent of the poetical she becomes for him in the course of his work on *Onegin*.

Tatiana begins as a name, grows into a heroine who counters convention but accommodates tradition, and is finally acknowledged as the author/narrator's own muse. In the course of his work on *Onegin*, Tatiana's development corresponds to Pushkin's personal and artistic searchings. The history of the poet's muse he provides in the final chapter reveals that here he does not look to the actual world where a muse might be discerned in a flesh-and-blood woman like A. P. Kern, or to literary models that can yield up inspiring heroine-muses like Lenore. He relies instead on his own imaginative energies to shape a source of inspiration for himself. There is great self-sufficiency but also great vulnerability in such intensely self-reflexive creative work. Pushkin's message is too profoundly personal and too cherished to bear public rehearsal before an unreceptive public like that described in "Conversation."

Pushkin's friend the poet Kiukhel'beker noted in his diary the distinct similarity he perceived between the author and his heroine:

> In his eighth chapter the poet himself resembles Tatiana. For one of his Lycee comrades, for a person who has grown up with him and who knows him inside out as I do, the feeling with which Pushkin is filled is noticeable everywhere, although he, like Tatiana, does not want the whole world to know about this feeling.[6]

Not everyone knew Pushkin "inside out" like Kiukhel'beker, and the resemblance between author and heroine of *Eugene Onegin* was easily overlooked. Indeed, what similarity could there be between a naive country girl or a princess of impeccable comportment on the one hand and a rakish poet with no mean Don Juan list under his belt on the other? And yet contrary to appearances, Pushkin has something far more profound in common with his heroine than with either Eugene or even the author/narrator to whom he is more easily compared, for it is she who exhibits that "cognitive receptivity of the mind to potentials" in terms of which, as Emerson notes, Pushkin himself defined poetic inspiration.[7] And it is Tatiana who, in Bethea's summary, "emerges as the 'poet' and the controlling subjectivity of the piece."[8] Tatiana and Pushkin are united in their unwavering dedication to the "other"—that is, to the imagination that infuses their actual surroundings with transcendent figurative significance, enabling them to achieve the seemingly impossible: to escape the contingencies of the here and now without loosening responsibility or breaking with form.

His heroine proved a highly effective disguise for Pushkin largely because the poetical qualities in question were not generally allowed either literary heroines or actual women. If the creative energy she shared with Pushkin was overlooked, Tatiana fit comfortably enough into prevailing categories of gender that are summarized in Belinskii's formula: "The life of a woman is concentrated predominantly in the life of the heart; to love means for her to live, and to sacrifice means to love."[9] Lost together with Tatiana's erotic energy, self-mastery, and expressivity was the creative vitality that sustained Pushkin's defense of poetry and fueled the potential for regeneration she held out for both the hero who played opposite her and the poet who created her. Tatiana became the progenitrix of a series of heroines doomed to sacrificial roles opposite passive heroes who—having failed to recognize that at the end of *Onegin* Tatiana promises a way out of superfluity—perpetuate Eugene's weaknesses rather than overcome them. Thus these heroes avoid the cul-de-sac of irony and cynicism in which late-romantic heroes end up, only to find themselves at another equally unpromising impasse. As for Tatiana, she is relegated to precisely that role which Liza of *A Novel in Letters* describes as having remained immutable in the course of three generations during which literary heroes underwent significant change (*PSS* 8:47–8).

In characterizations of even the strongest heroines who number among Tatiana's literary descendants—Goncharov's Olga (*Oblomov*), Turgenev's Anna Sergeevna (*Fathers and Sons*), Tolstoi's Anna Karenina, Bulgakov's Margarita (*Master and Margarita*), and Pasternak's Lara (*Doctor Zhivago*)—Tatiana's expressly poetical self-sufficiency recedes before their dependency on a male for self-realization. Ironically, a heroine who is Pushkin's own creative double is herself defined by and then engaged to reinforce those very categories of gender beyond which Pushkin advances her.

Diana Burgin has perceptively observed that Tatiana is "[p]erhaps the model for all Russian fictional woman writers, although she is usually acknowledged simply as the model for Russian fictional women."[10] We can now go one step further to consider the model Pushkin's heroine became for two actual woman writers, for Tatiana became a participant in a feminine poetic tradition whose strong if slender thread links the nineteenth and twentieth centuries. Responding to her poetic vigor, Karolina Pavlova and Marina Tsvetaeva engaged Pushkin's heroine to project their own artistic personae. In deriving creative impetus from Tatiana, Pavlova and Tsvetaeva draw precisely on those aspects of her constitution which we recuperate in the course of this study. The subsequent discussion of Tatiana's role in Pavlova's *Quadrille* and Tsvetaeva's "My Pushkin" reaffirms our Tatianacentric reading of Pushkin's *Eugene Onegin*. With no pretensions to exhaustiveness, this epilogue invokes Pavlova and Tsvetaeva to corroborate the productivity of this approach and to invite further study of Tatiana's role in the Russian feminine poetic tradition. We observe Pavlova and Tsvetaeva in direct confrontation with that inertia of convention that dictates how generic categories and gender roles are to be construed—those very dictates, in fact, that have hampered fuller appreciation of Pushkin's unique heroine and thus also the text that houses her. The dynamics are distinctly Pushkinian: in their own artistic affirmations of feminine creativity Pavlova and Tsvetaeva draw on Tatiana's creative energy and in so doing they revivify the heroine herself.

Women who sought recognition as poets in nineteenth-century Russia confronted a debate that raged, as Diana Greene describes, "throughout the nineteenth century in Russia and Europe . . . over whether women should write at all."[11]

Poetry in particular was held as the genre least suitable for the feminine pen. In lyric poetry intense desire and subjectivity combine with the rigorous exercise of formal control. Here women were at a distinct disadvantage, for in accordance with prevailing notions of gender, they were allowed neither the desire nor the self-mastery out of whose coincidence poetry springs. The antinomies the poet was to draw into productive simultaneity were thus situated beyond the woman's narrowed compass, and women who sought recognition as poets were open to attack on two fronts: they were criticized for lack of self control when their poems conveyed strong feelings, yet accused of being deficient in spontaneous emotional intensity when their poetry showed signs of technical mastery. Just how deeply ingrained such preconceptions were can be gauged by the poet Vladislav Khodasevich's casual but by no means anomalous dismissal of the nascent feminine tradition in a 1913 review:

Ведь читатель, конечно, согласится с нами, что стихи женщин . . . неизменно уступают стихам мужским в строгости формы и силе выражения. . . . От этого правила не ушли такие поэтессы как Каролина Павлова, гр. Ростопчина, Лохвицкая и даже Зинаида Гиппиус.[12]

[For the reader will surely agree with us, that the poems of women . . . are inevitably inferior to those of men in the strictness of form and power of expression. . . . This rule holds for poetesses like Karolina Pavlova, Countess Rostopchina, Lokhvitskaia, and even Zinaida Gippius.]

The unreceptive environment in which the woman writer found herself made her need to secure a place within an established literary tradition all the more urgent and generated what might be termed an "anxiety *for* influence." Imbuing a text with signs of influence of a recognized writer could serve as a means to secure artistic legitimacy and lend credence to the woman's literary enterprise. At the beginning of the nineteenth century this sought-after influence was, in the virtual absence of women poets, inevitably that of a male precursor, and it was only in the early decades of this century that the role of the male mentor on whom women writers traditionally depended could be augmented with support derived from female forebears.

This situation was further complicated by the fact that the woman had to confront not only those male writers who preceded her, but also the heroines they had created—heroines who generally upheld those very preconceptions that impeded the aspiring woman writer in her attempts at self-realization. The contest was clearly an uneven one, and yet it was by no means hopeless. By aligning herself with a well-known heroine, the woman writer could gain entry into the male literary tradition, and under the aegis of a luminary could destabilize constructs of gender that impeded her progress in it. The assimilation of a man's heroine into her life and texts afforded the woman writer an opportunity to situate herself within an existing literary tradition, reread in such a way as to accommodate feminine creativity.

Because in *Eugene Onegin* Tatiana is represented as a woman with her own story and yet also a poetical being, and because she came to be regarded as both a literary exemplar and a figure to be emulated by flesh-and-blood women, she emerged as a particularly promising model for woman poets. Given the crucial role Pushkin himself assigned his heroine and the extent to which he identified with her, it is not difficult to understand why Pavlova and Tsvetaeva should be drawn to her. The most influential heroine of Russia's most influential poet provided these women with an opportunity to establish ties to the poetic tradition over which Pushkin held uncontested sway and yet also to shape a poetic lineage that was distinctly their own.

In the context of the generic demands of poetry, Tatiana emerges as an eminently suitable ally, for her enactment of Pushkin's poetic principle depends on that very conjunction of intense emotion and perfect mastery of form generally denied women. Pavlova and Tsvetaeva responded to the autonomy and the creative potentialities with which Pushkin richly endowed his heroine and thereby countered the common tendency to consider Tatiana "only," to borrow from Virginia Woolf, "in relation to the other sex."[13] These two woman poets found in Tatiana something considerably more than the paragon of female virtue she was made out to be, indeed, something more than the image of a muse who inspired Pushkin himself. They recognized in her a woman who not only induced creativity, but was herself a creative individual. Here the focus was not on the responses Tatiana elicited from others (be they within *Eugene Onegin* or outside of it), but rather on how Tatiana herself responded to her surroundings. Tatiana's translation of her emotional energies not into matrimony, maternity, or death—the options that life, literature, and folklore afforded women—but into an imaginative world of her own design was duly appreciated, and her decision to lead a virtuous life was recognized as enabling rather than submissive. Reading Tatiana against the current of gender bias, Pavlova and Tsvetaeva focused on dimensions of *Eugene Onegin* that are slighted by conventional readings. Their responses to Tatiana show a receptivity to the poetical nature of Pushkin's heroine and reflect too the difficulty of their own negotiations between gender and calling. Two specific texts—Pavlova's *poema Quadrille* (1843–51, pub. 1859) and Tsvetaeva's essay "My Pushkin" (1937)—provide us with the opportunity to consider more closely the role these two poets assigned Tatiana.

In *Quadrille* the destinies of the woman in Russian society, the hero-ine in Russian literature, and the Russian woman writer are presented as parallel. Its title notwithstanding, there are five women's voices in *Quadrille*: the four heroines are joined by a markedly female author/nar-rator through whom Pavlova makes her own presence felt. The defense of women's imaginative and analytical capacities that is mounted by her heroines is crucial to Pavlova's own role as a writer of imaginative litera-ture. This defense is launched from within a restrictive social setting and imbedded in the literary tradition of Pushkin with specific reference to Ta-tiana, a heroine in whose imaginative compass and responsible social conduct Pavlova recognized a vital source of female autonomy.

Quadrille opens with a dedication to the master of the Russian *poema* Evgenii Baratynskii, after which the setting is described and the heroines are introduced. In the unmistakably *Onegin*-like digression that follows, the author/narrator of the piece establishes her femaleness and her allegiance to Moscow. She then goes on to invoke the phantom of her great male predecessor from Petersburg:

> Зачем, качая головою,
> Так строго на меня смотря,
> Зачем стоишь передо мною,
> Призрак Певца-богатыря?
> Ужели дум моих обманы
> Увлечь дерзнут мой детский стих
> В заветный мир твоей Татьяны,
> В мир светлых образов твоих.[14]

> [Why, shaking your head,
> Gazing at me so sternly,
> Why do you stand before me,
> Phantom of the Bard-hero?
> Can it be that my deceptive thoughts
> Will dare to draw my childish verse
> Into the secret world of your Tatiana,
> Into the world of your bright images.]

Lest her obeisance to Pushkin be construed as feminine timorousness, Pavlova concludes the passage with an assertion that all poets stand in awe of him:

> И все робеют и поныне,
> Поэта вспоминая вид:
> Все страшен ты певцов дружине,
> Как рати мавров мертвый Сид.[15]

> [And all quail to this day,

Recalling the guise of the poet:
You remain ever terrifying to the detachment of poets,
Like the dead Cid to the host of Moors.]

By means of this frankly admitted anxiety vis-à-vis Pushkin, Pavlova unites herself with all Russian poets who must similarly feel threatened by the ghostly presence of their larger-than-life predecessor. Yet at the same time, with her reference to Tatiana, she establishes a unique and privileged connection to Pushkin from which these other poets are excluded. Although in the course of *Quadrille* the author/narrator often consciously adopts an Onegian tone, she situates herself explicitly in Tatiana's feminine imaginative sphere ("zavetnyi mir tvoei Tat'iany" [the secret world of your Tatiana]). By this she means not only the text of *Eugene Onegin*, allusions to which abound in her *poema*, but specifically that inner world of Tatiana's own making that is shielded from public view and revealed only in her letter and her speech to Eugene. In the course of her *poema*, Pavlova's identification with Tatiana is mediated through the self-reflexive narratives of her fictional heroines. The impetus for their development derives from Pavlova's personal experience (in both her private and her literary life) and is informed by the exemplar she discerns in Tatiana. As she creates the heroines of *Quadrille*, Pavlova retains Pushkin's heroine in her mind's eye and encourages her reader to do the same. Like Pushkin before her, Pavlova too—and from a position more precarious than his—defends the place of the imagination in a harshly unreceptive world.

On a wintry Moscow night, four women on their way to a ball gather at the home of Countess Polina. As they sit in a tight circle around the fire, their conversation modulates from superficial social chatter to analytical introspective narration, which is precipitated, tellingly, by the question of gender roles in Russian society ("muzhchin i zhenshchin naznachen'e"). The heroines of *Quadrille* appear, as Susanne Fusso observes, "just past the crucial marriage age without having died or attained perfect happiness, as the standard Romantic heroine must."[16] They are described as having influential husbands, enviable social positions, and impeccable social grace, and in all of these particulars they resemble Pushkin's Tatiana when she, as Princess N, presides over St. Petersburg society. The next three hours—the remainder of *Quadrille*—are devoted to the recollection of formative events in their lives.

Within a structure of carefully balanced symmetries, Pavlova's heroines narrate stories in which commonplaces of the romantic imagination collide violently with commonplaces of the actual world. Thus, to draw on Fusso's summary, the first two narratives of *Quadrille* bring two Romantic archetypes into the gritty sphere of economic realism: Karl Moor becomes a common burglar, and Poor Liza becomes Not-Rich-Enough Liza.

The last two stories . . . deflate the Romantic hero in subtler and more original ways. Here it is the Romantic hero's rhetoric, not his behavior, that is exposed.[17]

Not romanticism itself, but its residue of mere convention and Onegin-like unwitting parody comes under attack as Pavlova distinguishes between convention-driven fantasy and the genuinely creative imagination. The self-analytical narratives of her heroines are recognizable variations on the plot of Tatiana's unconventional story, which centers not on matrimony but on a concern crucial to the creative artist: how the imaginative and the actual worlds might be responsibly interrelated. Counterposed to a harsh setting that leaves the woman virtually no options beyond marriage is the invented space of the woman's own making—one that, to apply Wallace Stevens's formulation, must have "the strength of reality or none at all,"[18] and which must somehow be reconciled with the concrete demands of the everyday.

Revealed to the reader in the stories these women tell is the emotional intensity underlying the perfect self-possession they maintain in public. The narrative model for their accounts is Tatiana's speech to Eugene, for each of Pavlova's heroines similarly takes stock of her situation in the context of significant events and images recalled from an earlier life that little resembles her present condition. The romantic equation of recollection with creativity is in full effect as Pavlova's heroines invent themselves anew through a reconstitution of their pasts. In the process of narration, isolated events are imbedded in the larger temporal context provided by retrospection to acquire new, expanded significance that promotes the women's heightened self-awareness. The interaction of two temporal frameworks—the time of the event and the time of the narration—replicates the conditions of Tatiana's final scene and similarly fosters self-realization. At the same time, the density of literary allusions draws our attention to another plane of the text: its author's assertion of her own identity as a writer, an identity that is closely bound up with the heroines whose self-creative process the reader observes.

Barbara Heldt has found the women's narratives in *Quadrille* to be "life stories of disillusionment, guilt, and helplessness."[19] They are that, to be sure, but Pavlova points beyond externally imposed restrictions placed on women and their outbursts of willful rebellion against them. Though nothing in the surrounding world or their circumstances in it is altered, through their narratives her heroines arrive at a point of vantage from which unthinking compliance with or rebellion against social demands and conventions is replaced with a fully responsible cognizance of their positions. This point is of utmost importance to her heroines and to Pavlova herself: the "smes' svoevol'ia i nevoli" (amalgam of willfulness and unfreedom) in terms of which Countess Polina describes women in Russian society is as ill suited to creative work as it is to the conduct of life. The primary purpose of Pavlova's *poema* is to ensure that this damaging combination be superseded by the responsible self-knowledge and voluntary self-mastery that Tatiana exemplifies and that lie at the heart of Pushkin's concept of genuine liberty in both life and art. Accordingly, the heroines' stories focus on self-assertion and not on victimization. Indeed, they are recounted in direct response to Polina's insistence on the woman's accountability:

> Признаемся, почти всегда
> Во всем мы виноваты сами.[20]

> [Let us admit, nearly always
> We are ourselves to blame for everything.]

Here a woman's voice replies to the question that resounded through Russia with the serialization of Herzen's *Who Is to Blame (Kto vinovat)* just when Pavlova was working on *Quadrille*. Provided in her *poema* is a distinctly feminine perspective on the moral and psychological blame that Herzen projects in his novel. Polina's pronouncement is important in its demand that a woman assume responsibility for her own life. Self-knowledge takes precedence over social change, and her rallying cry is that the woman must above all remain true to herself if she is to surmount those impediments to her fulfillment that society abundantly supplies. Thus Polina maintains to her gathered friends:

> Тех бедствий женщина могла бы
> Избегнуть, если бы она
> Сама себе была верна.[21]

> [These ills a woman could
> Avoid, if only she
> Would be true to herself.]

The question foregrounded with this assertion is which "self"—the publicly maintained or the privately fashioned—is true. This issue in particular evokes Tatiana's success in establishing a productive interdependency between her public and her private spheres and thus remaining genuinely true to both. Pushkin's alignment of the private world of his heroine with the countryside and her public persona with urban society in *Eugene Onegin* is replicated in the stories related by the heroines of *Quadrille*. The first two center on the woman's life of the imagination.

Narrated in them are private affairs played out in rural settings. The last two describe public spectacles in the city and focus expressly on the social constraints these women face.

Because, in the world Pavlova describes, existence outside of matrimony is virtually unthinkable for a woman, men become the subjects of extravagant fantasies. They alternately take on quasi-mythic proportions or are seen as objectifications both of the woman's inchoate longings and of her specific needs—whether physical, spiritual, emotional, or material. Under these circumstances it is only natural that a "tiazhkoe razuveren'e" (heavy loss of faith) should follow any actual relations with men. Marriage in particular must inevitably fall short of the preposterous hopes a woman attaches to it.

Nadina expects a soul mate who will coincide with the image confabulated in her fantasies. Her story ends, however, in a commonplace marriage of convenience. Liza, who like her namesake in Pushkin's "The Queen of Spades" is the victimized ward of a tyrannical old woman, sees her beloved (incidentally the only eligible male for miles around) as a liberator who will transform her solitary life of endless restrictions and humiliations into one of happiness and fulfillment. He, however, turns out to be not a knight but a fortune hunter who, upon learning that her inheritance is smaller than he expected, departs precipitously in search of a richer woman. Olga, who mistakes heightened excitability for love, feels that the attentions and promise of marriage of a newly met cavalier increase her self-worth and her social standing. In fact, she is the laughing-stock of those gathered, who understand, as Olga does not, that she has fallen for a deranged youth who courts and proposes to every woman he meets. For Countess Polina men are adversaries on the battlefield of society—a recurrent metaphor in Pavlova's writings that is realized when Polina witnesses the death of a fine, principled young man (described as being "both an Onegin and a Lenskii") in a duel fought on her behalf.[22]

Pavel Gromov echoes Herzen when he construes the central question that emerges from these stories in terms of blame: "Who then is more to blame," he asks, "for the troubles of a woman's fate—society or the woman herself?"[23] But Pavlova moves beyond this cliché of assigning blame to consider instead the creative energy that can be derived specifically from the excruciating incongruity between the imaginative and the actual that the woman confronts.

We have already traced Tatiana's course as she sees in Eugene a source of expanded possibility in an otherwise unremarkable world, experiences acute disappointment in the flesh-and-blood man who falls painfully short of this ideal, and arrives finally at an enabling reconciliation of these two seemingly incompatible figures—one a product of her imagination, one a creature of the actual world. Pavlova's heroines similarly progress beyond fixing all their hopes of escaping from their limited and limiting surroundings on a man whom they endow with an excess of significance. The discord between the imagined and the actual that lies at the core of each of their stories is correlative with the conflict between public and private—a concern that we have seen Pushkin address through Tatiana. The question, which took on even greater urgency at the time of Pavlova's composition of *Quadrille*, is whether the imagination fosters true cognizance of self and surroundings or precludes it. In Pavlova's work this debate is played out in fictional terms with particular emphasis on how it relates to women. Is the imagination, we are encouraged to ask together with the heroines, in fact a liberating force as Pushkin insists and Tatiana demonstrates, or is it yet another impediment to a woman's self-realization? Does allegiance to the imaginative realm constitute being true to one's self or is it a dangerous form of self-deception?

In Nadina's story the imagination is represented as being innate to a woman's nature. Just as Byron's Don Juan loves women despite his mother's enforced prohibition of any reading that "hints continuation of the species," so too does Nadina engage in flights of fancy even in the absence of those novels that served as catalysts for Tatiana's emotional and imaginative development. In direct contradistinction to Tatiana, Nadina authors her own fictional worlds. As she plies that very thread and needle Pushkin's heroine disdained in favor of books, Nadina's imagination attains Byronic proportions without the aid of literary stimulants:

> Мне незнаком был и Манфред и Лара,
> Но мне фантазия, поэт немой,
> Их создала.[24]

> [I knew neither Manfred nor Lara,
> But fantasy, the mute poet,
> Created them for me.]

Fusso sees this reference as a sign of limitation: "The sad aspect of the passage is that the products of her imagination, although free of outside influence, are identical to the products of Byron's imagination."[25] Yet it would seem that the allusions here are intended to foreground not the limitations of the feminine imagination, but rather three closely interrelated themes that are central to *Quadrille*: the silent woman's untold story, the woman's powerful emotions for which no outlet can be found, and the essentially poetic quality—inferior to no male writer's—of even those women's reveries that remain unexpressed. We may recall here that Kaled, the woman who loves Byron's Lara, dies "Her tale untold, her truth too dearly proved." Byron's *Manfred: A Dramatic Poem* masterfully protracts a story that is darkly hinted at but never related, revealing to the reader only its emotionally and spiritually devastating aftermath. These references to Byron thus reinforce the urgent need for self-expression that drives the stories narrated in *Quadrille* and highlights Pavlova's self-appointed role to speak on behalf of her "mute sisters," as she refers to women in *Dvoinaia zhizn'* (A Two-fold Life).[26]

Ultimately, like Pavlova herself, and like Pushkin's heroine who is invoked at the beginning of this *poema*, the four women of *Quadrille* must take an active role in defining themselves, and they must do so independently of the men in their lives. To this end the first pair of heroines, who represent the "nevolia" (unfreedom) part of Polina's formula, must realign their fantasies with actuality. The second two, examples of "svoevol'e" (willfulness), must disassociate themselves from the superficial norms of society to achieve a self-mastery dictated from within. In this regard, the two halves of *Quadrille* reproduce the oppositions that crystallize around Tatiana's story and which include most prominently rural-urban, private-public, and imaginary-actual. To a significant extent, the heroines of *Quadrille* are refractions of Tatiana through which Pavlova explores different facets of Pushkin's heroine and considers their relevance to the creative process.

In the course of recounting their stories, Pavlova's heroines demonstrate that, if successfully negotiated, the antinomies they confront can fuel self-knowledge and feed a creative (rather than a restrictive or self-deluding) imagination as suggested by Tatiana. In the clash between the imagined and the actual described in the four women's otherwise dissimilar stories, the imagination is not valorized. It is instead brought into productive alignment with actuality, and tempered by self-control. Only in such a configuration can the imagination provide the means to rise above societal restrictions, Pavlova insists through her heroines' narrative self-realizations and her own writing.

The stories they relate provide Pavlova's heroines a means for self-expression, which, like Tatiana's letter and speech to Eugene, focuses their creative energies and fosters self-knowledge. It is here that Pavlova disassociates herself from both Tatiana and her own heroines, for she alone arrives at the next stage of self-realization through writing. Pavlova's vacillation between identifying with the male author/narrator of *Eugene Onegin* and its heroine in the course of *Quadrille* suggests the difficulty she experienced as a woman who was a public practitioner of the art of poetry. It reminds us too of the enormous step it takes to embark on a poetic career that depends on the activation of those poetic principles Tatiana embodies in order to make public an inner landscape like the one she and the four heroines of *Quadrille* privately nurture. Like

Tatiana, Pavlova's heroines embody creative potentiality but do not themselves seek a broader audience as writers. Even as her heroines speak, Pavlova does not let her reader forget that it is she who enters their stories into the public domain. The poetic form in which *Quadrille* is couched interferes with the illusion that the characters author their narratives, and when Polina lapses into an Onegin stanza, we recognize Pavlova's need to assert her own mastery of this markedly Pushkinian form.[27]

In what is apparently an attempt to diminish the gap between her gender and her calling, Pavlova distances herself from other women in order that she be more readily accepted among poets who were predominantly male. Her divided allegiance to two selves that are made incompatible by the constructs of genre and gender under which she operates interferes not only with her self-realization as a poet, but also with her capacity to bond with other women. We see this, for example, in her hostile relations with her contemporary, the poet Evdokiia Rostopchina. We see it, too, in the way she relates to the heroines she herself creates. For Pavlova the conflict between woman and poet remains unresolved.

In this regard, Marina Tsvetaeva does significantly better. But then she has the advantage of precursors such as Pavlova, a poet in whose works she could study the intricacies, perils, and strategies of a woman's entry into the male domain of verse. Tsvetaeva's response to Tatiana is distinctly more poetical than sociological, and her assertiveness expands to include rather than exclude other women from the literary tradition. If Pavlova cannot fully reconcile being a woman and being a poet, Tsvetaeva, in establishing her own poetic identity, acts in quintessentially Pushkinian fashion not simply to overcome the impediments to such wholeness, but to successfully turn them to her own advantage. For Tsvetaeva, as we will see, the marginalized woman readily modulates into, indeed takes precedence over, what is by her definition the marginalized poet. Here Pushkin's Tatiana is once again enlisted as a crucial ally, as Tsvetaeva engages her male forebear's heroine to assert her own poetic credentials and to champion the vital role women play in the Russian poetic tradition.

Tsvetaeva first evokes Tatiana in "To, chto bylo" (That Which Was [1911–12, pub. 1991]), an early autobiographical piece that describes a tragicomic failure of life to imitate art. In it Tsvetaeva recounts how, as a young girl, following Tatiana's example, she dispatched a letter to the man who had captured her imagination and her heart—her younger sister's tutor. The recipient of this epistle proves even more unfeeling than Onegin. Marina's letter—which she has chosen to write in French—is returned with all her mistakes underlined in red. A significantly more elab-

orate reading of Tatiana—and this is the one that will concern us here—
appears in Tsvetaeva's essay "My Pushkin." Written on the eve of the cen-
tennial of Pushkin's death, this essay recreates, as Tsvetaeva wrote to a
friend, the Pushkin of her childhood.[28] Like so many of Tsvetaeva's prose
essays, "My Pushkin" defines the nature of poetry, and elaborates on the
responsibilities and destiny of the poet. Like virtually all of her memoirs,
it traces her own poetic becoming. As in so many of her other recollections, so too in "My Pushkin," Tsvetaeva recreates her childhood from
the vantage point of a full-fledged poet who reads incontrovertible signs
of poetic destiny back into details of her life. The essay holds a prominent
place in Tsvetaeva's artistic biography, for, as Alexandra Smith notes, "[i]t
is one of her last major works and crowns, together with 'Pushkin and
Pugachev,' the large corpus of her works relating to Pushkin."[29]

The possessive adjective of Tsvetaeva's title is not a claim on
Pushkin. It is rather her insistence on the highly idiosyncratic nature of
her reading of her "first poet."[30] What is doubtless a conscious echo of
the title under which a collection of essays by Valerii Briusov appeared in
1929[31] draws attention to Tsvetaeva's intensely personal response to
Pushkin that remains fiercely independent of intermediary texts—be they
scholarly or biographical. In the course of writing *her* Pushkin, Tsvetaeva
insists on the creativity inherent in the act of reading and foregrounds the
role of the reader on whom a poet ultimately depends. The Pushkin from
whom Tsvetaeva claims to have learned quintessential poetic truths is a
poet she (re)creates through her own reading of his texts.

Of all Pushkin's works that are discussed in this particular essay,
Tsvetaeva credits *Eugene Onegin* with exerting the most far-reaching
influence on her poetic development. It is from this work that she claims
to have derived the essential poetic truths that were to guide both her life
and her development as a poet. Indeed, as we will see, she maintains that
she is indebted to Pushkin's novel-in-verse for the very fact of her bodily
existence.

Yet even as she exuberantly embraces Pushkin as if he were her immediate predecessor—no generations intervening—Tsvetaeva is careful
to establish her own poetic autonomy. It is telling that, according to her
account, the *Eugene Onegin* she first encounters is not Pushkin's novel-
in-verse, but a scene from Tchaikovsky's opera, namely, Onegin's aria in
the last scene of act 1, which constitutes his response to Tatiana's letter.
From a musical evening she attended with her mother that featured scenes
from Dargomyzhskii's fanciful *Rusalka* and Serov's heroic *Rogneda*, the
six-year-old Marina—to her mother's openly expressed consternation—
singled out the scene between Tatiana and Onegin, where all the dramatic

action transpires beneath the surface. This choice, whose idiosyncrasy is immediately marked by the adult bewilderment with which it is met, signals the child's poetic destiny.

Distilled in this scene, as Marina perceives it, is the definition of a word she has already learned, as she explains, from her surreptitious reading of Pushkin's narrative poem *Tsigany* (*The Gypsies*). This word is "love," and the crucial lesson she now learns from *Eugene Onegin* is that of unrequited love. This lesson derives, significantly, neither from Pushkin's text nor from Tchaikovsky's music, but from Tatiana's body language:

> Моя первая любовная сцена была нелюбовная: он *не* любил (это я поняла), потому и не сел, любила *она*, потому и встала, они ни минуты не были вместе, ничего вместе не делали, делали совершенно обратное: он говорил, она молчала, он не любил, она любила, он ушел, она осталась. . . . (2:261)

> [My first love scene was non-love: he *didn't* love (that I understood), and that was why he didn't sit down; she *did* love, and that was why she stood up; they were not together a single minute, they did not do anything together, they did the exact opposite: he talked, she was silent, he did not love, she loved, he left, she stayed. . . .][32]

If the contradance she witnesses between Tatiana and Eugene is in itself unremarkable, the child's reading of it is exceptional, for Marina discerns the essential symmetries of *Eugene Onegin* that are encapsulated in this scene. She goes on, moreover, to see in Tatiana not merely a rejected woman, but an enabled heroine who, even in this vulnerable moment when she seems but the passive auditor of Eugene's just reproof, is in fact acting consciously to determine the course her life is to take. Eugene's refusal of Tatiana in this scene is translated by Tsvetaeva from a failure in life to a poetic victory for the heroine. Indeed, as she asserts later in the essay, the very fact that Tatiana falls in love with Eugene to begin with must be attributed to her certainty that for them mutually shared love is impossible. Tatiana chooses to love Eugene only because she knows full well that he cannot return her love:

> В том-то и все дело было, что он ее не любил, и только потому она его— *так*, и только для того *его*, а не другого в любовь выбирала, что втайне знала, что он ее не сможет любить. (2:262)

> [The whole matter rested in that alone—that he did not love her and only because of it did she love him *so much*, and only because of it did she choose *him* to love, that man and not another, because secretly she knew that he would not be able to love her.] (336)

In the context of the imperative that she love someone who is incapable of reciprocating her emotions, Eugene's "sermon" serves to confirm
that Tatiana has chosen correctly. When Eugene falls in love with her in
the latter part of the work, Tatiana acts to ensure that their love remain
unrequited. Thus, according to Tsvetaeva's reading, Tatiana's rejection of
the enthralled Onegin in the final chapter of Pushkin's work is motivated
neither by a desire for revenge nor by marital fidelity, but by Tatiana's
conscious, responsible choice of prolonged desire over its brief fulfillment.

For Tsvetaeva, Tatiana's strength lies in the fact that she can only
love, but not be loved. She describes Pushkin's heroine as determining to
remain

в зачарованном кругу своего любовного одиночества, тогда—
непонадобившаяся, сейчас—вожделенная, и тогда и ныне—любящая и
любимой быть не могущая. (2:262)

[in the enchanted circle of her own loneliness in love: then, a love deemed
unnecessary; now a love deeply desired; and then and now, a woman who
loves and cannot be loved.] (337)

In this way the three pivotal moments of Tatiana's story—her writing of
the letter to Eugene, her resigned reception of the lecture with which he
responds, and, finally, her rejection of his advances—come together in the
single exigency that, in Tsvetaeva's reading, governs Tatiana's life, and
which she adopts also for her own life and work:

Эта первая моя любовная сцена предопределила все мои последующие, всю
страсть во мне несчастной, невзаимной, невозможной любви. Я с той самой
минуты не захотела быть счастливой и этим себя на нелюбовь обрекла.
(2:262)

[That first love scene of mine foreordained all the ones that followed, all the
passion in me for unhappy, non-reciprocal, impossible love. From that very
minute I did not want to be happy and thereby pronounced the sentence of
non-love on myself.] (336)

Clearly discernible in this passage are the overtones of poetic destiny. It is
from Tatiana that Tsvetaeva claims to have learned the Orphic law of loss
according to which poets must live. The inexorable poetic interdiction of
satisfied desire is already in effect when she first falls in love with, or, more
accurately, when she chooses Eugene to be the object of her longing. Although Tsvetaeva does not discuss Tatiana's letter, in the context of her
reading it would have to be regarded as the heroine's conscious courting
of that loss without which the poetic imagination cannot endure. The letter to Eugene emerges not as the heedless gesture of a girl whose roman-

tic impulses lead her to transgress the bounds of social propriety, but as a necessary act that perpetuates the course of renunciation that she has chosen for herself. Accordingly, Tatiana is held up as a positive, creative counterexample to that unfortunate heroine who is impoverished by the satisfaction of her desire: "nashei drugoi geroini, toi, u kotoroi ot ispolneniia vsekh zhelanii nichego drugogo ne ostalos', kak lech' na rel'sy" (2:262) (that other heroine of ours, the one who from the fulfillment of all wishes had nothing left but to lie down on the rails [338]).

The Tatiana she recreates from Pushkin's text provides Tsvetaeva with an entire series of lessons that guide her own subsequent behavior and figure prominently in her self-definition as a poet:

Но еще одно, не одно, а многое, предопределил во мне Евгений Онегин. Если я потом всю жизнь по сей последний день всегда первая писала, первая протягивала руку—и руки, не страшась суда,—то только потому, что на заре моих дней лежащая Татьяна в книге, при свече, с растрепанной и переброшенною через грудь косой, это на моих глазах сделала. И если я потом, когда уходили (всегда уходили), не только не протягивала вслед рук, а головы не оборачивала, то только потому, что тогда, в саду, Татьяна застыла статуей.

Урок смелости. Урок гордости. Урок верности. Урок судьбы. Урок одиночества. (2:262)

[But there was still one more thing, not one but a great deal that *Evgeny Onegin* foreordained in me. If afterwards, a whole life long, and to this day, I was always the first one to write, the first one to stretch out my hand and my arms, not fearing judgment, it is only because at the dawn of my days, a Tatyana in a book, lying prone, by the light of a small candle, her braid tousled and thrown across her breast, before my eyes, did what she did. And if afterwards, when they went away (they always went away), I not only did not hold my arms outstretched after them, but did not turn my head, then it is only because *then*, in that garden, Tatyana grew rigid like a statue.

A lesson of courage. A lesson of pride. A lesson of fidelity. A lesson of fate. A lesson of loneliness.] (337)

These essential poetic lessons derived from Tatiana—here a feminine statue in Pushkin's gallery—dictate the surrender of self to overpowering emotion and yet also demand the renunciation of fulfillment. Already at the tender age of six, Marina chooses to follow Tatiana's path:

Между полнотой желания и исполнением желаний, между полнотой страдания и пустотой счастья мой выбор был сделан отродясь и дородясь. (2:262)

[Between the fullness of desire and the fulfillment of desires, between the fullness of suffering and the emptiness of happiness, my choice was made from birth—and before birth.] (338)

That a child so young, Tsvetaeva would have her reader understand, can discern messages of such profundity in a poetic text is the unmistakable sign of a poet. That a poetic text is allowed to exert such a powerful effect on the life of an individual is the sign of a woman reader. What Tsvetaeva describes as the prenatal ("dorodias'") choice of desire over fulfillment in the passage cited above is a reference to her mother who, according to the brief biography provided at this point, decided to forgo her own fulfillment in conscious emulation of Pushkin's heroine. Determined to follow Tatiana's example, Marina's mother chooses to marry not the man she loves, but the man who becomes Marina's father. Thus, as Tsvetaeva deduces,

> Татьяна не только на всю мою жизнь повлияла, но на самый факт моей жизни: не было бы пушкинской Татьяны—не было бы меня. (2:263)

> [Tatyana not only had an influence on my whole life, but on the very fact of my life: if there had been no Pushkin's Tatyana, I would not have come into existence.] (338)

Even as Tsvetaeva ascribes not only her poetic beginnings but the very fact of her birth to Pushkin's heroine, she notes: "Ibo zhenshchiny *tak* chitaiut poetov, a ne inache" (2:263) (For women read poets *that way* and not otherwise [338]).

This observation, particularly at this juncture in the text, is of tremendous import, for it insistently shifts the focus from the act of male writing to the act of female reading—a co-creative reading that imbues the text with significance beyond its author's ken. Our attention is drawn to the fact that Tsvetaeva's response to *Eugene Onegin* demonstrates her own extraordinary gift for that creative reading which is correlative with the virtuosic writing in this essay. This capacity to read is one that Tsvetaeva shares with Tatiana who, as we have seen, is Pushkin's model reader, and it is this capacity that marks the poetic potentialities of both women. "My Pushkin" demonstrates, above all, Tsvetaeva's own creative abilities, but it is of paramount importance that she ascribes to *all* women the capacity for intensely empathetic reading—a self-surrender to the text that accomplishes that very interpenetration of life and literature that Pushkin champions in his novel-in-verse.

In Tsvetaeva's emphasis on the woman reader we can recognize an important strategy of enablement: whether or not women are allowed to publish poetry, they are, in Tsvetaeva's representation, indispensable to its reception, which is to say, to the recreation in their own lives and on their own terms of poetic texts authored by men. Thus whether or not they are admitted into it as writers, they are vital to the tradition in which canonical texts come into being and endure.

As Tsvetaeva's creative reading of Pushkin becomes the material of the highly original writing in this essay, the act of reading and the act of writing are drawn together. Well before she takes up the pen to write, a poet is revealed already in the way she reads. The centrality Tsvetaeva ascribes to reading urges implicitly that Tatiana's extraordinary receptivity to literature be acknowledged as a sign of her creative capacities. In the course of shaping her own poetic identity, Tsvetaeva, with recourse to Pushkin's heroine, wins women a place in the literary tradition—even before they begin to write. Given the problematic status of writing women, the reading woman becomes a fitting model for the nascent woman poet. Through the reading Tatiana, Tsvetaeva aligns herself with the writing Pushkin.

Rather than disassociate herself from other women when she takes up the pen to write, as does Pavlova, Tsvetaeva insists on the poetic potentialities of all women. Although rooted perhaps in the ideals of the romantics and the post Symbolists, Tsvetaeva's notions depart from theirs in that she assigns women an active, responsible role within the literary tradition. In her account, they are neither the embodiment nor the essence of poetry; nor are they muses exciting creativity in others. They are instead those who—like Tatiana, like her own mother, and finally like Tsvetaeva herself—consciously choose to lead their lives according to the poetic imperative that demands the sacrifice of fulfillment in favor of its protraction.

In Tsvetaeva's conceptualization, the woman's erotic energies remain engaged, and she is given ascendancy even over Orpheus who translates unfulfilled desire into song. Indeed, from *her* Tatiana, Tsvetaeva derives a poetic model that supersedes the prototypical male poet. While Orpheus' loss of Eurydice is imposed by fate, Tatiana and the women who model themselves on her choose consciously to provoke loss and thereby to sustain the creative energy of their desire—whether this desire find public expression in poetry or not. If, elsewhere in her writings, Tsvetaeva explains the backward glance that loses the Greek bard his beloved as an *unconscious* gesture that privileges poetry over fulfilled desire,[33] she construes Tatiana's actions as the consequence of a fully *conscious* decision to forgo personal gratification. Following Tatiana, the women Tsvetaeva describes choose to remain true not simply to a spouse, but to a principle. For Tsvetaeva, the fact that neither Tatiana nor her own mother actually writes poetry matters little in light of the dependency of the poetic tradition on their capacity to read and to draw that reading into life. In any event, it is these two women—one fictional, one real—who have made *her* possible.

Pushkin's insistence on the productive cross-fertilization between life and literature that is compellingly demonstrated in *Eugene Onegin* is in full effect in Tsvetaeva's Pushkin essay. It is precisely to such cross-fertilization that Tsvetaeva ascribes her own birth and coming into being as a poet. And it is on the strength of such cross-fertilization that she styles herself as Tatiana's grandchild. Marina is not to be confused with that brood of children with which Belinskii hypothetically endows Tatiana in his haste to channel the creative energy of her desire into conventional maternity. Even as she creates herself in Tatiana's image, Tsvetaeva establishes a lineage of her own making. *Her* Tatiana—the Tatiana she reads and (re)creates—engenders not a child, but a woman poet.

Notes

Index

Notes

Foreword

1. For facsimiles of these pages, see A. S. Pushkin, *Polnoe sobranie sochinenii v 17 t.* (Moscow: Voskresen'e, 1996), vol. 18 (dopolnitel'nyi): Risunki [Drawings]. The 1824 "Tatiana" figures are on pp. 258–59; the 1823 Lensky on p. 182; and the famous sketch of Pushkin and Onegin on the Petersburg waterfront on p. 32.

2. For a brief survey, see V. I. Matsapura, "Rabota A. S. Pushkina nad obrazom Onegina (iz nabliudenii za chernovymi variantami romana v stikhakh)," *Voprosy russkoi literatury*, no. 2 (52), L'vov (1988): 67–75.

3. John Garrard, "Corresponding Heroines in *Don Juan* and *Evgenii Onegin*," *Slavonic and East European Review* 73, no. 3 (July 1995): 428–48, esp. 441. Garrard considers Tatiana a highly creative variant on Byron's Julia (who herself writes an excruciating letter to the adolescent lover who abandoned her, one of the few places in Byron's poem free of his corrosive irony), in part because "Tatiana possesses what Julia did not—an existence outside of passion" (444). Perhaps as a result of working with Pichot's "softened" French version of Byron's first cantos, Garrard suggests, Pushkin was inspired to create a female image unprecedented in the literature of his time. "It is through Tatiana that Pushkin channels his most fundamental critique of the Byronic hero, a character who does not develop and whose interior landscape never changes. . . . Here was potential indeed, enabling Tatiana to break out of the chrysalis of love as woman's whole existence" (447).

Introduction

1. Cited in Iurii Lotman, "K evoliutsii postroeniia kharakterov v romane *Evgenii Onegin*," in *Pushkin: Issledovaniia i materialy*, vol. 3 (Moscow-Leningrad: Akademiia Nauk, 1960), 161. "Poet v svoei 8–i glave pokhozh sam na Tat'ianu."

2. Monika Greenleaf, *Pushkin and Romantic Fashion: Fragment, Elegy, Orient, Irony* (Stanford: Stanford University Press, 1994), 206. Greenleaf goes on to say that Eugene is left "trapped in exitless solipsism," as "Tatiana and the poet move together into psychological and creative maturity." While I could not agree

more with the latter statement, I will argue in chapter 6 of this study that on the strength of Tatiana's creative energy new possibility opens for Eugene at the work's end.

3. J. Thomas Shaw, "The Problem of Unity of Author-Narrator's Stance in Puškin's *Evgenii Onegin*," *Russian Language Journal* 35, no. 120 (Winter 1981): 27.

4. Vladimir Nabokov details this triangular relationship in "Commentary" in Aleksandr Pushkin, *Eugene Onegin: A Novel in Verse*, trans. Vladimir Nabokov (Princeton: Princeton University Press, 1964), 2:129–30.

5. References to works by Pushkin will be provided with the volume and page number of *Polnoe sobranie sochinenii* (*PSS*) (Moscow: Voskresen'e, 1995) where the cited material appears.

6. For a reception history of *Eugene Onegin*, see J. Douglas Clayton, *Ice and Flame: Aleksandr Pushkin's "Eugene Onegin"* (Toronto: University of Toronto Press, 1985), Chap. 1, "The Repainted Icon: Criticism of *Eugene Onegin*." Tatiana's fate is traced in Geraldine Kelley, "The Characterization of Tat'jana in Puškin's *Evgenij Onegin*," Ph.D. diss., University of Wisconsin–Madison, 1976, 1–16.

7. For discussions of Pushkin's dialogue with his critics in regard to *Eugene Onegin*, see Paul Debreczeny, "Reception of Pushkin's Poetic Works in the 1820s: A Study of the Critic's Role," *Slavic Review* 28, n. 3 (1969): 394–415; Clayton, *Ice and Flame*, 9–22.

8. Clayton, *Ice and Flame*, 11.

9. Marina Tsvetaeva, *Izbrannaia proza v dvukh tomakh* (New York: Russica, 1979), 2:263. My translation.

10. Clayton, *Ice and Flame*, 4.

11. V. G. Belinskii, *Sobranie sochinenii v 9-ti tomakh* (Moscow: Khudozhestvennaia literatura, 1981), 6:399–426. F. M. Dostoevskii, *Polnoe sobranie sochinenii v tridtsati tomakh* (Leningrad: Nauka, 1984), 26:136–49.

12. Nabokov, "Commentary," 2:281.

13. Fedor Dostoevsky, "Pushkin," in *Russian Views of Pushkin's Eugene Onegin*, trans. Sona Stephan Hoisington (Bloomington: Indiana University Press, 1988), 59.

14. V. Sipovskii, *Pushkin: Zhizn' i tvorchestvo* (St. Petersburg: Trud, 1907), 555–618.

15. R. V. Ivanov-Razumnik, "Evgenii Onegin," in A. S. Pushkin, *Sochineniia* (St. Petersburg: Brokgaus-Efron, 1907), 3:205–34.

16. Geraldine Kelley gives Tatiana's autonomy its due in a study devoted entirely to this heroine. William Mills Todd's recognition that Tatiana's evolution is directly linked to the poet's own is a major contribution to our understanding of both the heroine and the text that houses her: William Mills Todd III, "*Eugene Onegin*: Life's Novel," in *Literature and Society in Imperial Russia, 1800–1914*, ed. Todd (Stanford: Stanford University Press, 1978), 203–235. Important too are those critical assessments that take questions of gender into account. Monika Greenleaf notes that "[t]hrough Tatiana, Pushkin is able to replay much of his own psychological material in a foreign, feminine key." Greenleaf, *Pushkin and Romantic Fashion*, 263. Feminist readings are offered by J. Douglas Clayton,

"Towards a Feminist Reading of *Evgenii Onegin*," *Canadian Slavonic Papers* 29 (1987): 255–65; Stephanie Sandler, *Distant Pleasures: Alexander Pushkin and the Writing of Exile* (Stanford: Stanford University Press, 1989), and particularly Diana L. Burgin, "Tatiana Larina's *Letter to Onegin*, or *La Plume Criminelle*," *Essays in Poetics* 16, no. 2 (1991): 12–23, which rescues Tatiana from the moribund image of self-sacrificing woman by insisting on the heroine's sexuality and creativity. Discussions of erotic elements in Tatiana's characterization contribute further to the increasing recognition of the complexity of the heroine: Richard A. Gregg, "Tat'yana's Two Dreams: The Unwanted Spouse and the Demonic Lover," *Slavonic and East European Review* 48 (1979): 492–505; Leonore Scheffler, "Tat'jana Larina," *Das erotische Sujet in Puškins Dichtung* (Tübingen: University of Tübingen Press, 1967), 178–200. Caryl Emerson's essay "Tatiana" celebrates the "dynamic poetic principle" that Tatiana enacts on Pushkin's behalf: Caryl Emerson, "Tatiana," in *A Plot of Her Own: The Female Protagonist in Russian Literature*, ed. Sona Stephan Hoisington (Evanston: Northwestern University Press, 1995), 6–20.

17. D. D. Blagoi, *Sotsiologiia tvorchestva Pushkina: Etiudy* (Moscow: Federatsiia, 1929).This view ran afoul of party dictates and was subsequently amended.

18. Ludolf Müller, "Schicksal und Liebe im *Jewgenij Onegin*." In *Solange Dichter Leben: Puschkin-Studien*, ed. A. Luther (Krefeld: Scherpe-Verlag, 1949), 148–63.

19. Leon Stilman, "Problemy literaturnykh zhanrov i traditsii v *Evgenii Onegine* Pushkina. K voprosu perekhoda ot romantizma k realizmu," in *American Contributions to the Fourth International Congress of Slavicists* (The Hague: Mouton, 1958), 321–67. The only departure of Tatiana's story from the stories of the heroines of her books is, Stilman observes, that Pushkin's heroine is spared the death to which her unhappy literary predecessors inevitably succumb.

20. Here we can cite particularly the important studies of the language and poetics of *Eugene Onegin* that Vinogradov, Vinokur, and Bakhtin carried out in Stalinist Russia in the face of what Clayton dubs a "'monolithic' acceptance of the neo-Belinskiian line of the decree," and the Structuralists' movement away from sociohistorical criteria to the text itself.

21. David Bethea in private correspondence.

22. Todd, "*Eugene Onegin*: Life's Novel," 214.

23. Emerson, "Tatiana," 13.

Chapter 1. Bildung

1. In a letter dated 4 November 1823, Pushkin wrote of his project to his friend the poet Viazemskii: "ia teper' pishu ne roman, a roman v stikhakh—d'iavol'skaia raznitsa" (I am now writing not a novel, but a novel-in-verse—a devil of a difference [*PSS* 13:73]).

2. Thus, for example, in Novalis's *Heinrich von Ofterdingen* where poems are imbedded into a prose text, Karolina Pavlova's *Dvoinaia zhizn'* (A Two-fold Life) that alternates passages of prose with poetry, and Pasternak's famous novel that culminates with Iurii Zhivago's poems, the novelistic and the poetical remain dis-

crete, and indeed are sensed to be in opposition. Even in Nabokov's *Dar (The Gift)* where verse is camouflaged in the prose of the novelistic text, its effect depends on the reader's recognition of the distinctiveness of the poetic passages. For a highly revealing discussion of Pushkin's own struggles with the novelistic form that overturns conventional platitudes on the subject, see Richard A. Gregg, "Pushkin's Novelistic Prose: A Dead End?" in *Slavic Review* 57, no. 1 (1998): 1–27.

3. J. Douglas Clayton, *Ice and Flame: Aleksandr Pushkin's "Eugene Onegin"* (Toronto: Toronto University Press, 1985), 184.

4. *Eugene Onegin* appears in vol. 6 of *PSS*. Henceforth I will supply chapter, stanza, and line numbers for each cited passage from *Onegin*. Unless otherwise indicated, the translations of passages from *Eugene Onegin* are those of James E. Falen. Alexander Pushkin, *Eugene Onegin* (Oxford: Oxford University Press, 1995). I draw on other translations when the passages under discussion demand a more precise rendering than Falen provides. Except where noted otherwise, the translations of Pushkin's prose are my own.

5. We can note here that in the introductory passage devoted to Olga, her name appears not in the nominative, but only in oblique cases (instrumental and genitive).

6. The text of the note (no. 13 in the 1833 and 1837 editions of *Eugene Onegin*) is as follows: "Sladkozvuchneishie grecheskie imena, kakovy, naprimer: Agafon, Filat, Fedora, Fekla i proch., upotrebliaiutsia u nas tol'ko mezhdu prostoliudinami" (*PSS* 6:192) (The most melifluous Greek names such as Agafon, Filat, Fedora, Fekla, etc., are used only by our common folk.)

7. William E. Harkins provides a valuable discussion of Pushkin's negation of "elaborated constructions" in his essay "The Rejected Image: Puškin's Use of Antenantiosis" in *Puškin Today*, ed. David M. Bethea (Bloomington: Indiana University Press, 1993), 86–98.

8. This translation is Charles Johnston's. Alexander Pushkin, *Eugene Onegin* (Harmondsworth: Penguin, 1979). I have retained Johnston's style of lowercasing.

9. For further discussion of the double heroine device see Geraldine Kelley, "The Characterization of Tat'jana in Puškin's 'Evgenij Onegin,'" Ph.D. diss., University of Wisconsin-Madison, 1976, 28–29. The double heroine device was already well established at the time of *Eugene Onegin*'s writing. Thus, for example, we find Rousseau's description in *The Confessions* of his own use of this device in creating the heroines of *La nouvelle Héloïse*: "Je fis l'une brune et l'autre blonde, l'une vive et l'autre douce, l'une sage et l'autre faible," Jean-Jacques Rousseau, *Les Confessions* (Paris: Imprimerie Nationale, 1995), 2:697. (I made one dark, the other fair; one lively, the other gentle; one sensible, the other weak [*The Confessions of Jean-Jacques Rousseau*, trans. J. M. Cohen (London: Penguin Classics, 1953), 400].) An excellent discussion of the double heroine device can be found in R. P. Utter and G. B. Needham, *Pamela's Daughters* (New York: Macmillan, 1936), esp. 195–206.

10. In an earlier draft Pushkin opened his description of Tatiana with the suggestion that the reader could easily picture his heroine, "but only with dark eyes" ("Vy mozhete druz'ia moi / Sebe ee predstavit' sami / No tol'ko s chernymi

ochami" [*PSS* 6:290]). Pushkin's decision to eliminate this concrete detail suggests his loosening of Tatiana's dependency on literary convention.

11. William Mills Todd III, "*Eugene Onegin*: 'Life's Novel,'" in *Literature and Society in Imperial Russia*, ed. Todd (Stanford: Stanford Univeristy Press, 1978), 207.

12. This detail is important on the one hand because it enacts Rousseau's ideas on upbringing and on the other because Pushkin was himself the product of similar benign neglect. Yet we must not lose sight of the fact that Tatiana's uniqueness does not depend exclusively on the laxity of her upbringing. Although reared presumably under the same circumstances, Olga does not develop along these lines and remains destitute of those exceptional features with which Pushkin endows Tatiana.

13. Here we may cite commentary as disparate as Dostoevsky's canonized Pushkin speech, F. M. Dostoevskii, *Polnoe sobranie sochinenii v tridtsati tomakh* (Leningrad: Nauka, 1984), 26:136–49. and Joanna Hubbs's more recent ethnographic reading, *Mother Russia: The Feminine Myth in Russian Culture* (Bloomington: Indiana University Press, 1993), 212–16 and 228.

14. Thus, for example, V. Sipovskii, *Pushkin: Zhizn' i tvorchestvo* (St. Petersburg: Trud, 1907), esp. 555–618.

15. This translation belongs to Walter Arndt. Alexander Pushkin, *Eugene Onegin* (New York: Dutton, 1981). I have only replaced his "conceits" with "deceits" for a more precise rendering.

16. Thus in 2:25, l. 14, Pushkin replaced "Sidela s knigoi u okna" with "Sidela molcha u okna" (*PSS* 6.290), making Tatiana's avid reading of Richardson and Rousseau that is noted in stanza 39 the first mention of her interest in books.

17. The question of heedless appropriation of literary models receives further elaboration in the discussion of the letter Eugene writes Tatiana in the final chapter of *Onegin*. (See chapter 6 of this study.)

18. In discussing the fact that heroines of novels have remained essentially unchanged, while heroes have undergone considerable transformation since the time of Richardson, Liza wonders: "Potomu li, chto sposoby nravit'sia v muzhchine zavisiat ot mody, ot minutnogo mneniia . . . a v zhenshchinakh—oni osnovany na chuvstve i prirode, kotorye vechny" (Can this be because in a man the means to be liked depend on fashion, on fleeting opinion . . . while in women they are based on feeling and nature, which are eternal [*PSS* 8:47–48]).

19. Samuel Richardson, *The History of Sir Charles Grandison* (London: Oxford University Press, 1972), 4:264.

20. Richardson, *Sir Charles Grandison*, 1:109.

21. Richardson, *Sir Charles Grandison*, 4:264.

22. For his account of Clementina's affliction, Richardson relied on the thenauthoritative Robert James, whose *Medical Dictionary* (1743, 1745) included, under the heading of "Mania," the following observation: "Among the Causes which dispose to the most violent Delirium, and . . . destroy the force both of the Mind and the Body, none is more powerful than an Excess of Love." Richardson, *Grandison*, 2:673.

23. Caryl Emerson, "Tatiana" in *A Plot of Her Own: The Female Protagonist in Russian Literature*, ed. Sona Stephan Hoisington (Evanston: Northwestern University Press, 1995), 13.

24. Dmitry Chizhevsky, "Commentary," in A. S. Pushkin, *Evgenij Onegin: A Novel-in-verse* (Cambridge: Harvard University Press, 1953), 229. For a list of Russian editions of Richardson's novels, see Iurii Lotman, *Roman A. S. Pushkina "Evgenii Onegin": Kommentarii* (Leningrad: Prosveshchenie, 1983), 199.

25. V. Sipovskii, *Pushkin: Zhizn' i tvorchestvo*, 565.

26. Chizhevsky, "Commentary," 229. Vladimir Nabokov, "Commentary," in Aleksandr Pushkin, *Eugene Onegin: A Novel in Verse*, trans. Nabokov (Princeton: Princeton University Press, 1964), 2:282. Lotman, *Kommentarii*, 198: "Ser'eznoe povedenie v detstve, otkaz ot igr—kharakternye cherty romanticheskogo geroia." (Serious conduct in childhood, refusal to play games are characteristic features of the romantic hero.)

27. Gottfried August Bürger, *Sämtliche Werke* (München: Carl Hanser Verlag, 1987), 1211.

Chapter 2. Love and Reading

1. William Mills Todd III, "*Eugene Onegin*: 'Life's Novel'" in *Literature and Society in Imperial Russia, 1800–1914*, ed. Todd (Stanford: Stanford Univeristy Press, 1978), 220.

2. See, for example, Pushkin's variant of "Otryvki iz pisem, mysli i zamechaniia" ("Excerpts from Letters, Thoughts and Remarks"), where he writes, "Russo zametil uzhe, chto ni odna iz zhenshchin-pisatel'nits [ne dokhodila dale] posredstvennosti—krome Safy i *eshche odnoi*, pisal Russo, razumeia Novuiu Eloizu, kotoruiu on vydaval za nevymyshlennoe litso" (Rousseau already noted that not one woman writer went beyond mediocrity—except Sappho and *one other*, wrote Rousseau, intending by this the New Eloise, whom he projected as an actual person [*PSS* 11:323]).

3. Among studies that focus specifically on Tatiana's reading are George Gibian, "Love by the Book: Pushkin, Stendhal, Flaubert" in *Comparative Literature* 8, no. 2 (Spring 1956): 97–109; Michael Katz, "Love and Marriage in Pushkin's *Evgeny Onegin*," *Oxford Slavonic Papers*, n.s., 17 (Oxford: Clarendon Press, 1984): 77–89; Stanley Mitchell, "Tatiana's Reading," *Forum for Modern Language Studies* 4, no. 1 (Jan. 1968): 1–21; V. Sipovskii, "Onegin, Tat'iana, i Lenskii," *Pushkin: Zhizn' i tvorchestvo* (St. Petersburg: Trud, 1907), 555–618; Leon Stilman, "Problemy literaturnykh zhanrov i traditsii v *Evgenii Onegine* Pushkina: K voprosu perekhoda ot romantizma k realizmu" in *American Contributions to the Fourth International Congress of Slavicists* (The Hague: Mouton, 1958), esp. 322–25, where Stilman assesses Sipovskii's work.

4. Mitchell, "Tatiana's Reading," 15.

5. Katz, "Love and Marriage," 80.

6. We can observe here that the epigraph for chapter 4 of *Eugene Onegin*, "La morale est dans la nature des choses," from de Staël's *Considérations sur la Révolution Française*, is identified by its author's maiden name Necker. Pushkin

thus preserves a distance between his own reading and that of his heroine, who is absorbed in her reading of de Staël's *Delphine*.

7. Mitchell, "Tatiana's Reading," 3.

8. Cited in Nabokov, "Commentary," in Aleksandr Pushkin, *Eugene Onegin: A Novel in Verse*, trans. Nabokov (Princeton: Princeton University Press, 1964), 2:317. For discussions of the significance of the story of Echo and Narcissus to Tatiana's story, see Geraldine Kelley, "The Characterization of Tat'jana in Puškin's 'Evgenij Onegin,'" Ph.D. diss., University of Wisconsin–Madison, 1976, 121–22; Riccardo Picchio, "Dante and J. Mafilâtre as Literary Sources of Tat'jana's Erotic Dream" in *Puškin: A Symposium on the 175th Anniversary of His Birth*, ed. Andrej Kodjak and Kiril Taranovsky (New York: New York University Press, 1976), 42–55; Irwin Weil, "Onegin's Echo," *Russian Literature Triquarterly* 10 (1974): 260–73.

9. Nabokov, "Commentary," 2:326.

10. We can observe here that the image of a poetic muse arises at the juncture of the actual world and the realm of the imagination, which she brings into productive interdependency. A manifestation of the poet's creative self, she is also a projected other in whom the familiar and the alien come together. As such, the muse comes into being only when the poet is alive to the possibility of such simultaneity.

11. This translation is Arndt's. Alexander Pushkin, *Eugene Onegin*, trans. Walter Arndt (New York: Dutton, 1981). I have only substituted "It is he!" for "So it's he!"

12. Some readers found Tatiana's love too precipitous to be convincing. Those readers who censured Pushkin for what seemed the improper haste with which his heroine fell in love with a man she scarcely knew apparently overlooked the emphasis on her preparation for this event and neglected also to note its effects on her imagination. See, for example, M. A. Dmitriev's review of *Eugene Onegin* for the journal *Atenei*, cited in J. Douglas Clayton, *Ice and Flame: Aleksandr Pushkin's "Eugene Onegin"* (Toronto: University of Toronto Press, 1985), 14.

13. Elsewhere Olga is described as rosy, which has led readers to envisage a pale Tatiana.

14. This system is delineated in the eighth line of 2:2: "I Noch', i Zvezdy, i Lunu" (And Night, and Stars, and Moon).

15. Monika Greenleaf, *Pushkin and Romantic Fashion: Fragment, Elegy, Orient, Irony* (Stanford: Stanford University Press, 1994), 248.

16. The other two are "Liudmila" (1808) and "Lenora" (1831). Bürger's *Lenore* was Zhukovskii's model at the beginning of his ballad career. Katenin who, as Pushkin describes it, decided to "show us Lenore in the energetic beauty of her original creation" ("vzdumal pokazat' nam Lenoru v energicheskoi krasote ee pervobytnogo sozdaniia" [*PSS* 11:221]) also created a Russian version of Bürger's ballad. His "Ol'ga" (1816) was a direct challenge to Zhukovskii, who had infused the original with a sentimental elegaic tone, smoothing over what seemed coarse to his ear. Katenin's intent was to capture the intensity of the less polished, energetic folk idiom of the original. The ensuing "Battle of the Ballad" divided

readers into two vigorously opposed camps. Zhukovskii supporters rallied around Gnedich while Griboedov headed those who favored Katenin. In 1833, Pushkin, recalling the dispute, expressed his preference for Katenin's version.

17. There is an appropriateness in what he does, inasmuch as this version of the ballad was intended by Zhukovskii as a wedding offering to his niece (the daughter of his half-sister), Aleksandra Andreevna Protasova, whom friends called "Svetlana" ever after. In connection with Bürger's *Lenore*, Pushkin wrote in an essay of 1833, "Ona byla uzhe izvestna u nas po nevernomu i prelestnomu poddrazhaniiu Zhukovskogo, kotoryi sdelal iz nee to zhe, chto Bairon v svoem Manfrede sdelal iz Fausta: oslabil dukh i formy svoego obraztsa" (It was already known to us from the unfaithful and delightful rendering of Zhukovskii, who did to it what Byron in his Manfred did to Faust: weakened the spirit and forms of his model [*PSS* 11:220–21]).

18. We can add here that Bürger drew his material from an ancient ballad, borrowed his heroine's name and strophic form from Johann Christian Günther's poem "To Leonore" ("An Leonore"), and claimed to have been affected in the writing of his own *Lenore* by myriad literary predecessors.

19. Vladimir and Olga's union had been foreseen while they were yet children. See 2:21, ll. 6–7.

20. Byron, *Don Juan*, 1:40, l. 7.

21. This position is not uncontested. Katz writes: "When Pushkin's young and foolish Tat'yana confesses to her nanny that she is in love, it is altogether likely that she conceives the possibility that her romantic love will culminate in a happy marriage" ("Love and Marriage," 85). There is nothing in the text, however, to lend concrete support to such a claim, and I would suggest that the assumption that Tatiana wants to marry is an importation into the text of conventional readerly expectations. It would appear that Pushkin goes to some trouble to suggest a different course for his heroine.

22. I resort here to Nabokov's literal translation, which conveys more precisely the images to which I refer. His capitalization and lowercasing have been retained.

23. Again, Nabokov's translation.

24. Germaine de Staël, *Delphine*, trans. Avriel H. Goldberger (DeKalb: Northern Illinois University Press, 1995), 27. "D'abord je crois en général, qu'un homme d'un caractère froid se fait aimer facilement d'une âme passionnée; il captive et soutient l'intérêt en vous faisant supposer un secret au-delà de ce qu'il exprime. . . ." De Staël, *Delphine* (Geneva: Librairie Droz, 1990), 1:124 . All references to *Delphine* will rely on this French edition and on Goldberger's translation.

25. As Sipovskii summarizes, "in him, the dreamy girl comes to love an ideal image she has herself created" ("v nem poliubila mechtatel'naia devushka ideal'nyi obraz, sozdannyi eiu samoi" [Sipovskii, "Onegin, Tat'iana i Lenskii," 568]).

26. Todd, "*Eugene Onegin*: 'Life's Novel,'" 229.

27. Germaine de Staël, *Letters on Rousseau*, "On the Letter on Spectacles," in *Major Writings of Germaine de Staël*, trans. Vivian Folkenflik (New York: Columbia University Press, 1987), 43.

28. Thus, for example, this notion, which is voiced in Richardson's *Clarissa*

and *Sir Charles Grandison* is repeated in Byron's *Don Juan*. In her writings de Staël bemoans repeatedly the fact that women are allowed only feelings and not productive activity.

29. This translation is Walter Arndt's. I have only replaced his "insidious" with the more literal "dangerous."

30. We know only of a variant of 1:9, ll. 1–4 that has some bearing on the discussion here: "Nas pyl serdechnyi rano muchit. / Ocharovatel'nyi obman, / Liubvi nas ne priroda uchit / A Stal' ili Shatobrian" (The fever of the heart torments us early. / Enchanting deceit, / We are taught love not by nature, / But by Staël or Chateaubriand [*PSS* 6:546, my translation]). We can observe here that as he develops his heroine, Pushkin abandons the opposition of nature and fiction to urge instead their dynamic interrelation.

31. Here it is worth noting that Nabokov's scathing assessment of *Delphine* is ill advised in light of the esteem in which Pushkin held de Staël, a woman whom, as he wrote in June of 1825, "Napoleon distinguished with persecution, monarchs with trust, Byron with his friendship, Europe with its respect" ("udostoil Napoleon goneniia, monarkhi doverennosti, Bairon svoei druzhby, Evropa svoego uvazheniia" [*PSS* 10:29]). Consider too the highly positive depiction of de Staël in "Roslavlev," Pushkin's (unfinished) polemic with M. N. Zagoskin's *Roslavlev, ili Russkie v 1812 godu* (Roslavlev, or Russians in the Year 1812) *PSS* 8:150–54.

32. Pushkin apparently read the 1777 edition of Prévost's translation of 1751 while in exile at Mikhailovskoe in 1824. See Iurii Lotman, *Roman A. S. Pushkina "Evgenii Onegin": Kommentarii* (Leningrad: Prosveshchenie, 1983), 199, and Nabokov, "Commentary," 2:346.

33. For an insightful study of these two novels, see Byron R. Wells, *Clarissa and la Nouvelle Héloise: Dialectics of Struggle with Self and Others* (Ravenna: Longo Editore, 1985).

34. Goldberger, 4 ("[l]es romans que l'on ne cessera jamais d'admirer" [80–81]).

35. This interrelatedness of Tatiana's novels can be further extended to include Benjamin Constant's *Adolphe*, with whose eponymous hero Eugene is aligned and which Tatiana is soon to read in his library. *Adolphe* is a lightly disguised account of Constant's own break with de Staël, with whom he entered into an extended, passionate relationship following their meeting in 1794.

36. Kelley, "Characterization of Tat'jana," 39–40.

37. Samuel Richardson, *The History of Sir Charles Grandison* (London: Oxford University Press, 1972), 1:25. Some five pages later this sentiment is repeated by Harriet's approving uncle, who commends her for remembering this "averrment" (1:30).

38. Robert James, cited in *Sir Charles Grandison*, 2:674.

39. Samuel Richardson, *Clarissa*, ed. George Sherburn (Boston: Houghton Mifflin, 1962), 76–77. Miss Howe's emphasis.

40. *Sir Charles Grandison*, 1:406.

41. Goldberger, 102 ("cette fête de mort, que les hommes ont nommée le mariage" [1:268]).

42. Goldberger, 98 ("Hé bien! Le sort d'une femme est fini quand elle n'a pas épousé celui qu'elle aime" [1:259]).

43. It seems likely that it was precisely Clarissa's extreme punctiliousness in the early part of the novel when she is drawn to Lovelace and first attracts his attention that precipitated Pushkin's comment in a letter to his brother of November 1824: "chitaiu Klarisu, mochi net kakaia skuchnaia dura" (I am reading Clarissa, an insufferably tedious fool [*PSS*, 13:123]). A somewhat kinder assessment of *Clarissa Harlowe* appears in his "Puteshestvie iz Moskvy v Peterburg" ("Journey from Moscow to Petersburg" [1831–34]), where Pushkin writes, "Mnogie chitateli soglasiatsia so mnoiu, chto Klarissa ochen' utomitel'na i skuchna, no so vsem tem roman Richardsona imeet neobyknovennoe dostoinstvo" (Many readers will agree with me that Clarissa is very tiresome and boring, but nevertheless Richardson's novel has exceptional merit. [*PSS*, 11:224]). Pushkin does not elaborate on the "exceptional merit," but we can speculate that it might have been the firm moral conviction that Clarissa developed over the course of the novel that he came to appreciate.

44. *Clarissa*, 452, Lovelace's emphasis.
45. *Clarissa*, 237.
46. *Clarissa*, 230, Lovelace's emphasis.
47. *Clarissa*, 473.
48. *Clarissa*, 464.
49. *Clarissa*, 499, Lovelace's emphasis.
50. Recent studies of *Clarissa* in particular have focused with considerable success on the question of letter writing and sexual expression. See, inter alia, Terry Castle, *Meaning and Disruption in Richardson's "Clarissa"* (Ithaca: Cornell University Press, 1982); Terry Eagleton, *The Rape of Clarissa* (Oxford: Basil Blackwell, 1982); Donnalee Frega, *Speaking in Hunger: Gender, Discourse, and Consumption in* Clarissa (Columbia: University of South Carolina Press, 1998); Brigitte Glaser, *The Body in Samuel Richardson's* Clarissa: *Contexts of and Contradictions in the Development of Character* (Heidelberg: Universitätsverlag C. Winter, 1994).
51. *Clarissa*, 256, Lovelace's emphasis.
52. *Clarissa*, 463, Clarissa's emphasis.
53. Judith H. McDowell, Introduction, Jean-Jacques Rousseau, *Julie, or the New Eloise*, trans. McDowell (University Park: Pennsylvania State University Press, 1968), 3.
54. Lotman writes, "Folk ethics permitted relative freedom in behavior prior to marriage, but regarded the faithlessness of a married woman as a heavy sin." For women of the gentry class, however, a "fall" prior to marriage was deemed disastrous while adultery was "a virtually legalized phenomenon." Lotman, *Komentarii*, 219.
55. Nabokov, "Commentary," 2:338.
56. McDowell, 405. The original reads: "Mon ami, je fais cet aveu sans honte; ce sentiment resté malgré moi fut involontaire; il n'a rien coûté à mon innocence; tout ce qui dépend de ma volonté fut pour mon devoir: si le coeur qui n'en dépend pas fut pour vous, ce fut mon tourment et non pas mon crime. J'ai fait ce que j'ai dû faire; la vertu me reste sans tache, et l'amour m'est resté sans remords." Jean-Jacques Rousseau, *Julie ou la nouvelle Héloïse* (Paris: Garnier Frères, 1960), 728–29.

57. McDowell, 83 ("Mon regret est bien moins d'avoir donné trop à l'amour que de l'avoir privé de son plus grand charme." "Nous avons recherché le plaisir, et le bonheur a fui loin de nous" [76]).

58. McDowell, 83 ("Notre jouissance était paisible et durable, nous n'avons plus que des transports: ce bonheur insensé ressemble à des accès de fureur plus qu' à de tendres caresses. Un feu pur et sacré brûlait nos coeurs; livrés aux erreurs des sens, nous ne sommes plus que des amants vulgaires; trop heureux si l'amour jaloux daigne présider encore à des plaisirs que le plus vil mortel peut goûter sans lui!" [76]).

59. McDowell, 85 ("Je te dirai ce soir les moyens que j'imagine d'avoir d'autres occasions de nous voir . . ." [77]).

60. McDowell, 123 ("Je donne le change à mes transports en les décrivant" [122]).

61. De Staël, "On Literature," in *Major Writings*, 203.

62. Goldberger, 198 ("La morale, qui défend de jamais causer le malheur de personne, est au-dessus de tous les doutes du coeur et de la raison" [1:453]).

63. Goldberger, 211 ("la socéité, la Providence même peut-être, n'a permis qu'un seul bonheur aux femmes, l'amour dans le mariage . . ." [1:478]).

64. *Sir Charles Grandison*, 1:64.

65. Goldberger, 54. "La passion fait tourner toutes nos forces contre nous-même . . ." [1:178]).

66. McDowell, 78 ("Peut-être l'amour seul m'aurait épargnée; ô ma cousine! C'est la pitié qui me perdit" [70]).

67. Goldberger, 239 ("Léonce exerce sur moi la tout-puissance, que lui donnent à-la-fois son esprit, son caractère et son amour. Il me semble que je suis née pour lui obéir, autant que pour l'adorer; seule, je me reproche la passion qu'il m'inspire; mais en sa présence le mouvement involontaire de mon âme, est de me croire coupable quand j'ai pu le rendre malheureux" [1:533]).

68. It is worth noting here that however removed these heroines are from our times, recent studies in adolescent behavior reveal the persistence of this very model of behavior for girls in our society. Thus, for example, Carol Gilligan's findings demonstrate convincingly that adolescent males tend to base their moral decisions on abstract notions of rights or justice, while the moral judgments of adolescent females are led by personal considerations and individual responsibility. These tendencies are shown to persist into adulthood. See Carol Gilligan, *In a Different Voice* (Cambridge: Harvard Univeristy Press, 1982); Carol Gilligan, Janie Ward, and Jill Taylor, eds., *Mapping the Moral Domain* (Cambridge: Harvard University Press, 1988).

69. Jean-Jacques Rousseau, *The Confessions*, trans. J. M. Cohen (London: Penguin Classics, 1953), 405. "Qui tient radicalement à tout l'ordre social" (Jean-Jacques Rousseau, *Les Confessions* [Paris: Imprimerie Nationale, 1995], 1:704).

70. Goldberger, 3 ("c'est un obstacle a l'expression des sentimens vrais, que l'importun souvenir des ecrits insipides qui nous ont tant parlé des affections du coeur" [79]).

71. Sipovskii, "Onegin, Tat'iana i Lenskii," 558.

72. Sipovskii, "Onegin, Tat'iana i Lenskii," 558. We may observe here that

nearly a century later the poet Marina Tsvetaeva was to describe the significance to her own development as a poet of her illicit youthful reading of works by Pushkin that had been forbidden by her mother.

73. The subsequently deleted stanza 11 that appeared at this juncture in the fair copy of *Eugene Onegin* described the sequentiality of fashion and linear time, and thus provided a telling contrast that highlighted the synchronicity Tatiana achieved. "Uvy! Druz'ia! Mel'kaiut gody— / I s nimi vsled odna drugoi / Mel'kaiut vetrenye mody / Raznoobraznoi cheredoi— / Vse izmeniaetsia v prirode / Lamush i fizhmy byli v mode / Pridvornyi frant i rostovshchik / Nosili pudrenyi parik" (*PSS* 6:577). In Nabokov's translation this passage reads: "Alas, friends! The years flicker by, / and with them one after another / flicker the giddy fashions / in varied sequence. / All things in nature change: / patches and panniers were in fashion; / the court fop and the usurer / wore powdered wigs." Nabokov, "Commentary," 2:349.

74. Walter Arndt's translation, again with the replacement of his "insidious" by "dangerous."

75. Iurii Lotman, "The Structure of *Eugene Onegin,*" in *Russian Views of Pushkin's* Eugene Onegin, trans. Sona Stephan Hoisington (Bloomington: Indiana University Press, 1988), 98.

76. Johnston's translation. Alexander Pushkin, *Eugene Onegin* (Harmondsworth: Penguin, 1979).

Chapter 3. Tatiana's Letter to Onegin

1. This translation is Nabokov's, with a minor adjustment. Aleksandr Pushkin, *Eugene Onegin: A Novel in Verse* (Princeton: Princeton University Press, 1964).

2. Nabokov, "Commentary," in *Eugene Onegin*, trans. Nabokov, 2:352.

3. Thus, to cite but one of many possible examples, Lotman summarizes the content of this stanza as characterizing Pushkin's evolution to prose: "V strofe namechen put' evoliutsii Pushkina k proze" (Charted in this stanza is the path of Pushkin's evolution to prose.) Iurii Lotman, *Roman A. S. Pushkina* "Evgenii Onegin": *Kommentarii* (Leningrad: Prosveshchenie, 1983), 215.

4. *Don Juan*, in *Byron: Complete Poetical Works* (Oxford: Oxford University Press, 1970), 659. In *Beppo* Byron's author/narrator similarly notes: "I've half a mind to tumble down to prose" (629).

5. Lotman, *Kommentarii*, 216.

6. Byron, *Don Juan*, 659.

7. Leon Stilman, "Problemy literaturnykh zhanrov i traditsii v *Evgenii Onegine* Pushkina: K voprosu perekhoda ot romantizma k realizmu," in *American Contributions to the Fourth International Congress of Slavicists* (The Hague: Mouton, 1958), 366.

8. Thus Johnston. Alexander Pushkin, *Eugene Onegin* (Harmondsworth: Penguin, 1979).

9. Peter Brang, relying on variants of *Eugene Onegin,* suggests that Pushkin develops deliberate similarities between Tatiana's nurse and the nurse in

Karamzin's "Natal'ia, boiarskaia doch'." See his "Natal'ja, bojarskaja doč" und Tat'jana Larina," *Zeitschrift für slawische Philologie* 2 (1959): 348–362.

10. "Vecherom slushaiu skazki moei niani, originala niani Tatiany, vy kazhet-sia raz ee videli, ona edinstvennaia moia podruga—i s neiu tol'ko mne neskuchno" (In the evening I listen to the fairy tales of my nanny, the prototype of Tatiana's nanny, I think you once saw her, she is my only friend and it is only with her that I am not bored). Pushkin to D. M. Shvarts, December 1824, in *PSS* 13:129.

11. Johnston's translation.

12. It is telling that the particular word she uses for "times"("chereda") is a noun that indicates "turn" or "succession." She now finds herself in the "bad times" devoid of a past.

13. Lotman, *Kommentarii*, 218–20.

14. The similarity between the description of Praskov'ia's arranged marriage and that of Tatiana's nanny has been noted by Michael Katz. See his "Love and Marriage in Pushkin's *Evgeny Onegin*," in *Oxford Slavonic Papers*, n.s., 17 (Oxford. Clarendon Press, 1984). 85.

15. Lotman notes similar descriptions of the application of just such remedies to enamored young ladies in Karamzin's "Natal'ia boiarskaia doch'" and Bestuzhev's "Roman i O'lga." *Kommentarii*, 216–17. As in Tatiana's novels, so too in these works love is deemed a malady for which a cure must be found. Tatiana's nurse is, of course, innocent of these literary precedents and acts according to custom.

16. Kelley notes this departure from European literary tradition but sees in it a touch of humor: "The failure of Tat'jana's nurse to fill the roles of clever and bawdy confidante, teacher in the art of love, and go-between is one of the amusing and distinctive features of her characterization." Geraldine Kelley, "The Characterization of Tat'jana in Puškin's *Evgenij Onegin*," Ph.D. diss., University of Wisconsin–Madison, 1976), 110. The tonality of the scene between Tatiana and her nanny is gentle and affectionate. I would venture to suggest that those who find it comical are under the sway of Juliet's scenes with her nurse in *Romeo and Juliet*. For all the apparent similarities, a significant difference prevails between Shakespeare's and Pushkin's nurses. Juliet's understands and encourages the desires that grip her ward. Her feigned incomprehension is but a brief withholding of the support she willingly lends to the project of seeing that those desires are fulfilled. The scene is humorous precisely because under the nurse's professed ignorance we (unlike Juliet who is taken in by it) recognize a knowing and experienced woman. This comical touch is absent from Pushkin's text, however, for Tatiana's nanny has in fact completely lost touch with—indeed has never been allowed to experience—those gripping emotions her ward describes. Tatiana's nanny does not withhold. She has nothing to give.

17. Commentary on the significance of this threefold repetition of "in love" varies. Thus, for example, A. L. Slonimskii attributes the first utterance to Tatiana's sense of amazement at discovering the designation for her feelings, the second to growing self-confidence, and the third to ecstasy. *"Evgenii Onegin,"* in

Masterstvo Pushkina (Moscow: Gosudarstvennoe izdatel'stvo khudozhestvennoi literatury, 1963), 349–51. Kelley, who perceptively notes that such a reading can scarcely account for the "gorest'" (bitterness) that describes Tatiana's second repetition, suggests more plausibly that with each repetition Tatiana is drawing further back into herself in disappointment over her failed attempt to engage her nurse (Kelley, "Characterization of Tat'jana," 115–16).

18. Tatiana is discussed as an author in her own right by Diana L. Burgin, whose important study has contributed much to my own reading. See her "Tatiana Larina's *Letter to Onegin* or *La Plume Criminelle*," *Essays in Poetics* 16, no. 2 (1991): 12–23.

19. Stilman, "Problemy literaturnykh zhanrov," 351–52.

20. The "translation" of Tatiana's letter has received considerable scholarly attention. Here I will consider translation primarily in connection with how it relates to Tatiana's characterization. For further discussions see, inter alia, Sergei Bocharov, "The Stylistic World of the Novel" in *Russian Views of* Eugene Onegin, trans. Sona Stephan Hoisington (Bloomington: Indiana University Press, 1988), esp. 149–58; and V. V. Vinogradov, *Iazyk Pushkina* (Moscow/Leningrad: Academia, 1935), 222–30.

21. "Avtor skazyval, chto on dolgo ne mog reshit'sia, kak zastavit' pisat' Tat'ianu bez narusheniia zhenskoi lichnosti i pravdopodobiia v sloge." P. A. Viazemskii, *Polnoe sobranie sochinenii* (St. Petersburg, 1879), 2:23.

22. Viazemskii, *Polnoe sobranie sochinenii*, 2:23.

23. In his sketch "Prichinami, zamedlivshimi khod nashei slovesnosti" ("Causes Retarding the Development of Our Literature"), written in 1824, the year in which he worked on this chapter of *Onegin*, Pushkin complained: "Proza nasha tak eshche malo obrabotana, chto dazhe v prostoi perepiske my prinuzhdeny *sozdavat'* oboroty slov dlia iz"iasneniia poniatii samykh obyknovennykh" (our prose is still so unpolished, that even in simple correspondence we are forced to *create* turns of phrase to describe the most common concepts [*PSS* 11:21]).

24. For a discussion of the significance and reception of this "invention" and an analysis of the language of Tatiana's letter, see Vinogradov, *Iazyk Pushkina*, 222–26.

25. George Sherburn, Introduction, Samuel Richardson, *Clarissa* (Boston: Houghton Mifflin, 1962), iv.

26. Jean-Jacques Rousseau, *The Confessions*, trans. J. M. Cohen (London: Penguin Books, 1953), 400. "Je me figurai l'amour, l'amité, les deux idoles de mon coeur, sous les plus ravissantes images. Je me plus à les orner de tous les charmes du sexe que j'avais toujours adoré" Jean-Jacques Rousseau, *Les Confessions* (Paris: Imprimerie Nationale, 1995), 2:697.

27. It would be plausible to explain the similarities that have been noted between Tatiana's letter and an elegy of 1819 by Marceline Desbordes-Valmore as a sign that Pushkin studied a text written by a woman in preparation for creating his heroine's letter. Concerning these similarities, see Lotman, *Kommentarii*, 228–29 and Nabokov, "Commentary," 2:392.

28. As Stilman convincingly argues, this is the emotional basis for the im-

mutability of a woman's role in the novels read by the heroine of *A Novel in Letters*. Stilman, "Problemy literaturnykh zhanrov," 350–51.

29. Monika Greenleaf, *Pushkin and Romantic Fashion: Fragment, Elegy, Orient, Irony* (Stanford: Standford University Press, 1994), 257. See also p. 258, where Greenleaf describes "the deliberately protracted representation of the difficulty of the literary act" that she discerns in the many-layered translation of Tatiana's letter and describes as an allegory of "the perilous journey from the foreign country of the poet's psyche into the equally foreign country of legible language."

30. See chapter 2, n. 16, above.

31. Bocharov, "Stylistic World of the Novel," 151.

32. All of the known sketches, drafts, and reworkings are in Russian. Nabokov has noted that the Russian "translation" of Tatiana's letter "slips beautifully into French." "Commentary," 2:387.

33. Vinogradov, *Iazyk Pushkina*, 222. "V roli reformatora: on sozdaet normy 'ideal'nogo' iazyka russkoi zhenshchiny-dvorianki, a ne vosproizvodit ego."

34. Vinogradov, *Iazyk Pushkina*, 223.

35. On the question of an original, see Vinogradov, *Iazyk Pushkina*, 222.

36. Bocharov, "Stylistic World of the Novel," 152. Bocharov regards the concept of translation as an embodiment of "the profound *compositional idea* of [Pushkin's] novel which is conscious of being only a 'translation' of the real world." "Pushkin the translator," Bocharov concludes, "does not compete with the 'original' of reality." While the concept of translation Bocharov projects is a fruitful one, I submit that if Pushkin's translation does not in fact *compete* with reality, it is only because it is *one* with it. Thus, as we will see, Tatiana's letter and its translation ultimately fuse within the text of *Eugene Onegin*.

37. *PSS* 6:3314. See also P. Annenkov, *A. S. Pushkin. Materialy dlia ego biografii i otsenki proizvedenii* (St. Petersburg, 1873), 132–33.

38. In his study devoted to the interplay of the poetic and the prosaic in Pushkin's text, Iurii Tynianov overlooks this peculiar instance of poetry being passed off successfully as prose in the two letters (particularly in Eugene's which is purportedly a verbatim rendering). That the reader so readily accepts these deviations from the Onegin stanza to signal epistolary prose demonstrates the ease with which conventional expectations operating in concert with suspended disbelief can override actual generic features.

39. Lotman argues that in the latter half of the twenties Pushkin countered romantic subjectivity with a realism that presupposed an objective hero who acted independently of the author's will. It was the character's own psychology and not the author, Lotman maintains, that dictated his actions. See Iu. M. Lotman, "K evoliutsii postroeniia kharakterov v romane *Evgenii Onegin*," in *Pushkin: Issledovaniia i materialy*, vol. 3 (Moscow-Leningrad: Akademiia Nauk, 1960), 163. Lotman is certainly right to note that Pushkin sought to create for his reader a sense that the actions of his characters in *Eugene Onegin* depended on something other than his own authority. Yet the characters' single-mindedness (this with the

notable exception of Tatiana and the author/narrator), one might even say tunnel vision, makes the argument for realism less compelling. Extraordinary is the fact that in his novel-in-verse Pushkin succeeds in making his characters and settings seem so very credibly "real" when, in fact, they are highly stylized.

40. Bocharov, "Stylistic World of the Novel," 151.

41. Cited in Dmitry Chizhevsky, "Commentary," in A. S. Pushkin, *Evgenij Onegin: A Novel-in-Verse* (Cambridge: Harvard University Press, 1953), 243.

42. Richard A. Gregg, "Rhetoric in Tat'jana's Last Speech: The Camouflage That Reveals," *Slavic and East European Journal* 25 (1981): 6.

43. Gregg, "Rhetoric in Tat'jana's Last Speech," 1.

44. Quoted according to Nabokov's translation, "Commentary," 2:391. "Esli vprochem smysl i ne sovsem tochen, to tem bolee istiny v pis'me; pis'mo zhenshchiny, k tomu zhe 17 letnei, k tomu zhe vliublennoi" (*PSS 13:26*). Pushkin refers here to his heroine's use of the word "neliudim" (unsociable), but his observation is relevant to the letter in its entirety.

45. "[O]na ne umela by ni poniat', ni vyrazit' sobstvennykh svoikh oshchushchenii, esli by ne pribegla k pomoshchi vpechatlenii, ostavlennykh na ee pamiati plokhimi i khoroshimi romanami, bez tolku i bez razbora chitannymi eiu. . . ." V. G. Belinskii, *Sobranie sochinenii v 9–ti tomakh* (Moscow: Khudozhestvennaia literatura, 1981), 6:416.

46. V. Sipovskii, "Onegin, Tat'iana i Lenskii," in *Pushkin: Zhizn' i tvorchestvo* (St. Petersburg: Trud, 1907), 569–76.

47. Nabokov, "Commentary," 2:391–94.

48. John Garrard, "Sravnitel'nyi analiz geroin' 'Don Zhuana' Bairona i 'Evgeniia Onegina' Pushkina," *Voprosy literatury* (Nov.–Dec. 1996): 153–77.

49. Cited in Garrard, "Sravnitel'nyi analiz geroin'," 155.

50. Byron's choice of name for his heroine underscores her ties to Rousseau's Julie, even as the subsequent fate of her letter debunks the sentimenal school that informs it.

51. Garrard perceptively notes that Julia is the only character in *Don Juan* who is allowed her own voice by the overbearing narrator and calls the text of her letter one of Byron's most refined lyric poems. "Sravnitel'nyi analiz geroin',"156.

52. Sipovskii, "Onegin, Tat'iana i Lenskii," 569.

53. Vinogradov, *Iazyk Pushkina*, 229.

54. Stilman, "Problemy literaturnykh zhanrov," 321–22. "Nasyshchennost' 'Evgeniia Onegina' literaturnymi materialami, osobaia oshchutimost' v nem literaturnoi stikhii, poniatno, niskol'ko ne iskliuchaet sviazei proizvedeniia s deistvitel'nost'iu, tochno tak zhe, kak vozdeistvie na 'Evgeniia Onegina' razlichnykh literaturnykh istochnikov ne iskliuchaet ego glubokoi khudozhestvennoi original'nosti."

55. Garrard suggests that in initiating the correspondence Tatiana is behaving like Byron's Julia ("Sravnitel'nyi analiz geroin'," 170). Yet it would seem that the radical differences that prevail in their respective situations overwhelm this point of similarity. (Julia is an experienced woman who writes her letter to bid a final farewell to her departing lover.)

56. Caryl Emerson, "Tatiana," in *A Plot of Her Own: The Female Protagonist in Russian Literature*, ed. Sona Stephan Hoisington (Evanston: Northwestern University Press, 1995), 8.

57. Burgin, "Tatiana Larina's *Letter to Onegin,*" 12–23.

58. Belinskii, *Polnoe sobranie sochineni*, 6:416 ("bednaia devushka ne znala, chto delala").

59. Burgin, "Tatiana Larina's *Letter to Onegin,*" 15.

60. It is interesting to observe that it is precisely this frame, which he quotes in full, that Belinskii singles out for especial praise in his essay on Tatiana. Belinskii, *Polnoe sobranie sochinenii*, 416–17.

61. Onegin, as we will see, subsequently avails himself of this power at Tatiana's name day festivities.

62. This version is Arndt's. Alexander Pushkin, *Eugene Onegin* (New York: Dutton, 1981).

63. Krystyna Pomorska, "Zametiki o pis'me Tat'iany," in *Alexander Puškin, Symposium II* (Columbus: Slavica Publishers, 1980), 64. The four works are: "Tatiana's Letter" (1824), the lyrics "Ty i vy" (1828) and "Ia vas liubil" (1830), and the short story "Vystrel" (1830).

64. Burgin, "Tatiana Larina's *Letter to Onegin,*" 18.

65. Burgin, "Tatiana Larina's *Letter to Onegin,*" 19.

66. Nabokov, "Commentary," 2:368.

67. We can recall here that the appearance of a muse is predicated on adequate preparation. Thus, for example, in the second half of Pushkin's lyric "Ia pomniu chudnoe mgnoven'e" ("I Remember the Wondrous Moment"), the muse does not occasion the reawakening of the persona's soul. Rather, she reappears to him only once that reawakening has already been accomplished, and he is once again prepared to recognize her.

68. The rendering is Nabokov's.

69. Tatiana's letter was written between February and June of 1824.

70. Cf. "Ia pomniu chudnoe mgnoven'e: / Peredo mnoi iavilas' ty, / Kak mimoletnoe viden'e." In addition to the rhymed "mgnoven'e"-"viden'e" and the fleeting quality of the inspired visions, we can observe that the metrical similarity between Tatiana's lines and Pushkin's further enhances this connection.

71. Nabokov's translation.

72. Sipovskii, "Onegin, Tat'iana i Lenskii," 574.

73. Kelley, "Characterization of Tat'jana," 130.

74. This is how Lotman construes Tatiana's opposition. (*Kommentarii, 230*).

75. Unlike her mother, who did not know the difference between Lovelace and Grandison because she did not read any of Richardson's novels, Tatiana knows Richardson well enough to recognize this shared quality of these otherwise dissimilar characters. Here is what the author/narrator says of the elder Larina:

Она любила Ричардсона.
Не потому, чтобы прочла
Не потому, чтоб Грандисона
Она Ловласу предпочла; 14

[It wasn't that she'd read him, really,
Nor was it that she much preferred
To Lovelace Grandison. . . .]
(2:30, ll. 1–4)

The note (no. 14) which Pushkin appends to this passage is pointedly laconic and does nothing to distinguish the two heroes: "Grandison i Lovlas, geroi dvukh slavnykh romanov" (Grandison and Lovelace, heroes of two renowned novels.)

76. The translation is Nabokov's, the emphasis is mine.

77. Burgin, "Tatiana Larina's *Letter to Onegin*," 19.

78. This rendering is Nabokov's.

79. We can observe here that the willingness to imbue a seemingly arbitrary sign with great import is a trait Tatiana shares with the superstitious author who created her.

80. This emphasizes once again that Tatiana is not slavishly imitating her novels.

81. The translation is Arndt's.

82. Burgin, "Tatiana Larina's *Letter to Onegin*," 19.

83. Nabokov, "Commentary," 2:368.

84. Kelley, "Characterization of Tat'jana," 85.

85. Nabokov's translation.

86. Nabokov, "Commentary," 2:407. Pushkin's works provide other examples of women's songs interpolated into his texts, among which are the Circassian girls' song in *Kavkazkii plennik*, the Tartar song sung by the harem in *Bakhchisaraiskii fontan*, and Zemfira's song in *Tsigany*.

87. On the stylistic peculiarities of this song, see Lotman, *Kommentarii*, 232–33; Chizhevsky, "Commentary," 245; Nabokov, "Commentary," 2:407–9.

88. The "nets" of enticement appeared also in the description of Onegin in 1:12, l. 6, which describes his plans for the coquettes: "Kakie seti im gotovil!" (What nets he prepared for them!). This image appeared also in an earlier variant of 2:9, where Pushkin described Lensky as refraining from "glorifying the nets of voluptuousness" ("Ne slavil seti sladostrast'ia" [*PSS* 6:270]).

Chapter 4. Aftermath

1. Vissarion Belinsky, "*Eugene Onegin*: An Encyclopedia of Russian Life," in *Russian Views of Pushkin's "Eugene Onegin*," trans. Sona Stephan Hoisington (Bloomington: Indiana University Press, 1988), 34.

2. Stanzas 1–4, which Pushkin ultimately chose to omit from *Eugene Onegin*, had appeared in *Moskovskii vestnik* in 1827 under the heading "Women—A Fragment" and were thus already familiar to Pushkin's contemporary readers. Stanzas 5–6, which appear never to have existed, are described by Lotman as a "mystification" on Pushkin's part. Iurii Lotman, *Roman A. S. Pushkina "Evgenii Onegin": Kommentarii* (Leningrad: Prosveshchenie, 1983), 235. Nabokov comments that in light of the fact that in 1833 Pushkin himself had been married for two years, he was wise to omit these stanzas with their cynical view on relations with women. Vladimir Nabokov, "Commentary," in Aleksandr Pushkin, *Eugene Onegin: A Novel in Verse* (Princeton: Princeton University Press, 1964), 2:414–18.

Neither Nabokov nor Chizhevskii refers to the fact that there had been no stanzas 5–6. Dmitry Chizhevsky, "Commentary," in A. S. Pushkin, *Evgenij Onegin: A Novel-in-Verse* (Cambridge: Harvard University Press, 1953), 247.

3. V. V. Vinogradov, *Iazyk Pushkina* (Moscow-Leningrad: Academia, 1935), 229.

4. Nabokov, "Commentary" 2:423.

5. The translation is Nabokov's.

6. This accords with Eugene's preference for economics over poetry that is noted in stanza 7 of chapter 1. "Branil Gomera, Feokrita; / Zato chital Adama Smita / I byl glubokii ekonom" (Homer, Theocritus disdaining, / From Adam Smith he sought his training / And was no mean economist.) Alexander Pushkin, *Eugene Onegin*, trans. Walter Arndt (New York: Dutton, 1981).

7. Falen's translation. Alexander Pushkin, *Eugene Onegin* (Oxford: Oxford University Press, 1995).

8. Even Nabokov succeeds in ferreting out only one connection (to Senancour's *Obermann*) ("Commentary," 2:422), a connection Lotman dismisses (*Kommentarii*, 236).

9. Caryl Emerson has observed that "Pushkin (in contrast to Rousseau before him and Tolstoy after him) did not value *embarrassment*—the public disclosure of one's private indiscretions or vice—as a literary virtue." See her "Pushkin, Literary Criticism, and Creativity in Closed Places" in *New Literary History* 29, no. 4 (Autumn 1998): 656.

10. The reflections of *Adolphe* in Pushkin's writings are analyzed by Anna Akhmatova. See "*Adol'f* Benzhamina Konstana v tvorchestve Pushkina," in *O Pushkine* (Leningrad: Sovetskii pisatel', 1977), 50–88. Akhmatova notes that Pushkin's copy of *Adolphe* (3rd edition of 1824) bore copious pencil marks and notes (55).

11. Thus Nabokov.

12. We can note here the telling insistence on the verb "meniaet" (changes) in Pushkin's various drafts of this passage. Whatever alterations were made to the text, Onegin's emphasis on replacement remained at the forefront in this section. *PSS* 6:349–50.

13. Compare also the closing couplet of 1:29, where the author/narrator explains: "Ia eto potomu pishu, / Chto uzh davno ia ne greshu" (I am writing this because / I have long since stopped sinning).

14. "I will observe only that the less one loves a woman, the more certain is one to possess her. But this amusement is worthy of an old ape of the eighteenth century."

15. William Mills Todd III, *The Familiar Letter as a Literary Genre in the Age of Pushkin* (Princeton: Princeton University Press, 1974), 144.

16. Cf., e.g., "otlozhim— / Liubvi my tsenu tem umnozhim / Vernee v seti zavedem" ("we will postpone / We will thus increase the value of love / Will lead them more certainly into our nets" [3:25, ll. 5–7]).

17. This translation is Johnston's. Alexander Pushkin, *Eugene Onegin* (Harmondsworth: Penguin, 1979).

18. It is extremely unlikely that Eugene has read any of Richardson's novels.

Here he presumably invokes Lovelace much as Tatiana's mother invokes Grandison—on the strength of hearsay alone. Richardson's hero's name had by Onegin's time become a commonplace to describe libertines. Indeed, Pushkin refers to it in various letters to his friends and even adopts it as a cognomen for himself (see, e.g., *PSS* 13:71, 14:33, 14:49, 16:104).

19. This translation is Arndt's.

20. Once again Arndt. I have only substituted "tongue" for his "voice" (for *iazyk*) because of the significance of the specific reference to the language of the letter.

21. Arndt's translation.

22. This translation is Nabokov's.

23. Lotman, *Kommentarii*, 236.

24. Onegin is not startled by Zaretskii's visit on the morning after the festivities not because he anticipates the delivery of Lensky's challenge, but simply because he and Zaretskii, as the author/narrotor is careful to explain at this point, habitually get together (6:8, ll. 5–8).

25. Here I do not deny the complex social and psychological significance of dueling in Pushkin's era. I suggest only that as Pushkin represents the particular situation here in *Eugene Onegin,* the duel between Eugene and Vladimir underscores the arbitrariness and inflexibility of the code that dictates it. Onegin's personal inclinations are described as being distinctly at odds with the behavior forced on him by fear of public opinion (6:11). This suggests that Eugene sacrifices his friend to his own public image. I am prepared to suggest that underlying this situation are Pushkin's own growing doubts about this ironclad, ever-repeated ritual.

26. J. Douglas Clayton, *Ice and Flame: Aleksandr Pushkin's "Eugene Onegin"* (Toronto: University of Toronto Press, 1985), 140.

27. Lotman, *Kommentarii*, 236–37.

28. This holds true for the *Belkin Tales* as well.

29. Abram Terz (Andrei Sinyavsky), *Strolls with Pushkin*, trans. Catherine Theimer Nepomnyashchy (New Haven: Yale University Press, 1993), 65. "V desiatkakh variatsii povestvuet Pushkin o tom, kak u suprotivnika roka oblamyvaiutsia roga, kak vopreki vsem ulovkam i proiskam sud'ba torzhestvuet pobedu nad chelovekom, putaia emu karty ili podkidyvaia siurpriz" (*Progulki s Pushkinym* [London: Overseas Publications Interchange, 1975], 36).

Chapter 5. Tatiana's Dream

1. O. N. Grechina, "O fol'klorizme *Evgeniia Onegina*," in *Slavianskie literatury i fol'klor, Russkii fol'klor* 18 (Leningrad: Nauka, 1978), 19. Grechina's study provides a detailed discussion of the implications of the folk rituals that Pushkin includes in *Eugene Onegin*. Although I do not concur with her exclusive focus on Tatiana's "narodnost'" (national character) in connection with this material and disagree too with some of the particulars of her reading (e.g., that Tatiana is focused exclusively on determining the possibility of her future happiness with Eugene), the ethnographic material of this article has greatly assisted in the development of my own ideas on the significance of the folk rituals in the text.

2. Grechina has pointed out that Tatiana's saint's day (12 January by the Julian and 25 January by the Gregorian calendar) was traditionally celebrated in the countryside with fortune-telling rituals, so that her very name is linked with winter and divination. "O fol'klorizme *Evgeniia Onegina*," 23.

3. Geraldine Kelley, "The Characterization of Tat'jana in Puškın's *Evgenij Onegin*," Ph.D. diss., University of Wisconsin–Madison, 1976, 143.

4. "Strashnye rasskazy / Zimoiu v temnote nochei / Pleniali bol'she serdtse ei" (but grisly stories / Quite charmed her heart when they were told / On winter nights all dark and cold [2:27, ll. 6–8]).

5. Johnston's translation. Alexander Pushkin, *Eugene Onegin* (Harmondsworth: Penguin, 1979).

6. Dmitry Chizhevsky, "Commentary," in A. S. Pushkin, *Evgenij Onegin: A Novel-in-Verse* (Cambridge: Harvard University Press, 1953), 257.

7. Grechina, "O fol'klorizme *Evgeniia Onegina*," 30.

8. Grechina, "O fol'klorizme *Evgeniia Onegina*," 31–32.

9. Iurii Lotman, *Roman A. S. Pushkina "Evgenii Onegin": Kommentarii* (Leningrad: Prosveshchenie, 1983), 264–65.

10. Grechina, "O fol'klorizme *Evgeniia Onegina*," 32.

11. Somewhat earlier in Russian history, divination by dream entailed a more concrete risk: under Catherine the Great it was made a criminal offense. See W. F. Ryan and Faith Wigzell, "Gullible Girls and Dreadful Dreams: Zhukovskii, Pushkin and Popular Divination," in *Slavonic and East European Review* 70, no. 4 (1992): 666.

12. Faith Wigzell, *Reading Russian Fortunes: Print Culture, Gender, and Divination* (Cambridge: Cambridge University Press, 1998), 71.

13. Both Lotman (*Kommentarii*, 266) and Grechina ("O fol'klorizme *Evgeniia Onegina*," 32) comment on the significance of the removal of the belt, which may seem like a redundant detail in Pushkin's text in light of the preceding statement that Tatiana disrobed. V. I. Smirnov elaborates on this type of ritual in his *Narodnye gadaniia v Kostromskom krae* (Kostroma, 1927) where he writes: "before auguries with mirrors, the augurer unties all the knots on her person. . . . The knot impedes human contact with the force to which she turns during fortunetelling with the request for aid in learning his fate" (cited in Grechina, 32).

14. Lotman in his *Kommentarii* (268) notes that this is corroborated by a variety of (unspecified) sources.

15. Grechina, "O fol'klorizme *Evgeniia Onegina*," 32.

16. Richard A. Gregg, "Tat'yana's Two Dreams: The Unwanted Spouse and the Demonic Lover," *Slavonic and East European Review* 48, no. 113 (October 1970): 492.

17. Michael Katz, "Dreams in Pushkin," *California Slavic Studies* 11 (Berkeley: University of California Press, 1980), 71.

18. Valda Nesaule reminds us that the idea that the dreamer creates his own dream has held since ancient times. See her "Tatiana's Dream in Pushkin's *Evgenij Onegin*," *Indiana Slavic Studies*, vol. 4, ed. William B. Edgerton (Bloomington: Indiana University Press, 1967), 119–20.

19. Ryan and Wigzell, "Gullible Girls and Dreadful Dreams," 665–66.

20. Roman Jakobson, "Marginal Notes on *Eugene Onegin*," in *Roman Jakobson: Selected Writings* (The Hague: Mouton Publishers, 1979), 290.

21. William Mills Todd III, "*Eugene Onegin*: Life's Novel," in *Literature and Society in Imperial Russia, 1800–1914*, ed. Todd (Stanford: Stanford University Press, 1978), 214.

22. Todd, "*Eugene Onegin*: Life's Novel," 215.

23. Todd, "*Eugene Onegin*: Life's Novel," 217.

24. Caryl Emerson, "'The Queen of Spades' and the Open End," in *Puškin Today* (Bloomington: Indiana Univeristy Press, 1993), 32.

25. Emerson, "'Queen of Spades,'" 32–33.

26. Emerson, "'Queen of Spades,'" 36.

27. Ralph E. Matlaw, "The Dream in Yevgenij Onegin," *Slavonic Review* 37 (1959): 89, 487; Katz, "Dreams in Pushkin," 74.

28. Cited in Chizhevsky, "Commentary," 258; Matlaw, "Dream in Yevgenij Onegin," 487; Katz "Dreams in Pushkin" 73–74. Schubert's extremely popular book was translated into Russian in 1814. Whether or not Pushkin was familiar with this particular work—and it remains unclear as to whether he did in fact read it—the ideas expressed in it would certainly have been known to him through his readings of the romantics. (The work is not listed in Modzalevskii's catalogue of Pushkin's library.)

29. Katz, "Dreams in Pushkin," 74.

30. Katz, "Dreams in Pushkin," 74.

31. Most commentators acknowledge the erotic nature of Tatiana's dream. The most extensive treatment of its erotic imagery can be found in Richard Gregg's "Tat'yana's Two Dreams"; Georgii Gachev's "Russkii eros" in *Natsional'nye obrazy mira: Kosmo/Psikho/Logos* (Moscow: Progress Publishers, 1995), 242–50; G. A. Kharazov, "Son Tat'iany. Opyt tolkovaniia po Freidu" in *ARS*, (Tiflis), no. 1 (1919): 9–20; and J. Douglas Clayton, "Towards a Feminist Reading of *Evgenii Onegin*," *Canadian Slavic Papers* 29, nos. 2 & 3 (June-September 1987): esp. 262–64.

32. Grechina, "O fol'klorizme *Evgeniia Onegina*," 35.

33. Lotman, *Kommentarii*, 272.

34. Lotman, *Kommentarii*, 270.

35. Various scholars have commented on the similarity between the creatures of Tatiana's dream and those depicted in representations of *The Temptation of St. Anthony* by Bosch, Murillo, and on a Russian *lubok*. Lotman notes that Pushkin had a print of the Murillo painting at his Mikhailovskoe estate (*Kommentarii*, 272).

36. Vladimir Nabokov, "Commentary," in Aleksandr Pushkin, *Eugene Onegin: A Novel-in-Verse* (Princeton: Princeton University Press, 1964), 2:501.

37. For a study of this aspect of Bosch's works, see M. A. Bax-Botha, *Hieronymous Bosch: His Picture-Writing Deciphered*, trans. D. Bax (Rotterdam: A. A. Balkema, 1979). I thank Ieva Vitins for acquainting me with this work.

38. Grechina, "O fol'klorizme *Evgeniia Onegina*," 37.

39. Faith Wigzell notes Pushkin's own familiarity with such books. "In

1827," she writes, "a dreambook was seen on the poet Pushkin's desk at Mikhailovskoe and his Petersburg library contained a cartomantic guide" (*Reading Russian Fortunes*, 71).

40. Katz, "Dreams in Pushkin," 94.

41. Matlaw, "Dream in Yevgenij Onegin," 500.

42. This translation is Johnston's.

43. Again, Johnston.

44. Note the "vlastvovat'" in Eugene's speech and the "vlast'" in the description of Tatiana.

45. Johnston's translation.

46. J. Thomas Shaw, "The Problem of Unity of Author-Narrator's Stance in Puškin's *Evgenii Onegin*," *Russian Language Journal* 35, no. 120 (Winter 1981): 33.

47. Lotman, *Kommentarii*, 287.

48. That Dostoevsky apparently profited from Pushkin's psychological astuteness can be deduced from similar unconsciously motivated behavior on the part of some of his major characters at crucial junctures in their stories (cf., e.g., Goliadkin, Raskolnikov, Myshkin).

49. See *PSS* 6:434. George Gibian observes that "The care lavished by Pushkin on this brief passage is shown by the fact that we have four preparatory versions." For a discussion of these versions, see his "Love by the Book: Pushkin, Stendhal, Flaubert," *Comparative Literature* 8, no. 2 (Spring 1956): 100–101. Notes on the drafts can be found also in Nabokov, "Commentary," 3:96–101 and Lotman, *Kommentarii*, 316–20.

50. Gibian, "Love by the Book," 100.

51. Thus Arndt. Alexander Pushkin, *Eugene Onegin* (New York: Dutton, 1981).

52. Gibian, "Love by the Book," 101.

53. Todd, "*Eugene Onegin*: 'Life's Novel,'" 226.

54. Anna Akhmatova observes that Viazemskii translated *Adolphe* not to acquaint Russian writers with the novel, which they could easily have read in the original, but in order to provide them with language suitable for writing a psychological novel. She goes on to describe that Pushkin took considerable interest in this translation, which was dedicated to him and which he described as a "translation of the refined, metaphysical, subtly sensual *Adolphe* into our uncultivated language" ("perevod svetskogo, metafizicheskogo tonko-chuvstvennogo *Adol'fa* na nash neobrabotannyi iazyk"). See her "*Adol'f* Benzhamina Konstana v tvorchestve Pushkina," in *O Pushkine* (Leningrad: Sovetskii pisatel', 1977), 59.

55. David Bethea, *Realizing Metaphors: Alexander Pushkin and the Life of the Poet* (Madison: University of Wisconsin Press, 1998), 39.

56. In the same spirit Pushkin ascribed considerable significance to Gnedich's Homer translations as well.

57. This in a letter to his wife (dated 23 January 1828), which he wrote upon reading this chapter when it appeared in the *Moscow Herald*. Cited in Nabokov, "Commentary," 3:121.

58. See, e.g., Lotman, *Kommentarii*, 331.

59. Chizhevskii, "Commentary," 281.

60. The translation is Arndt's with the exception of the last two lines, which I have altered to convey the habitual quality of his appearance that is denoted by the imperfective verb.

61. This translation is Nabokov's. Aleksandr Pushkin, *Eugene Onegin: A Novel-in-Verse* 1:249.

Chapter 6. Tatiana's Glory

1. This felicitous formulation, which perfectly describes *Eugene Onegin*, appears in Albert Gleizes and Jean Metzinger, "Cubism," in *Modern Artists on Art* (Englewood Cliffs, N.J.: Prentice Hall, 1964), 12.

2. Iurii Lotman, *Roman A. S. Pushkina "Evgenii Onegin": Kommentarii* (Leningrad: Prosveshchenie, 1983), 336-37.

3. J. Thomas Shaw, "The Problem of Unity of Author-Narrator's Stance in Puškin's *Evgenii Onegin*," *Russian Language Journal* 35, no. 120 (Winter 1981), 30.

4. Lotman, *Kommentarii*, 336–37.

5. Johnston's translation. Alexander Pushkin, *Eugene Onegin* (Harmondsworth: Penguin, 1979).

6. Leslie O'Bell, "Through the Magic Crystal to Eugene Onegin," in *Puškin Today* (Bloomington: Indiana University Press, 1993), 162.

7. Thus Arndt. Alexander Pushkin, *Eugene Onegin* (New York: Dutton, 1981).

8. This translation is Arndt's.

9. This translation is Nabokov's. Aleksandr Pushkin, *Eugene Onegin: A Novel-in-Verse* 1:292.

10. Cf. *Don Juan*, 13:84–88 and *Eugene Onegin*, 8:24–26.

11. D. Blagoi, *Masterstvo Pushkina* (Moscow, 1955), 198. "Ustonavlivalo polnuiu simmetriiu v otnoshenii razrabotki osnovnoi liubovnoi fabuly romana."

12. Thus Arndt.

13. Lotman, *Kommentarii*, 361. "Onegin i Tat'iana ispol'zuiut odni i te zhe formuly, odnako smysl i funktsiia etikh formul v ikh upotreblenii gluboko razlichny."

14. Lotman, *Kommentarii*, 362. "Chto v pis'me Onegina raskhozhie formuly perestaiut byt' sviazannymi s *opredelennym* tekstom, a prevrashchaiutsia v fakt obshchego upotrebleniia. Tak, naprimer, dlia vyrazheniia 'milaia privychka' (*douce habitude*) mozhno bylo by ukazat' desiatki 'istochnikov'. Na samom zhe dele eto vyrazhenie uzhe otorvavsheesia ot liubogo iz nikh. No imenno potomu, chto Onegin upotrebliaet eti vyrazheniia, ne zadumyvaias', otkuda oni prishli k nemu, chto sami po sebe eti vyrazheniia dlia nego nichego ne znachat, oni okazyvaiutsia tesno sviazannymi s ego real'noi biografiei."

15. Lotman, *Kommentarii*, 362. "Kak v poezii, zdes' vyrazhenie est' odnovremenno i soderzhanie."

16. This translation is Johnston's.

17. Here I concur with Lotman's opinion on the subject. *Kommentarii*, 363–64.

18. Again Johnston.

19. Faith Wigzell describes the significance of games of chance, which "were played almost exclusively by men, and, far from being regarded as 'innocent en-

tertainment,' were seen in aristocratic society as a dangerous duel with chance which young men took up as a challenge to their manhood." *Reading Russian Fortunes: Print Culture, Gender, and Divination* (Cambridge: Cambridge University Press, 1998), 118. See also Iurii Lotman, *Besedy o russkoi kul'ture. Byt i traditsii russkogo dvorianstva (XVIII-nachalo XIX veka)* (St. Petersburg: Iskusstvo, 1994), 141–45.

20. Vladimir Nabokov, "Commentary," in Aleksandr Pushkin, *Eugene Onegin: A Novel-in-Verse* (Princeton: Princeton University Press, 1964), 3:227.

21. J. Douglas Clayton, *Ice and Flame: Aleksandr Pushkin's "Eugene Onegin"* (Toronto: University of Toronto Press, 1985), 112.

22. This rendering is Arndt's.

23. The elusive presence in this passage of the "ideal" that slips just beyond Eugene's reach is created by the reference to *idol mio* in the acoustic environment of the rhyming "i ronial—to zhurnal." These acoustic clues work together with the context to suggest the word *ideal*, which is strongly felt, although not actually present in the text. Note too that the "svorotil" of 8:37, l. 13 brings Eugene acoustically close to the creativity of its perfect anagram "sotvoril."

24. Caryl Emerson, "Tatiana," in *A Plot of Her Own: The Female Protagonist in Russian Literature*, ed. Sona Stephan Hoisington (Evanston: Northwestern University Press, 1995), 14–20.

25. Emerson, "Tatiana," 16.

26. William Mills Todd III, *Fiction and Society in the Age of Pushkin: Ideology, Institutions, and Narrative* (Cambridge: Harvard University Press, 1986), 129.

27. Richard A. Gregg, "Rhetoric in Tat'jana's Last Speech: The Camouflage That Reveals," *Slavic and East European Journal* 25 (1981): cited phrases on pp. 1, 6, and 9, respectively. The eloquence of Gregg's argument cannot disguise the fact that even as he meticulously scrutinizes Tatiana's speech for inaccuracies, he is content to take everything said by Eugene and even the notoriously unreliable author/narrator at face value. It thus transpires that Eugene's and the author/narrator's distortions are rallied as proof of Tatiana's "dubeity." It appears that it is against the privileged male voice that Tatiana's (feminine) veracity is to be judged.

28. Abram Terts, *Progulki s Pushkinym* (London: Overseas Publications Interchange, 1975), 102. Siniavskii/Terts provides a superb discussion of the significance of memory in Pushkin's creative process on pp. 101–7.

29. This felicitous formulation is Clayton's (*Ice and Flame*, 185).

30. Gregg, "Rhetoric in Tat'jana's Last Speech," 8.

31. The theme of the irrevocability of matrimonial vows in Pushkin's works receives close attention in Ludolf Müller, "Schicksal und Liebe im *Jewgenij Onegin*." In *Solange Dichter Leben: Puschkin-Studien*, ed. A. Luther (Krefeld: Scherpe-Verlag, 1949), 148–63.

32. Stephanie Sandler, *Distant Pleasures: Alexander Pushkin and the Writing of Exile* (Stanford: Stanford University Press, 1989), 207.

33. Gregg notes that Tatiana "uses the first person pronoun thirty-five times in her seventy-seven line speech." "Rhetoric in Tat'jana's Last Speech," 12, n. 11.

34. My translation.

35. William Mills Todd III, "*Eugene Onegin*: 'Life's Novel,'" in *Literature and Society in Imperial Russia, 1800–1914*, ed. Todd (Stanford: Stanford Uni-

versity Press, 1978), 228–29. See also William Edward Brown, *A History of Russian Literature of the Romantic Period* (Ann Arbor: Ardis, 1986), 82.

36. Thus, for example, Belinskii. See his "Stat'ia deviataia. 'Evgenii Onegin' (Okonchanie)," in *Sobranie sochinenii v 9-ti tomakh* (Moscow: Khudozhestvennaia literatura, 1981), 6:424.

37. One such example is Michael Katz, who writes: "When an older and wiser Tatiana declares her abiding love to Onegin and simultaneously announces the intention to honor her marriage vows, she is in one sense re-enacting the denoument of Rousseau's romantic novel. There can be little doubt that she vaguely recalls the fates of her favorite heroines. . . . But it would seem that it is Julie's *superficial conjugal fidelity* combined with her abiding love for Saint-Preux which stands as the closest model for Tat'yana's decision"(my emphasis). See "Love and Marriage in Pushkin's *Evgeny Onegin*," in *Oxford Slavonic Papers*, n.s., 17 (Oxford: Clarendon Press, 1984): 80.

38. It is similarly a readerly assumption and not an explicit given in the text that makes the letter Tatiana is reading when Eugene bursts in on her one of those that he has written to her.

39. Although she did not marry out of love, it seems that Tatiana has grown attached to her husband. Pushkin refrains from overt commentary on this score, but he does provide unmistakable signs of intimate understanding and trust between husband and wife. Thus, for example, in the midst of a crowded social event, a glance from Tatiana is sufficient to communicate her needs to her husband (8:19, l. 13); moreover the Prince does not appear jealous or threatened by the attentions Eugene pays his wife.

40. Clayton's observation is very much to the point here: "The real drama of the poem is, I would suggest, not Onegin's and Tat'iana's love for each other, but Pushkin's love for Tat'iana . . ." (*Ice and Flame*, 189).

41. A similar proclamation of allegiance to a distant other found its way into Pushkin's 1833 "Skazka o mertvoi tsarevne i o semi bogatyriakh"("The Tale of the Dead Princess and the Seven Knights"). In this fairy tale, the Princess responds to the suit of the seven knights for her hand in marriage with the confession: "No drugomu ia navechno / Otdana" (But I am given / dedicated to another forever [*PSS* 3:548]).

Here the Princess refers to her intended, but it is significant that during her sojourn with the knights, she never once mentions him, nor seeks to return to him. Confronted with a choice between the brave knights with their immediate offer of love and marriage, and a distant, by now rather abstract betrothed of whom she knows nothing, the Princess unhesitatingly chooses the latter. This choice having been made, the *ménage à huit* returns to its daily routine, no effort made toward a possible reunion of the parted couple. In this regard the Princess, like Tatiana, opts for unrealized potential over the promise of immediate fulfillment.

42. Clayton, *Ice and Flame*, 189.

43. "Poeziia vyshe nravstvennosti," Pushkin wrote in the margin of an article by Viazemskii. Cited in Terts, *Progulki s Pushkinym*, 170.

44. Walter Vickery, *Alexander Pushkin* (New York: Twayne, 1970), 129.

45. Leon Stilman, "Problemy literaturnykh zhanrov i traditsii v *Evgenii Onegine* Pushkina: K voprosu perekhoda ot romantizma k realizmu," in *American Contributions to the Fourth International Congress of Slavicists* (The Hague: Mouton, 1958), 363–65.

46. Stanley Mitchell, "Tatiana's Reading," *Forum for Modern Langauge Studies* 4, no. 1 (Jan. 1968): 7.

Epilogue

1. Caryl Emerson, "Pushkin, Literary Criticism, and Creativity in Closed Places," *New Literary History* 29, no. 4 (Autumn 1998): 665.

2. Iurii Lotman, "*Aleksandr Sergeevich Pushkin. Biografiia pisatelia. Predislovie k pol'skomu izdaniiu*," in *Lotmanovskii sbornik* (Moscow: ITs-Garant, 1995), 87. "Zakon iskusstva—vozrastanie vozmozhnostei vybora."

3. Emerson, "Pushkin, Literary Criticism, and Creativity," 666.

4. Boris Gasparov, *Poeticheskii iazyk Pushkina kak fakt istorii russkogo literaturnogo iazyka* (Vienna: Gesellschaft zur Forderung slawistischen Studien, 1992), 80. "Zhivaia sviaz' so stilisticheskim, zhanrovym, psikhologicheskim stroem minuvshego veka, v sochetanii s burnymi novatorskimi ustremleniiami sovremennoi Pushkinu epokhi, dali unikal'nyi tvorcheskii fenomen, nepovtorimye svoistva kotorogo pozvolili ego tvorchestvu stat' odnim iz samykh moshchnykh tvorcheskikh impul'sov v istorii russkoi kul'tury."

5. David Bethea, in private correspondence.

6. Cited in Lotman, "K evoliutsii postroeniia kharakterov v romane *Evgenii Onegin*," in *Pushkin: Issledovaniia i materialy*, vol. 3 (Moscow Leningrad: Academiia Nauk, 1960), 161. "Poet v svoei 8–i glave pokhozh sam na Tat'ianu. Dlia litseiskogo ego tovarishcha, dlia cheloveka, kotoryi s nim vyros i ego znaet naizust', kak ia, vezde zametno chuvstvo, koim Pushkin preispolnen, khotia on, podobno svoei Tat'iane, i ne khochet, chtob ob etom chuvstve znal svet."

7. Caryl Emerson, "Tatiana," in *A Plot of Her Own: The Female Protagonist in Russian Literature*, ed. Sona Stephan Hoisington (Evanston: Northwestern University Press, 1995), 11.

8. David Bethea, in private correspondence.

9. Vissarion Belinskii, "Stat'ia deviataia. 'Evgenii Onegin' (Okonchanie)," in *Sobranie sochinenii v 9-ti tomakh* (Moscow: Khudozhestvennaia literatura, 1981), 6:424. "Zhizn' zhenshchiny po preimushchestvu sosredotochena v zhizni serdtsa; liubit'—znachit dlia nee zhit', a zhertvovat' znachit liubit'."

10. Diana L. Burgin, "Tatiana Larina's *Letter to Onegin*, or *La Plume Criminelle*," *Essays in Poetics* 16, no. 2 (1991): 13.

11. Diana Greene, "Nineteenth-Century Women Poets: Critical Reception vs. Self-Definition," in *Women Writers in Russian Literature*, ed. Toby W. Clyman and Diana Greene (Westport, CT: Praeger Publishers, 1994), 96.

12. Vladislav Khodasevich, *Sobranie sochinenii*, ed. John Malmstad and Robert Hughes (Ann Arbor: Ardis Publishers, 1990), 2:133.

13. Virginia Woolf, *A Room of One's Own* (San Diego: Harcourt Brace, 1957), 82.

14. Karolina Pavlova, *Polnoe sobranie stikhotvorenii* (Moscow: Sovetskii pisatel', 1964), 310. The translation that follows is my own.

15. Pavlova, *Polnoe sobranie*, 310.

16. Susanne Fusso, "Pavlova's *Quadrille*: The Feminine Variant of (the End of) Romanticism," forthcoming in *Karolina Pavlova* (Evanston: Northwestern University Press, 1999).

17. Susanne Fusso, "Pavlova's *Quadrille.*"

18. Wallace Stevens, *The Necessary Angel: Essays on Reality and the Imagination* (New York: Vintage Books, 1951), 7.

19. Barbara Heldt, *Terrible Perfection: Women and Russian Literature* (Bloomington: Indiana University Press, 1987), 112.

20. Pavlova, *Polnoe sobranie*, 312.

21. Pavlova, *Polnoe sobranie*, 312.

22. The similarity of this duel to the last one Pushkin fought is noted in Fusso, "Pavlova's *Quadrille.*"

23. Pavel Gromov, Introduction, in Karolina Pavlova, *Polnoe sobranie*, 44–45.

24. Pavlova, *Polnoe sobranie*, 315.

25. Susanne Fusso, "Pavlova's *Quadrille.*"

26. Barbara Heldt has translated this work as *A Double Life*, but inasmuch as Pavlova takes its title from the opening words of Byron's poem "The Dream," "Our life is two-fold," it seems desirable to preserve this reference.

27. The passage in question opens with the following lines, which make the reference to *Onegin* unmistakable:

> Мой дядя, старый князь Арсений,
> В то время летом и зимой
> Жил, предаваясь сельской лени,
> В своей деревне под Москвой . . .

> [My uncle, aging prince Arsenii,
> Those days in winter and in spring,
> Lived in his village just near Moscow,
> Content with doing not a thing.]

There is a trace of rebellion here too, for having strictly adhered to the given form for a full twelve lines, Pavlova chooses not to close out the stanza with the couplet anticipated in lines 13–14.

28. Marina Tsvetaeva, *Pis'ma k Teskovoi* (Jerusalem: Versty, 1982), 148. "*Moi* Pushkin—eto Pushkin moego detstva: tainykh chtenii golovoi v shkafu" (*My* Pushkin—is the Pushkin of my childhood: of clandestine readings, my head in the bookcase).

29. Alexandra Smith, *The Song of the Mockingbird: Pushkin in the Work of Marina Tsvetaeva* (Berne: Peter Lang, 1994), 107. My purpose here is neither to consider the larger questions raised in Tsvetaeva's Pushkin texts nor to offer an exhaustive analysis of "My Pushkin," but only to consider Tsvetaeva's particular response to Tatiana offered in this text. Readers interested in a fuller account of Tsvetaeva and Pushkin are encouraged to consult Smith's outstanding study.

30. Marina Tsvetaeva, *Izbrannaia proza v dvukh tomakh* (New York: Russica, 1979), 2:250. All subsequent citations of "My Pushkin" will be according to this edition. Hereafter the page numbers will appear in the text.

31. Valerii Briusov, *Moi Pushkin* (Moscow/Leningrad: Gosudarstvennoe izdatel'stvo, 1929), is a posthumous publication of essays the Symbolist poet devoted to Pushkin. On Tsvetaeva's strained relations with Briusov, see Alexandra Smith, *Song of the Mockingbird*, 11–22.

32. This, like all subsequent translations of Tsvetaeva's Pushkin essay, is taken from Marina Tsvetaeva, *A Captive Spirit: Selected Prose*, ed. and trans. J. Marin King (Ann Arbor: Ardis, 1980), 336. Henceforth page numbers referring to this edition will appear in the text.

33. For a study of the significance of the Orphic model to Tsvetaeva's self-definition and to the images of the poet she developed, see Olga Peters Hasty, *Tsvetaeva's Orphic Journeys in the Worlds of the Word* (Evanston: Northwestern University Press, 1996).

Index

DATE DUE
